8008

Our Land
and
Heritage

Our Country

by Gertrude Stephens Brown

with Ernest W. Tiegs and Fay Adams

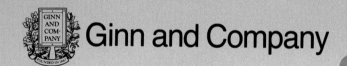 Ginn and Company

Contents

1 Our beginnings

© Copyright, 1979,
by Ginn and Company (Xerox Corporation)
All Rights Reserved
Home Office: Lexington, Massachusetts 02173
0-663-36156-7

2 How we began a nation

3 How our country grew

4 How our country changed

5 Binding the nation together

6 Looking at our great nation

7 Our American neighbors

Maps

Charts and diagrams

1

Our beginnings

People from Europe come to the New World

The Vikings

Leif Ericson sat high up in his ship staring across the waves. All at once he began to shout excitedly to a young sailor below. "Dag! Look up ahead! See those birds! Maybe they're heading for the same land we are."

"Let them lead the way. We'll follow where you take us, Leif," said Dag. "You always guide us well!"

"Come, now! The North Star guides us at night and the sun by day." But Leif was pleased just the same. "We all do our part together, you know. That's the Viking way. Now, back to our jobs!"

Dag nodded. "Aye, Leif," he replied, pulling his hooded cape close against the cold wind.

Ericson studied the view to the west again. After a while he shouted, "Yo ho, friends! I see land far off!"

The sailors ran to the rails, cheering wildly. They loved the sea. But after a long and dangerous journey, they were always happy to see land again.

The Vikings were bold people who lived in northern Europe long ago. Find Europe on the global map on page 10.

The Vikings (vī′kingz) lived along the shores of what are now the countries of Norway, Sweden, and Denmark. These people were expert shipbuilders. Their ships glided easily over the waves when winds filled the big sail. But when the wind died down, the sailors had to row.

These skilled sailors were brave. They were not afraid of fierce storms or of being lost at sea. They accepted such problems as tests of courage.

Even before the year 1000, a group of these daring explorers had wandered far out on the Atlantic Ocean. They found the islands of Iceland and Greenland. Locate them on the map on page 10.

Viking settlements were started on these islands. Growing up in one of them was a boy named Leif Ericson. He was named Ericson because he was the son of Eric the Red, a daring leader.

Young Leif heard many stirring tales of Viking voyages. One, he never forgot. It was about a Viking ship that had set out for Greenland. It was blown off course by stormy winds. The captain lost his way. After many days he sighted a land that he had never seen before. It had green forests at the edge of the sea.

The captain knew that this was not the bare rocky coast of Greenland. So he turned back. When he reached Greenland, he told people about the land he had seen.

Ericson wondered if the tale was true. Some day he would find out.

Leif Ericson discovered America about a thousand years ago. He had persuaded a group of thirty friends to sail with him. They hoped to find the unknown land described by the Viking captain.

Ericson's party probably landed on the shores of Newfoundland. This is an island off the coast of North America. Find Newfoundland on the map on page 10. Notice how near it is to North America.

Ericson called this land Vinland because it seemed to be covered with grapevines. Groups of Vikings settled in Vinland. One of these groups was led by Leif's relative Gudrid with her husband. None of the groups, though, stayed longer than three or four years. People in other parts of Europe did not learn about the Viking voyages to America.

Africans may have come

Africans may have come to North America after the Vikings had come. Stories tell how Africans set out in large sailing canoes even before Columbus. They hoped to learn what lands lay beyond the sea. Little is known about their travels. It is thought, though, that some Africans may have landed far south on the continent of North America. They may have remained there among the Native Americans.

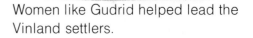

Women like Gudrid helped lead the Vinland settlers.

The first Americans

People came from Asia in small groups many thousands of years ago. This is why they are often known as the Native Americans.

Locate Asia on a map or globe. Find the place where Asia and North America are closest together. Notice that a small body of water separates them. This was not always so. At one time Asia and North America were connected here by a narrow strip of land.

Groups of Asians came across this strip of land into America. They were hunters. They caught wild game for food. They used animal skins for clothes. They had to move often to follow the animals.

During thousands of years, these people scattered over most of North America and its islands. Some roamed into South America. In some places the people settled into villages. Some of the villages grew into large towns. Great nations developed. This all took place long before people in Europe knew about America.

But in those distant times the Native Americans were not called Indians. They were given the name Indian by Columbus. What brought Columbus to America? Let's find out.

9

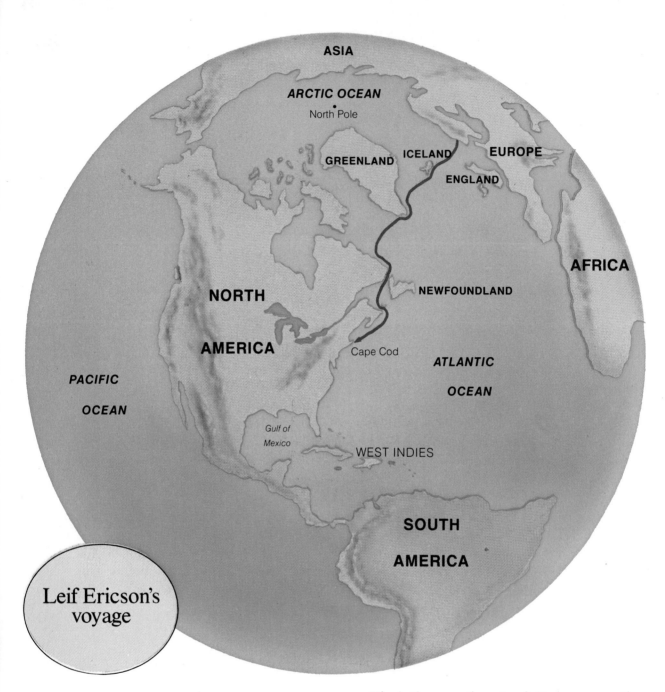

ASIA

ARCTIC OCEAN

• North Pole

GREENLAND

ICELAND

EUROPE

ENGLAND

AFRICA

NORTH

AMERICA

NEWFOUNDLAND

Cape Cod

ATLANTIC

OCEAN

PACIFIC

OCEAN

Gulf of
Mexico

WEST INDIES

SOUTH

AMERICA

Leif Ericson's
voyage

The earth is nearly round like a ball. A small model of the earth is called a *globe*. A globe shows correctly the sizes and shapes of bodies of land and oceans. When you look at a globe, you can see only half of the earth. The global map above shows you almost half of it.

Find the continent of Europe on the global map above. West of Europe is the Atlantic Ocean. It separates Europe from North America. Find the Atlantic Ocean on the global map.

The Viking explorers sailed across the Atlantic Ocean from Greenland to Newfoundland. African explorers may have crossed the Atlantic. Later, European explorers crossed it.

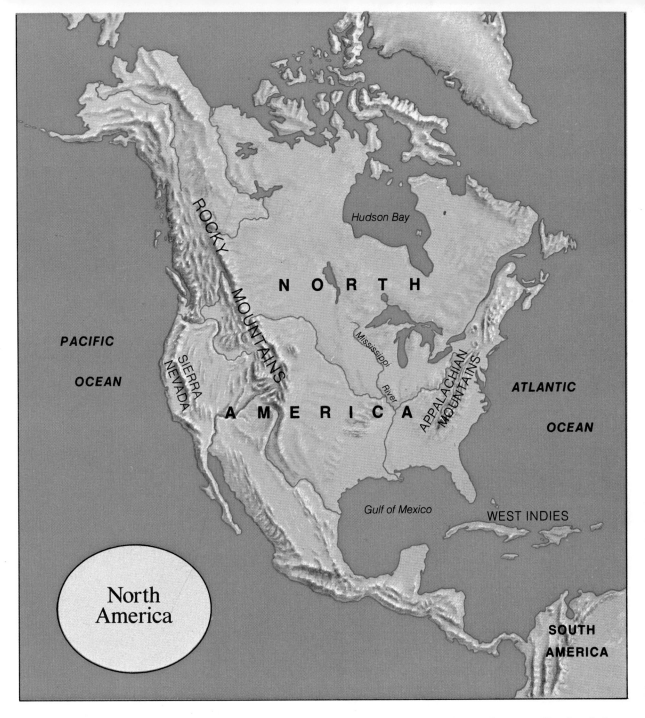

ROCKY MOUNTAINS

SIERRA NEVADA

PACIFIC

OCEAN

NORTH

Hudson Bay

Mississippi

River

APPALACHIAN
MOUNTAINS

ATLANTIC

OCEAN

A M E R I C A

Gulf of Mexico

WEST INDIES

North
America

SOUTH
AMERICA

This map shows the continent of North America. Notice how it extends from the Atlantic to the Pacific Ocean. Find the long Mississippi River, which flows through the middle of the land. Locate the mountains on the continent.

The map above is different from a global map. Maps like this one are usually more useful when studying a small part of the earth. For example, on a globe, North America is usually quite small. A globe would have to be huge to show all of the rivers and mountains in North America.

A globe, however, can show the exact shape of a body of land or water. This cannot be done on a map. To see why, press the rind of half an orange out flat. The edges break as it flattens out. It looks different. The same thing happens when a map is made.

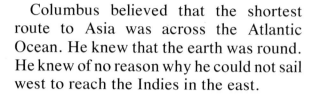

Wanted! Treasures from the Indies!

The people of Europe were interested in trading with the Indies. They found out about the fine goods produced in the Indies. From the Indies they wanted spices to help make food taste better. They wanted silks, jewels, and gold and silver articles.

These goods were expensive and hard to get in Europe. Only wealthy people could afford them. Even a small box of pepper cost a great deal of money. A look at a map will help explain why.

The Indies were very far away from Europe. The name Indies was given to lands in eastern Asia. They included India, China, and the Spice Islands. Find these lands on a map or globe. Now find Europe.

Travel between Europe and the Indies was slow. Goods were carried part way by mules over mountain trails. Camel caravans hauled the goods across hot deserts. Finally, the treasures were loaded on boats for the last part of the long journey.

Some goods never arrived. Robbers lay in wait along deserted trails. Sometimes pirates seized the goods at sea. No wonder, then, that people in Europe wanted a safer, shorter route to the Indies.

The country of Portugal sent ships southward down the west coast of Africa to search for a new route to Asia. The Portuguese hoped to sail eastward around the tip of Africa and up the east coast to the Indies.

One daring man thought a new route to the Indies was in another direction. He was a sea captain from Italy named Christopher Columbus.

Columbus believed that the shortest route to Asia was across the Atlantic Ocean. He knew that the earth was round. He knew of no reason why he could not sail west to reach the Indies in the east.

The voyages of Columbus

On a globe trace a route between Europe and the Indies by moving west. Notice that North and South America are in the way. Notice also that the huge Pacific Ocean is between the Americas and the Indies. Columbus did not know about these things.

Columbus had spent many years planning a westward route to the Indies. However, he could not afford to hire sailors and to buy ships and supplies. Only kings, nobles, and rich merchants could pay for such expensive voyages.

Over and over, Columbus asked for help. Each time he was turned away. Finally, after he had given up hope, he was called to the Spanish palace. Queen Isabella of Spain had decided to help him after all.

Columbus set sail one sunny day in August 1492. His three small ships—the Santa María (san′tə mə rē′ə), the Niña (nē′nyä), and the Pinta—sailed from a busy harbor in Spain. Their route led south and west across the Atlantic Ocean.

In those days many people feared the wide Atlantic Ocean. They called it the Sea of Darkness or the Unknown Sea. But not Columbus! He had learned much about it and its currents and winds. A *current* is a flow of water. *Winds* are currents of air that move over the earth.

Columbus knew that a current flowed westward from the coast of Africa across

This is a model of the *Santa María,* Columbus's largest ship.

the Atlantic. He had learned that winds blew westward above it. He was sure that these currents and winds would move the ships westward.

Columbus kept a careful record of the voyage. Some days the weather was fine, and the sea was calm. At other times angry storms sent huge waves crashing across the decks.

Some sailors complained bitterly. They were afraid of the dreadful storms and of being far out at sea. Never before had they been so long at sea without seeing land. They were afraid that they could not find their way back to Spain. They begged Columbus to turn back, but he refused. At last on October 12, 1492, the ships reached land.

Columbus claimed the land he found for Spain. As soon as they landed, Columbus pushed his sword into the sand. Then he raised the flag of Spain.

Columbus and his crew soon met the Arawak people, who lived there. They were friendly and traded parrots, balls of cotton thread, and darts for glass beads, tiny bells, and red caps.

Columbus had discovered an island near North America. But he thought he had reached lands near Asia. He named the island San Salvador, which means ''Holy Savior'' in the Spanish language. He thought San Salvador was the Indies. He called the people he met there *Indians.*

13

Today San Salvador and its neighbor islands are known as the West Indies. Find the West Indies on the map on page 17.

Columbus returned to Spain, where he was welcomed as a hero. He made several other voyages to the new lands. He visited many islands in the West Indies and reached the coast of South America. But Columbus never found a route to the silks, spices, and jewels of the Indies.

The lands that Columbus discovered were not named for him. Instead they were named America after an Italian seaman and writer, Amerigo Vespucci (ä′mər rē′gō ve spü′chē). Several years after Columbus had reached America, Vespucci sailed along the northeast coast of South America. He wrote letters about the lands he had seen. He claimed that they were a new continent and not a part of Asia. A writer of a geography book read one of these letters. The writer suggested that the lands across the sea be called America in honor of Amerigo Vespucci. The name America was given first to South America and later to North America, too.

14

Do you know the word?

Write 1 to 6 on paper. Then write for each sentence the correct word or words.

1. The first European to come to America whose name we know was _____ .
2. He came to a place that he named _____ .
3. This place was probably _____ .
4. He sailed from _____ .
5. He was followed by a group of settlers led by _____ .
6. The first Americans were groups of people who came to North America from _____ .

See if you remember

1. Who were the Vikings?
2. What Viking leaders discovered America and started settlements in America? About how long ago was it?
3. What people found America first? How did this happen? What "route" did they take?
4. Why did leaders in Europe want a new trade route to Asia?
5. Why did Columbus give the name Indians to the people of San Salvador?

A look at two global maps

This book contains dozens of maps. They will help you learn much about the places, events, and topics mentioned in the book.

A small model of the earth is called a *globe*. A globe shows sizes and shapes of the bodies of land and water. A global map shows how the earth would appear if you were looking at it from space.

Look at the two global maps on page 14. Each one shows one half of the earth, or a *hemisphere* (hem′ ə sfir′). The map on the left shows the *Western Hemisphere*. The one on the right shows the *Eastern Hemisphere*. Use these maps to help you answer the following questions.

1. In which hemisphere is North America? In which hemisphere is Europe?

2. Find the North Pole. The South Pole is not shown on these maps. Halfway between the poles is the *equator*. It is an imaginary line around the earth halfway between the North Pole and South Pole. Every place on the equator is the same distance from each pole. Find the equator on the global map on page 14. Does the equator run through North America?

3. The largest bodies of land are called *continents*. There are seven continents: Asia, Africa, North America, South America, Europe, Australia, and Antarctica. Which six continents are shown on these global maps? On which continent do you live? What continent lies south and east of the continent on which you live?

4. The largest bodies of water are called *oceans*. Seven tenths of the earth's surface is covered by ocean water. The largest ocean is the Pacific. Find it. The second largest is the Atlantic Ocean. Find it. Which ocean is nearest your home? Find the Indian Ocean. Is it in the Eastern or the Western Hemisphere? Find the smallest ocean, the Arctic. Which pole does it surround?

A closer look at your book

This book tells how our nation was born and how it grew. It tells about our government and many of the country's leaders. It explains how the work of many people has helped our nation become great.

This book describes the wide plains, fertile valleys, beautiful mountains, rivers, and seacoasts of the United States. It explains how our use of natural resources has helped it to become a strong nation.

The following activities will help you to get better acquainted with the book.

1. Find the *Contents*. On what page does it begin? What information does it give you?

2. Look at the contents again. Notice that the book is divided into seven parts. On what page does part one begin? What is it about?

3. Find the list of maps. What kinds of information can you get from the list?

4. Find the *Index*. On what page does it begin? Use the index to find the pages that have information about Leif Ericson, about Spain, and about Native Americans.

5. Before the index is the *Geography dictionary*. Turn to it. What information can you get from this dictionary?

2
People from Europe and Africa explore North America

How Florida was found

Juan Ponce de León (pons′ də lē′ən) was a Spanish soldier and explorer. He had sailed to America on Columbus's second voyage.

Ponce de León became the governor of an island in the West Indies. But he thought his job was dull and soon got tired of it. He wanted to search for gold—and especially for the Fountain of Youth.

Stories said that anyone who drank the fountain's magic waters might become young and strong again. It was also said that gold was hidden near the fountain.

One day in 1513 Ponce de León and his men set out to hunt for the marvelous fountain. They landed on the shore of a low, flat land. They saw graceful palm trees, pine forests, and beautiful flowers. They named this land Florida, a Spanish word meaning "full of flowers."

Cortés brought cattle and horses with him to America.

The explorers tasted the waters of many lakes and streams. But they did not grow younger. Just as disappointing, they did not find gold. At last they gave up and returned to the West Indies. Still, Ponce de León had claimed a large area of land for Spain.

The Spanish in North America

Other Spanish explorers sailed west from Spain. Like Columbus, they hoped to find a shorter route to Asia and bring back great treasures.

The Spaniards took guns, cannon, and horses with them. The Native Americans had never seen horses. At first they thought that a horse and rider were one creature. They had never seen guns and cannon either. You can see then why such strange, frightening new things puzzled them. Later they learned to use horses and guns. They traded furs and other valuable things for them.

"We want gold," the Spaniards demanded of the Native Americans by sign language. They answered, "We have no gold. You may find some far away from here." This encouraged the Spaniards to search and search.

Cortés was a very successful treasure hunter. Cortés (kôr tez′) was a bold Spanish leader. He guided several shiploads of soldiers from the West Indies to Mexico. Around the year 1519 he conquered the powerful Aztecs, who ruled much of Mexico.

The Aztecs had rich gold and silver mines. Cortés seized vast amounts of this treasure. He sent shipload after shipload of

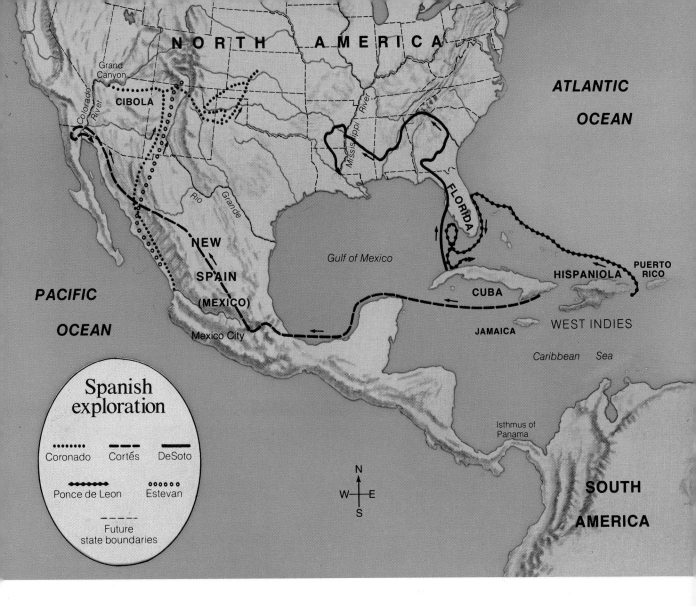

Spanish exploration

- •••••• Coronado
- – – – Cortés
- ——— DeSoto
- •••••• Ponce de Leon
- ○○○○○ Estevan
- – – – Future state boundaries

gold and silver to Spain. Gold from America helped Spain to become a very rich country. Still, the hunt for more gold continued.

In 1538, De Soto arrived in Cuba as the new governor. Cuba is the largest island in the West Indies. Columbus had visited it and claimed it for Spain.

De Soto thought that the job of governor was dull, and he soon tired of it. He wanted to search for gold. He had heard that Florida, which was nearby, was "a land of gold."

De Soto sailed to Florida with about 600 men and women. He did not find gold there. He then led his people northward through what are now the states of Georgia and South Carolina.

De Soto's party met Native Americans along the way. They were mainly Cherokees, Chickasaws, Creeks, and Natchez. Much of the land was thickly forested. At times, traveling was difficult. Still, the Spaniards pushed on and on. They traveled through areas that are now the states of North Carolina, Tennessee, Alabama, and Mississippi. On the map trace with your finger De Soto's route.

As the months passed, many explorers became ill and died. At last the weary

17

group reached the banks of a wide river. They had arrived at the mighty Mississippi. It was the largest river De Soto had ever seen. Still, he was not very excited. What he wanted to find was gold. He had been hunting it for three long years.

De Soto camped on the bank of the Mississippi. There his people built boats. They rowed across the river and continued on west into what is now Arkansas. They saw many Native Americans and vast lands but no signs of gold. Finally, they turned back. By the time they returned to the Mississippi, De Soto was ill. Before long he died. His followers buried him in the great river. He and his people were the first Europeans to see the Mississippi River.

About this time another search for gold was going on. After the Spaniards had seized Mexico's riches, they ruled this land. They called it New Spain. They heard stories about the seven gold cities of Cibola, supposedly to the north of New Spain. Two parties set out to find them.

The first party was led by a Spaniard named Estevan. He was a black man. There were black people in nearly every Spanish exploring party. Estevan guided his party across what is now New Mexico. One day he saw what he thought was a shining city in the distance. Estevan traveled toward it, but he was killed before he reached it.

Later, some Spaniards learned that this shining city was a small village. It was carved out of bright-colored cliffs. The sunlight had made it shine like gold.

The second party that set out to find the cities was led by Coronado (kôr′ə nä′dō). In 1540 he set out from New Spain with a group of more than a thousand men. They traveled north across rugged mountains and some scorching deserts. Find Coronado's route on the map.

Disappointed when they could not find Cibola, Francisco Coronado *(left)* and his party returned to Mexico *(page 18)*.

After many weeks, Coronado saw dazzling buildings in the distance. "Ah! See!" he shouted. "One of the rich cities of Cibola! I'm sure of it!"

The excited men galloped closer. But the "city" was another small village made golden by the sunlight. Coronado did not give up. He divided his men into several groups to search in different directions.

Coronado himself led a group east over present-day Texas and north into what is now Kansas. Another group traveled west. It discovered the Grand Canyon of the Colorado River. None of them found gold.

Coronado and his men returned to New Spain empty-handed. However, they had claimed enormous lands for Spain.

Find a map of southwestern United States. Notice how many cities and bodies of water have Spanish names. This entire area was once part of the lands claimed and later settled by Spain.

Do you know the answers?

1. What land did Ponce de León explore?
2. What group of Native Americans did Cortés conquer in Mexico?
3. What two leaders explored large areas north of New Spain?
4. Why did Spanish explorers hunt for the cities of Cibola?
5. What part of our country has many Spanish place-names? Why does it?

Can you match the words?

Copy these words in a column on paper.

Indies	De Soto
Vespucci	Cibola
Ponce de León	Coronado
Cortés	

Now write one of the words below beside the word on your paper that it matches.

Grand Canyon	spices
Mexico	Florida
cliff dwellings	Mississippi River
America	

The French in America

In 1534 the French king sent Jacques Cartier (kär tyā′) to America. He was a well-trained French sea captain. He was told to look for gold and for a shorter route to Asia.

Cartier's two ships landed on the shores of what is now eastern Canada. He planted the French flag and claimed the land for France. The next year he returned and sailed far up a great river. You can follow his voyage on the map on page 21. He named this river the St. Lawrence. He hoped it was a waterway leading to Asia. He finally reached some *rapids*, which are swift, churning waters that tumble over rocks. He could go no farther.

Cartier made several other voyages west, but he failed to find gold or a route to Asia. The explorer Marguerite de Roberval was on one of these voyages. She became marooned on an island. Alone and with no supplies, she kept herself alive for more than a year. She was finally rescued.

Champlain is known as "the Father of New France." For about seventy years the French almost forgot Canada. Then they became interested again when they saw that Spain was settling much of America. They decided they must start a colony of their own. A *colony* is a group of settlers called *colonists* who go to live in another land owned by their country. Samuel de Champlain was to be in charge of the colony in New France.

In 1608 Champlain started the first successful French settlement. It was built near the cliffs on the St. Lawrence River. It was called Quebec. Champain was the governor of New France.

Champlain helped the colonists build a fort and plant crops. He urged the colonists to trade with the Native Americans for furs. The furs were shipped to France and sold for high prices.

Champlain spent much time exploring and making maps of the lands and waterways around the St. Lawrence River. On one trip, he explored two of the Great

La Salle and his party start out on their journey to explore the Mississippi.

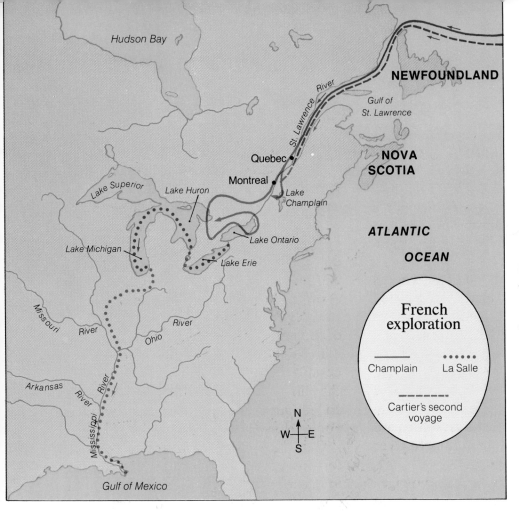

Hudson Bay

NEWFOUNDLAND

St. Lawrence River

Gulf of St. Lawrence

NOVA SCOTIA

Quebec

Montreal

Lake Superior

Lake Huron

Lake Champlain

Lake Michigan

Lake Ontario

Lake Erie

ATLANTIC

OCEAN

Missouri River

Ohio River

Arkansas River

Mississippi River

Gulf of Mexico

French exploration

Champlain ········ La Salle

- - - - - Cartier's second voyage

N W—E S

French explorers traveled throughout New France. What did they hope to learn?

Lakes—Huron and Ontario. On another trip, he found and named Lake Champlain. Find these lakes on the map of New France.

Champlain chose a site for the colony. This site became the city of Montreal. A woman, Jeanne Mance, wanted to help start the colony. There was a rule that said women could not go on the trip. Jeanne tried to change the rule. Finally she did. Jeanne was a leader of the first colonists who went to Montreal. She was the colony's business manager. She started and ran a hospital, too. Her hospital, Hôtel-Dieu, has become one of the great hospitals in Montreal.

The fur trade brought more and more young people to New France. One was Robert de La Salle, age 23, a member of a French noble family. La Salle came to New France in 1666. He started a trading post on the banks of the St. Lawrence River. He built a good fur-trading business with the Native Americans. They told him about a great river to the south and west. La Salle was curious. Could it be a waterway leading to the Pacific Ocean? He decided to find out.

La Salle made the long journey. He guided his men all the way down the Mississippi River to its mouth. The *mouth* of a river is the place where it empties into a body of water.

The Mississippi River, with some of its branches, is shown on the map above. Locate its mouth. Near this area, La Salle raised the French flag. He claimed for France all of the land drained by the Mississippi River. He then named the land Louisiana in honor of the king of France.

21

Cabot landed on Newfoundland close to where the Vikings had landed.

The English in America

In 1497 the king of England sent John Cabot to America. Cabot was from Italy, but he had been living in England. In fact, he had taken an English name. Like Columbus, Cabot believed that he could sail west to reach the Indies. He decided to sail a shorter route than the one Columbus had followed. The map shows Cabot's route. Notice that he sailed almost straight west from England. Notice how his route differed from the one that Columbus took.

One summer day Cabot reached the cool shores of a large island. It lay along the northeast coast of North America. It was the island now called Newfoundland. Cabot thought that he was near China. Still he did not see any splendid cities with shining gold towers. Nor did he see any camel caravans loaded with silks and spices.

Cabot had found a different kind of wealth. He noticed that the shallow waters off the large island were alive with fish. There were so many fish that they could be scooped up in baskets. Fish was an important food for many Europeans. Cabot knew that Europeans, who earned money by fishing, would welcome news of these rich fishing grounds.

Cabot claimed the land he found for England.

The king of England was pleased by the news that Cabot had almost reached China! A second voyage was planned. This time Cabot was to take five ships west. He said that they would return loaded with treasures from China.

Cabot could not keep his promise. He once again reached the east coast of North America. He was nowhere near Asia. But Cabot did explore farther than before. He claimed more land for England along the Atlantic coast.

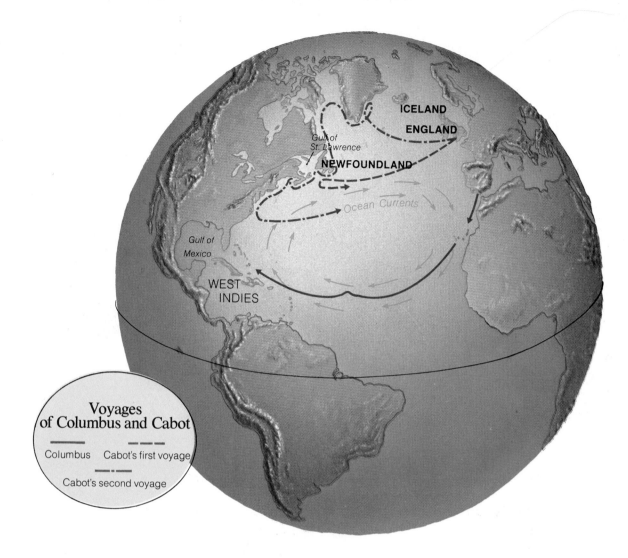

Vopages
of Columbus and Cabot

——— — — —
Columbus Cabot's first voyage

— · —
Cabot's second voyage

Later, Cabot's claim to land in America became very important to England. It was along the east coast that England's colonies grew. In fact, this is where the United States began.

The first two English colonies in America failed. In the late 1500s three shiploads of English people sailed to America. They started England's first colony on Roanoke Island, off the coast of what is now North Carolina. They had a hard time in this new land. After a year they gave up and went back to England. Find Roanoke Island on the map on page 35.

Soon a second group of settlers arrived on the island. This group of 150 men and women was led by an able governor, John White. A few weeks later, Eleanor White Dare gave birth to a daughter, Virginia, the first English child born in America.

Before long, the governor had to return to England for supplies. England was at war before he was ready to return. When he sailed back to the Roanoke Island colony three years later, he found the small village in ruins and its people gone.

He could not tell what had happened. Had the people starved or wandered away? The sad governor could not tell. He found one clue. The word "Croatoan" was carved on a tree. This was the name of the friendly Native Americans nearby. He wondered if the settlers had joined them. The mystery was never solved. This group of early English settlers is still known as the Lost Colony.

23

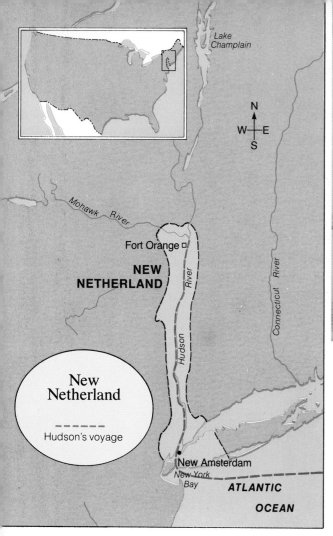

New Netherland

- - - - - - Hudson's voyage

New Amsterdam became the main Dutch settlement. Today it is called New York City.

The Dutch in America

The Dutch people live in a small European country, the Netherlands. It is located west of West Germany. Find the Netherlands on a globe. The Netherlands had many skilled traders and merchants. Like other trading peoples, the Dutch were eager to find a shorter route to the Indies.

In 1609 a Dutch trading company sent Henry Hudson west. He was told to search for a route to Asia through America. Hudson was a skillful English sea captain.

On part of his journey, he sailed about 140 miles up a beautiful river. He hoped it would lead him to the Pacific, but he was disappointed. The river now bears his name, the Hudson River.

Find the Hudson River on the map. It flows through what is now the state of New York to the Atlantic Ocean, not to the Pacific. Because Henry Hudson explored this river for them, the Dutch claimed the lands around it.

The Dutch started a colony they called New Netherland. Find the colony on the map. Dutch fur traders soon arrived in New Netherland. They built trading posts along the Hudson River.

At the mouth of the Hudson River was an island. Peter Minuit had bought it from the Manhattans, who lived on it. He had paid them with goods worth about $24. The goods included axes, kettles, knives, and bright-colored beads.

The island became known as Manhattan Island, the name it still has today. On the southern tip of the island, the Dutch built a fort, a mill, and some houses. They named the place New Amsterdam after the largest city in their homeland. Because of its good harbor and location, New Amsterdam grew steadily.

Do you know?

1. Who changed the rule against women and started a great hospital in Montreal?
2. Who was the explorer who has a great eastern river named for him?
3. Where was the Lost Colony settled?
4. What did Peter Minuit buy?
5. From whom did he buy it?
6. Who was the "Father of New France"?
7. Which country was interested in exploring for gold more than for anything else?
8. Which explorer was most interested in the country of the Great Lakes and Mississippi River?

A map of persons

On thin paper, trace an outline of North America. Trace the map on page 11. Write the names of these persons on the map where you think they should be.

Ericson   Ponce de León
Cortés   La Salle
De Soto   Mance
Cartier   Hudson
Champlain   Cabot

Making an explorer story

You may find it interesting to make a true story about one of the explorers. Choose one of them from the map you made. Find out what you can about this explorer. Look in books in your schoolroom, the library, and at home. Write sentences giving the story.

A time line of exploration

Across a sheet of paper, draw a line ten inches (25 cm) long. Divide the line into 10 equal spaces. Label the marks for the spaces with years. Your line should look like the one below. Of course your line will be much longer. And you will finish writing the years. What will the latest year be? You are making a time line of exploring.

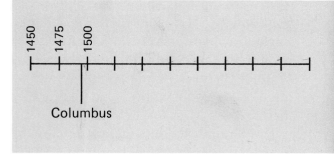

Below the line in the correct spaces, write the explorers shown in the list below. Be sure to write them in the right order. The first explorer is shown above.

Cabot   De Soto
Cartier   Estevan
Champlain   Hudson
Columbus   La Salle
Coronado   Ponce de León
Cortés

You may have to look back in the book to know when the exploring was done.

Why can you not put Ericson on your time line?

3
People the explorers found here

The Mound Builders

Let's flash back to the time before the explorers came to America. In your imagination flick a time clock back hundreds and hundreds of years. Go back before Columbus's time. Go back even earlier than Leif Ericson.

Suddenly it is the year 900. We are in beautiful eastern North America. Here are gently rolling hills, pleasant valleys, and huge forests. Here and there are villages. Farther away are some larger towns. The people in these villages and towns are Mound Builders. That is our name for them. We do not know what they called themselves.

The Mound Builders included many different tribes of Native Americans. A *tribe* is a large group of people who speak the same language and who follow the same customs.

Each tribe of Mound Builders was made up of smaller groups called bands. A *band* was like a large family. Its members might have lived together in a village. Or they might have moved together from one place to another. They hunted and fished together and shared other work.

Some of these people probably built mounds as far back as the year 600. How many centuries ago was that? A century is 100 years.

The Mound Builder tribes were spread over a large part of America. They lived on land from present-day New York, west to what is now Kansas and Nebraska, and from Wisconsin south to the Gulf of Mexico. Look at the map of the United States on pages 254-255. Find the area settled by the Mound Builders.

The clay figure of a mother and child came from a burial mound in Illinois. The serpent mound is in Ohio.

The Mound Builders built thousands of mounds. A large number of the mounds have survived down to our time. More than 10,000 have been found in Illinois and in Ohio. There are also mounds in Indiana, Georgia, Mississippi, West Virginia, and Wisconsin. Have you visited any mounds? If so, where?

Mounds were made of dirt heaped up in various shapes. Some were made in the shape of snakes or birds. Some looked like giant cones turned upside down. Others were shaped like rounded hills or steep hills flattened on top. Some were very large.

The workers who built the mounds started by digging up the dirt. They then carried it, basket by basket, to the building place.

B.C. | A.D.

Christopher Columbus arrives in New World

Leif Ericson arrives in Vineland

1000   100 | 100   600   1000   1500

Pueblos

Mound Builders

Cliff Dwellers

These people built temples and places for tribal meetings on top of some of the mounds. They used other mounds as forts. They built most of the mounds as burying places for their dead.

The Mound Builders buried food, and tools, with their dead. Scientists have learned many things from these buried objects, called artifacts. An *artifact* is something that was made by humans.

Scientists have found stone hoes and spades. So they know that some of the Mound Builders raised crops. They have found axes and hatchets made of flint. They think that these might have been used to cut down trees.

Scientists have also found carved stone figures. Because of these, they know that some of the Mound Builders were expert sculptors. They have found carved stone pipes, which might have been used to smoke tobacco.

Scientists have found bone needles, necklaces of bone and shell, jars of pearls, and bracelets made of copper. What might be learned about the Mound Builders from these artifacts?

During the 1500s, the building of mounds ended. For centuries, though, it had been important. Mound building influenced the customs of many different groups of Native Americans.

27

The ways of Native Americans

Native Americans were scattered all over America. Some of these groups are named on the map on page 29. Which of these groups are familiar to you? What do you know about them?

Not all groups were alike. Some were very different from each other. This was partly because of geography. Not all of these groups settled on the same kind of land.

Some Native Americans lived in forests and some on grassy plains. The forest people built houses of logs and planks. Usually wild game, fish, and nuts were plentiful near their homes.

Those that lived on the grasslands had a different way of life. They were mainly big-game hunters. They hunted buffalo, antelope, deer, and elk. They ate the meat and used the skins for clothes. Many of the plains peoples were nomadic. That is, the bands moved from place to place. They used tepees as houses because they could move them easily.

Native Americans who lived in the desert had still another way of life. *Deserts* are dry places. They are too dry for most trees to grow. Some desert people built houses of earth and brush. Others used adobe bricks to build thick-walled houses. They made the bricks from clay and straw and dried them in the sun. Why might thick walls be helpful in a hot, dry area?

One group of desert dwellers, the Pueblos, carved apartments out of cliffs. The ruins of some cliff dweller houses can be found in southwestern Colorado. Find the Pueblos on the map.

This picture, painted by a European artist, shows a Native American village.

The various groups had different ways of life. The Mayas and Aztecs built large cities. They built fine palaces and temples. Centuries ago they lived in what are now Mexico and Central America. Find this area on the map. You will read more about the Aztecs and the Mayas (mī′əz) later.

Even before 1600 some groups joined together. The groups were known as the Iroquois Nation. It was made up of six groups. Each group took care of its own affairs. Each, though, promised not to go to war unless the other groups agreed. On the map find where the Iroquois lived.

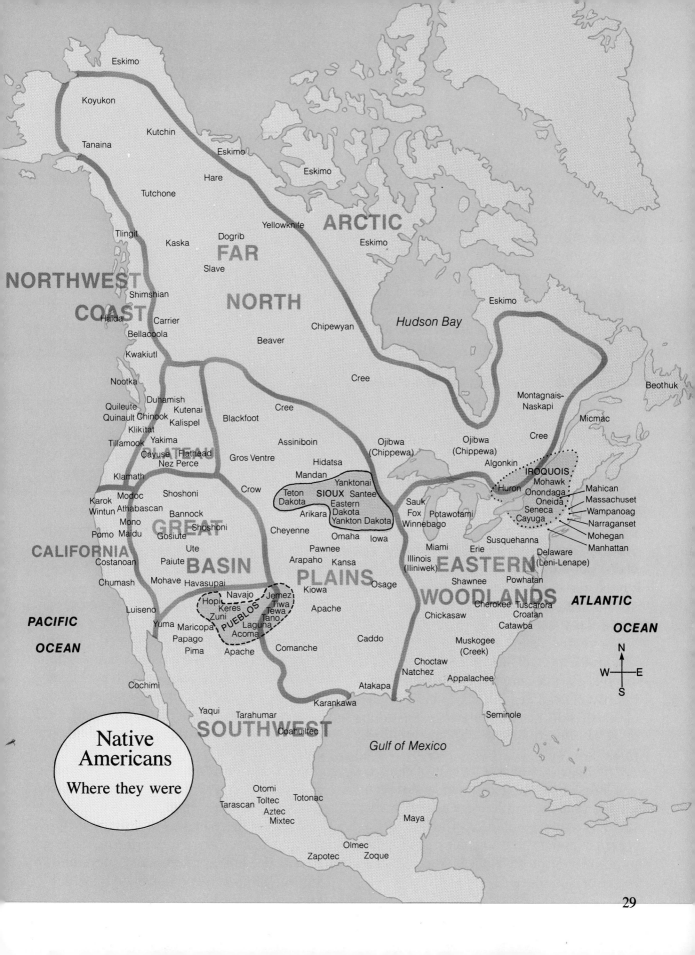

Eskimo

Koyukon

Kutchin

Tanaina

Eskimo

Hare

Tutchone

Yellowknife

ARCTIC

Tlingit

Kaska

Dogrib

FAR

Eskimo

Shimshian

Slave

NORTH

Eskimo

NORTHWEST

COAST

Haida

Carrier

Chipewyan

Hudson Bay

Bellacoola

Beaver

Kwakiutl

Cree

Montagnais-
Naskapi

Beothuk

Nootka

Duhamish

Cree

Ojibwa
(Chippewa)

Ojibwa
(Chippewa)

Cree

Micmac

Quileute
Quinault Chinook
Klikitat
Tillamook Yakima

Kutenai

Kalispel

Blackfoot

Algonkin

IROQUOIS

Mohawk

Mahican

Cayuse Flathead
Nez Perce

Gros Ventre

Assiniboin

Huron
Onondaga
Oneida
Seneca
Cayuga

Massachuset
Wampanoag
Narraganset
Mohegan
Manhattan

Klamath

Hidatsa

Mandan

Karok Modoc
Wintun Athabascan
Mono
Pomo Maidu
Costanoan

Shoshoni

Crow

Yanktonai

Teton
Dakota

SIOUX Santee
Eastern
Dakota
Yankton Dakota

Sauk
Fox Potawotami
Winnebago

Susquehanna

Delaware
(Leni-Lenape)

Bannock

GREAT
Shoshoni
Gosiute

Arikara

CALIFORNIA

Ute

BASIN

Cheyenne

Omaha

Iowa

Miami

Erie

Powhatan

Paiute

PLAINS

Pawnee

Arapaho Kansa

Osage

Illinois
(Iliniwek)

EASTERN

WOODLANDS

ATLANTIC

Chumash

Mohave Havasupai

Kiowa

Shawnee

Cherokee Tuscarora
Croatan
Catawba

OCEAN

PACIFIC

Luiseno

Hopi Navajo Jemez
Keres Tiwa
Zuni Tano
Yuma Maricopa PUEBLOS Tewa
Laguna
Papago Acoma

Apache

Chickasaw

OCEAN

Pima

Apache

Comanche

Caddo

Muskogee
(Creek)

Cochimi

Choctaw
Natchez

Appalachee

N

Karankawa

Atakapa

W   E

S

Yaqui

Tarahumar

SOUTHWEST

Coahuiltec

Seminole

Native
Americans

Where they were

Gulf of Mexico

Otomi

Tarascan

Toltec

Totonac

Aztec

Mixtec

Maya

Zapotec

Olmec

Zoque

29

What animals on these totem poles are from British Columbia?

Native Americans of the northwest coast

Many groups lived on the northwest coast of North America. The area where they lived was along the Pacific Ocean. It included land from northern California to Alaska. Hills and mountains rise steeply back from much of this coast. It is a cool, rainy area that is green with forests. Find the land of the northwest coast people on the map on page 29.

They lived in villages that were made up of large wooden houses. Several families lived in each of them. The houses were built of huge cedar logs cut into planks. Each house had a high slanting roof with a smoke hole in the middle. The houses often had carved and painted doorposts. Some of them showed the brave deeds of a person who lived in the house. Many had a carving of Thunderbird. He was the Indian god of thunder and lightning. They said that the storm clouds were his shadow.

Sometimes they brought a giant cedar log from the forest. They decorated it with carvings of spirits and animals. The carvings showed the history of a family. Finally they painted the log. Such a carved log is called a *totem pole*.

These people would set up a totem pole in front of a house to show its owners. They used totem poles as tombstones. They also used them to support the roofs of houses.

The richest man of the village was its chief. He owned the most blankets, canoes, and tools.

Every few years a chief might hold a large gathering, which we call a potlatch. The more important a chief was, the more people he would invite to it. Sometimes a chief would invite friends from far away.

During the potlatch the chief gave each person a present. He gave valuable presents to the chiefs of the other groups. Other people got fewer, less valuable presents. Of course, he would expect to receive many expensive presents when he was invited to the next potlatch.

There was plenty of food for these northwest coast people. They caught fish in the sea. They caught the salmon in the rivers. They scooped up the salmon in nets or speared them. They dried or smoked much salmon for future meals.

The men hunted for deer, elk, caribou, and bear. The women preserved the meat by salting it or by smoking or drying it. They also gathered roots and berries.

Northwest coast people made dishes from shells, horns of animals, and stone. They made large serving bowls of wood.

They sometimes carved the bowls with fancy designs and used them at potlatches.

These northwest coast people were expert boat builders. They made wooden canoes, large and small, from cedar logs. They began by hollowing out a log with fire and tools. Next they filled the log with water. Then they heated stones and dropped them into the water. The hot water softened the wood so that it could be shaped.

Their ocean-going canoes were from thirty to sixty feet (9m to 18m) long. They were decorated with brightly painted carvings. One group might use some of its canoes to exchange goods with other groups. They used other canoes for whale-hunting, far out at sea.

In the early 1800s explorers and fur traders came from Europe. They visited the land of the northwest coast people. These traders traded their iron tools and other goods for furs. The Europeans brought many changes to the Native Americans' way of life. In time, their special way of life began to disappear.

Gifts from the Native Americans

Native Americans taught the colonists many things. The Native Americans knew how to grow and use foods that were new to the colonists. These foods were corn, peanuts, beans, peppers, squash, sweet potatoes, and tomatoes. The settlers learned how to take sap from maple trees and to make maple syrup and sugar from it.

Native Americans have given America hundreds of place names. Chicago comes from their word *checagou*. Seattle is named for a friendly chief. More than half of the states have Native American names. Does yours? If it does, learn its meaning.

You probably use some Native American words once in a while. Words like canoe, chipmunk, and moccasin are examples.

Perhaps you have heard someone say "Let's bury the hatchet!" Those wise words come from our Native American friends and mean, "Let's stop quarreling and live at peace with one another."

Native Americans of the Northwest were great seafarers. They traveled far from home in their canoes.

Do you remember?

1. Who were the Mound Builders? What are mounds? How were they built? How were they used?
2. What are artifacts? Name some of the things scientists have learned about the Mound Builders from artifacts.
3. How were the peoples who lived in forests, on the plains, and in deserts different from each other? Why are they different?
4. Describe a northwest coast Native American village. Be sure to include what the houses looked like, what the people ate, and some things that they made.

What words do you need?

Write the numbers 1 to 9 on paper. After each number, write the word or words you need to complete each sentence.

1. An _____ is something made by humans.
2. A century is _____ years.
3. About 10,000 mounds have been discovered in the states of _____ and _____ .
4. Many mounds were used as _____ , or burial places.
5. The _____ carved homes out of cliffs.
6. The _____ and _____ built splendid cities.
7. Native Americans of the northwest coast carved handsome _____ to tell of their brave deeds.
8. Native Americans introduced Europeans to some important favorite foods, including _____ , _____ , and _____ .
9. More than half of the _____ have Native American names.

What is your idea?

1. Over the years our government moved Native Americans away from the settlers to reservations. A famous chief, Cochise, said, "Let my people mingle with the whites on their farms and in their communities. Let us be one people." How do groups of people mingle in your community? How can you help to encourage it?
2. Native American ways of living were the result of the kind of area in which they lived. How does the geography of the place you live affect your ways of living?

Things to do

1. Make a list of things, such as places, words, foods, that make you think of the Native Americans.
2. Are there any mounds near your home? If so, learn what you can about them. Write on paper what you learn. Share your information with your class.

Using pictures

1. Study the pictures in this chapter. Which picture did you enjoy most? Why? What are some things you learned from it?
2. Use the map on page 29 and an encyclopedia to get information about Native American people. Then chart on paper what you learn. Use three columns. In one column write the names of the groups of Native Americans. Use one column to tell where they lived. And use one to tell what kind of house they lived in.

How we began a nation

Building the thirteen English colonies

A colony is started

The colony of Virginia began at Jamestown in 1607. It was spring, and Virginia was a pleasant place. Flowers were blooming in the grassy meadows. There were patches of wild strawberries. Deer, bears, and foxes roamed through the woods.

What a welcome sight for the 104 men and boys! They had left England in December! Sixteen of their companions had died on the four-month trip across the Atlantic. They were here to start a colony.

The men and boys had signed up to work for the London Company. It was formed by a group of English merchants. They sent three ships west. The colonists were to hunt for gold and silver and to raise crops.

Finally the ships sailed into Chesapeake Bay and up a quiet river. The leaders named it the James River in honor of King James I. He had given the company permission to start a colony.

The tired colonists eagerly left their boats. They settled on a low swampland along the river. They cut down trees and built a rough fort and a few huts. They named this new settlement Jamestown. Find Jamestown on the map on page 35. Soon the settlers realized that Jamestown was not a good place to live. It was damp and swampy. There were mosquitoes everywhere.

The colonists did not build sturdy houses. They drank swamp water instead of digging wells for pure water. They did not raise crops for food. They wanted to look for gold. They did not want to farm.

Soon the food supplies ran low, and there was not enough to eat. Many colonists became ill. A large number died. It seemed that the new colony of Virginia would fail. Then Captain John Smith took command.

Captain John Smith became the leader of Jamestown. He made friends with the Native Americans who lived nearby. He arranged to trade with them for corn. He told the colonists to stop searching for gold

By the time John Smith left the colonies, settlers were clearing lands outside the fort at Jamestown.

and plant crops. He said that all colonists must work if they wanted to eat.

Captain Smith had many exciting adventures. Once, he was captured and taken before Chief Powhatan (pou′ ə tan′). Powhatan decided that the captain was a dangerous enemy and must die. But Powhatan's daughter Pocahontas (pō′kə-hon′təs) begged her father to spare the captain's life. Her wish was granted. Captain Smith was allowed to return to Jamestown. Later, Pocahontas married one of John Smith's friends, John Rolfe. After a time they went to England to live.

Captain Smith could not solve all of Jamestown's problems. The colonists were discouraged and homesick. At last they decided to give up and return home.

They boarded ships and started down the river. On the way they met some ships arriving from England. These ships carried supplies and many new colonists. Some were women. So the Virginians turned their ships around and led the way back to Jamestown. Later, a ship brought many more women to Virginia.

Soon there was more good news. No longer did the colonists have to work entirely for the London Company. Instead, each settler was given land near Jamestown to farm.

The colonists became successful farmers. They learned from the Native Americans how to grow corn and tobacco. They raised corn for food and tobacco to sell to England.

Jamestown was the first permanent English settlement in America. It became the capital of the colony of Virginia. At Jamestown, self-government in the American colonies began.

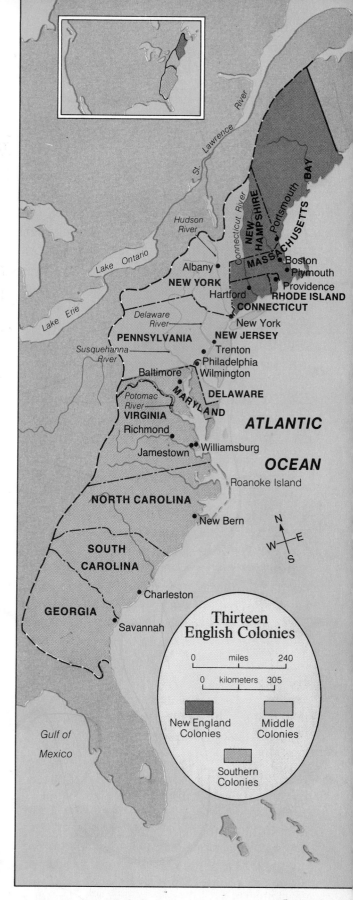

Thirteen English Colonies

0   miles   240

0   kilometers   305

New England Colonies

Middle Colonies

Southern Colonies

The beginning of self-government

The Virginia colonists were ruled by a governor chosen by the king. They had to follow laws made in England. The colonists had no one to *represent,* or act for them, in England. They thought that this was unfair. Some of them asked, "How can people far across the Atlantic Ocean decide what laws we need?" They wanted the freedom to make their own laws. They asked for this right, over and over.

One English leader sided with the colonists. He worked hard to change the way that England ruled the colony. Other English leaders agreed with him.

In 1618 a new governor arrived in Virginia. He brought good news. The colonists were going to help make their own laws. A group of colonists met with the new governor to plan an election.

Two people from each settled area were chosen to be the lawmakers. The lawmakers were called *burgesses.* They represented the people of the districts or places where they lived. When the burgesses met together, their group was known as the House of Burgesses.

The House of Burgesses first met in July in 1619. They met in the church in the little village of Jamestown. The meeting lasted six days.

Each morning, just after sunrise, a drum signal called the burgesses together. The summer weather was hot and humid. But these men wore coats and hats, just the same. They were copying the custom for lawmakers in England, where the weather was much cooler.

The burgesses discussed what laws were needed. Every burgess had a chance to speak. A person who spoke while another was speaking could be fined 100 pounds (45 kg) of tobacco. That was a stiff fine because tobacco sold for a high price in England.

The burgesses passed a law that healthy people must work. If they did not work, they would be punished. They passed several laws about crops. For example, each planter wanted to grow as many acres of tobacco as possible. But food was needed, also. One law required planters to raise food for their families and workers.

The House of Burgesses was the first group of representatives to meet in America. Its meetings started the kind of government the United States has today.

The growth of the southern colonies

Five colonies were started along the southern Atlantic coast. They were Virginia, Maryland, North Carolina, South Carolina, and Georgia. The five colonies became known as the southern colonies.

These colonies were on a wide strip of low flat land along the coast. Such low flat land is called a *plain.* When it extends along a seacoast, it is a *coastal plain.*

The southern coastal plain reached inland for a great distance. It was thickly forested. Wide rivers moved slowly through it. One was the James River. Jamestown was located on its banks.

The Virginia settlers became successful farmers. They learned from the Native Americans how to plant tobacco. Tobacco became the colony's chief crop.

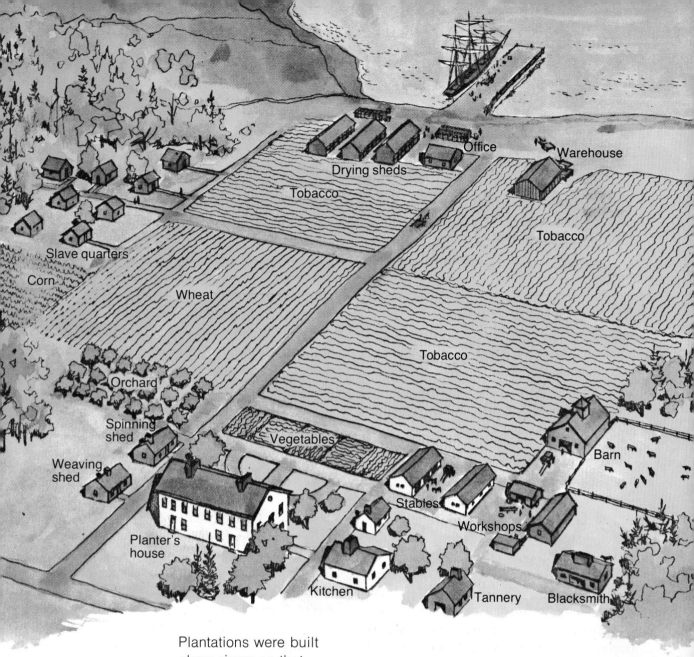

The following labels appear on the illustration:

Drying sheds
Office
Warehouse
Tobacco
Slave quarters
Corn
Wheat
Tobacco
Tobacco
Orchard
Spinning shed
Vegetables
Weaving shed
Barn
Stables
Workshops
Planter's house
Kitchen
Tannery
Blacksmith

Plantations were built along rivers so that planters could get their crops to market.

The tobacco plant took many minerals from the soil. Fields, planted in tobacco, wore out quickly. Most farmers did not put plant food back into the soil. They did not fertilize their fields as farmers do today. Instead, when fields wore out, farmers would cut down trees and plow new fields. They could do this because there was so much land.

In time a few people owned large pieces of land. Such lands were called *plantations*. The owners were called *planters*.

Most plantations extended back from rivers. Many had their own river-front and wharf. There, ships from England could bring supplies and load.

A planter could not farm a plantation alone. It was too large. Many workers were needed. So some planters began to buy African slaves to do the work. But most farms had few acres and few, if any, slaves.

In colonial times the governor of Virginia lived in the Palace at Williamsburg.

Plantations were very much like small villages. The plantation family lived in the large house. Nearby were the buildings where cooking, spinning, weaving, and laundry were done. There were barns and stables and several kinds of workshops.

The houses of the richest planters had many rooms. Almost every room had a fireplace to provide heat during the winter. Such houses had furniture and drapes brought from England. Food was served on fine English china.

Cooking was done over the hot coals in fireplaces. For light, the people used candles or lamps which burned whale oil.

Men usually ran the outside work of the plantations. Women ran the households. The women planned the meals and directed the spinning, weaving, and sewing.

Eliza Lucas Pinckney was a South Carolina planter. She was the first to raise indigo in the colonies. She did this when she was 21 years old. She was managing three plantations at the time.

The slaves lived in very small cabins. They did most of the work on the plantation. Some slaves were house servants. Others were expert carpenters, bricklayers, mechanics, and shoemakers. The largest number of slaves worked in the fields. They raised crops such as tobacco, rice, sugar cane, and indigo for blue dye.

In 1699, Williamsburg became the capital of the colony of Virginia. It was located seven miles from Jamestown, on higher, drier ground. It was the home of one of the first colleges in the United States. Find Williamsburg on the map of the colonies on page 35.

Years later, the capital was moved to Richmond. Then, Williamsburg began to fade. Today, Williamsburg has been restored. It looks much like it did in the old days. Many people visit Williamsburg every year.

The colony of Maryland began north of Virginia in 1634. It was founded by a wealthy nobleman, Lord Baltimore. The king of England had given him the right to start a colony. Lord Baltimore named the colony Maryland in honor of Queen Mary of England.

In 1670 the English king gave eight men a charter for a colony. The colony they started was named Carolina. It was located in a large forested region south of Virginia. In 1729 Carolina was split into two colonies. They were North Carolina and South Carolina. North Carolina was made up of many small farms. South Carolina had good harbors. The settlers in South Carolina grew crops to sell to other countries. South Carolina's busiest seaport was Charleston. It became one of the largest cities in the southern colonies.

In 1733 the last southern colony, Georgia, began. By this time Spanish settlers were living in Florida, farther south. The English king was afraid that Spain would seize nearby lands. To prevent this, he asked James Oglethorpe to start a new colony. Oglethorpe and a group of colonists settled at a place that they called Savannah. In time Savannah became a busy seaport. Thousands of colonists settled in Georgia. Many were poor people who came there to make a better life.

Many settlers came to live in the five southern colonies. People in England heard about the long hot summers and good rainfall in the south. They found that fine crops could be raised there. Some were crops that could not be grown in England, such as rice and indigo.

Some colonists, like the tobacco planters in Virginia, owned large plantations. Other settlers moved inland from the coast and started small farms. They cut down trees, built their cabins, and began raising crops. Farming became the main industry in the southern colonies.

Oglethorpe tried to make sure that the Native Americans were treated fairly. Here he introduces Chief Tomo-Chi-Chi to Georgia lawmakers.

Do you know?

1. When was the first permanent English settlement started? Where?
2. What were some problems the first settler families faced?
3. Who was the leader of the first English settlers? What made him a good leader?
4. What was the House of Burgesses? When did it first meet? Why were its meetings important?
5. Which were the five southern colonies?
6. How did climate and geography affect ways of living in the southern colonies? How do they affect your way of living?

Things to do

1. Learn who represents your area in the state *legislature*, or lawmaking body. Find out how your representative is chosen.
2. In what part of the book is the Index located? Notice that it uses several pages. It contains names of many important people, places, and things in alphabetical order.

   Look in the *J* section for *Jamestown.* On what pages of this book can you read about Jamestown? To find *Captain John Smith,* find the *S* section. An index always lists a person's last name first. On what pages of this book can you read about Captain Smith?

   Find *Williamsburg.* In what section will you look? On what pages of this book can you read about Williamsburg? Look for *James Oglethorpe.* Will you turn to the *J* section or the *O* section? On what pages of this book can you read about James Oglethorpe?
3. Look in the library for more information about the Jamestown settlement. Draw a picture showing what it looked like.

The New England colonies

The Pilgrims began the settlement of New England. Their story begins in England in the early 1600s. A new law ordered all the people to attend the Church of England. Some people refused to obey the law. They wanted to worship God in their own way. So they held meetings in secret. When the king learned of this, he was angry. He stopped the meetings and put the leaders in prison. Many of these people moved to the Netherlands. There they could worship as they pleased. They were known in the Netherlands as the Pilgrims.

The Pilgrims lived in the Netherlands for several years. Their children began to speak the Dutch language and to follow Dutch customs. Their parents were unhappy about this. They wanted their children to follow English customs. So they decided to leave the Netherlands.

Some of the leaders said that the Pilgrims should go to America. There they could worship God as they chose, yet live like English people.

A modern copy of the *Mayflower* sails the Atlantic Ocean. *(far left)* Photos of an outdoor museum at Plymouth show how the Pilgrims built thatched roofs and had fun. *(above)*

Months of planning were needed. Then the Pilgrims set out across the Atlantic. They sailed in a small ship named the *Mayflower*. The voyage took more than nine weeks. One cold wintry day in 1620, the Pilgrims reached the coast of America.

Before going ashore, the Pilgrims signed an agreement known as the *Mayflower Compact*. They agreed to obey the laws made by their leaders. They also agreed to elect representatives and to choose a governor. The Pilgrims were the first colonists to set up their own democratic government.

The Pilgrims called their settlement Plymouth. They said, "Here we shall build our homes and a new England. It will be a strong new England for our children and our children's children." Even today, the northeast corner of the United States is known as New England.

The Pilgrims had a bad time that first winter. The weather was very cold. They had to cut down trees and build shelters against the cold. Their supply of food was low. Nearly everyone was sick. Half of the Pilgrims died. But they did not give up. They were determined to build a strong Plymouth colony.

In the spring, Native Americans taught the Pilgrims how to plant corn and vegetables. They taught them how to take care of the corn while it was growing. They also taught them how to harvest it and to prepare it for eating.

The colonists hunted game in the forests and caught fish in the sea. As time passed, the Pilgrims built better houses. Slowly Plymouth grew.

The Pilgrims at Plymouth began the custom of celebrating Thanksgiving. They set aside a time in the fall to feast and give thanks for their harvest. This custom has been continued to the present day. Thanksgiving Day is now the fourth Thursday of each November.

41

The Puritans were another religious group who came to New England. The Puritans, too, were English. Many were leaders in the country. Like the Pilgrims, they did not agree with all the ideas of the Church of England. They wanted to make it more "pure," so they were called the Puritans.

But the king would not allow them to change the rules of the Church of England. As a result, many Puritans sailed to America. They brought tools, seeds, household goods, cattle, and horses.

The Puritans started the Massachusetts Bay Colony in 1629. They started the city of Boston. Locate Boston on the map of the colonies. Boston has one of the best harbors on the Atlantic coast. It soon became a busy seaport and trading center.

Within a few years, thousands of Puritans joined the first settlers. Some of them started little villages near Boston.

The Puritans worked hard. They did not approve of lazy people. They thought that wasting time was a sin.

The Puritans made almost everything that they needed. They made their own furniture from trees they cut down. They grew their own food and preserved it for the winter months. They raised cows and sheep for food and clothing. They raised chickens for eggs and meat. They spun thread on spinning wheels and wove cloth on looms. They made candles and soap.

The Puritans cooked their food in big iron pots in huge stone fireplaces. Sometimes they roasted meat on spits, or rods, that could be turned.

Everyone did a share of the work. Even young children had jobs to do. At the end of each busy day, Puritan families gathered to read from their Bibles and to say their evening prayers. They went to bed early. The children often shared small rooms up under the eaves of the houses.

The Massachusetts Bay Colony grew larger and larger. In time, the smaller Plymouth Colony became part of the larger Massachusetts Bay Colony. Together, the two became the colony of Massachusetts.

The Puritan leaders ran the colony of Massachusetts. Only church members were allowed to vote. The rules were strict, and people were punished for breaking them. One rule was that everyone must attend the Puritan church. The Puritans wanted to worship God in their own way. They were not willing, though, to give this freedom to others.

Some people began to dislike the Puritan government. These people left Massachusetts to start new colonies. Rhode Island was one of the new colonies. Find Rhode Island on the map of the colonies.

Rhode Island was founded in 1636 by a young minister named Roger Williams. He felt that people should be allowed to worship as they wished. He thought that the laws should be made by the people rather than by a few church leaders.

Williams preached these ideas in his church. This caused trouble. The Puritan leaders were so angry that they decided to ship him back to England. Friends warned him that he was about to be arrested. That night Roger Williams left his village.

He traveled through the snow-covered forests to a Narraganset (nar⁄ə gan′ sit) village. There he spent the rest of the winter. He learned the Narraganset language. He came to like and respect the Narraganset people.

(left) Roger Williams was welcomed by the Naragansets.

(below) Anne Hutchison led meetings of people who disagreed with the Puritan leaders.

The next spring, Williams paid the Narraganset for some land along the bay. This was unusual. Most settlers at that time did not believe that Native Americans should be paid for their land.

Williams founded a village on the land he had bought. He believed that God had provided a good place for his settlement. So he named the new village Providence. Find Providence on the map of the colonies. Soon many other people moved to this village. Today, Providence is Rhode Island's capital and largest city.

Anne Hutchinson was another founder of Rhode Island. She was a religious leader in the Massachusetts Bay Colony. Like Williams, she was unhappy with the Puritan government. She spoke against it. She believed that women could also tell people about God. The Puritans told her she had to leave the colony. She started a settlement on the island of Aquidneck. It later became part of the colony of Rhode Island.

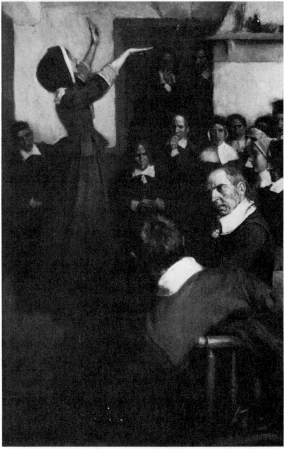

Blacksmith shop

Church

Inn

Carpenter's shop

Sawmill

Meeting house

School

Grist mill

Common

New England settlers lived in villages that looked somewhat like this.

Thomas Hooker was also unhappy with the Puritan government. So he left the Massachusetts Bay Colony. Hooker led his followers into the valley of the Connecticut River. The rich wide valley attracted many settlers. In 1638 they formed a separate colony called Connecticut. They laid out a town they called Hartford. Later, it became the capital.

Mary Dyer was a Quaker in Hartford. She was forced to leave Hartford. She was twice ordered to be hanged for her beliefs. The second time she did not get released. She died as an example to others.

New England's early settlers lived in small villages. Most of them had come from villages in England. So they liked living close together. And they could share farm tools more easily. They also could have more land for planting if people lived together in small areas.

Families lived on narrow lots in the villages. They built houses at the fronts of the lots. Behind them they planted fruit trees and gardens and built cowsheds. They planted crops in fields that they had cleared. They also planted orchards of fruit trees.

In a New England village some houses faced a square grassy field called a *common*. All of the villagers owned this public pasture. They owned it "in common." That is how it got its name. On the common the cattle could graze safe from the wild animals.

Each village had a church, a school, and a meeting house. It also had a blacksmith shop, an inn, and a grist mill. In the grist mill the farmers' wheat was ground into flour. The meeting house was very important. There the people planned the laws for the village. There they chose their leaders.

New Englanders had a share in making laws for their colony. They elected representatives to their colony's lawmaking body, or *legislature*. But these were English colonies. So the English king chose the governors and some other leaders. The people did not have as much say about their laws as they wished. This sometimes led to quarrels with the king's leaders.

The land in New England was difficult to farm. Much of the land was filled with large rocks. These had to be cleared away before crops could be planted. The land was covered by hills and low mountains. The valleys between them were usually small. As a result, the growing fields were small.

New England did not have a good climate for growing crops. Deep snow covered the ground for months at a time. The warm weather of spring came late. So the growing season was short. It begins when the heavy frosts of spring are over. It lasts until killing frosts come in the fall.

It was also hard to find people to work on the farms. And farm equipment was hard to find too.

New Englanders grew many different kinds of crops. They grew corn, wheat, barley, and hay. They grew cabbages, turnips, squash, onions, beans, parsnips, carrots, pumpkins, and cucumbers. They

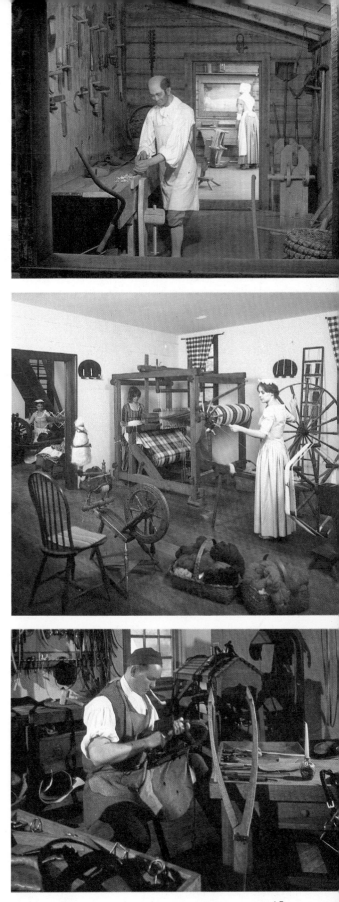

Colonists made their living in different ways. Each trade had its own tools. What tools and materials are these people using? What are they making?

45

grew fruits, such as apples, cherries, plums, and pears.

New Englanders grew almost all their own food. But because farms were small, they did not have crops left over to sell. Many people found other ways to earn their living.

Some New Englanders earned their living by lumbering. New England was covered with thick forests. Some settlers cut down forest trees for timber. They floated the logs down the swift streams. At mills the logs were sawed into lumber. The lumber was shipped to England. Lumber became a good money crop.

Some New Englanders became skilled shipbuilders. Along harbors and on the banks of rivers, colonists worked at shipbuilding. They used the tall straight pines for ship masts. They used New England lumber for other parts of the ships.

Other people of New England made their living by fishing in the ocean. There are dozens of bays along the New England coast. These bays provide shelter for boats. The coastal waters of New England were rich with cod and other fish. The fish were dried or salted and stored for a long time. Fish sold well in Europe and also in the colonies. Fishing became an important industry.

As time passed, the colonies in New England grew and grew. More and more people settled there. By 1700 there were three colonies on this land. They were

Salem, Massachusetts had two ports, one for the summer and one for the winter.

The busy harbor in New York made it one of the most important cities in the English colonies. Ships from all over the world brought their goods to this busy port.

Massachusetts, Connecticut, and Rhode Island.

New Hampshire and Maine started out as part of Massachusetts. Colonists from the Massachusetts Bay Colony settled these areas. In 1741 New Hampshire became a separate colony. Maine did not become a separate colony. It became a state in 1820.

Thousands of people also settled south of New England in the middle colonies.

The middle colonies

There were four colonies known as the middle colonies. They were New York, Pennsylvania, Delaware, and New Jersey. Find each one on the map on page 35.

Only one middle colony, Pennsylvania, was founded by English people. New York, Delaware, and New Jersey were started by people from other countries. The first settlers in this middle region were Dutch people from the Netherlands.

New York began as the Dutch colony of New Netherland. The Dutch built fur trading posts and forts along the Hudson River. They drained and filled the swampy areas around New Amsterdam. They built streets and roads. They traded with the Native Americans, and they shipped goods to other countries.

The settlements grew steadily under Dutch rule. In time, though, the king of England came to believe that New Netherland was on English lands. In 1664 he sent ships to New Amsterdam to capture the city. Most of the Dutch were farmers and traders. They had only a few soldiers and could not protect themselves. They had also become unhappy with Dutch rule. They surrendered the colony of New Netherland to the English.

The name, New Netherland, was changed to New York in honor of the English Duke of York. New Amsterdam was given the name New York City.

New York City grew rapidly. One reason was its location. It was on Manhattan Island, at the mouth of the Hudson River. It has one of the finest harbors in the world. Ships from many parts of the world called at its port. They carried away lumber, furs, and grain. Today, New York City is the largest city in the United States.

Pennsylvania was first settled by Swedish and Dutch people. Later a large group of English people called Quakers settled there. Like the Pilgrims, the Quakers did not want to attend the Church of England. When they worshiped in their own way in England, they got into trouble. Some were put in prison, and others were fined large sums of money.

In 1681 the king of England gave William Penn permission to start a colony. Penn was a Quaker. The colony was named Pennsylvania. "Sylvania," means woodlands.

Penn made sure that the colonists in Pennsylvania had freedom of religion and freedom to make their own laws. He also made sure that the Native Americans who lived nearby were treated fairly.

The first Quaker settlement was a village named Philadelphia. It means "City of Brotherly Love." Philadelphia was located a hundred miles (160 km) up the Delaware River.

Penn planned Philadelphia with care. He laid out straight wide streets and parks and gardens. Philadelphia was one of the most beautiful towns in all of the colonies. Its avenues were tree-shaded. They were lined with neat red brick houses with shining marble steps.

Philadelphia grew into a shipping center. Many ships visited its docks. They brought goods from England. They carried away crops, lumber, and other products.

New Jersey's first settlers came from several places in Europe. They were English, Swedish, Dutch, and the Scotch-Irish. New Jersey was first part of the colony of New York and later part of Pennsylvania. In 1702 New Jersey became a separate colony with its own government.

Delaware's earliest settlers came from Sweden and Finland. They called their settlement New Sweden. The Swedes and Finns had always lived near forests. They knew how to build houses of logs. In America they built the same kind of log cabins they had used in Europe. These were the first log cabins in America.

Other settlers admired these strong, warm log houses. They were easy to build and comfortable to live in. Many settlers began to build such houses. In time, thousands of them dotted the colonies.

New Sweden became first a part of New Netherland. Later it was part of New York, then of Pennsylvania. In 1704 Delaware became a separate colony. Find Delaware and New Jersey on the map of the colonies.

Many people in the middle colonies were farmers. In Europe, their ancestors had farmed the land for hundreds of years. The new settlers were pleased with their good farmland.

Broad lowlands spread over New Jersey and Delaware. Rich deep soil covered the wide valleys that reached back along the rivers of the middle colonies. The summers were warm and long. Plenty of rain fell. So large crops of fruit, barley, corn, and wheat could be grown. The region began to ship boatloads of grain to Europe.

Logs split for doors and floors

Logs notched for walls

Notched logs fit together to form corners

Moss, clay, or mud fill cracks in walls

Rough wooden shingles made from logs cover roof

Fieldstone used for fireplace

Swedish settlers taught other colonists how to build log cabins. Soon log cabins were all along the American frontier.

Some settlers had learned special trades in their homelands. When they moved to America, they found jobs as carpenters, painters, and bricklayers. Some workers knew how to build entire houses of brick.

Women and men earned their living as traders and shopkeepers. Some of them took charge of shipping goods to Europe. Those who liked to travel into the wilderness became fur traders. They paddled canoes far up the streams. The furs they brought back sold quickly to wealthy people in Europe.

The middle colonies prospered. The people there worked hard, but they liked life in America. They enjoyed owning their own farms and businesses. They were proud of their freedom to take part in the government.

People in the middle colonies chose representatives to help make their laws. This freedom was prized throughout the thirteen colonies.

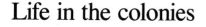

Life in the colonies

Long distances separated the thirteen colonies. These colonies extended from Maine on the north to Georgia on the south. They covered about 1600 miles (2575 km) along the Atlantic coast. You can measure this distance. Use the scale of miles or the scale of kilometers on the map on page 35.

See how well you can use the scale of distances. Imagine that you live near the coast in New Hampshire. About how many miles away is Georgia? Find out. Place a ruler on the map. Notice that the distance on the map between Georgia and New Hampshire is about four inches. On this map, one inch is for about 350 miles. Four inches then would be for about 1000 miles. That tells you that Georgia is about 1000 miles from New Hampshire.

Now use the kilometer scale. On this map, the distance is almost 11 centimeters. One centimeter is about 150 kilometers. So the distance is about 1650 kilometers.

The colonies had different kinds of lands and climates. The southern colonies had wide flat lands. The warm climate and long growing season were excellent for raising tobacco, rice, and other money crops. Many people lived on plantations and farms. Agriculture was the chief business in the southern region.

The New England colonies were on hilly, rocky lands. The winters were long and cold. The growing season was short.

Farming did not pay very well. However, thick forests covered the hills and mountains. There were millions of fish in the waters off the coast. There were good natural harbors. Many people fished, cut wood, and built ships.

The middle colonies had more level lands and much rich soil. Their growing season was long enough for a lot of crops. The deep rivers and harbors were good for trading and shipbuilding.

Many colonists came to America as indentured servants. Indentured servants were men and women who could not afford to pay their own way to America. A colonist paid the fare. In return, the servant agreed to work for the colonist for a few years. Often indentured servants learned trades or farming from their masters. After a time, usually four to seven years, the servants were free to leave. Usually there was some payment at that time. It was often clothing, tools, and a supply of food. In some places the freed servant got a plot of land.

For many years about half of the new arrivals to the colonies were indentured servants.

This is an agreement between John Henry Coats, an indentured servant, and his master, John Humphries. Coats agreed to work for nine years and seven months. In return Humphries agreed to teach Coats the trade of shoemaking and reading, writing, and arithmetic.

In 1619 a Dutch trader brought the first blacks to Virginia as indentured servants.

During the 1600s and early 1700s, many black people came. At first, a few came as indentured servants. They came to all parts of the colonies. After they were free to leave, they became farmers, mechanics, sailors, shopkeepers, traders, and musicians.

There were also black people in the colonies who never became free. They were slaves. At first slaves were brought to all of the colonies. In time, though, slavery died out in New England and the middle colonies. It did not pay there.

The number of slaves in the southern colonies increased rapidly. By the middle of the 1700s, there were nearly half a million slaves in America. Most lived in the south. Some colonists became concerned about slavery. They began to speak out against it. But the number of slaves continued to grow.

Match the names and places.

Match each person or group listed in column 1 with a colony listed in column 2. Copy the items in column 1 on paper. Then write opposite each one the correct colony from column 2. You may use some of the items from column 2 more than once.

Column 1	Column 2
William Penn	Massachusetts
Puritans	Georgia
Lord Baltimore	Connecticut
Roger Williams	Pennsylvania
Thomas Hooker	Maryland
Quakers	Rhode Island
Anne Hutchinson	Virginia
Pilgrims	South Carolina
Captain John Smith	
James Oglethorpe	
Eliza Lucas Pinckney	

Try to remember

1. What three groups of colonies were first established in the United States by England? Name the colonies in each group.

2. Who were the Pilgrims? Why did they come to America? Where did they settle? What was the Mayflower Compact?

3. Name some of the hardships that the New England colonists faced. Why do you think they stayed in America instead of returning home?

4. How was New York settled?

5. How did the colony of Pennsylvania begin? Do you think Pennsylvania would have been a good place to live? Why?

Use a map

Use the map and key on page 35 to help you answer the questions below.

1. Which of these is the *title* of the map?

   An inset map
   Thirteen English Colonies

2. How many groups of colonies does the *key* tell about?

3. Look at the *direction finder* on the map. What does *N* stand for? Which of the thirteen colonies extended farthest north? Which was farthest south? Draw a direction finder on a piece of paper and write the letters of the four main directions in the correct places.

4. There are four main directions. There are others too. Northeast is between north and east. Southwest is between south and west. In what direction is New York from Pennsylvania?

5. Look at the *scale of miles* and the *scale of kilometers*. How many miles does one inch stand for on this map? About how many miles is it from New York City to Richmond? from Boston to New York City? from Philadelphia to Boston?

   How many kilometers does one centimeter stand for? How many kilometers is each of the above distances?

Things to do

1. List some of the kinds of work the people in the colonies did. Put a check mark (✓) before each kind of work in your list that is shown in a picture in chapter 4.

2. On an outline map, label each of the thirteen colonies. Color the New England colonies light green, the middle colonies yellow, and the southern colonies orange. Make a key for your map.

3. On paper, make three columns. Head the first "southern colonies," the second "New England colonies," and the third "middle colonies." In each column write as many words or phrases as you can for that group of colonies. For example, under "southern colonies" you might write "plantations"; under "New England colonies" you might write "rocky soil."

4. Choose one of the thirteen colonies. Imagine that you must convince people to settle in your colony. Make a poster showing some of the good things about the colony.

5. It took the Pilgrims over nine weeks to cross the Atlantic Ocean. Find out how long it takes to cross the ocean today by sea and by air.

5
The thirteen English colonies win their independence

A ride spoiled a secret

The British soldiers planned to sneak out of Boston one April night in 1775. They planned to go to Concord, near Boston. They would seize the guns and ammunition stored there.

On the way, the soldiers planned to stop at Lexington to arrest two trouble-makers hiding there. They were Samuel Adams and his friend John Hancock.

But the British plan had leaked out! One colonist who heard it was Paul Revere, a Boston silversmith. He earned his living by making silverware, silver bowls, church bells, and copper articles.

Paul Revere belonged to a group who wanted to be free of English rule. He often carried messages for the group around Boston. He also took messages to other cities, such as New York and Philadelphia.

That April night in 1775, Paul Revere was ready to ride again. But he did not know which way the British would come. Would they march by land, the long way from Boston? Or would they choose the short-cut and cross the Charles River?

Revere and his friends agreed on a lantern signal, high in the tower of North Church. One lantern meant the British were coming by land. Two lanterns meant that they were taking the short-cut across the river.

Suddenly, two lanterns shone from the church tower. Revere set out. Quietly, two friends rowed him across the river. Another friend met him with a horse.

Revere sped toward Lexington. On his way, he drew up at every farmhouse, shouting, "Awaken, everyone! The British are coming."

In honor of Paul Revere's ride, Boston put up this statue in front of the Old North Church.

He arrived at Lexington about one o'clock in the morning. He found colonial guards protecting the house where Samuel Adams and John Hancock were asleep. When he first called out his warning, the guards said, "Be quiet! Our guests need their rest. We can't have noise at this hour."

"Noise?" answered Revere. "You'll soon have a worse noise! The British are coming, I tell you!" Then he banged on the door and warned Adams and Hancock to flee for their lives.

Another rider, William Dawes, also helped to spread the alarm. Look on the

54

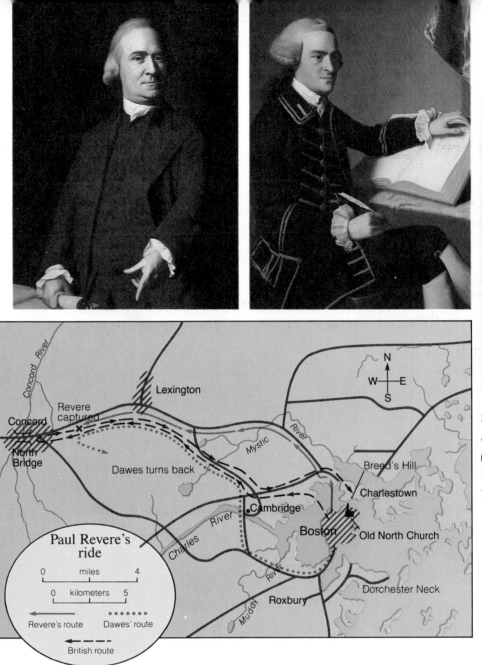

Samuel Adams *(left)*, John Hancock *(center)*, and Paul Revere *(right)* worked for independence.

map and study the routes taken by Revere and Dawes. Notice that they met at Lexington.

British soldiers stopped the two messengers at Lexington. Dawes escaped. Revere was captured. In a short time he was released but without his horse.

Meanwhile, the colonists were up and busy, preparing for the British. About seventy men gathered on Lexington Green, the village common. They were called *minutemen* because they had agreed to be ready to fight "at a minute's notice." They

had been drilling for months in many villages and towns.

The minutemen at Lexington that early morning had no uniforms and only a little training. But they were brave and determined. Their captain warned them not to fire first. "Don't fire unless fired upon," he ordered. "But if they want a war, let it begin here."

Many events had led up to this first battle of an important war. We will come back to this battle after we have read about these events.

King George III had the support of the English people in his fight against the rebellious colonies.

The colonists quarrel with England

Each colony's governor was appointed by the king in England. For years, though, the colonists governed themselves almost completely. They chose the legislatures that made the laws, even the tax laws.

The colonies were located about 3000 miles (4800 km) across the Atlantic Ocean. To get in touch with the colonists required a long sea voyage. It took three or four months to send a message and get an answer. It seemed easier to let the colonists be on their own.

As the years passed, the colonists did more and more the way they pleased. This was freedom, and they liked it. The colonists were proud, too, that they were growing stronger. They were raising fine crops and trapping many animals for furs. They were taking lumber from the forests and fish from the sea. And they were earning money by trading with other countries. The colonies were doing well even though England tried to control their trade.

From time to time the English government had passed Trade Laws. These laws said the colonists must ship goods such as sugar, cotton, tobacco, furs, and lumber only to England. They were to buy certain manufactured goods from England. These included tools, nails, buttons, and woolen cloth. The colonists were not allowed to make these things for sale to other colonies or to other countries. Also, they could not buy goods directly from other countries. Products had to be sent to England first, where a tax was added.

The Trade Laws were supposed to help England grow strong. England would get things that it needed from the colonies. English industry would make money selling goods to the colonists. The English government would get money from the taxes on the trade.

Some parts of the Trade Laws pleased the colonists. But they didn't like the limits on where to trade. The colonists wanted to sell a product wherever it brought the highest price. If they could get a better price in France or Spain, why sell to England? And they wanted to buy goods at low prices. The shipment of goods, for example, from France to England and then to America raised the cost. Both higher freight charges and English taxes made things cost more.

The colonists soon began to ignore the Trade Laws. England was far away. And even along the English coast there was much smuggling in those days. To *smuggle* is to bring goods into a country against the law. In the colonies the trade officials did not enforce the Trade Laws. So the colonists carried on a good business with other countries.

England tried to gain more control of the colonies. King George III and his advisers thought the colonists owed England a great deal. The English kings had given them permission to start colonies in the first place. English soldiers had protected the colonies. Now the colonies were making money. The English wanted a share. The king and his advisers thought of a way to get it.

By 1763 England decided the colonists must really obey the Trade Laws. One reason was that England had been fighting a long war with France. This war had cost a lot of money. England was also spending much money to keep an English army in America. The army was there to protect the colonists. The English people were already paying high taxes. So they thought that the colonists also should pay more taxes.

This was bad news. Obeying the Trade Laws meant an end to the colonists' trade with other countries. It also meant paying high prices for British goods. Then, to make matters worse, Parliament passed a new law.

In 1765 Parliament passed the troublesome Stamp Act. It required a special stamp on each newspaper printed in the colonies. Stamps were necessary on calendars, licenses, important papers, and even on playing cards. The stamps had to be bought from the British government.

When the colonists heard about the Stamp Act, they were very angry. For a hundred years they had been making their own tax laws. They were afraid that Parliament would pass other tax laws. This would take away much of their freedom.

The colonists sent a message to the king. They asked that they be allowed to help make the tax laws. But the king would not listen.

Then many Americans became bitter. They complained, "This is taxation without representation. That isn't fair!"

English goods like these were sold throughout the colonies.

Anna Catherine Green spoke out against the Stamp Act in her newspaper the *Maryland Gazette.*

Soon, colonists were fighting the Stamp Act. Some broke into the stamp offices and destroyed stamps. Others formed clubs. They held meetings and planned ways to work against the Stamp Act. One of the clubs was called the "Sons of Liberty." Paul Revere was a member of it. Another club was the "Daughters of Liberty."

Some brave newspaper publishers

spoke out against the Stamp Act. Anna Catherine Green, the publisher of the *Maryland Gazette*, was one of these brave people.

Colonists refused to buy English goods. This hurt England's business. Therefore, English merchants begged Parliament to give up the Stamp Act.

Some leaders in England felt that this law was unfair. They spoke in Parliament against the Stamp Act. Parliament agreed to do away with it, or repeal it.

Less than two years later, though, Parliament passed other taxes. These were taxes on lead, paint, glass, paper, and tea. These new taxes angered the colonists just as the old ones did. At that time they were also angry about something else. England had decided that British soldiers sent to America would live in the colonists' homes.

In 1770 there was a fight between a crowd of colonists and a group of British soldiers. The soldiers fired at the crowd. Crispus Attucks, a sailor and former slave, was killed. He is sometimes called the first person to die for American independence. The colonists called the fight the "Boston Massacre." It made them even more determined not to pay new English taxes.

Soon the taxes on everything except tea were repealed. But three years later, England placed new taxes on tea and other goods. Special tax officers were put in charge. They were ordered to punish anyone who broke the laws.

This stirred the colonists to new action. In dozens of towns and villages, the Sons of Liberty and the Daughters of Liberty met. They got the settlers not to buy the taxed goods. The British tea companies

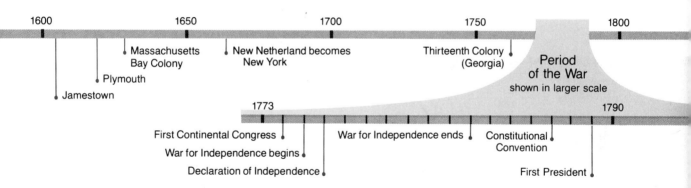

Timeline (top scale):
1600 | 1650 | 1700 | 1750 | 1800

- Jamestown
- Plymouth
- Massachusetts Bay Colony
- New Netherland becomes New York
- Thirteenth Colony (Georgia)
- Period of the War — shown in larger scale

Timeline (lower scale):
1773 | 1790

- First Continental Congress
- War for Independence begins
- Declaration of Independence
- War for Independence ends
- Constitutional Convention
- First President

lost much business. They begged Parliament to repeal these laws.

Parliament took off the taxes on most goods. But the tea tax stayed. This showed that the colonists still had to pay taxes.

Business improved for most English merchants. But the biggest English tea company was losing money. To help this company, Parliament let it sell tea in the colonies at a low price. But the colonists still had to pay a tax on this tea. They refused. Instead they made trouble for the company's tea ships.

Then one night some colonists held a Boston Tea Party. They sat in a candle-lit room near the Boston waterfront. They were members of the Sons of Liberty. Paul Revere was there. Their planning might have gone like this.

"The tea ships are still in the harbor!" said one.

"And they'll stay!" grumbled another. "The governor refuses to send them back to England. He says the tea will be unloaded."

"We'll not buy it nor pay one penny tax on it!" declared their leader, Samuel Adams.

"That's the truth!" agreed a third man. "But what can we do?"

"Sarah Fulton says we should get rid of it. That sounds like a good idea to me," said Adams.

So these Sons of Liberty agreed on a daring act. They planned to dump the tea into the harbor.

On a cold December night in 1773, more than forty colonists met. Then they rushed down the dark streets to the wharf and boarded the tea ships.

With loud cries, the Sons of Liberty went to work. They used sharp hatchets to open dozens of chests of tea. They then tossed the tea overboard. Before long, they had dumped 342 chests of tea into the harbor.

When King George III heard about this "Boston Tea Party," he was furious. "The colonists will be punished," he stormed. "I shall send General Thomas Gage and an army to Boston. He will close the Boston harbor to all ships. He will govern Massachusetts. He'll teach those colonists a lesson! They will pay for every pound of tea they have destroyed!"

British tea ships had also been unwelcome in some other harbors in the colonies. They had not been allowed to land in Philadelphia or New York. In Charleston, South Carolina, the tea had been seized. It was stored in damp cellars to spoil.

The trouble over tea was caused by a quarrel over taxes. For a long time the thirteen colonies and England had argued about taxes. By 1773 these arguments had grown into a bitter quarrel.

59

The colonists work together

Newsletters helped to draw the colonists together. Some groups were formed to write newsletters. They were called Committees of Correspondence. Samuel Adams had formed the first one in Boston. Within a short time, others were at work in several colonies.

The groups met regularly to discuss the latest news. The members talked over problems that faced the colonies. Then they put the news in newsletters.

Riders delivered the newsletters. They rode from village to village in all kinds of weather. At each stop, a friendly welcome awaited the messenger. Colonists were eager to hear the latest news.

The Committees of Correspondence had already warned that General Gage and his troops were landing in Boston. Now Boston's own committee sent out news of the stern British rule there.

General Gage's rule in Massachusetts alarmed the colonies. For one thing, General Gage sent the members of the Massachusetts legislature home. Then he began to govern the colony himself. He boasted, "I'll teach these hot-headed Americans to obey orders!"

Gage also closed Boston's harbor. This was a sad event for the busy seaport. Many people made their living by shipping and fishing. With ships idle, hundreds of workers had no jobs.

General Gage's troops wore handsome uniforms with bright red coats and high leather boots. The colonists called them "Redcoats." Some people made fun of the soldiers behind their backs.

Other colonists were quite polite and accepted the British soldiers. These colonists still were loyal to England. They were known as *Loyalists* or *Tories*. They said, "We came from England. We are living in English colonies. We must obey the king."

Another group of colonists were known as *Patriots*. They were upset by unfair tax laws and Boston's loss of freedom.

The Patriots were angry with General Gage. He had seized control of Massachusetts and had closed Boston's port. They declared, "If the British can take away Massachusetts' freedom, watch out! The other colonies are in danger, too. We must talk together and decide what to do."

The colonial leaders met at the First Continental Congress. It began in September 1774 in Philadelphia. The city was about halfway between the northern and southern colonies. Find Philadelphia on the map of the thirteen colonies.

Fifty-six delegates came from every colony except Georgia. Some delegates had traveled to Philadelphia by boat. Others had made the journey by stagecoach. A few had come several hundred miles on horseback.

The meeting of the First Continental Congress was important for many reasons. It was the first time that leaders from so many colonies had gathered. Before this, the thirteen colonies had been acting on their own. Each one was like a separate nation. Each one took care of its own affairs. By 1774, however, the colonies were starting to think more alike. Now their delegates met to talk over their problems with England.

The delegates to the Congress knew why they were meeting. But no one was sure what would be decided. There was excitement in the air. Samuel Adams, George Washington, Patrick Henry, and many others were at this meeting.

Patrick Henry was a member of Virginia's House of Burgesses. He was a Patriot and spoke out boldly against England. He pleaded for the colonies to stand together. He urged that they defend their rights and freedoms. But he warned that this might lead to war.

Most of the delegates were opposed to war. When war was mentioned, many shook their heads and said, "No! No! Not that!" One man turned to his neighbor, "Surely we can settle things with England without war!"

The First Continental Congress lasted for seven weeks. During that time many matters were discussed. The delegates were loyal to England. But they made it clear that they would not give up their rights. They would not buy goods from England or ship goods there until certain laws were repealed. Then the delegates agreed to meet again in May 1775.

Most of the delegates went back to their homes. They hoped that the quarrel with England could be settled peacefully. They wanted the right to trade freely with other countries. But they wanted to remain citizens of England as well. A few delegates thought that the colonies should break away from England.

Some Patriots began to work for independence. They hoped that some day the colonies would form a new nation. One of these Patriots was Samuel Adams. He got many colonists to help work for freedom.

Another was his friend John Hancock. A third was Paul Revere. These Patriots lived

George Washington, Patrick Henry, and Richard Henry Lee attended the First Continental Congress. What did the Congress discuss?

in Massachusetts. Already they had had trouble with British soldiers.

Patrick Henry was also speaking out for freedom. One day in March 1775 he spoke to a group of Virginians. They had gathered in St. John's Church in Richmond, their capital city. His stirring words rang out, "Gentlemen may cry, 'Peace! peace!' but there is no peace! The war is actually begun!"

Later on in his speech, Patrick Henry spoke words which have become famous, "Is life so dear, or peace so sweet, as to be purchased at the price of chains and slavery? . . . I know not what course others may take; but as for me, give me liberty or give me death!"

In the meantime, people in Boston got set for more trouble. Quietly, Patriot leaders arranged for colonists in many towns and villages to drill together. These minutemen were training in secret, almost under General Gage's nose.

General Gage had heard that two of the boldest Patriots were Samuel Adams and John Hancock. They had stirred up much bitter feeling against England. They were working for independence. The king called them rebels and ordered them arrested.

General Gage learned that Adams and Hancock were staying at Lexington, a few miles northwest of Boston. Gage also heard that Patriots had hidden guns and ammunition at Concord, near Lexington.

The British general sent nearly a thousand British soldiers to Lexington and Concord that April night in 1775. They were to capture Adams and Hancock. They were to take the supply of arms hidden in Concord. You read earlier how Paul Revere and William Dawes warned the people.

A shot at Lexington began an important war. At dawn, hundreds of British soldiers marched into Lexington. There about 70 colonists were waiting. The surprised British captain told the minutemen to lay down their arms. But the Americans would not do so. Then a shot was fired. It began a long war. Because the colonies were revolting against British rule, this is called the *Revolutionary War*. It is also called the *War for Independence*.

The handful of Patriots fought bravely at Lexington. But they were no match for hundreds of trained soldiers. After several colonists were killed, the Patriots gave up and scattered.

The British expected no more trouble. They marched on to Concord to search for guns and gunpowder. But news of their

The outnumbered colonists refused to lay down their arms. Instead, they fired on the British at Lexington. What happened next?

The colonists attacked the British near Concord's North Bridge. How did the fight at Concord differ from that at Lexington?

coming had spread. Four hundred Patriots attacked them at North Bridge.

News of the fighting stirred many minutemen to action. Some were plowing when they got the word. But they did not finish their furrows. Nor did they stop to unhitch their animals from the plows. Shouldering their guns, they hurried off to join other Patriots.

Many of these colonists lined up along the road that led back to Boston. They hid behind trees, fences, and buildings.

Then they attacked the returning soldiers with gunfire and rocks. Dozens of British soldiers fell by the roadside. Others stumbled wearily on. General Gage sent fresh troops to their rescue.

That night many campfires burned brightly around the edge of Boston. From a distance they seemed to twinkle like harmless fireflies. But the fires meant trouble for General Gage and his soldiers. There were Patriots camped around Boston. Some blocked the roads so that the British could not leave to get food. Some watched the movements of British ships in the harbor. A few Patriots were full of mischief as well as daring. They went to the door of General Gage's home. There, they tacked up this message, "Come out and fight!"

The news of the battles at Lexington and Concord spread quickly. Soon, colonists from New Hampshire to Georgia had heard it. Some people sided with the Massachusetts minutemen. Others thought that they had been too eager to fight. However, everyone knew there were serious problems ahead.

Could the colonies get England to deal with them more fairly? Or should they become independent? The colonists sent their leaders to another meeting of the Continental Congress. They were to decide what should be done.

Can you match A and B?

On paper, write each of the items in List A. Each item is the first part of a sentence. Be sure to leave space for the rest of the sentence. Find the rest of the sentence in List B and write it on your paper after the beginning of the sentence.

List A

Paul Revere	Lexington
Minutemen	Tories
First Continental Congress	Samuel Adams
	Sons of Liberty
Patrick Henry	Daughters of Liberty
General Gage	The Stamp Act

List B

organized the first Committee of Correspondence.

was a meeting of leaders representing the colonists in 1774.

was a law that put a tax on important papers.

said, "Give me liberty or give me death."

were colonists who were loyal to England.

held meetings to work against the Stamp Act.

is the place where the War for Independence began.

watched for the lantern signals. They were one if by land, two if by sea.

was sent to Massachusetts to punish the colonists after the Boston Tea Party.

were a group of colonists ready to fight "at a minute's notice."

Some questions to answer

1. Why were the colonists angry with the English government? List as many reasons as you can.
2. The colonists were afraid that England was trying to take away some of their freedom. List some things that the colonists were free to do.
3. Who were the Tories, or Loyalists? Who were the Patriots? How were the two groups different? How were they alike?

What is your opinion?

1. Why do people want to govern themselves?
2. What do you think these words mean— "taxation without representation"? How do we have taxation *with* representation in our country today?
3. What is meant by the words "price of freedom"? What price did the colonists pay?

Make a then-and-now chart

Use the pictures in this chapter to discover how people dressed in colonial times. Make a chart of dress then and now. On it, list ways people dressed "then" and some ways they dress "now." Discuss with your class the differences your chart shows.

The colonists declare independence

The Second Continental Congress met in Philadelphia in 1775. The meeting place was a brick building called the State House.

Again, the leaders of the colonies met. George Washington was there. John Hancock became the president of the Congress. Other delegates were Benjamin Franklin, Samuel Adams and his cousin, John Adams. Thomas Jefferson and Patrick Henry were there too.

This Congress tried once more to settle the problem with England. It sent a message to the king, but he refused it. Instead, he called the colonists rebels. He told of new plans to punish them. Then the Congress voted to have an army.

The Continental Congress chose George Washington to head its army. They asked him to be the commander-in-chief. Washington was a trained soldier and officer. He was also a respected leader, deeply interested in the colonies. Congress felt that he could lead the soldiers from the different colonies. George Washington had many experiences that prepared him to be a leader.

George Washington was a surveyor and soldier. He was born on a plantation in Virginia. He rode horseback ten miles every day to attend school. He liked mathematics and enjoyed working out of doors. He learned to be a surveyor. A surveyor measures lands. Young Washington was hired to survey wilderness lands in the Appalachian (ap/ə lā/chən) Mountains.

Beyond the Appalachians is the Ohio River. It flows through a wide valley of

As a young man, George Washington worked as a surveyor.

rolling hills and fertile plains. Both England and France claimed this vast region.

England's colonists wanted the rich Ohio Valley. They dreamed of settling this land. The French wanted the Ohio Valley too. They wanted to keep on trapping furs and trading with the Native Americans. They did not want English settlers in the valley. They feared that their fur business would be ruined. So the French began to build forts from Lake Erie to the Ohio River.

This news alarmed Virginia's British governor. He asked George Washington to carry a message to the French. The message was that the French must get out of the Ohio Valley. If they did not, the English would put them out.

By now, Washington had become an officer in the Virginia army. Already he was proving that he was a good leader.

65

One cold mid-winter day in 1753, Washington and a small party set out. For weeks they traveled west over ranges of snow-covered mountains. At last they reached the French fort.

The commander was polite. But he said he would not leave the Ohio Valley. Washington took this answer back to the governor of Virginia.

Washington fought in the French and Indian War. Soon, Washington was sent west again. This time, he led a band of soldiers. They were to help defend a fort built by the English. It was at the place where the Allegheny and Monongahela rivers join to form the Ohio River. Find this place on the map on page 67. The country that controlled this "gateway" could control the entire valley.

Washington and his men got there too late. French soldiers had taken the fort. They had renamed it Fort Duquesne. Some Native Americans had joined the French soldiers. They, too, wanted to keep English settlers out of the valley.

Fighting began between Washington's soldiers and the French forces. Washington was forced to surrender.

The news of the battle spread. England sent General Edward Braddock and many soldiers to fight the French. Washington became one of Braddock's officers.

General Braddock had a large army. He had heavy cannon and supply wagons. He wanted to attack Fort Duquesne. It was a long distance inland across rugged mountains. There was no road, so one had to be built.

A group of colonists began this back-breaking task. Day after day, for weeks they chopped down trees. Braddock's sol-

diers followed along behind the workers. The long lines of soldiers moved only a short distance each day.

As the soldiers came near the French fort, sharp cries rang through the forest. The French forces were hiding behind trees. The British fired their guns. But they could not see the enemy. General Braddock refused to let his soldiers break their lines. Washington came close to being wounded. General Braddock was killed. The battle for Fort Duquesne ended in a crushing defeat for the British.

Four years later, however, George Washington helped the British capture this fort. In time, the British won the French and Indian War.

After the war, Washington and other colonial soldiers returned to their homes with new feelings. They had learned how to defend themselves in war. They had also made friends with soldiers from other colonies. In time, such friendships helped to draw the colonies closer together.

After the war was over, Washington went back to Virginia. He married Martha Custis. They went to live on his large plantation, Mount Vernon.

Washington spent much time managing the plantation. He served as a member of the Virginia legislature, the House of Burgesses. It met at Williamsburg. Washington also was a delegate to the First and Second Continental Congresses.

CANADA

Lake Superior

Lake Michigan

Lake Huron

Lake Ontario

Lake Erie

Fort Dearborn
(Chicago)

Mississippi River

Missouri River

Ohio River

Fort Kaskaskia

FRENCH
TERRITORY

Tennessee River

Claimed by
England
and U.S.

Lexington
and
Concord

NEW
HAMPSHIRE

M A S S A C H U S E T T S

Saratoga

Breed's Hill

Boston

NEW YORK

RHODE ISLAND

CONNECTICUT

West
Point

New York

APPALACHIAN MOUNTAINS

River

Allegheny River

PENNSYLVANIA

Valley Forge

Trenton

NEW JERSEY

Fort Pitt
(Fort Duquesne)

Philadelphia

Monongahela River

MARYLAND

DELAWARE

Mount Vernon

VIRGINIA

Richmond

Yorktown

ATLANTIC

OCEAN

NORTH CAROLINA

SOUTH
CAROLINA

Charleston

GEORGIA

Savannah

Claimed by Spain and U.S.

SPANISH TERRITORY

N
W   E
S

New Orleans

Gulf of Mexico

The
New Nation

0	miles	200

0	kilometers	250

Thirteen
original
states

Lands gained
from England
at the close
of the revolution

■ Early
forts

✴ Battle

The Second Continental Congress declared independence. The Congress met in the State House in Philadelphia in 1776. Conditions were growing steadily worse. The British would not give the colonies the rights that they wanted. A few bloody battles had been fought.

To make matters worse, the English king had hired German soldiers to fight the colonists. This made them very angry.

By June 1776, many members of the Congress said that the colonies should be independent. Richard Henry Lee, of Virginia, declared boldly, "These united colonies are, and of right ought to be, free and independent states."

The Congress chose a committee to write a declaration. Thomas Jefferson was named its leader. He was a lawyer from Virginia. He had studied government and was a brilliant thinker and writer. Other members of the committee were Benjamin Franklin, John Adams, Roger Sherman, and Robert Livingston.

Franklin was one of a family of seventeen children. He went to work when he was ten years old. He studied before work in the morning and after work, late at night. He was a printer, writer, and inventor.

John Adams was a lawyer from Massachusetts. One day he got a letter from his wife. Abigail Adams thought that the Congress would need to make some new laws. She asked John to "remember the ladies. . . . Do not put such unlimited power into the hands of the husbands." She warned that women would rebel. We will not be bound, she said, "by any laws in which we have no voice."

Roger Sherman was a delegate from Connecticut. He had been a shoemaker.

By studying nights, he had become a lawyer and judge. Robert Livingston was a lawyer from New York.

This committee helped Jefferson write the Declaration of Independence.

On July 2, 1776, the members of the Congress met to vote on independence. Each colony was allowed one vote. Twelve colonies voted for it.

A hush fell over the room as the Declaration of Independence was read. It said "that all men are created equal" and have the right to "life, liberty, and the pursuit of happiness." It stated that a fair government was needed. It explained that, when a government is unfair, it is time to set up a new one.

The Declaration then listed many ways in which England had been unfair to the colonies. It announced that, "We, therefore, . . . declare, That these United Colonies are . . . Free and Independent States."

After the Declaration had been read, the audience cheered. Some delegates rushed up to praise Jefferson. Some shook hands with the other members. Then, each part of the Declaration was discussed.

On July 4 the delegates from twelve colonies voted for the Declaration. Soon, the thirteenth colony voted for it.

Later, many in the town met outside the State House to hear the Declaration read. Afterwards they cheered. Then a large bell high in the tower rang out the good news.

Copies of the Declaration of Independence were printed. Mary Katherine Goddard was asked to print the official copy. Copies were rushed to all of the colonies. The Congress wanted everyone to hear it read as soon as possible.

The Second Continental Congress appointed a committee to write the Declaration of Independence.

After the Declaration of Independence was signed, the colonies were called states. They were Massachusetts, New Hampshire, Connecticut, Rhode Island, New York, New Jersey, Pennsylvania, Delaware, Maryland, Virginia, North Carolina, South Carolina, and Georgia.

The State House in Philadelphia became known as Independence Hall. It is still standing. Thousands of people come to see it every year. Its huge bell is called the Liberty Bell. This bell is now on display in Independence Hall.

The Fourth of July is called Independence Day. It is a national holiday.

On July 4, 1776, the Liberty Bell was rung to announce the adoption of the Declaration of Independence. It cracked in 1835 as it was tolling for the funeral of Chief Justice John Marshall.

In 1777 the Continental Congress adopted a flag. The flag had thirteen red and white stripes. There was a circle of thirteen stars on a field of blue. One star and one stripe stood for each of the thirteen states.

The people in the thirteen states knew that their fight for independence had just begun. They did not realize, though, how long it would take to win freedom.

The colonists win independence

The War for Independence had started in 1775 at Lexington and Concord. Then the bitter Battle of Bunker Hill was fought near Boston. The battle ended when the Americans ran out of ammunition. The British took the heaviest losses though. At Bunker Hill many American lives were saved by a former slave named Peter Salem. He shot the British major who was leading an attack on the Americans. For a short time the British were confused. This gave the Americans time to retreat.

Soon George Washington took command of the American army. His army was very different from the British army. For one thing there were few "regular" soldiers. His soldiers joined up for short periods of time. So the army was always changing.

The regular soldiers were helped by the state militias. They were made up of soldiers who served during times of danger. After a danger had passed, these soldiers would go back home.

There were 5000 slaves, former slaves, and free black people in the American army and navy. Some slaves were forced

Mary Hays, also known as Molly Pitcher, took her husband's place at the cannon after he was wounded.

to fight in place of their masters. Others were freed for fighting in the army.

Many wives came along when their husbands joined the army. They cooked, sewed, and nursed the wounded. Margaret Corbin was one of these women. She and her husband John fought with the army in New York. John was killed in battle. Margaret then took over his job as cannon loader. She was wounded and captured by the British.

Mary Hays was another brave Patriot. In the middle of a raging battle, she carried pitchers of cold water to the soldiers. They called her "Molly Pitcher." When her husband was wounded, she grabbed his gun and fought on in his place.

Deborah Sampson went to war alone. She dressed herself as a man and joined the

Peter Salem, like other blacks, fought bravely at the Battle of Bunker Hill.

army. She served for nearly eighteen months before she was found out and sent home. For the rest of her life, she suffered from the two wounds she had received in battle.

Three women, Parnell Panter, Marya Allen, and Polly Daggett, helped the cause. One night a British ship lost its mast in a storm. The British came to Martha's Vineyard where these women lived. They wanted to take the town's liberty pole to use as a mast. In the dark of the night, these three daring women blew up the liberty pole. The British were stranded on the island, unable to help the siege of Boston.

Several officers were soldiers from Europe. Marquis de Lafayette (mär′-kwis di lä′fē et′) was a wealthy Frenchman. He had been trained as a soldier in France. He believed in the Americans' fight for freedom and admired their courage. He wanted to help them.

Lafayette made plans to sail to America to join Washington. The king of France learned of Lafayette's plans. He had not yet decided to help the Americans. He told Lafayette to stay in France.

But Lafayette had made up his mind. He bought supplies and a ship. He kept the ship hidden in a quiet Spanish harbor until he was ready to sail west. He was afraid to cross France in his coach, however. So he dressed as a poor messenger. He galloped ahead of his carriage and finally reached Spain. He then sailed to America.

Lafayette became a general in the American army. He served without pay until the end of the war.

71

Thaddeus Kosciusko helped the Americans during the Revolutionary War.

Baron de Kalb (di kalb′) was a friend of Lafayette. He had been born in Germany but was living in France. Soon after Lafayette, de Kalb joined the American army.

Count von Steuben was also from Germany. He taught the soldiers about discipline and fighting.

Count Pulaski (pù las′kē) and Thaddeus Kosciusko (kos′ē us′kō) were both born in Poland. Early in the War for Independence they came to America to help lead the army.

The American soldiers caused trouble for the British in Boston. Finally, the Redcoats boarded ships and sailed from Boston to Canada.

George Washington led his soldiers to meet other British forces in New York. But his army was too small to face the large British army. The British captured New York City. The American army barely got away.

Washington needed to find out what the British would try next. Nathan Hale volunteered to act as a spy to find out.

He dressed as a Dutch teacher and went to the British lines. He talked with the Redcoats and laughed at their jokes. They liked him so much that they talked freely of their plans. They did not dream that they were telling secrets to an enemy.

About the time Hale was ready to leave, a Tory recognized him. Hale was captured. The British tried to buy off the young American. They offered him money and a chance to be an officer in their army. Hale remained loyal to Washington. He was sentenced to death. Before he was hanged, he was asked if he had anything to say. Calmly, he made a short speech. It ended with these words, ''I only regret that I have but one life to lose for my country.''

The British pushed the American army back into Pennsylvania. Hessian soldiers set up camp at Trenton, on the Delaware River. Find Trenton on the map of the new nation. The Hessians were from a part of Germany. They had been hired by the British to fight the American soldiers.

In December 1776 the fight for independence seemed hopeless. Then Washington had a daring plan. Christmas was near, and he knew that the enemy would have holiday parties. He planned to attack them then. He knew an attack was not expected.

So one night Washington led about 2000 soldiers to the banks of the Delaware. They crowded into open boats, and steered their way carefully through broken chunks of ice floating down the river.

The American victory at Saratoga was a turning point in the war.

When the soldiers landed on the other side, snow was falling. They began their nine-mile (15 km) march to Trenton. When the shivering troops reached the city, the Hessians were asleep after a merry feast. Victory came quickly. The Americans won much ammunition and food as well.

The British leaders now decided to end the war with one crushing blow. The troops of General Burgoyne (bər goin′) were camped in Canada. They were to march south through New York. Other British troops were to move in from the west. Still others were to sail up the Hudson River from the south. The British armies would close in on the Americans like the jaws of a huge trap. Thus they would take the state of New York.

New York was a "key" state. If it fell, New England would be cut off from the other states. You can see how this would happen if you look at the map of the new nation. The British thought this would end the war.

Burgoyne's troops headed south. But they went very slowly. They ran into many problems. The land was thick forest. There were many lakes and swamps. There were no roads. It was hard to move a large army and its supplies through such an area.

Burgoyne's troops finally reached the middle of New York. But they did not meet other British troops. Instead, near Saratoga (sar′ ə tō′gə), American soldiers surprised them. Fierce fighting lasted for days. At last the British general surrendered his 5000 soldiers. This was a key victory for the colonies.

73

France decided to help the Americans win. Benjamin Franklin had sailed to France to ask for help. France was bitter about losing the recent war with England. So the French king listened to Franklin. But he was not ready to help. He did not think the Americans could win a war against England.

The news of the big victory at Saratoga changed the king's mind. He invited Franklin to a party in the palace. There, he said France would help the Americans.

Washington's soldiers spent a terrible winter at Valley Forge. Find Valley Forge on the map of the new nation. It was located about twenty miles (32 km) from Philadelphia. The British were staying in comfortable homes and inns in this city.

The American army was crowded into small wooden huts. The weather was bitterly cold. Icy winds piled snow in deep drifts around the cabins.

Washington's soldiers had a very hard time. They were half-starved. They had no beds and only a few blankets. They did not have warm clothes. The shoes of some

Benjamin Franklin was warmly greeted by the French king and his court.

Mary Murray talked to the British officers and learned about their plans. How did other women help?

were so worn that their bruised feet left bloody tracks in the snow.

Some soldiers died, and many others were sick with fever. Yet those who were able drilled all winter long. They still felt that they would win the war.

Many times, Washington was discouraged. But he did all he could for the soldiers. Martha Washington was at Valley Forge also. She helped make warm clothing. Martha and George spent their own money to buy food and supplies for the soldiers.

The War for Independence affected everyone in some way. Each person had to choose to help the Americans or to be loyal to England. Some families had members who helped the Americans and members who helped the British.

For example, Mary Murray was a loyal Patriot. Her husband was a Tory and a friend of the British officers. She learned of a British plan to capture Washington's army. She invited the top British officers to a dinner party. While they were at her house, Washington's army escaped.

Terrible shortages developed in the colonies. Items made of lead or pewter went to the army for bullets. Goods were no longer coming from England. So the Americans had to make everything for themselves.

Sometimes the British took food to feed their troops. One brave woman, Catherine Schuyler from New York, burned her entire wheat crop to keep it from being used by the British.

Sometimes people's houses were taken over by British officers. Lydia Darrah's house in Philadelphia was one of these. She listened while the officers were making plans. She then risked her life to tell those plans to Washington.

The War for Independence was fought in the western wilderness, too. The English had taken the French forts west of the Appalachians. British soldiers were stationed there. During the War for Independence they made trouble for western settlers by stirring up the Native Americans.

One day, George Rogers Clark visited Patrick Henry, the governor of Virginia. Clark told him that the pioneers in the west were under attack. He volunteered to raise a force of 200 men to seize the British forts.

He asked Governor Henry for money to buy supplies. Henry agreed to help Clark.

Clark and his soldiers boarded boats. They went down the Ohio River for many miles. Then they hid their boats and marched across Illinois. They were headed for Fort Kaskaskia on the Mississippi River. Locate the fort on the map of the new nation.

After dark, Clark's troops stole up to the fort. The surprised British gave up without firing a shot.

Clark hoped to capture other British forts. But they were many miles apart. So he had to make careful plans and get help from some of the Native Americans. Clark visited their campfires. He proved to the chiefs that he was a fair and bold leader. He persuaded them to help him.

Clark and his soldiers marched from one fort to another. They traveled across the snowy plains in very cold weather. They waded through icy streams. Their clothes became thin and ragged. Often they did not have enough food. But in time, Clark's brave band took many British forts.

George Rogers Clark surprised the British at Ft. Kaskaskia. His victories in the west helped our country win the Northwest Territory.

John Paul Jones's *Bonhomme Richard* was heavily outgunned by the *Serapis*. It looked like the Americans would lose the fight. How did the battle end?

The War for Independence was also fought at sea. Captain John Paul Jones took part in many sea battles. As a boy, John Paul had lived on the west coast of Scotland. He saw many ships come and go. He dreamed of the day when he would be a sailor. That day came when he was twelve years old.

Some of John Paul's trips took him to America. One day he decided to settle there. About this time he added Jones to his name. From then on he was called John Paul Jones.

When the Revolutionary War began, Jones offered to serve at sea. At first the states did not have a navy. They put guns on trading ships and fishing vessels. This was the start of the American navy. But it was no match for England's fine navy.

A famous sea battle was fought between Captain Jones's ship and an English ship. His ship was old and clumsy, and the English ship was fast and heavily armed. The two vessels shot at each other for hours. At last Jones's ship caught fire and began to sink. Things looked hopeless, but John Paul Jones would not give up.

Instead, he shouted, "I have not yet begun to fight!" Jones brought his sinking ship close to the English vessel. Then his sailors tied the two ships together. They climbed aboard the English ship and forced its crew to give up.

The war ended when General Charles Cornwallis surrendered. In October 1781 the Americans won a very big victory. The battle took place at Yorktown where Cornwallis had led the British troops. Yorktown is on the York River, near Chesapeake Bay. Locate Yorktown on the map of the new nation.

When Cornwallis set up camp, Lafayette moved his troops in to cut off escape by land. Meanwhile, Washington's army had marched south to help. French ships blocked Chesapeake Bay to stop escape by sea.

Fighting went on for three weeks. Cornwallis surrendered when he saw that his army was trapped. This ended the war. At last the colonies had won their long, hard struggle for freedom!

George Washington's *(top)* rapid march to the Chesapeake took Cornwallis *(bottom)* by surprise. After several weeks of fighting at Yorktown *(left),* the British surrendered.

Soon a peace treaty was made. In it, the British agreed that the thirteen colonies were free and independent. Also the British gave up their claim to lands west to the Mississippi River. This meant that American territories reached from Canada to Florida and from the Atlantic to the Mississippi.

By this time, the states often called themselves the United States. But they did not yet have a plan for a government.

Some questions to answer

1. What is the Declaration of Independence? Describe some ideas that are in it.
2. Describe some of the hardships suffered by the soldiers in the American army. Why do you think they kept on fighting?
3. Name some ways that colonists who were not in the army helped to fight the War for Independence.
4. Out of all the people talked about in this chapter, which one do you think did the most heroic thing? Describe what this person did.

Fun with a map

Turn to the map on page 67. Study the *key*.

1. What color shows

the first thirteen states?

the lands gained from England west of the Appalachians?

2. A *symbol* is a kind of sign, or tiny drawing, that stands for something else. What symbol on the map stands for

a fort?

a city?

a place where a battle was fought?

3. Look at the scale of miles on the map. How many miles does one inch represent on this map? About how many miles is it from Philadelphia

to New York City?

to Charleston?

to Richmond?

4. Now use the scale of kilometers. How many kilometers does 1 cm represent? Find the three distances above in kilometers.

Things to do

1. Use the index to find the names of the people listed below. On paper, write the names and the numbers of the pages in this book where they are discussed.

George Washington	Mary Murray
Mary Hays	Thomas Jefferson
Nathan Hale	Lafayette
Martha Washington	Deborah Sampson
Crispus Attucks	Peter Salem
George Rogers Clark	

2. Think of the meaning of each word below. If you don't know a meaning, look the word up in a dictionary. Write a sentence using each word.

wilderness	Patriot
representative	tax
repeal	delegate
independence	minutemen
smuggle	militia

6
The thirteen states become a nation

The Americans form a government

One evening in 1786, two Connecticut neighbors were talking.

"How did you get along selling your apples in New York City?" asked Martha.

"Badly," replied Mark. "I lost money. I hauled the apples to the coast and hired a boat. I unloaded at the wharf, but that cost a stiff tax. They said it was because I was from another state."

"Any trouble selling?" asked Martha.

"No. The merchant paid me with paper money. New York prints the money though. They charged some kind of special tax. I have a little New York money left, but it isn't worth much in our village."

"It makes me angry that states can print their own money," said Martha.

"But who can stop them?" asked Mark. "The Congress can't. It doesn't have the power. The states are running things about as they please. Look at the way they're quarreling over boundaries. They even argue about who'll use the rivers. Some states even want to make agreements with countries in Europe."

"Never!" said Martha. "That must never happen. We'd better wake up and form a national government."

Many people felt as Martha and Mark did. Among them were George Washington and Benjamin Franklin.

The leaders planned for a constitutional convention. This was in the fall of 1786. The convention was to be in Philadelphia's State House. Each state was asked to send delegates. There were 55 in all.

The delegates gathered in late May. They were respected leaders, and most of

Benjamin Franklin, printer, author, inventor, diplomat, and scientist, was admired by the other delegates.

them had taken part in the government. Some had been members of the Continental Congress and had worked together. They knew each other well.

George Washington had been given a hero's welcome when he arrived at the convention. All of the bells in Philadelphia were rung in his honor. He was elected chairman of the convention.

Before long, the delegates began to disagree. Some were afraid that a strong national government would have too much power. Others were afraid that the large states would run things. Some delegates said that the states with the largest number of people should have the most representa-

George Washington presided over the signing of the Constitution.

tives. And who would head the new nation? Some said that a president should be in charge. But others thought of a president as a king. One person said that a president should hold office for life. Many of the delegates shouted against this idea. So Washington had to rap for order.

Planning went on through the long, hot summer. The delegates argued with each other. Some gave up and went home.

One delegate, Benjamin Franklin, knew how to calm the storms. By this time he was 81 years old. But he was still a sharp thinker. His stories often set the delegates to laughing. Franklin earned the nickname "Peacemaker of the Convention."

At last in September the new plan of government was finished. It was called the *Constitution of the United States*. Most of the delegates signed it. Then each state voted on it. Some states were not happy with the new Constitution. In time enough voted for it to make it the law of the United States.

Some people were still afraid that a strong national government might take away their rights and freedoms. In 1791, some additions, or *amendments*, to the Constitution were made. These ten amendments are called the Bill of Rights. One deals with freedom of religion, speech, and press. The other nine protect other basic rights.

The Constitution set up three branches of government. This was to make sure that no person or group would get too much power. The three branches are the *executive*, the *legislative*, and the *judicial*.

The *executive* branch makes sure that the laws are enforced. An executive is a kind of manager. The President is the chief executive of the United States and is elected by the voters of the country.

The *legislative* branch makes the laws. It is called the Congress. Congress is divided into two parts, the Senate and the House of Representatives. The members of both parts are elected by the people.

The *judicial* branch decides what the laws mean and when people are breaking them. Its members are appointed, or chosen, by the President. The judges must also be approved by the Senate.

George Washington became the first President. The election was held in 1789. Washington did not want the office of President. He was weary from his years of service and longed for a quiet life at Mount Vernon. He was elected, though, and gave up his own plans.

One early spring day, Washington left Mount Vernon in a horse-drawn coach. He was on his way to New York City, the new capital of the United States. As he traveled through towns and villages, people lined the streets to cheer him. Some had closed their shops. Others had left their fields. Children were out of school. People were dressed in their best clothes for this day. Many people threw flowers in front of Washington's coach.

The people in New York made special plans to honor Washington. They sent a boat to carry him across the bay. Thirteen

When Washington was rowed across New York Harbor on the way to his inauguration, brightly decorated warships greeted him.

men, one for each of the thirteen states, rowed the boat.

When Washington reached the shore, he was greeted by a mighty welcome. Cannons boomed! Bands played! Church bells rang! While people cheered, the tall, quiet leader walked down a long red carpet.

Washington became President on April 30, 1789. This was *Inauguration Day*, the day that the President took the oath of office. Washington placed his hand on an open Bible. Then he promised to serve the country faithfully and see that its laws were obeyed.

Many people listened as Washington took the oath of office. Members of Congress and other leaders stood nearby.

Crowds cheered as George Washington took the oath of office. The nation's first President was sworn in on a crowded balcony overlooking New York's Wall Street.

Thousands of excited Americans gathered to cheer for their new President.

Some Americans wanted to call Washington, "Your Highness" or "Your Majesty." Others objected, saying, "We fought a war to be rid of kings." It was decided that "Mr. President" would be Washington's title. The Chief Executive is still called "Mr. President."

Washington was President for eight years. He served two terms of four years each. Soon after he was elected, Congress decided that New York City was too far north to be the nation's capital. So Philadelphia was made the capital.

In the meantime it was decided that a new capital would be built. It was to be on the banks of the Potomac River. The land for the capital was given by Maryland and Virginia. It was to be called the District of Columbia.

Washington guided the plans for the new capital. He hired Pierre-Charles L'Enfant, a skilled French builder who had fought in the War for Independence. L'Enfant suggested that the first government building, the *Capitol*, be the heart of the new city. It would be at the center, with wide avenues going out like spokes in a wheel. This plan was used.

83

Architect Benjamin Banneker planned Washington, D.C.

Washington also hired Benjamin Banneker as a surveyor. He was a black American scientist and inventor. Banneker planned the streets and buildings of the new capital.

Congress named the new capital Washington in honor of George Washington.

George Washington died at Mount Vernon in 1799 at age 67. He had served others for much of his life. As a young man, he had surveyed new lands to the west. He had been a soldier in the French and Indian War. He had been a member of the House of Burgesses in the colony of Virginia.

Washington had been a member of the Continental Congresses. He had served as the commander of the American army. He had been the chairman of the important Constitutional Convention. And finally he had become the first President of the United States. He served as President for eight years. George Washington's birthday is a national holiday.

84

Choose the correct endings

Three endings are given for each of the incomplete sentences below. Write the numbers 1 to 7 on paper. After each number write the ending that completes the sentence correctly.

1. At the close of the Revolutionary War, the colonies (worked together.) (argued with each other.) (were ruled by England.)

2. One central government was needed (to unite the states.) (to give more power to each state.) (to choose a king.)

3. The Constitutional Convention elected as its leader and chairman (Benjamin Franklin.) (Thomas Jefferson.) (George Washington.)

4. The new plan of government was called (the Bill of Rights.) (the Constitution of the United States.) (the Declaration of Independence.)

5. The purpose of the legislative branch is (to make laws.) (to enforce the laws.) (to punish lawbreakers.)

6. The city of Washington was planned by (Pierre-Charles L'Enfant.) (Benjamin Franklin.) (General Lafayette.)

7. The laws of the United States are made by (Congress.) (the states.) (the President.)

Things to do

1. Find out more about one of these people.

   Martha Washington   John Adams
   Benjamin Franklin   Abigail Adams
   Thomas Jefferson   Benjamin Banneker

   Be ready to share with your class some of the interesting information you learn.

2. Choose one event in the life of George Washington. Act out a short play about it.

In what order

Below is a list of important events. On paper, write the numbers 1 through 8 in a column. Then write the important words of the event that happened first after number 1. Write each letter after a number to show the order in which the events happened.

a. The First Continental Congress was held.

b. The English began to settle the Massachusetts Bay Colony.

c. George Washington was inaugurated President.

d. Cornwallis surrendered.

e. Washington was elected President.

f. The Constitutional Convention was held.

g. The War for Independence began.

h. Abigail Adams tells John Adams to "remember the ladies."

Can you answer these questions?

1. What were some of the problems that faced the Americans after the War for Independence?

2. What three branches of government were set up by the Constitution? Describe each of the branches.

3. What city was the first capital of the United States? What was the second capital of the United States?

4. Where and why was a new capital laid out?

5. What is the Bill of Rights? Why was it added to the Constitution?

To help you dramatize

It is fun to make a play about some event in our lessons. We call this dramatizing. It is a good idea to keep such plays very simple. So it is not necessary to make scenery or costumes or to memorize parts.

First, help your class choose an event to dramatize. Then quickly get all the information you can about that event. Read the story material carefully and study helpful pictures. While you are doing this, pretend you are one of the characters and think what you would do and say in the play.

7
Our wonderful country

A huge and varied land

The Navajos are one group of Native Americans. Long ago the Navajos traveled south from what is now Canada. They came to the southwestern part of what is now the United States.

The Navajos settled on desert lands of little rain. The summers are long and burning hot. It takes great skill and knowledge to live in such an environment. *Environment* includes all of the things around us.

The Navajos lived in harmony with their environment. They learned how to survive in the dry, unfriendly land and to use nature's gifts wisely. They had a saying.

The frog does not
Drink up
The pond in which it lives.

What does this saying mean to you?

Most Native Americans had a special feeling about the land. They loved and respected nature's gifts of
air,
land and water,
oceans, rivers, and lakes,
mountains and plains,
rain and sunshine,
plants and trees,
birds, fish, and other animals.
They realized how much they depended on nature's gifts.

They said, "We are a part of nature. We cannot live without nature's gifts. We must honor, respect, and protect these gifts. If we don't, we will suffer."

Do people today feel this way about nature's gifts? How are you helping to care for nature's gifts? What else can you do to protect these gifts? Think about these

Navajos began herding sheep soon after the Spaniards introduced sheep and horses to the Southwest. Earlier the Navajos had been hunters and farmers.

questions as you read about the great country that is the United States.

The land the Navajos knew is only a small part of this country. The United States reaches from the Atlantic Ocean on the east to the Pacific Ocean on the west. It reaches from Canada on the north to Mexico on the south.

Still more lands are a part of our country. They are the far-distant states of Alaska and Hawaii. Alaska is our northern most state. See the map on page 327. Hawaii is a group of islands far out in the Pacific Ocean. Find it on the global map on page 341.

Zebulon Pike and his party discovered Pikes Peak as they were exploring the Arkansas and Red rivers. Ninety years later, the top of Pikes Peak inspired Katherine Lee Bates to write "America the Beautiful."

The United States has many different kinds of land. There are wide plains, fertile valleys, and rolling hills. There are high plateaus and ranges of mountains.

These kinds of lands are shown in the pictures in this chapter. They show the kinds of land you would see if you traveled along the red line on the map on pages 90-91.

Where are these various kinds of land in the United States? What are they really like? Let's take a closer look and find out.

The United States has both high lands and low lands. You can see this on the map on pages 90 and 91. The mountain peaks are the highest lands. One of the tallest mountains is Pikes Peak. Pikes Peak is in the Rocky Mountains. The altitude of Pikes Peak is 14,109 feet (4300 m). *Altitude* is the height of land above the level of the sea. Mount McKinley, in Alaska, is much higher. It has an altitude of 20,300 feet (6187 m). Mount McKinley is the highest point in the United States.

Another word for altitude is *elevation.* Elevation figures often appear on road signs. For example, if you were driving into Chicago, you might see a sign that says this: "Chicago, elevation 610 feet." That tells us that Chicago is 610 feet (186 m) above the level of the sea.

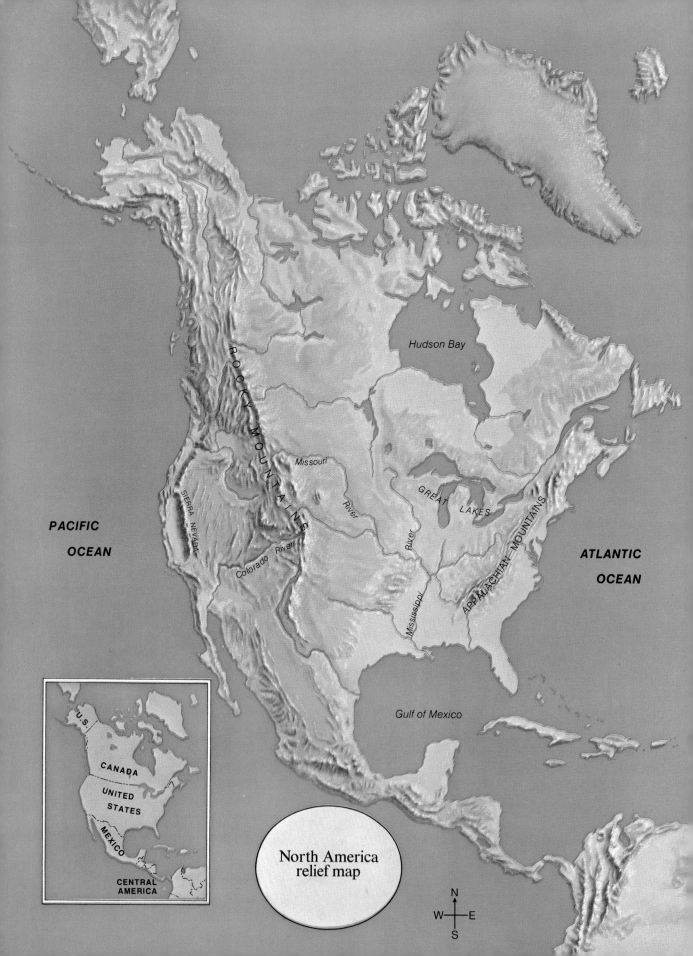

Hudson Bay

Missouri

River

GREAT LAKES

River

Mississippi

APPALACHIAN MOUNTAINS

ROCKY MOUNTAINS

SIERRA NEVADA

Colorado River

PACIFIC OCEAN

ATLANTIC OCEAN

Gulf of Mexico

North America
relief map

U.S.

CANADA

UNITED STATES

MEXICO

CENTRAL AMERICA

N
W E
S

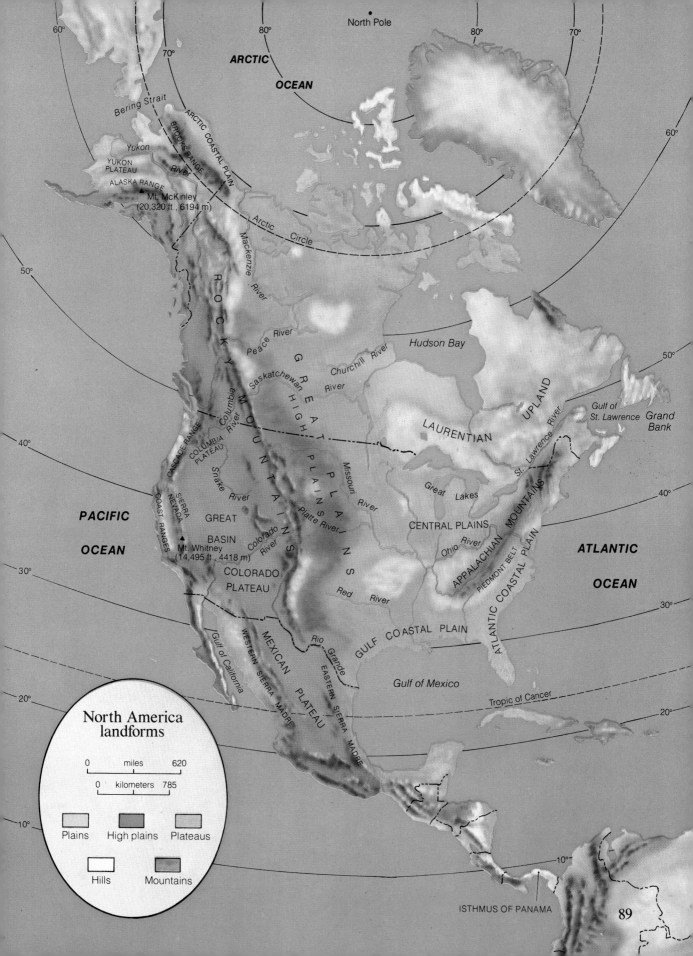

North Pole

ARCTIC

OCEAN

60°

70°

80°

80°

70°

60°

60°

Bering Strait

ARCTIC COASTAL PLAIN

BROOKS RANGE

Yukon

YUKON
PLATEAU

Yukon

River

ALASKA RANGE

▲ Mt. McKinley
(20,320 ft., 6194 m)

Arctic   Circle

Mackenzie

River

R
O
C
K
Y

M
O
U
N
T
A
I
N
S

50°

Peace River

Saskatchewan

River

Churchill River

River

Hudson Bay

G
R
E
A
T

H
I
G
H

P
L
A
I
N
S

50°

40°

CASCADE RANGE

COLUMBIA
PLATEAU

Columbia
River

LAURENTIAN

UPLAND

St. Lawrence River

Gulf of
St. Lawrence

Grand
Bank

40°

Snake

River

SIERRA
NEVADA

COAST RANGES

GREAT

▲ BASIN

Mt. Whitney
(14,495 ft., 4418 m)

COLORADO

PLATEAU

Platte River

Colorado
River

Missouri

River

Red   River

Great   Lakes

CENTRAL PLAINS

Ohio River

APPALACHIAN MOUNTAINS

PIEDMONT BELT

ATLANTIC COASTAL PLAIN

40°

PACIFIC

OCEAN

30°

ATLANTIC

OCEAN

30°

Gulf of California

WESTERN SIERRA MADRE

MEXICAN
PLATEAU

EASTERN SIERRA MADRE

Rio

Grande

GULF COASTAL PLAIN

Gulf of Mexico

Tropic of Cancer

30°

20°

20°

ISTHMUS OF PANAMA

10°

10°

10°

North America
landforms

0   miles   620

0   kilometers   785

Plains   High plains   Plateaus

Hills   Mountains

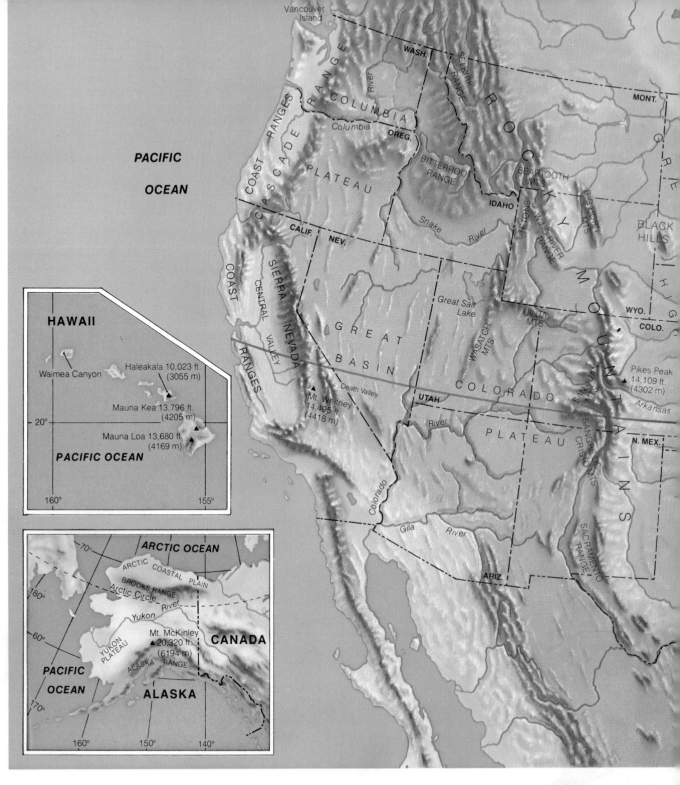

PACIFIC

OCEAN

WASH.

COLUMBIA

River

Columbia

OREG.

PLATEAU

CALIF.   NEV.

COAST RANGES

CASCADE RANGE

Snake

BITTERROOT
RANGE

IDAHO

ROCKY

SELKIRK
RANGE

MONT.

BEARTOOTH
MTS

BIG HORN
MTS

BLACK
HILLS

River

SNAKE RIVER RANGE

WIND RIVER RANGE

MOUNTAINS

GRE

WYO.

COLO.

Great Salt
Lake

UINTA
MTS

WASATCH MTS

GREAT

BASIN

COLORADO

Pikes Peak
14,109 ft.
(4302 m)

Arkansas

UTAH

PLATEAU

N. MEX.

Mt. Whitney
14,495 ft.
(4418 m)

Death Valley

River

Colorado

Gila

River

ARIZ.

SACRAMENTO
RANGE

SANGRE DE CRISTO MTS

SIERRA NEVADA

CENTRAL VALLEY

COAST

RANGES

Vancouver
Island

HAWAII

Haleakala 10,023 ft.
(3055 m)

Waimea Canyon

Mauna Kea 13,796 ft.
(4205 m)

Mauna Loa 13,680 ft.
(4169 m)

20°

PACIFIC OCEAN

160°   155°

ARCTIC OCEAN

70°

ARCTIC COASTAL PLAIN

BROOKS RANGE

Arctic Circle

River

180°

Yukon

CANADA

60°

YUKON
PLATEAU

Mt. McKinley
20,320 ft.
(6194 m)

ALASKA RANGE

PACIFIC

OCEAN

170°

ALASKA

160°   150°   140°

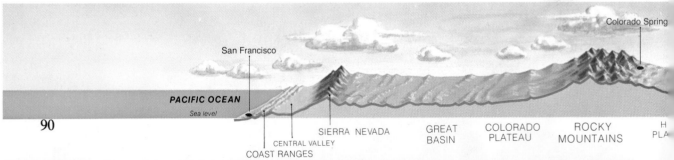

Colorado Spring

San Francisco

PACIFIC OCEAN

Sea level

COAST RANGES

CENTRAL VALLEY

SIERRA NEVADA

GREAT
BASIN

COLORADO
PLATEAU

ROCKY
MOUNTAINS

H
PLA

90

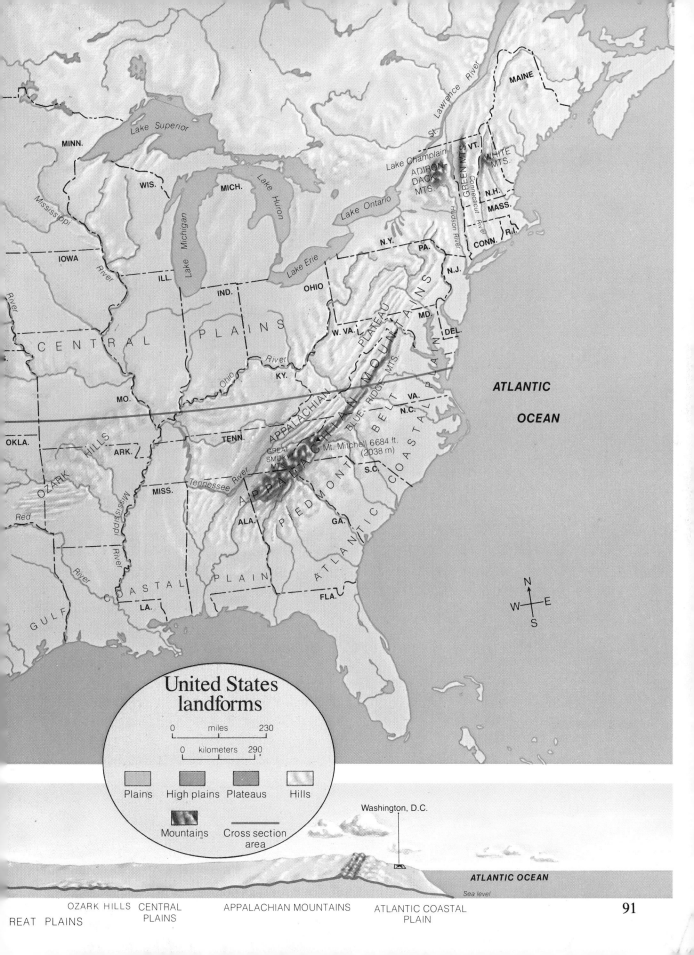

United States landforms

MINN.

Lake Superior

WIS.

MICH.

Lake Huron

Lake Michigan

Mississippi River

IOWA

ILL.

IND.

OHIO

Lake Erie

Lake Ontario

St. Lawrence River

MAINE

Lake Champlain

VT.

ADIRON-
DACK
MTS.

GREEN MTS.

WHITE
MTS.

N.H.

MASS.

Hudson River

Connecticut River

CONN.

R.I.

N.Y.

PA.

N.J.

C E N T R A L   P L A I N S

River

MD.

DEL.

W. VA.

KY.

Ohio River

P L A T E A U

A P P A L A C H I A N   M O U N T A I N S

VA.

BLUE RIDGE MTS.

N.C.

A T L A N T I C   C O A S T A L   P L A I N

ATLANTIC

OCEAN

MO.

TENN.

GREAT
SMOKY
MTS.

Mt. Mitchell 6684 ft.
(2038 m)

OKLA.

H I L L S

ARK.

S.C.

O Z A R K

MISS.

Tennessee River

Mississippi River

A P P A L A C H I A N

P I E D M O N T

B E L T

S.C.

ALA.

GA.

Red River

River

LA.

G U L F   C O A S T A L   P L A I N

A T L A N T I C   C O A S T A L   P L A I N

FLA.

N
W   E
S

United States landforms

0   miles   230

0   kilometers   290

| Plains | High plains | Plateaus | Hills |

| Mountains | Cross section area |

Washington, D.C.

ATLANTIC OCEAN

Sea level

REAT PLAINS

OZARK HILLS

CENTRAL
PLAINS

APPALACHIAN MOUNTAINS

ATLANTIC COASTAL
PLAIN

The Great Smoky Mountains are part of the Appalachians. Where are the Appalachians?

Large areas of the United States are plains. *Plains* are mostly level lands. Some plains are shown in the picture on page 97. Notice how flat they are.

Plains are usually good farmlands. Most areas on plains are fertile. They can produce large amounts of food. It is easier to build roads and railroads on plains than over mountains.

Some parts of the United States are plateaus. A *plateau* is a broad, high area of land. It may be partly flat and partly hilly. It may have steep slopes on one or more sides.

On the map on pages 90 and 91, two large plateaus are shown. Find them. Plateaus in the western part of the United States are often very dry lands. How are plateaus different from the central plains?

Hills extend through many parts of the United States. *Hills* are rolling lands that are not as tall as mountains.

Look at the hills in the picture on page 94. See how rounded they are. Hills are often rounded because rain, wind, snow, and ice have been grinding them down for millions of years.

Hills are difficult to farm. But they are often wooded and beautiful. The map on pages 90 and 91 shows two well-known groups of hills. Find them on the map.

The United States has many beautiful mountains. *Mountains* are higher than hills. See the pictures on these two pages. Are there any mountains in the state which you live?

Look again at the map on pages 90 and 91. What color on the map shows mountains? Sometimes the word highlands is used for land that has hills and mountains. Find the Appalachian Highlands. The Ap-

The rugged peaks of the Rocky Mountains dominate the western part of the United States. How are the Rockies different from the Appalachians?

palachians are very old mountains. They are rounded and include range after range of mountains. A range is a row of connected mountains. The Appalachians run from Canada south to Alabama. These mountains have different names in different places.

The Great Smokies and the Blue Ridge Mountains are a part of the Appalachians. So are the Adirondacks and the White Mountains. Do any of the Appalachians come into your state? If so, which ones?

Now locate the Rocky Mountains. Which mountains are higher, the Appalachians or the Rockies? How is this shown on the diagram on the bottom of pages 90-91?

The Rocky Mountains stretch from Canada to Mexico. The Rockies also include many different ranges with names of their own. Among them are the Grand Tetons and the Wind River Mountains.

Farther west, near the Pacific Ocean, is another great group of mountains. This group includes the Sierra Nevada, the Cascade Range, and the Coast Range. Find them on the map and on the diagram. Which is higher, the Sierra Nevada Range or the Coast Range?

Fertile valleys lie between some ranges of mountains and hills. Locate a valley on the map on pages 90 and 91. There is a long, wide valley in California. It's between the Sierra Nevada and the Coast Range. What is it called?

Many valleys were carved out by rivers rushing down from mountains and hills. As water drains off mountain and hill slopes, it washes earth away. Many little streams cut their way down the slopes. Gradually the streams carve out small valleys. Farther on, larger valleys are carved out as streams join together to become larger. Finally the streams join a river.

A large valley looks nearly flat. Actually, the sides slope so that water drains into the river flowing through the valley.

The Ohio River is an important part of our transportation system.

There are many rivers and lakes in the United States. A river may start high in the mountains when melting snow and ice form little streams. It may begin at a place where underground water bubbles up to form a spring. The place where a river begins is called its *source*.

The streams join together and grow larger. In time they become a river. Most rivers flow to the sea. A river, together with its tributaries, is called a *river system*.

Two large rivers that empty into the Atlantic Ocean are the Hudson and Connecticut rivers. They begin in mountains which are a part of the Appalachian Highlands.

Many streams hurry down the western side of the Appalachians. They join the Ohio River. When rivers flow into a larger river they are called its branches, or tributaries. The Ohio is a large river itself. But it empties into a larger river, the Mississippi. Therefore, the Ohio is a tributary of the Mississippi.

The long, winding Missouri is another tributary of the Mississippi. It journeys about 2700 miles (4345 km) on its way to the Mississippi.

The Mississippi is a mighty giant. But no wonder, it has so many branches! You can see this on the map on pages 90-91. The name Mississippi comes from a Native American word meaning "great river."

Several important rivers flow through the western part of the United States. Two are the Colorado and Columbia rivers. Locate the Colorado River on your map. In what mountains does it begin?

The source of the Columbia is high in snowy mountains in Canada. This river winds southwestward. It finally becomes part of the boundary between the states of Oregon and Washington. With your finger, trace its course on your map.

There are many other rivers in the United States. What one is best known to you? Is it used as a waterway? Does it provide power for making electricity or irrigation water for crops? Does it furnish water for cities to use?

Lakes are also a natural resource. The five Great Lakes extend along a part of our northern boundary. Locate them on the same map. We share four of these lakes with Canada. Which one lies entirely within the United States? The Great Lakes and the St. Lawrence River together form a valuable waterway.

There are thousands of other lakes scattered through the United States. Rivers and lakes are useful as well as beautiful.

Lake Michigan *(top)*, Alaska's Noatak River *(left)*, and Utah's Great Salt Lake *(right)* show the variety that can be found among our country's waterways.

These pictures should make you think about important natural resources. What resources are shown? How are these resources used?

The United States has many valuable natural resources. These resources include air, water, soils, climate, forests, oil, and coal. What other natural resources can you name?

For a long time we have used many of our natural resources carelessly. Clean air is necessary for our health. Yet we have allowed our air to become dirty, or *polluted*, with gases, smoke, and other wastes. We have let harmful chemicals and waste materials get into our streams, rivers, and lakes. Even the oceans are being affected by the harmful wastes dumped into them. So, today, water pollution is a big problem.

Later in this book we shall talk more about pollution problems. We shall also discuss *conservation*, or ways of using our natural resources more wisely.

By now, you should realize that we live in a wonderful country. You know that nature has given us many marvelous gifts.

But natural resources alone did not make this country a great country. The people of this country have been our greatest resource.

The Native Americans loved this land. They learned to live with the land and not just on it. They respected the land and everything on it. When the Europeans came to North America, many of these Native Americans helped them learn about the land. They taught them to live with it.

People came to the United States from all of the world's countries. Many came

because they wanted to. Others had no choice—they were forced to come. But all of these people had a part in the building of our country.

Today, the number of people living in the United States is growing. We are using up our natural resources. People became careless. It seemed that the United States was so rich in resources that they would never be used up. But most of these resources will take hundreds or thousands of years to replace. Some, like oil and natural gas, can never be put back.

We must conserve those resources that cannot be replaced. We must learn to develop new ones.

Solar energy is heat from the sun. The United States gets lots of heat from the sun. The amount of energy the country gets from one hour of sunlight would supply its needs for about three years. The problem is how to collect, store, and use this power. Some scientists are working in the field of solar energy. A number of scientists are working on projects in desert areas. Why do you think this is a good place to do this work?

What are some ways you can help conserve natural resources? Can you think of other ways in which you can help fight pollution and conserve resources? All of us must help do this. That is the only way we will be able to help the earth support all the people who live on it. That is the only way that we will be able to keep on enjoying nature's gifts to us.

Finding and using maps

1. Find a relief map in this chapter. On which page is it?
2. Which page has the landforms map of our country? On this map locate where you live. What is the main kind of landform in your area?
3. Find a page that shows an inset map.
4. Where do you find an elevation sketch?
5. Where is the landforms map of our continent located?
6. On which page in this chapter are there maps with keys?

Test your reading

Write the numbers 1 to 6 on paper. After each, write the word or words needed to complete the sentence.

1. A _____ map gives us a general idea of where the land is hilly and where there are plains.
2. A _____ map shows the location of plains, hills, plateaus, and mountains.
3. The streams and rivers that flow into a large river are called its _____.
4. The five largest lakes in the United States are _____.
5. The place where a river begins is called its _____.
6. Nature's gifts such as climate and soil are called _____.

Things to do

1. Find pictures of the many types of land and water described in the unit. Cut out the pictures. Use them to make a booklet about the geography of the United States.
2. Use salt and flour, clay, sawdust, or other material to make a relief map of the United States. You may need to look in library books to find out how to do this.
3. Make a diorama showing the land occupied by Native Americans in the southwestern United States.

What do you think?

1. Why do we say that our country is rich in natural resources? How can we help to conserve them?
2. Why do we have more and more pollution in our environment?
3. How can we help to clean up our air and water? Why is it important for us to do this?
4. How could Native Americans live in an area for thousands of years without hurting it? What kinds of things do you think they did to protect the animals and the land around them? What things *didn't* they do?
5. An *ecologist* (e kol′ə jist) is one who studies what happens to animals and plants when the place in which they live changes. An ecologist also studies how changes around humans affect them. What kind of books would you read if you wanted to be an ecologist?

3

How our country grew

8
Pioneers cross the mountains

Daniel Boone looks westward

Daniel Boone and John had become good friends. They met while driving supply wagons for General Braddock's army.

In the evenings Daniel, John, and other drivers sat around a campfire. One night a driver spoke up, "John, I hear you've been west, over the mountains."

"That I have," John replied, nodding. "You all ought to go! It's grand meadowland country!"

"Good hunting out yonder?" asked another driver.

"I should say so!" replied John. "Great hunting! The buffalo are so big that, when they walk, the meadows sink in. I saw so many deer and elk I couldn't count them in a week! There were millions of turkeys, too! They had to take turns flying!" John went on and on spinning his tall tales.

Twenty-year-old Daniel sat spellbound. Later he asked, "What's the name of that wonderland out west, John?"

"The Indians call it Kentuck, Daniel," John said. "You should see it someday."

"Could be I will," answered Daniel. From then on, Daniel Boone dreamed of exploring Kentucky.

Daniel Boone was born in a small Pennsylvania settlement in 1734. His parents were Quakers. They had a small farm, a blacksmith shop, and a weaving business. Each of their many children had special work to do. Daniel herded the cows and helped raise the crops. He went through the woods like a hunter. He spent hours at target practice and became a fine marksman.

Native Americans lived near the settlement. They taught Daniel some hunting secrets. They taught him how to move through the forests silently. He learned how to make the sounds of birds and animals to draw wild game close.

At age 15, Daniel with his family moved far south. They settled along the Yadkin River on the North Carolina frontier. Find this area on the map. A *frontier* (frun tir′) is the edge of a settled area. People who settle on a frontier are called *pioneers* (pī′ə-nirz′). Most of the settlers from Europe didn't know that Native Americans had

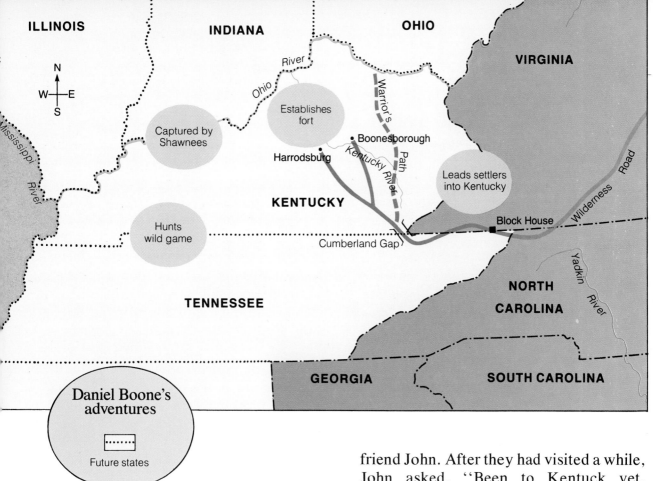

Daniel Boone's adventures

▭┈┈┈┈

Future states

already explored and settled many parts of the continent. The European settlers thought of it as empty land.

Daniel helped build a log cabin and clear land for crops. He hunted and trapped in the forests. His favorite job, though, was exploring. Later, he went north to drive an army supply wagon.

After Boone returned home, he married Rebecca Bryan. She was the daughter of a neighbor. They built a log cabin and began to farm. But Daniel was not happy and he was restless. He turned to hunting and trapping for a living. Daniel was away for months at a time. Rebecca took care of their home, family, and farm alone. She had courage and was handy with a gun.

One day a peddler came by. He was selling needles and cloth. Daniel was at home. He saw that the peddler was his old friend John. After they had visited a while, John asked, "Been to Kentuck yet, Daniel?"

"Not yet, friend," answered Daniel. "But I'm aiming to go someday."

"Better you don't wait!" said John. "It's likely that land fever will take settlers out there before long. Then it'll be crowded."

Daniel and John began to make plans to explore Kentucky.

In 1769 Boone and several friends headed west. They carried supplies such as warm bearskin blankets, salt, a small kettle or two, and their guns.

They crossed range after range of tree-covered Appalachians. At last they got to Cumberland Gap. A *gap* is an opening, or low place, through a mountain range. Find Cumberland Gap on the map about Daniel Boone.

Boone's party went through the gap. Then they took an old trail into Kentucky. Hunters had named this trail the Warrior's

Path. It led to the hunting grounds of some Native American peoples. Find the Warrior's Path on the map.

Boone and his friends made camp. Kentucky was all they had dreamed. They liked its wooded hills and green meadows. Long before, there had been trees just about everywhere. The Native Americans had burned off some trees so that more grass would grow. Grassy meadows brought deer and other wild game.

Boone's party hunted many animals for their furs and skins. They knew that furs would bring a good price back home.

But the Cherokees had taken this hunting ground. It had been theirs for hundreds of years. They were angry when a stranger killed animals they needed for food and furs. They attacked Boone's party and took its furs and skins. The leader of the Cherokees warned the men to leave.

Boone did not leave. For many months he explored Kentucky by himself. He found rich soil that would grow good crops. He dreamed of leading settlers to this new frontier.

Boone knew that it would not be easy to settle in Kentucky. It was a dense wilderness. There were no roads. It was far from towns and cities. Also, many Native Americans lived in this region. They would fight to protect their lands. Life for the settlers would be hard and full of dangers.

Pioneers settle Kentucky and Tennessee

The first frontier had been along the Atlantic coast. It was the wilderness where the earliest settlers lived. It, too, had been a land of dangers and hardships.

Yet it was a good land. So the colonists stayed.

As the years passed, more and more people settled along this coast. Thousands of people came from Europe. Also, the colonists had large families. As their children grew up, many of them started farms. By the 1780s the best land along the Atlantic coast was being used.

Then there was another problem. Much of the land had been farmed for a long time. Tobacco and some other crops had worn out the soil. Some farmers could hardly make a living on the poor soil. People had to move farther west to find fertile land. The best new lands with rich soils lay beyond the Appalachian Mountains.

But lands west of the Appalachians were to be kept for Native Americans. Some groups had lived there a long time. Others had gone there when the colonists settled the lands near the coast.

Hunters were the first colonists to cross the Appalachians. The mountains rose like high walls, one beyond the other. Their slopes were steep and covered with thick forests. There were only a few gaps through the ranges. So trails wound up and down the slopes.

Hunters were often on the move looking for wild game. So they found out much about a region. They learned about the native peoples. They discovered the best places to cross rivers. They found the trails and the gaps through the mountains.

Some explorers of the frontier marked cuts, or blazes, on trees along the way. Such explorers were called trailblazers. Daniel Boone was a famous one. He made many trips over the mountains to trap for furs and to claim land.

In 1775 Boone began to carve out a route to Kentucky. Boone and 28 workers started across the mountains. He rode ahead to show the way and blaze the trail. For part of the way, he followed the old Warrior's Path. The workers swung their mighty axes to chop down trees and clear away brush.

Building a route through the Appalachians was hard work. But each day the workers pushed on a little farther. At last the 300-mile path was finished. It became known as the Wilderness Road. It was narrow, rocky, and often steep. It was full of tree stumps. Find the road on the map about Daniel Boone. The Wilderness Road led to the heart of Kentucky. Boone's party camped near the Kentucky River. There they started a settlement.

Boone and his friends built the town of Boonesborough. How did the settlers protect their homes?

Boone and his friends built Boonesborough. Find it on the map on page 101. Boonesborough was built like a fort. Log cabins were lined up around a center yard. They had no doors or windows in their back walls. The cabins were joined by a heavy wall of logs called a *stockade*.

At each corner stood a two-story blockhouse with narrow windows. The pioneers could fire their guns through them.

103

Huge log gates led into the fort. They were closed at night and in times of danger. Children often tended livestock outside the walls during the day. The cattle and horses were kept inside the stockade at night for safety.

The settlers cleared away the hiding places near the fort. They cut down most of the trees but left one old elm standing. On hot days it spread cooling shade. This elm served as a kind of town hall. Under it the people discussed their problems and plans. There they made the laws for their little settlement.

Planning together was the way of life in Boonesborough. Working things out together is a part of what is called *democracy* (di mok′rə sē). Democracy means that people govern themselves.

Many tales about Kentucky were told by hunters and trappers. They told about buffalo hunts and other adventures. They spread news about the fertile land. Many people were thinking about moving west. They wanted to learn more about the land beyond the Appalachians.

Here is a story about a family that decided to move west. The Fosters lived in Virginia on a tobacco farm. They were poor people. Their land was so worn out that only small crops could be grown. The Fosters were often ready to give up and move away.

One evening, a weary traveler knocked at the Foster cabin. "I've just come from the west," he explained. "Could you let me stay here for the night?"

The Fosters asked the stranger in. This was the custom in those days. While the stranger talked, the family cooked supper. It was the light meal of the day. Tonight it

Boonesborough's old elm served as a town meeting place. In its shade, settlers discussed their problems and plans.

was corn-meal mush topped with honey and milk. The mush was cooked in a large kettle in the fireplace.

After the meal, the Fosters and their bearded guest sat around the cheery fire. He told the family about Kentucky.

He said that Kentucky had land for sale for about two dollars an acre. A *deed* was given to a person who bought land. A deed was a paper that showed who owned a piece of land.

"Of course," said the stranger, "some people think that frontier land should be free. They don't bother to buy it. They settle where they please and clear the land and plant crops. They are called squatters. They are living on land they don't own or rent. This is against the law."

"What happens to squatters?" asked Matthew.

"Oh, they're forced to move, once the government finds out about them," an-

Families like the Fosters moved west to start a new life.

swered the hunter. "The smartest folks buy the land and get a deed for it."

Many ambitious settlers were preparing to move west. The Fosters and some of their neighbors decided to join them. They bought land near Boonesborough and received their deeds.

One winter evening, after months of planning, Mr. Foster said, "Well, it's all settled now. When spring comes, we'll head west. There'll be about fifty of us."

Packing was a big job. There were so many things to take to a new home. They had to take clothing, the soft feather beds, the butter churn, and the spinning wheel. They would need the table and chairs and their dishes and iron kettles. There would be no place to buy supplies. So they would take tea, salt, sugar, flour, corn meal, and bacon. They would need corn and potatoes

to plant. And, of course, they must have guns and gunpowder. Some things could not be moved.

"The trail is rough and steep," Mr. Foster said. "We can't take wagons, so we'll have to pack all of our things on horses."

"Everything?" asked Matthew.

"Everything we take," answered his mother. "Better give away the things we can do without. That tall chest and our heavy furniture can't go."

"But, Mother, that tall chest was a wedding present from your grandmother!" said Matthew. "I would like it."

"I wish you could have it," answered Mother. "That chest came from England when Virginia was still a young colony. But it's too heavy to load on a horse."

Moving west on the Wilderness Road

The Fosters and their friends set out for Kentucky. They were led by a guide who had followed the Wilderness Road several times. Some people rode on horses. Others walked. Some drove cattle. Others carried rifles and guarded the party.

At night the travelers camped beside streams and cooked their meals. They slept under the stars wrapped in blankets. Pioneers and their dogs stood guard.

The journey took many weeks. At last the Fosters and their friends came to Boonesborough. They stayed there until they could build a fort and homes of their own nearby. The Fosters and other brave pioneers helped make new towns in the Kentucky wilderness.

The Kentucky wilderness became a territory and then a state. A *territory* of the United States is a part of the country that is not yet a state. When enough people settle in a territory, it can have its own legislature. A *legislature* is a group of leaders elected by the people to make their laws. The governor and other officers of a territory are chosen by the President of the United States and Congress. When a territory has enough people, it may ask to become a state. At one time, all but the first thirteen states were territories.

Kentucky was the first territory west of the Appalachians to become a state. It became a state in 1792. Its people then had more say in their government. They could vote for the President. They could also elect members of Congress.

Many pioneers settled on the rich lands of Tennessee. Find Tennessee on the map. In what direction is it from Kentucky?

James Robertson urged pioneers to settle in Tennessee. As a young man, he had gone there from North Carolina. He was pleased with its fertile lands.

Robertson led many families across the mountains into Tennessee. Hundreds of other settlers also moved into this region. In 1796 Tennessee became a state.

Find Kentucky and Tennessee on the map on page 107.

Settlers move into the Ohio Valley

The Northwest Territory was north of Kentucky and Tennessee. It stretched west all the way to the Mississippi River. Find this territory on the map on page 107. It was separated from Kentucky by the winding Ohio River.

During the Revolutionary War, George Rogers Clark and his soldiers had captured British forts in this wilderness. The forts had been built by the French. Then the French had lost them in the French and Indian War. After the War for Independence, the Ohio Valley became part of the new United States.

The wide wilderness north of the Ohio River had wooded hills and rolling plains. It had plenty of good land for farming. But it was not an easy land to settle. The powerful Eries, Potawatomies, and Winnebagos lived there.

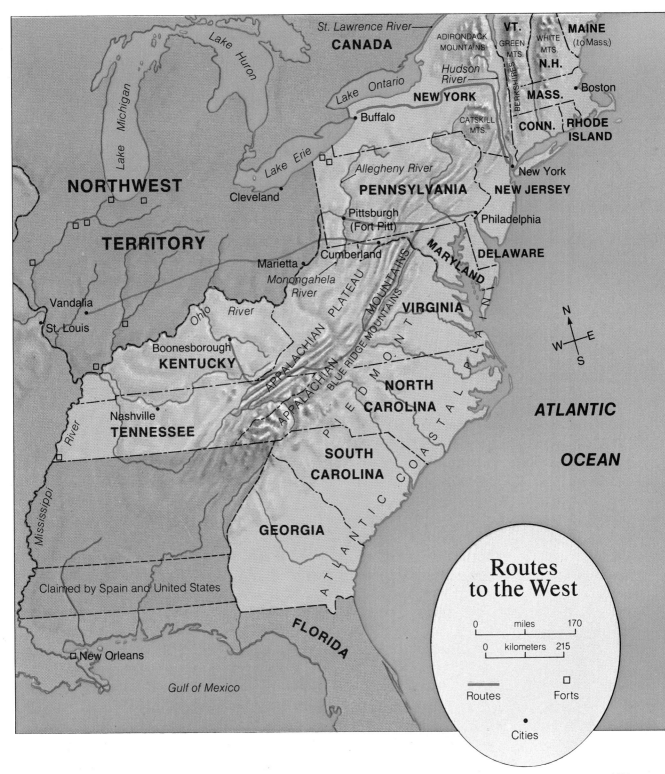

St. Lawrence River
CANADA
ADIRONDACK
MOUNTAINS
VT.
GREEN
MTS.
WHITE
MTS.
MAINE
(to Mass.)
N.H.
Hudson
River
BERKSHIRES
MASS.
Boston
Lake Ontario
NEW YORK
CONN.
RHODE
ISLAND
CATSKILL
MTS.
New York
Lake Erie
Buffalo
Allegheny River
PENNSYLVANIA
NEW JERSEY
NORTHWEST
Cleveland
Pittsburgh
(Fort Pitt)
Philadelphia
Lake Michigan
Lake Huron
TERRITORY
Cumberland
Marietta
MARYLAND
DELAWARE
Monongahela
River
PLATEAU
MOUNTAINS
VIRGINIA
Vandalia
Ohio
River
APPALACHIAN
BLUE RIDGE MOUNTAINS
PIEDMONT
St. Louis
Boonesborough
KENTUCKY
APPALACHIAN
NORTH
CAROLINA
ATLANTIC
Nashville
TENNESSEE
APPALACHIAN
SOUTH
CAROLINA
ATLANTIC COASTAL PLAIN
OCEAN
River
Mississippi
GEORGIA
N
W   E
S
Claimed by Spain and United States
FLORIDA
New Orleans
Gulf of Mexico

Routes to the West

| 0 | miles | 170 |
| 0 | kilometers | 215 |

—— Routes   ☐ Forts

• Cities

Tecumseh tried to stop the westward movement of white settlers. After his warriors were defeated, he joined the British.

In anger they saw or heard that settlers had taken over the Kentucky hunting grounds. They saw them scare away the game. They knew settlers now were chopping down forests and laying out farms in the Ohio Valley. They did not plan to give up the Ohio country too. They began to raid the boats and wagons that brought settlers into their lands.

Tecumseh tried to save the ancient Ohio Valley homelands. He was a tall, proud Shawnee chief. He dressed in buckskin and stuck a tomahawk and a silver-handled hunting knife in his belt.

Tecumseh fought the settlers with words and with weapons. He spoke against the chiefs who signed peace treaties with the settlers. He said that land was like air and water. It belonged to everyone. So the chiefs had no right to give it away. Native Americans could be strong if they lived in their own ways and worked together.

Tecumseh got a number of tribes to form a *confederation,* or union. It would try to stop the settlement of the Ohio Valley. This confederation of a few thousand warriors joined with the British to fight the United States in the War of 1812.

Once Tecumseh marched his warriors single file across a clearing in the woods. It looked as though there were a lot of them. The United States commander surrendered Fort Detroit to Tecumseh.

Later Tecumseh led all the British and Indian forces, even though he was wounded. But then he was killed in battle.

After Tecumseh's death, his people gave up fighting the settlers. They agreed to move west of the Mississippi River. They left the Ohio Valley.

Congress had sold millions of acres of Ohio land to land companies. They were to survey and advertise it and sell it cheaply. Soon, many pioneers were settling in the Ohio Valley. To their friends ''back east'' they sent letters like this one.

I am delighted with Ohio. Wild game is plentiful, and the climate is fine. Land is cheap, and the rich soil grows wonderful crops. Come west and see for yourself. But hurry! People are pouring into this Ohio country.

By the way, we have good news from Congress. The Ohio country is now a territory. But Congress has passed a law to divide it into states as soon as it is settled. The new states will have the same rights as the other states. Isn't that good news?

In time thousands of pioneers traveled west to the Ohio Valley. The map on page 107 shows the three routes they traveled. Many from Virginia took the Wilderness

Conestoga wagons were built to haul freight over bad roads. Broad wheels stopped them from sinking into the mud. Curved wagon beds kept the contents from moving. What did the canvas tops do?

Road through Cumberland Gap. People from New England and the Middle Atlantic states used two northern routes.

One route began in New York and followed the Hudson and Mohawk rivers. It led to the land near Lake Ontario and Lake Erie.

The second route went west across Pennsylvania. Over it creaked hundreds of covered wagons called Conestoga wagons. The wagons were often painted red and bright blue and had white canvas tops. They were pulled by teams of horses or oxen. Some pioneers could not afford teams. They pulled their own wagons.

The Pennsylvania route led to Pittsburgh. Pittsburgh had grown up around

Cooking and washing utensils

Driver's seat

Packing cases

Water

Tool box

Extra water

Beds on top of packing case and trunk

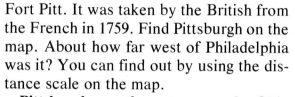

Fort Pitt. It was taken by the British from the French in 1759. Find Pittsburgh on the map. About how far west of Philadelphia was it? You can find out by using the distance scale on the map.

Pittsburgh was the gateway to the Ohio Valley. It was located where the Allegheny (al′ə gā′nē) and Monongahela (mə-non′gə hē lə) rivers meet to form the Ohio River. From Pittsburgh it was easy to float down the Ohio to the lands of the new west. Thousands of pioneers passed through Pittsburgh on their way to the lower Ohio Valley.

Boat building was one of Pittsburgh's chief industries. There were small boats and large ones for sale. Hunters and trappers wanted canoes. But farmers bought or built flatboats, rafts, and keelboats.

Here are some parts of a diary. It tells about one family's trip into the Ohio Valley by boat.

July 25: *We have been busy building a large raft. It is eighty feet long.*

July 30: *The cabin on the raft is done. We will be very comfortable in it.*

August 1: *We are loading the raft tomorrow. We will store our food, clothing, and furniture in the cabin. The raft is large enough to carry our covered wagon and livestock.*

August 2: *At last we are on our way! We are drifting down the river with the current. We take turns guiding the raft with the long sweeps.* (A sweep was a long oar used to push and steer boats.)

August 4: *We had trouble today! Our raft got stuck in the sand. We must always watch so we don't scrape against rocks or buried logs and brush.*

August 6: *It is hot! Even so, Mary has spent long hours drawing pictures of the birds and animals along the river. There are so many that we've never seen before.*

August 8: *Father is sharpening tools today and mending harness. We must be ready to work when we reach Ohio.*

August 10: *The haystack on our raft is getting smaller and smaller. But no wonder! Our horses and cow eat hay all day.*

August 18: *We are nearing the end of our journey. Tomorrow we will roll the wagon off the raft and load it once more. Then we will take our raft apart. Every nail and piece of lumber will be used for building our new home.*

More and more settlers moved west. By 1803, so many settlers had come to Ohio that it became a state. It was the third state west of the Appalachians.

As time passed, many settlers traveled even farther west. They went to lands that are now a part of Indiana and Illinois. Pioneers from the south settled the lands west of Georgia. Find these frontiers on the map of the routes west. Pioneers pushed the frontiers farther and farther west. Their farms and villages sprang up all the way to the Mississippi.

Settlers push the Native Americans west

Native Americans east of the Mississippi became fewer. Many of them were forced to move. Some had to move into lands where others already lived. Bitter wars broke out between them.

Many had to change their way of life. Some of these people had lived for centuries in wooded mountain areas. Now they had to learn to live on the plains. Some had lived in mild climates. Now they had to get used to cold weather. Often the people suffered greatly before they could learn new ways.

Many caught diseases brought into their lands by the settlers. They could not fight these diseases, so a great number died.

The Creek nation, made up of many groups, had about fifty towns. The towns were scattered through what are now Georgia and Alabama. The Creeks had given up some lands when the colony of Georgia was started.

Later, more settlers came and pushed the Creeks even farther west. The Creeks saw their forests cut down. They saw the animals of the forests killed. They saw their crops ruined.

Some Creeks tried to stop the settlers. They formed raiding parties. Some joined Tecumseh's confederation and fought with him in the Ohio Valley. In time the Creeks had to move west of the Mississippi.

Another large confederation was that of the Cherokees. They lived in what is now western North Carolina and eastern Tennessee. The Cherokees (cher′ə kēz′) often helped the settlers. They learned the settlers' ways of farming, weaving, and house building. They built roads and schools. They set up a government like that of the United States.

Sequoya was a great Cherokee leader. He had never been to school. But he invented a way of writing in the Cherokee language. This took him twelve years, but he did not give up.

Most of the Cherokees learned to read and write. They printed a weekly newspaper and many books.

Sequoya, who invented a system of writing in the Cherokee language, was also a silversmith and painter.

In the early 1800s, many settlers began moving into Cherokee lands. Some Cherokees gave up and moved to Tennessee. Others would not leave.

After a time, the United States ordered the Cherokees to move farther west, across the Mississippi River. The Cherokees went to the highest court in the United States. The judges said they did not have to give up their land. But the President said the Cherokees would have to leave anyway.

They were forced to move during the winter of 1838–1839. Most had to walk all the way to Oklahoma. Almost a fourth of the 18,000 who started out died along the way. Some froze to death. Some became sick and had to be left in the wilderness. This move of the Cherokees is known as the Trail of Tears.

Choose the right answers

Below are some sentences with three endings. Copy each sentence with its correct ending.

1. The Cumberland Gap was a low place in the (Rocky Mountains.) (Appalachian Mountains.) (White Mountains.)
2. Boone and his friends built a fort and village called (Pittsburgh.) (Big Lick.) (Boonesborough.)
3. Working things out together is a way of self-government called (business.) (territory.) (democracy.)
4. To prove that a settler owned a piece of land the United States government required (a cabin.) (a deed.) (some animals.)
5. People who settled on land they did not own were called (hunters.) (fur traders.) (squatters.)
6. The first territory west of the Appalachians to become a state was (Kentucky.) (Ohio.) (Tennessee.)
7. Fort Pitt was the gateway to (Kentucky.) (the Ohio Valley.) (the lands along the Hudson River.)

Organizing notes

It is important to take notes when you read about a topic. You should also organize them.

If you are taking notes on the life of a person, list the main events. Write them in the order in which they happened.

If you are taking notes on a topic such as keelboats, list the main ideas. Leave space under each one for details.

Some questions to answer

1. Many pioneers traveled on rivers to reach new lands. Looking at a map will show you that these were the long routes. Why didn't the pioneers follow shorter routes?

2. What was the Wilderness Road? Why was it important? How was it different from roads today?

3. Why did the pioneers want to move west? Give as many reasons as you can.

4. What would you have liked about being a pioneer? What would you have disliked about it?

5. What were some of the things that happened to the Native Americans when settlers pushed west into their lands?

Let's use a map

Turn to the map of the Routes to the West on page 107. This is a *political* map. Such a map shows into what countries, states, and territories a land is divided. This political map shows the United States in 1800. How many states had been added to the first thirteen?

The map also acts as a *relief* map. A relief map shows the heights of the land by shading a color. What shade shows the highest parts of the Appalachian Mountains?

This is also a *route* map. The title tells you this. What symbol stands for a route? Trace the route between Philadelphia and Pittsburgh. What symbol is used to show a town?

What fort is located at Pittsburgh? What is the symbol for fort?

What route led to Kentucky? To what settlement did it go? Which of the three routes led farthest inland? On which one could pioneers travel farthest by boat?

Working together

Group activities give you a chance to work with others. Working with others in the classroom is just as important as it is on a baseball team. Here are suggestions to keep in mind.

1. Decide what jobs are to be done and list them on the board.

2. Choose a committee to complete each big job.

3. Elect a leader for each committee.

4. Cooperate with the leader and others.

5. Be ready to share materials.

6. Work quietly, quickly, and well.

7. Be ready to share what you have done with the other members of your class.

Things to do

1. Visit a library. Find reference books such as encyclopedias and an atlas. An *atlas* is a book of maps. Review how to use the card catalog.

2. Find information in the library about one of the following.

Daniel Boone	Sequoya
Rebecca Boone	Wilderness Road
Boonesborough	keelboats
Cherokee Trail of Tears	James Robertson
Appalachian Highlands	Conestoga wagons
Tecumseh	

3. Read the paragraph on page 112 about "Organizing Notes." Take and organize notes on the topic you read about in item 2 above.

9

The Louisiana Territory and Florida

The need for a peaceful port

One afternoon young May Judson stopped at the country store.

"Howdy, May!" greeted Mr. Jenkins, the storekeeper. "What can I sell you today? Say, you look upset! What's happened?"

"Plenty!" exclaimed May. "And I'm fighting mad! Did you hear about my brothers?"

"You mean the ones that haul lumber and grain down the Mississippi on their flatboat?" asked Mr. Jenkins.

May nodded. "They got to New Orleans all right. But this time the port was closed. The Spanish guards wouldn't let them unload. They even took the boats and ran my brothers out of town. They told them that if they came back, they'd go to prison!"

"That's terrible!" said Mr. Jenkins, shaking his head.

"It sure is!" answered May. "We should buy that port and be done with it! What do you think, Mr. Jenkins?"

"What you say is right, May," the storekeeper replied. "For years bad things have been happening in New Orleans, some of them dangerous. We need a peaceful port. But it looks like we'll have trouble as long as France or Spain holds New Orleans. Yes, May, I think we should buy New Orleans."

Many people thought just as May and Mr. Jenkins did. See if you agree with them as you read on.

La Salle had claimed the Mississippi River lands for France. He named this huge region Louisiana. Later, the French started a settlement near the mouth of the

May Judson and Mr. Jenkins discuss the New Orleans problem.

Mississippi. This town was named New Orleans. Find it on the map on page 117.

After the French and Indian War, France had to give England some lands. They were between the Appalachians and the Mississippi. After the War for Independence, these lands became a part of the United States.

Spain had helped France during its long war with England. So, as payment, France gave New Orleans and its Louisiana lands

114

Under my wings everything prospers

The port of New Orleans became a part of the United States in 1803. How did this help western farmers and traders?

west of the Mississippi to Spain. This vast area was known as the Louisiana Territory. It was in the center of what is now the United States. It covered the area from the Gulf of Mexico to Canada and from the Mississippi River to the Rocky Mountains. Its main settlement was New Orleans.

The Louisiana Territory was under Spanish rule for several years. All boats had to get permission to load and unload goods at New Orleans. They also had to pay a special tax.

By 1800 a French general, Napoleon, ruled France. He forced Spain to give New Orleans and the Louisiana Territory back to France.

This worried the people. They knew that Napoleon had made France a strong nation. He had conquered much of Europe and had sent soldiers to the West Indies. The Louisiana Territory was next to the United States. The pioneers worried about what Napoleon would do with it.

Thousands of pioneers had settled west of the Appalachians. The farmers grew corn, wheat, and other crops. They raised cattle, hogs, and sheep. Some pioneers roamed the woods to trap wild animals for the furs. Others started sawmills for sawing logs into lumber. So the settlers had crops, meat, wool, hides, furs, and lumber to sell.

The people east of the Appalachians were ready to buy the settlers' goods. But there were no good roads for sending the products over the mountains. The Wilderness Road was too steep and rough for wagons. Another route was needed.

The pioneers had begun to use the Mississippi River as a highway. Find this river on the map. One of its chief branches is the long, winding Ohio River. Find the place where the Ohio River joins the Mississippi. Boats could float down the Ohio River to the wide waters of the Mississippi. Then they could go on down the Mississippi to New Orleans.

Crops were shipped on slow, clumsy flatboats. The boats were guided to the middle of the river. They drifted southward with the current. At last they reached New Orleans.

After the boats were unloaded, some were taken apart and sold as lumber. Others were used to carry back needed goods. The trip up the river was very hard. Poles were used to push the boats upstream against the current. At some places they were towed by ropes from the river bank.

As the years passed, more flatboats traveled up and down the Mississippi River. They were the chief cargo carriers for the Ohio and Mississippi valleys. They carried goods that were worth millions of dollars.

Mississippi shipping helped New Orleans become a busy port. This port was a gateway to the sea and to eastern United States. Goods were unloaded at New Orleans and stored there. Then they were loaded on ships. The ships sailed to cities along the Atlantic coast, to the West Indies, and to Europe.

There was a threat to the growth of New Orleans as a port. The farmers of the Ohio Valley worried about sending their goods there. So President Jefferson decided to try to buy New Orleans.

116

The United States buys a huge territory

A meeting was held in Paris, France, about the Louisiana Territory. In 1803 two Americans, Robert Livingston and James Monroe, met with Napoleon's officials. They were ready to offer France two million dollars for New Orleans.

During their talks one French leader asked, "Why doesn't the United States buy the whole Louisiana Territory? We will sell it and all of New Orleans for $15,000,000."

Louisiana celebrated becoming a part of the United States with a ceremony in New Orleans's main square. How did Louisiana become a part of our country?

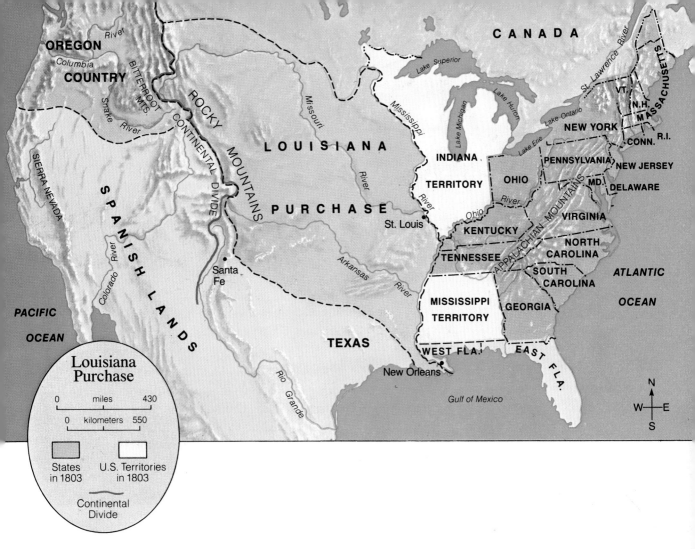

Livingston and Monroe were amazed at this surprising offer. Getting the Louisiana Territory would nearly double the size of the United States. The price for the land was about three and a half cents an acre. They had not dreamed of buying so much land at such a low price. Besides, they did not have the government's permission to do so.

There was no way to talk over the matter with President Jefferson and Congress. There was no telegraph or telephone.

Livingston and Monroe did not send a letter to ask what to do. It would have taken too long. They dared not wait weeks for an answer. Instead, they took France's offer. This business deal became known as the Louisiana Purchase.

The Louisiana Purchase added a huge area to the United States. It pushed its borders west to the Rocky Mountains. It gave the United States the whole Mississippi River and New Orleans. Find this area on the map.

The Louisiana Purchase pleased some people but not others. The farmers west of the Appalachians were pleased. Hunters and trappers were happy about the Louisiana Purchase, too.

But many people who lived east of the Appalachians were not pleased. They grumbled that fifteen million dollars was too much money for wilderness. They did not know how rich the land was. They did not know that someday thirteen states would be formed from this large territory.

117

Florida becomes part of the United States

Ponce de León had claimed Florida for Spain early in the 1500s. The Spaniards started the fort and village of St. Augustine in 1565. It was Florida's first permanent settlement. It was founded forty-two years before Jamestown.

The Spaniards kept Florida for about two hundred years. But then a change came. After the French and Indian War, Spain gave Florida to England. In return, Spain got the port of Havana, Cuba.

The English divided Florida into East Florida and West Florida. Find the Floridas on the map on page 117. In which one is St. Augustine located? *(See page 283.)*

West Florida reached to the Mississippi River along the Gulf of Mexico. This strip of land was from eight to forty miles (13 to 64 km) wide. The Mississippi Territory was north of West Florida.

Locate East Florida on the map. Notice how far south it reached. It was mostly a peninsula. A *peninsula* is a large body of land almost surrounded by water.

The Seminoles lived in the Floridas. The Seminoles had come from an area farther north. They had been driven off their lands by the settlers. But they were at peace with the English rulers of Florida.

England wanted planters to settle on the fertile Florida lands. Some planters came from the southern colonies. When the War for Independence began, many of the Loyalists fled to East Florida. The Loyalists were those people who stayed loyal to England.

In 1783 England gave the Floridas back to Spain. Spain could not keep order in the land. The Floridas became hiding places for pirates and other lawbreakers. Robbers roamed about, attacking, stealing, and killing. The settlers lived in fear. They did not dare to ship crops down the rivers.

West Florida was added to the United States in 1810. For several years many Florida settlers had urged this. So had the pioneers who lived in the Mississippi Territory to the north. They could not send their crops down the rivers safely. Nor were their plantations safe from attack.

The United States knew that it must protect its settlers. To make sure this was done, it tried to buy West Florida. When Spain would not sell, the United States took this region. West Florida and the Mississippi Territory became part of three new states. They were Louisiana, Mississippi, and Alabama.

St. Augustine, Florida, the oldest city in the United States, was built by Spain's Admiral de Avilés and his troops in 1565 *(top left)*. A hundred years later Spain built the Castillo de San Marcos. For more than 150 years the fort's cannons guarded the Spanish settlers *(top right)*. St. Augustine's oldest house is shown *(bottom)*.

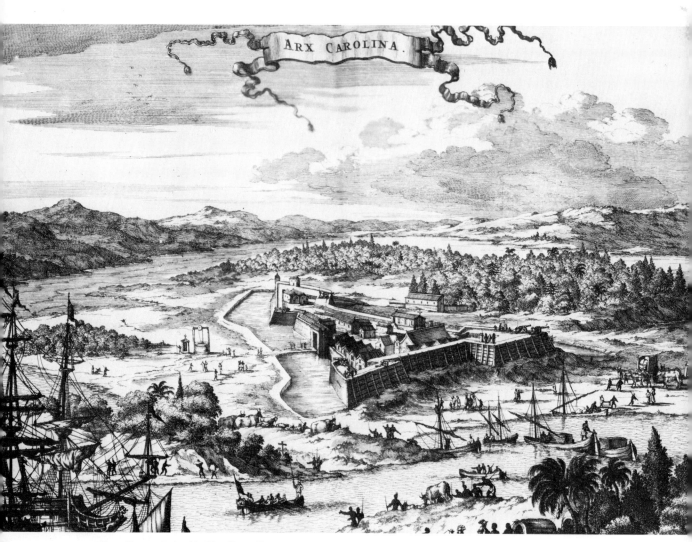

The French built Ft. Caroline on Florida's St. Johns River in 1564. How was the fort protected? Despite these strong defenses, Spain captured Ft. Caroline the year after it was built.

The United States bought East Florida in 1819. Problems came up there, too. Raiders came north into Georgia. The United States government asked Spain to stop these attacks. But little was done. At last Spain agreed to sell the peninsula. The United States paid five million dollars for the peninsula.

East Florida is now the state of Florida. St. Augustine is in this area. It is the oldest city in the United States.

A few hunters and trappers had traveled beyond the Mississippi. They brought back amazing tales of vast grassy plains and huge herds of buffalo. They told of towering mountains and rushing rivers. They told about many groups of Native Americans that lived on the plains.

Pioneers who had settled near the Mississippi heard these tales first. After the Louisiana Purchase, President Jefferson got Congress to agree that the new lands west of the Mississippi should be explored.

Do you know?

1. Why did the United States want to buy New Orleans?
2. Why was the Mississippi River such an important waterway?
3. What thirteen states have been formed from lands in the Louisiana Purchase?
4. How did the United States get Florida?

What do you think?

1. The Louisiana Purchase is sometimes called the greatest bargain in history. Why do you think it is called this?
2. What were some of the gains of adding vast new lands to the United States? What were some problems this might have caused?
3. Why aren't all rivers used for transportation?

Things to do

1. Learn more about one of the following.

   New Orleans   Seminoles
   James Monroe   Louisiana Purchase
   St. Augustine   Robert Livingston
   Take notes on what you read.

2. Use the Geography Dictionary to review the meaning of *peninsula*. Draw the Florida peninsula. Color the land green and the water blue.

3. On paper write these events in the order in which they happened.

   The United States purchases the Louisiana Territory

   Kentucky becomes a state

   Daniel Boone blazes the Wilderness Road

   The United States buys East Florida

   The United States takes West Florida

A matching game

Ten items are in List A. Write them in a column on paper. Be sure to leave space at the right of each one to write one or two long words.

For each item you have written, find the one in List B that belongs with it. Write it where it belongs. You will not use all of the items in List B.

List A

1. A seaport on the Mississippi River
2. Land bought from France
3. The President of the United States when the Louisiana Purchase was made
4. A famous French general
5. The business deal with France
6. The price paid for the Louisiana Territory
7. The oldest city in the United States
8. Land nearly surrounded by water
9. When the United States gained West Florida
10. Land added to the United States in 1819

List B

West Florida	New Orleans
James Monroe	East Florida
Spain	1776
a peninsula	Louisiana Territory
Napoleon	England
island	Thomas Jefferson
St. Augustine	Louisiana Purchase
$20,000,000	West Florida
$15,000,000	1810

10
Exploring and settling the new lands

A Shoshoni girl grows up

The Shoshoni lived west of the Mississippi. Most of them were nomadic. That is, they moved from place to place. They looked for grass for their horses and food for themselves. They ate mostly seeds, roots, fish, and small animals.

They lived in small groups during the winter. That way there would be enough food. In summer they got together for dances and ceremonies to celebrate the season of new plant and animal life.

Grass Woman was a Shoshoni. One day, when she was eleven, she and other Shoshoni were gathering roots and berries. Suddenly loud shrieks filled the air. An enemy group captured eight of the Shoshoni children. Grass Woman was one of them.

Grass Woman worked hard in her new home. After a time she was treated almost as a daughter.

One day a French fur trader came to visit. He bought Grass Woman. He took her to live with the Mandans.

The Mandans lived on the northern part of the plains, as is shown on the map on page 29. They built villages of earth-covered homes along the Missouri River (page 125). They raised corn, beans, squash, and tobacco on their rich soil. They traded their farm products for buffalo hides and meat, horses, and other kinds of goods.

The Mandans gave Grass Woman a new name. They called her Sacajawea (sak´ə-jə wē´ə). The name means Bird Woman. Sacajawea learned to make robes from buffalo hides. She made clothing and moccasins from deer skins. She found how to use herbs, roots, and barks as medicines. Sacajawea learned other Native American languages. By the time she was sixteen, she and the fur trader had become husband and wife.

Sacajawea grew restless. She missed moving from place to place. She wished for more adventure. Before long that wish came true. She took a long journey that made her famous. That part of the story begins many months earlier in Washington, D.C.

The Mandans taught Sacajawea to make robes from buffalo hides.

President Jefferson chose William Clark *(left)* and Meriwether Lewis *(right)* to explore the Louisiana Territory.

Lewis and Clark explore the northwest

President Jefferson sent for his secretary, Captain Meriwether Lewis. Let's imagine what they said.

"Captain Lewis," began the President, "I've been eager to learn more about the Louisiana Territory. It's time to find out what we have bought."

Captain Lewis nodded. "Yes, Mr. President, I agree."

"You are the person to explore this region," Jefferson continued. "You are a good leader and a trained soldier. You know the ways of the wilderness. I want you to lead a party west."

"That would be a big job, Mr. President. But I'm as anxious as you to learn more about this vast territory," answered Captain Lewis.

"Good!" exclaimed Jefferson. "Then begin plans at once. Choose some strong helpers and get ready to leave next spring. I want you to bring back reports and maps of the lands you see. Plan to explore the Missouri River and other rivers. I want to know if there is a good water route to the Pacific. Also, I want to know about the plant and animal life. And learn as much as you can about the people."

"I'll do my best, Mr. President," answered Captain Lewis.

Jefferson asked another soldier, William Clark, to be Lewis's partner. Lewis and Clark were close friends.

Lewis and Clark began to choose people to go along with them. In all, forty-five people would start the trip. Some were soldiers and skilled hunters. Two had experience with boats. One was a blacksmith. Some were expert builders. One

123

This part of the Missouri River looks much as it did in 1805.

was a cook. Another could speak a few Native American languages. Two took along their fiddles to make music when there was spare time.

That winter the group got ready for the long, hard trip. They took hikes and practiced shooting. Some gathered supplies. In strong boxes they packed guns, gunpowder, buckskin clothing, and warm blankets. They packed corn meal, flour, salt, tea, medicines, and notebooks for sketches and reports. They also decided to take along bracelets, small mirrors, needles, and other presents for the people they would meet. Lewis studied about plants and animals so that he could keep records of those seen in the west.

In May 1804 the Lewis and Clark party set out. Captain Lewis took along his large black dog, Scannon. Later on, Scannon saved his master's life when a grizzly bear attacked.

They left from St. Louis. Find St. Louis on the map. It is located on the Mississippi River, near where the Missouri River flows into the Mississippi.

The group moved slowly up the Missouri, against its swift currents. Some of the explorers were on a large keelboat. Some paddled the two canoes.

Lewis often walked along the river bank. He took notes about the plants, trees, and wildlife. His dog, Scannon, was with him.

124

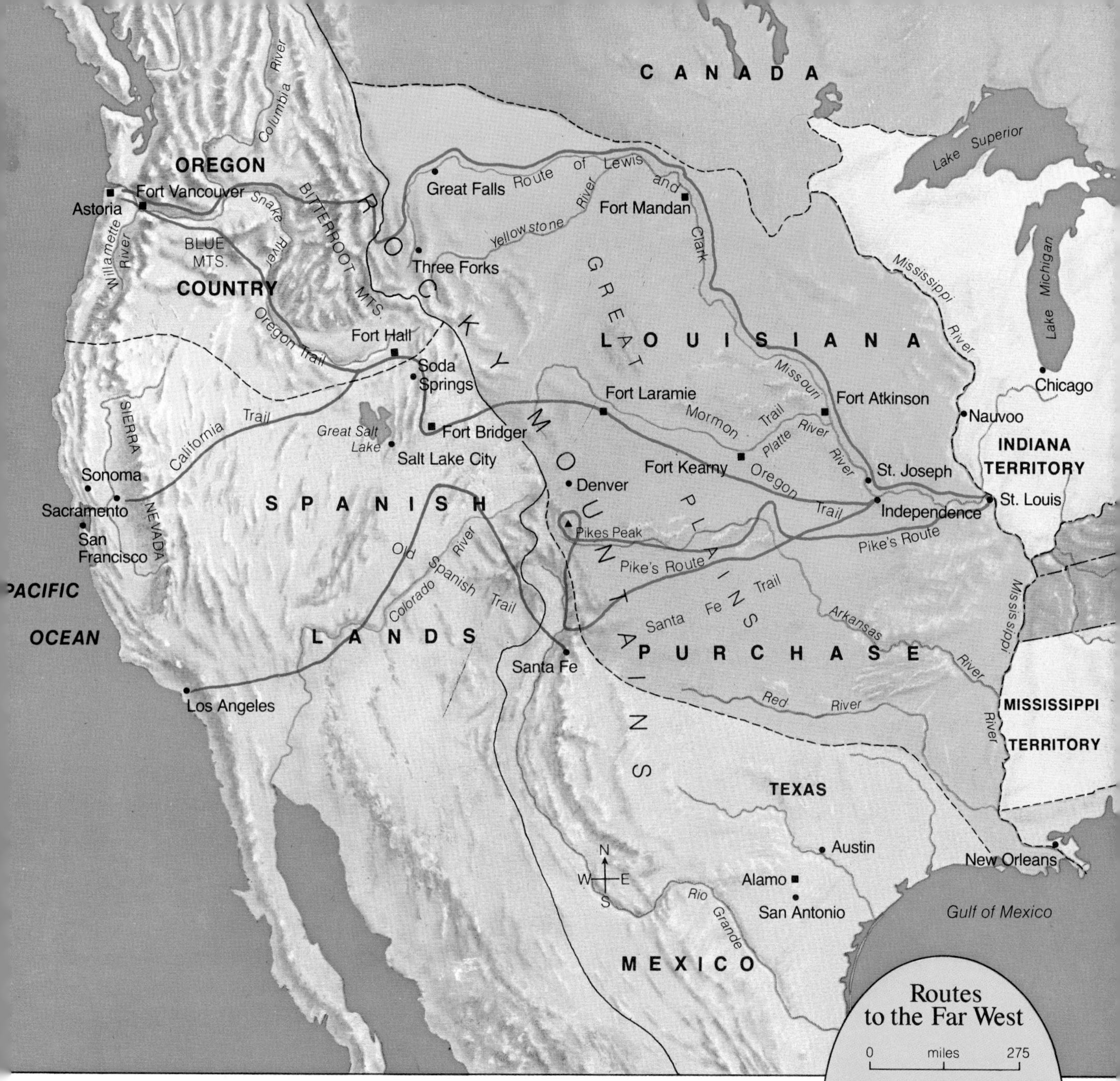

The map shows "Routes to the Far West" with various geographic labels:

Bodies of water and geographic features: PACIFIC OCEAN, Columbia River, Willamette River, Snake River, Yellowstone River, Missouri River, Platte River, Colorado River, Arkansas River, Red River, Rio Grande, Mississippi River, Gulf of Mexico, Lake Superior, Lake Michigan, Great Salt Lake, BLUE MTS., BITTERROOT MTS., ROCKY MOUNTAINS, SIERRA NEVADA, GREAT PLAINS, Pikes Peak.

Regions: CANADA, OREGON COUNTRY, LOUISIANA PURCHASE, SPANISH LANDS, INDIANA TERRITORY, MISSISSIPPI TERRITORY, TEXAS, MEXICO.

Forts and towns: Astoria, Fort Vancouver, Great Falls, Fort Mandan, Three Forks, Fort Hall, Soda Springs, Fort Bridger, Salt Lake City, Fort Laramie, Fort Atkinson, Chicago, Nauvoo, Sonoma, Sacramento, San Francisco, Denver, Fort Kearny, St. Joseph, St. Louis, Independence, Los Angeles, Santa Fe, Austin, Alamo, San Antonio, New Orleans.

Trails/Routes: Route of Lewis and Clark, Oregon Trail, California Trail, Mormon Trail, Old Spanish Trail, Santa Fe Trail, Pike's Route.

Routes to the Far West

0 — miles — 275

0 — kilometers — 350

Continental Divide — Trails/Routes

■ Forts ● Towns

Usually Clark stayed on one of the boats. He made notes and sketches of the river and nearby land. Both Lewis and Clark kept journals, or diaries, as did others in the party.

At night the group camped by the river. By the light of campfires, Lewis, Clark, and others wrote in their journals.

Mosquitoes and tiny gnats are swarming about us. Will they never stop? We are miserable with them. Very hot today.

By November the group had gone up the Missouri River for about a thousand miles (1600 km). They had reached the wind-swept plains of what is now North Dakota.

125

The explorers camped on the northern plains for the winter. They built a stout log shelter and called it Fort Mandan. Look for Fort Mandan on the map. The Mandans lived nearby. They brought gifts of beans, corn, pumpkins, and squash.

The Mandan people told many stories. Some were about high western mountains. We know that they were telling about the Rocky Mountains.

Other stories were about the Pacific Ocean. They called it "Everywhere Salt Water." The Mandans told of lots of rivers. Lewis and Clark were glad to hear tales of the "Mighty River of the West." They knew there was a river that emptied into the Pacific Ocean. Its wide mouth had been found nearly ten years before by a sea captain. The captain had named it the Columbia River for his ship, the *Columbia.*

Lewis and Clark asked the Mandans many questions about the Columbia River. They wanted to know where it began and through what kinds of lands it flowed. But the Mandans did not know. The Mandan chief said they should go west to find out. That is just what the explorers planned to do when spring came.

Lewis and Clark came to know a French trapper and his wife, Sacajawea. She knew some parts of the west. So Lewis hired her and her husband as guides.

In April when the snows were melting, the party set out. Its smallest member was Sacajawea's two-month-old baby boy. Sacajawea carried him strapped to her back.

The explorers paddled north and west up the narrowing Missouri River. They crossed present-day Montana. As the river cut through the hills and mountains, its water flowed more swiftly. One of the explorers wrote:

Our boats tipped over today, and we saw our valuable records sink out of sight! It seemed that they were lost forever. But Sacajawea dove into the cold water and rescued them. How thankful we are!

One morning the travelers reached thundering falls. They had to leave the river and tramp overland around the falls. To carry their boats, they built carts with slices of logs for wheels. On the river again, the explorers rowed once more. At last they came to the place where three rivers joined the Missouri. The Native Americans called this place "Three Forks." Sacajawea knew that the Shoshoni lived nearby.

As the party moved upstream, it became harder to row the boats. Lewis and Clark knew they must soon leave their boats. They needed horses to carry the supplies. But they did not know where to get them.

Then the explorers met a group of Shoshoni. Sacajawea knew the leader. He was her brother, the chief of his tribe. They greeted each other warmly. He gave the party supplies, horses, and a guide.

The explorers continued west through the Rockies. One diary tells about some of their hardships.

We have been making our own trails. So many rocks push through the rough ground that our moccasins are worn through. Our feet are cut and bleeding. The nights are cold and sharp. We are very hungry, but game is scarce here.

The mountains rise higher and higher. A heavy snow fell today. Slippery paths caused us a bad accident. Some of our horses fell down the mountainside and we

could not save them. Our men must now carry more supplies.

After many weeks the explorers reached the snow-covered *Continental Divide*. It is a high place where the streams divide. Some flow eastward from the mountains. Some flow westward. Those on the east side of the Continental Divide flow toward the Mississippi River. Their waters finally reach the Gulf of Mexico. Most of the streams on the west side flow toward the Pacific. One of these is the Columbia River. Locate it on the map on page 125.

At the Continental Divide, the explorers looked west. They saw mountains stretching on and on, range after range. The map shows these mountains.

The explorers did not have maps or a compass to guide them. They were tired and nearly starved, yet they pushed on. After many days they climbed down the

When they reached Three Forks, Sacajawea told Lewis and Clark that the Shoshoni lived nearby. How did the Shoshoni help the explorers?

last steep slopes. Ahead were low green hills, pleasant meadows, and a shining river. On its banks they camped and rested. There they built five canoes.

The explorers paddled far down the river. They found that it joined a broader waterway, the Snake River. Find the Snake River on the map. They followed it for many days. At last it poured into an even wider river. This was the "Mighty River of the West," the Columbia River.

With great skill the explorers guided their canoes through rapids and rough waters. Lewis and Clark knew when they were getting close to the Pacific Ocean. The air had a salty taste and a thick ocean

Lewis and Clark built Ft. Clatsop at the mouth of the Columbia River. Here their party spent the winter of 1805-1806.

fog hung low. When this thick fog cleared, the explorers saw white-capped waves breaking against the shore.

At last after a year and a half, the brave band had reached its goal. With glad hearts, they gave thanks for their success. One leader wrote, "The ocean is at last in view. Oh, what joy!"

During the winter of 1805-1806, the explorers camped near the Pacific. For shelter they built cabins inside a strong stockade. They spent much time hunting. There were lots of deer and elk for meat. The skins were used for new moccasins and clothing. The party spent many days exploring. This region had rainy winters. It had fine fertile valleys. Its hills were covered with trees. The Oregon country was a good land for fur traders and settlers.

The next spring the explorers started eastward. Their notebooks were full of reports, sketches, and maps. Their boats carried samples of skins, furs, and rocks. In September the tired explorers reached St. Louis, their starting point. Their travels had taken nearly two and a half years. They had gone about 8000 miles (12,900 km) through all kinds of wild country.

The United States now had a claim to the Oregon country. The explorations of Lewis and Clark made this claim possible. The Oregon lands were west of the

Louisiana Territory. Find these lands on the map. The Oregon country stretched from California to Alaska. It extended about 800 miles (1290 km) inland from the Pacific Ocean.

Lewis and Clark brought back useful facts about the great lands west of the Mississippi. They told about the plains, mountains, rivers, and trails. They told about Native Americans and much wild game.

These reports stirred up much interest. Hunters and trappers were very happy to have news of fur-bearing animals. Hunters and trappers soon took a chance and went west.

The journals kept by members of the Lewis and Clark party included drawings as well as written descriptions. Why did the explorers keep journals?

Some questions to answer

1. Why were Lewis and Clark sent on an expedition? How did they get ready for it?

2. What route did Lewis and Clark take? Why did their journey take so long?

3. Who was Sacajawea? In what ways did she help Lewis and Clark?

4. Why was the journey of Lewis and Clark important?

Things to do

1. Pretend that you were a member of the Lewis and Clark party. Write a journal about some of your experiences.

2. Look at the map on page 125, which shows the route taken by Lewis and Clark. Then make a mural about the lands and animals that Lewis and Clark saw.

   A mural is a long band of pictures extending across a wall. To make a mural, use wide strips of heavy wrapping paper. Fasten the papers along a blackboard. Plan what will be shown on the mural. Sketch the main ideas on paper. Use chalk to sketch the pictures on the mural. Then color the pictures.

3. Read in another book about Sacajawea, the Shoshoni, or the Mandans. Take notes and be ready to share what you learn.

Traders and trappers travel to the Northwest

Since 1787, American trading ships had visited northwest harbors. They sailed around South America and up the Pacific coast to the Oregon country. There they traded with the Native Americans.

When a trading ship entered a harbor, many canoes met it. The Native Americans had plenty of velvet-like sea otter skins and other rich furs to trade. They were traded for bright cloth, glass beads, and knives. The knives were needed to do the fine carving on their houses and totem poles. The knives were also used to prepare food. The cloth and beads were used to make clothes.

John Jacob Astor built a trading post in Oregon. He was a New York businessman. He had become rich buying and selling furs. Astor heard about the fur-bearing animals Lewis and Clark had seen in the Northwest. He decided to build a trading post there.

Astor sent one group of traders and trappers overland to Oregon. Another group went by boat around South America. At the mouth of the Columbia River, the two groups met. They built the settlement of Astoria. Find it on the map that shows the routes to the far west. As-

toria did not succeed as a trading post. But it helped make strong the claim of the United States to Oregon.

In a few years, many people explored the great Northwest. Most of the first ones were fur traders and trappers.

Traders and trappers roamed far inland to set traps and trade. They explored rivers and valleys. They found passes through the mountains. These people were pathfinders and trailblazers. They found the easiest places to cross rivers. They located and marked the easiest routes across the plains and mountains. The knowledge they gained opened the way for pioneer settlers.

Settlers come to the Oregon country

Missionaries were the first settlers in the Oregon country. Some Native Americans had heard about the Christian religion from the fur trappers and traders. In 1831 the Nez Percés and another group sent four delegates to St. Louis. They looked for missionaries to teach their people to read and write. They also wanted to learn about the Christian religion.

Soon a missionary named Jason Lee and his helpers journeyed west with some trappers. Lee settled in the Willamette Val-

Trains of fur traders crossed the sun-baked plains in the 1830s.

ley near what is now Salem, Oregon. He built a mission and started a school for the Native Americans.

Lee was certain that the fertile Willamette Valley would be a fine place for settlers. When he got back east, he told glowing tales of the Oregon country. Later he returned with fifty settlers.

Meanwhile other missionaries had journeyed to the Oregon country. Two of them were Marcus and Narcissa Whitman. The Whitmans started a mission in eastern Washington. Dr. Whitman went east for supplies. He, too, told of the rich Oregon country and urged people to move west.

Happy settlers wrote letters to their friends. Trappers and travelers carried the letters back east. Here is what one of the letters might have said:

Truly we have come to a wonderful land! The soil is rich and grows crops all year round. We raise tall wheat and large fruit. The fields are high with grass. There is more than enough to feed many horses, cattle, and sheep.

Huge forests of oak, pine, cedar, and fir grow here. We are cutting trees and putting up cabins as fast as we can. Salmon swim up the Columbia River and are very good to eat. The climate is pleasant and mild. It never gets very cold. We have plenty of rain.

Such letters were passed from one family to another in the east. Some were even printed in newspapers. Some people decided to move to the Oregon country. They planned to follow the Oregon Trail.

Pioneers travel west on the Oregon Trail

The Oregon Trail began at Independence, Missouri. This town was in western Missouri on the Missouri River. Find Independence on the map that shows the Oregon Trail. See page 125.

People from many states came to Independence in covered wagons. They camped there until forty or fifty wagons were ready to go on together. A group of wagons was called a *wagon train*.

The long trip to Oregon took a wagon train about five months. The pioneers had to take large amounts of food and other supplies. They bought these things in Independence.

Among the foods that they purchased were flour, sugar, smoked meats, coffee, salt, and dried fruit. They bought extra shoes and boots, seed potatoes, spare wheels and other wagon parts, and ammunition. From their homes the pioneers

Because traders and trappers knew the easiest routes across the plains and mountains they often acted as guides for wagon trains.

usually brought feather beds, blankets, dishes, and other household goods.

The Oregon Trail wound northwest for about 2000 miles (3200 km). It crossed the Great Plains, hot deserts, and high mountains. Trace the Oregon Trail on the map.

May seemed the best month for starting out. By that time the days were sunny and warm. Fresh new grass covered the plains. The pioneers needed grass for their cattle, sheep, oxen, and horses.

A wagon train often hired a guide. Guides knew the trails. Guides knew the best places to cross the rivers and to make camp. Each wagon train chose one captain, or leader. A committee was chosen to help make the rules.

Men, women, and children shared the dangers and the hard work. Everyone had jobs to do. Some people guided the wagons. Others drove the livestock. Blacksmiths kept the wagons fixed and greased the wheels with bear or wolf fat.

Skilled hunters shot game for meat. They also kept watch as guards.

Women worked hard to make the trip possible. They cooked the food. They washed the clothes. They cared for the children and the sick people.

The travelers began their days at four o'clock in the morning. Guards fired their guns to wake up everyone. Breakfasts were cooked over campfires, and horses and cattle were rounded up.

After breakfast the bedding was put away. Then the wagons were loaded and the oxen were hitched to them. Most wagons were pulled by teams of oxen. These big animals were stronger than horses.

About seven o'clock a bugle blew the signal for the start of the day's march. Then one by one the wagons creaked down the trail. They often stirred up great clouds of dust. At noon the party stopped for lunch. Their animals grazed and rested nearby. Soon, though, the wagons were rumbling on again. In late afternoon the pioneers guided their wagons into a large circle. They built campfires and cooked the evening meal within this safe circle.

After supper the children played and the older people talked. Some evenings some of them sang and danced. A few played violins. At last, when the campfires burned low, the people often sang a hymn.

The pioneers traveled through the Great Plains and crossed many rivers. The plains were west of the Mississippi River. They stretched to the Rockies. Those nearest the Mississippi were gently rolling lands with patches of trees. They were covered with tall grass. They were called *prairies.*

West of the prairies, the pioneers came to drier lands, the Great Plains. Find them

on the map on page 125. Little rain fell here. By early summer its short grass began to burn in the sun's heat.

The Oregon Trail followed the Platte River for many miles. Find the Platte River on the map. There were no bridges over the rivers along the trail. Where the water was low, the oxen and other animals splashed through very easily. Crossing a deep river was hard. Sometimes, each team of oxen was chained to the wagon in front as well as to its own wagon. The oxen then swam across the river, pulling the floating wagons.

If the river was very deep, the pioneers built rafts to carry their wagons. Now and then a raft tipped over and supplies were lost.

At the river's edge, the travelers often saw wild animals drinking. There were deer and antelope. But the buffalo were the animals the pioneers feared. Millions of them fed on the grass of the plains. At times, a loud noise might make them

Watching traders leave for the west was always exciting. This 1830 caravan included two carriages and ten supply wagons. What kinds of goods might the traders have been carrying?

charge across the land. This was a buffalo stampede. It was a thing all pioneers feared. Here is a story of such an event.

As the Scotts were eating breakfast, huge clouds of dust swept toward them.

"It's a buffalo stampede!" shouted Ida Scott. "Quick! Into the wagons!"

The clouds of dust rolled closer. The thunder of hoofs shook the ground. The great dark animals charged ahead. The Scotts fired their guns in the air. The shooting of the guns caused the buffalo herd to turn just as it neared the wagons. A few animals stumbled and fell. The others plunged on until the last ones roared by.

The pioneers used the dead animals. There were enough hides to make many robes. There was meat for days and days.

To keep the meat from spoiling, the pioneers cut it into long thin strips. They dried them over a bed of coals. The dried meat was called jerky. Native Americans had taught the pioneers to keep meat in this way.

Buffalo hides sold for good prices in those days. Some pioneers became buffalo hunters. They killed thousands of the animals just for their hides. Slowly the great herds of buffalo began to disappear. So life became harder and harder for the Native Americans. They needed the buffalo for food, shelter, and clothing. Now they had to ride a long way to find food. Often what they found was not enough for their families.

Beyond the plains towered the snow-peaked Rockies. The Native Americans called them "the Shining Mountains" because their snowy peaks shone in the sun.

As the map on pages 90–91 shows, these mountains stretch from Canada into Mexico. They pass through Montana, Wyoming, Colorado, Utah, and New Mexico.

The highest slopes in the Rockies have no trees. There, the weather is too cold for trees to grow. The place where the trees stop growing is called the *timber line*. The pioneers could see where this timber line began.

The Oregon Trail led through a pass in the Rocky Mountains. The map on page 125 shows where it crossed the mountains. Here's what might have happened as the Scotts' wagon train neared the mountains.

As the high peaks loomed up, eleven-year-old John Scott was worried. "How can our wagons go over those steep mountains?" he asked.

"Never fear, my boy!" replied the guide. "We'll not climb the high peaks. There is a better way through a pass! We'll climb a little at a time, up for a while and down! We'll go through a high valley. Then we'll go up again and down! We'll crawl along, but we'll make it!"

After many weeks, the pioneers reached the Continental Divide. The guide pointed west and said, "Out there is the Oregon country."

"Way over there?" asked Mary. "Is all that land the Oregon country?"

"Indeed it is," replied the guide. "It extends for many weeks of travel from here to the Pacific Ocean. It's now about a two months' journey to the Willamette Valley where you'll settle."

One day, the Scott party rested at the bottom of a steep slope. "Look, Mother," exclaimed Mary. "There's a plow rusting over there!"

There were no bridges across the rivers along the Oregon Trail. Here pioneers ford the Platte River in their watertight wagons. Notice how many oxen are used to pull the wagons.

"And a bedstead!" added Ida. "Why were they left?"

"To make the wagons lighter, I suppose," answered Mrs. Scott. "The hills ahead are rough and steep."

At that moment, Mr. Scott called, "We're in trouble. The wagons are too heavy."

"What can we leave behind?" Mrs. Scott asked. "We've nothing we can do without."

"I guess we'll have to leave the maple bed and dresser," answered Mr. Scott sadly.

Other families had to unload some goods, too. Then the cows were hitched with the oxen to help pull the wagons.

135

The long journey to Oregon was full of hardships. The pioneers crawled along rough, dusty trails for months. They lived through the long hot days of summer heat. They crossed swift rivers and high mountains.

Good water was always hard to find. Some days there was only a little to drink. At times, the only water found was bitter and made many people sick.

The travelers had to eat the same kinds of food day after day. They got tired of eating dried meat and corn cakes. Some began to complain.

There were no doctors to take care of the sick. The women took care of babies that were born on the way. Many animals died on the trail.

Most of the pioneers were farmers. They knew that in Oregon they could buy good land cheap. So they braved the hardships willingly. Still they were glad when the end of the trip was near.

One cool October night the Scotts and their friends sat around their cheerful campfire. They were happy. Captain Scott had just said that soon they would reach the Columbia River. There they would load their wagons on rafts and float down into the Willamette Valley.

As the campfires died down, Captain Scott began to speak. "The land of promise is just a few days away. Let us be thankful for our safe journey."

Two days later, the tired party reached the valley. "Hooray!" shouted Ida. "We made it all the way to Oregon!"

Oregon becomes a state

More and more pioneers moved to the Oregon country. Some went to hunt and trap. The largest number were settlers. They built towns and laid out farms.

But their land was not a state. Its settlers could not vote for the President of the

Large murals in the state capitol at Salem show scenes from Oregon's history. Here Captain Robert Gray trades with Native Americans.

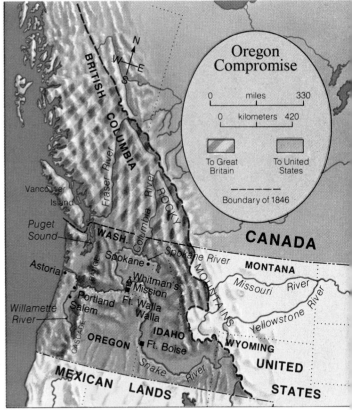

United States or for members of Congress. They could not choose their governor.

Both the United States and England had claimed the Oregon country. And each nation had good reasons for its claim. Sir Francis Drake, the English explorer, had visited the Oregon coast in 1589. In 1778, Captain James Cook had claimed Oregon for England. And the English had built trading posts in the valley of the Columbia River.

The United States also claimed Oregon. Captain Robert Gray had been there. He discovered the Columbia River. Lewis and Clark had explored part of the Oregon country. John Jacob Astor had built the trading post, Astoria, in Oregon. Fur traders had mapped routes through the area.

And many of the pioneers had settled in Oregon.

Neither country was willing to give up its claim. Some leaders felt that the matter should be settled by war. Others wanted to talk things over at a conference, or meeting. Finally, in 1846, a conference was held.

The United States and England decided to divide the Oregon country. Representatives of the two countries agreed on a compromise. In a *compromise* each party gives up part of what it first wanted.

England agreed that the United States should have the land south of what is now Canada's border. The United States agreed that Great Britain should have the northern part of the Oregon country.

In 1853 the Washington Territory was formed from part of the Oregon country. In 1859 Oregon became a state. At last the settlers of the Oregon country had all of the rights of citizens. They welcomed this news with loud cheers and singing.

Chief Joseph, in the center, meets with Alice Fletcher, a missionary.

The United States defeats the Nez Percés

About 6000 Nez Percés lived in the Oregon country. In 1855 the Nez Percés agreed to live on a reservation. It was a large one. It took in most of their old hunting and fishing lands. The treaty, or agreement, gave the Nez Percés these lands forever.

In 1860, gold was discovered on the Nez Percé reservation. Miners and settlers quickly moved into the area. The treaty did not stop them. United States officials then decided to make a new treaty. The new treaty took away about three-fourths of the Nez Percé reservation.

Many chiefs would not accept the new treaty. Chief Wellamotkin was one of them. He was also called Joseph. He and his followers went on hunting and fishing in the Wallowa Valley. After Chief Wellamotkin's death, his son, also called Joseph, led the Wallowa Valley people.

Meanwhile, settlers began to move into the Wallowa Valley. Chief Joseph would not leave. In 1877 a war broke out. For five months 5000 United States troops chased Chief Joseph's band of 300 through the rugged mountains. The Nez Percés won some battles, but were beaten as they tried to flee to Canada.

Here is part of Chief Joseph's speech of surrender.

I am tired of fighting. Our chiefs are killed . . . . It is cold and we have no blankets. The little children are freezing to death. My people, some of them, have run away to the hills and have no blankets, no food . . . . I want . . . to look for my children . . . . Maybe I shall find them among the dead . . . . My heart is sad and sick. From where the sun now stands I will fight no more forever.

After the Nez Percés had been defeated, they were moved out of the Northwest. They were sent to a reservation in Oklahoma.

What do you think?

1. What is a compromise? How is it useful in settling disputes?

2. Most explorers and pioneers did not turn back even though they suffered many hardships. Why didn't they give up? Why was it so important to them to complete their journey?

Things to do

1. Learn all you can about buffaloes. Find out how the United States government protects these animals today.

2. Among the dances and games that the pioneers enjoyed were:

   Pop Goes the Weasel   Captain Jinks
   Little 'Liza Jane   Sandy Land
   Here We Go Round the Mountain

   Help your class learn how to play these pioneer games.

3. The Lewis and Clark party and the pioneers on the Oregon Trail took different routes west. On an outline map of the United States, show these two routes.

4. Discuss with your class the meaning of this sentence: "The settlers' frontier kept moving farther and farther west into the lands of the Native Americans." Use a map of the United States to help you explain its meaning.

Is it true or false?

Write the numbers 1 to 10 on paper. Read the following sentences carefully. If a statement is true, write *true* after its number. If it is not true, write *false*.

1. The Lewis and Clark party set out in 1804.

2. The Lewis and Clark party followed the Mississippi River.

3. Sacajawea was a valuable guide.

4. Lewis and Clark finally reached the Pacific Ocean.

5. A large group of covered wagons is called a wagon train.

6. Only the United States had good reasons for claiming the Oregon country.

7. The United States kept its agreement with the Nez Percés.

8. John Jacob Astor built the trading post of Astoria in Oregon.

9. The trip overland to Oregon took about two months.

10. The route that led to the Northwest was called the Oregon Trail.

11
Gaining the Spanish Southwest

Pioneers from Mexico settle the Southwest

Mexican colonists reached the Southwest in 1598. This was before the colony of Virginia began.

Juan de Oñate (ō nyä′tā) was a governor in Mexico. He decided to explore lands to the north. He wanted to start a colony there. He wanted to find gold and the great riches that were said to be hidden in the Southwest.

Oñate made careful plans. He even spent a lot of his own money. It cost him almost a million dollars to start the colony.

Oñate's wife was Cortés's granddaughter. She was much admired for her skills and cheerful courage.

In the spring of 1598 the large party set out. There were the Oñate family and nearly 130 settlers. Native American guides led the way.

Most of the colonists rode horses. Supplies and belongings were packed on mules and in 83 two-wheeled carts. Of great importance were the books, dishes, and seed for starting crops and orchards.

The colonists drove more than 7000 animals, too. There were extra horses and mules and many cattle and sheep. Oñate's wagon train was almost four miles (7 km) long. The huge party moved along slowly, day after day.

In a few months the party reached a pleasant place in northern Mexico. There they started what would be the first permanent European settlement in the Southwest.

This Spanish colony came to be New Mexico. Oñate was its first governor. He built a mission school. There people could learn to read and write Spanish. Spanish music and trades were taught. And people could learn about the Christian religion.

The Mexicans taught the Native Americans how to build carts and how to weave woolen cloth. They showed them how to grow wheat, oats, peas, and onions. These

Before the Spaniards came, the Native Americans wove woolen cloth on a loom like this.

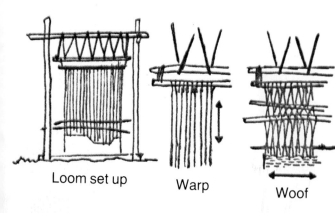

Loom set up   Warp   Woof

crops were new to the Southwest Native Americans. The Mexicans also helped the Pueblo people start fruit orchards.

The Native Americans shared their know-how about ways of living in their high, dry land. They showed the Mexican colonists how they dug ditches to bring water to their lands. This way of watering is called *irrigation*. They showed the colonists where to find honey, nuts, and salt, and where to hunt for deer and elk. The Native Americans brought presents of food to the colonists.

Oñate led a party across the plains. His record-keeper told about grasslands that could feed thousands of cattle and sheep. He told of the rich soil in which fine crops could be grown.

Oñate was not lucky in his search for gold. But he learned much about the Southwest. He captured Apaches and Comanches and brought them back to work as slaves.

Santa Fe's Palace of Governors was built by the Spanish in 1610. It was at one time New Mexico's state capitol. The building is now a historical museum.

The city of Santa Fe was established in 1610. Santa Fe (san′tə fā′) became the capital of New Mexico. It is the oldest capital in the United States. Find Santa Fe on the map of the Routes to the Far West on page 125.

The most famous building in Santa Fe was built in 1610. This was ten years before the Pilgrims came to America. It is called the Palace of the Governors. It is the oldest government building in the United States.

The *architecture* (är′kə tek′chər), or design, of this building is partly Spanish-Mexican and partly Native American. The colonists used some ideas from their Spanish ancestors. The palace had very thick walls. There were covered walkways around the building.

141

Native Americans did the work of building the Palace of Governors. They used some of their ideas of architecture. One was to have the logs that hold up the roof stick out from the walls. In time, this style of building came into wide use in the Southwest.

Pike explores the Southwest

In 1807 Santa Fe had some surprising visitors. Zebulon Pike and a party of explorers were taken there by guards who saw them nearby. They thought that the explorers were spies. After a time, they were let go and sent back to the United States.

Zebulon Pike had grown up in wilderness country. His father had been an army officer serving west of the Appalachians.

Young Zeb, as he was called, liked living on the frontier at the edge of the wilderness. He came to know some of the Native Americans who lived there. When he was fifteen, he joined the United States Army. He began to serve under his father.

In July 1806 the army sent Pike to explore some lands farther west. He was to learn more about the Arkansas and Red rivers. He was to find the source of each one. He had twenty-two soldiers and a doctor in his group. Many of them had been with Pike on earlier trips. They had asked to go with him this time.

Pike traveled across the Great Plains. Grasslands stretched as far as the explorers could see. Often they saw buffalo and antelope grazing. They saw thousands of prairie dogs. People in Osage and Pawnee villages gave them horses. They told them about the mountain they would cross. And they served them a feast. You can trace Pike's route on the map on page 125.

At last the party reached the Arkansas River. Winter had set in. The river was rough. Some of their boats tipped over, and a lot of their supplies were lost. They hunted and traded for food with an Osage band that was camped for the winter along the river.

One day Pike saw a strange-looking "cloud" in the distance. He soon knew that it was a huge snow-crowned mountain. It was a part of the Rockies. Its peak stood out because it reached so high.

Pike and his party set out to climb the high peak. There was no trail, and deep snow blocked the way. So they had to turn back. Pike's goal was not forgotten. Today this mountain is named Pikes Peak.

For many weeks Pike searched for the source of the Arkansas River. Snow fell day after day, and cold winds blew. There was no food for the horses. The explorers had to carry their own supplies through snowdrifts. Hunting was poor. The explorers were often hungry as well as half frozen. But they did find the source of the Arkansas River. It began in a canyon (kan′yən) in the Rockies. A *canyon* is a narrow valley with sides that are high and steep. The river began as just a small stream tumbling over rocks.

The explorers then went southwest to find the source of the Red River. The map shows where they went. They entered a part of New Spain. They called it the Spanish territory or the Spanish Southwest. Find the Spanish lands on the map. Notice how these lands reached west to the

Pacific Ocean and north to the Oregon country. Coronado's party had claimed these lands for Spain long before.

Pike met Native Americans in the Spanish Southwest. Some lived in villages of apartment-like buildings. The Spanish word for village is *pueblo*. So the people came to be called the Pueblos. Among them were the Hopi, Zuni, Acoma, and Laguna people. Before the Spanish came, there were 60 villages. When Pike saw them there were only 19.

The thick walls of the Pueblo buildings were made of mud brick, or adobe. Each building had many rooms. A different family lived in each room. There was a firepit for cooking and a hole in the roof for the smoke to go out. The rooms on the ground

While Pike and his party were exploring, they were captured by Spaniards. The Spaniards thought that the explorers were spies sent by the United States. The explorers were taken to Santa Fe as prisoners.

floor had no doors. To enter a room, people climbed up a ladder to a porch above. Then they climbed down another ladder through the smoke hole. In times of danger, the ladders were taken down.

The Pueblos were farmers and sheep herders. They grew corn and cotton in irrigated fields. They raised sheep and goats for meat and wool. They wove beautiful baskets and handsome blankets. They also made fine pottery.

The Navajos and the Apaches were other Southwestern people. Both groups raised some corn and other vegetables. They lived in family groups in houses that were made of logs and covered with earth or branches. The Navajos also herded sheep and goats.

Traders find the Southwest

When Pike's party returned east, they reported what they had seen. Traders were eager to hear Pike's reports. Pike told them that he thought Santa Fe's people wanted American goods. He said a trader could make money in this town. But he warned that traders might be put in jail. Santa Fe was a part of Mexico. It was governed by Spain. It was against the law for people in Spanish territories to trade with outsiders.

In 1821 Mexico won its freedom. The people in Santa Fe then welcomed visitors.

Many traders made the long trip to Santa Fe. The first traders loaded their goods on mules. From Missouri they traveled southwest about 800 miles (1280 km) to Santa Fe.

The traders led their mules into the town's *plaza*, or central square. Many people crowded around. They bought cloth, nails, tea, salt, tobacco, knives, rib-

Native Americans built many different kinds of houses. Navajo hogans were built of logs covered with earth. Apache wickiups were constructed of brush.

A modern-day wagon train follows the same route once taken by traders and settlers to reach Santa Fe.

bon, and other things. They paid for these goods in silver, gold, hides, wool blankets, furs, and livestock. Business was so good that some traders planned to take wagon trains of goods to Santa Fe. "A wagon train could make a fortune!" said one trader.

Other traders thought that the journey to Santa Fe would be too hard for wagon trains. But some people were set on going. They blazed the Santa Fe Trail.

The Santa Fe Trail became the chief route to the Southwest. Find it on the map on page 125. It started at Independence, Missouri. It crossed plains cut by deep rivers. It led across hot deserts dotted with cactus and gray-green sagebrush.

Along the Santa Fe Trail, traders saw herds of buffalo and many antelope. They saw rattlesnakes and long-tailed lizards. At night they heard the cries of wildcats and the sharp yips of coyotes.

The trip was long and hard. The traders feared the sixty-mile (96 km) stretch of hot, dry, sunbaked desert. There, they could not find water for themselves or their animals. Kiowas and Comanches sometimes attacked the wagon trains. Still, some traders were able to guide their wagons over the Santa Fe Trail, year after year.

Meanwhile, exciting things were taking place in Texas. At that time Texas was ruled by Mexico. But thousands of people from the United States were settling there.

145

Pioneers settle in Texas

Moses Austin had opened the way for pioneers in Texas. He had traded with Spaniards and Native Americans in Texas. He had often traveled across the rolling plains where wild horses and wild game roamed.

In the southern part of Texas, Spanish priests had built churches called *missions*. There they taught Native Americans the Christian religion as well as trades. The Spanish built forts near the missions. Small towns grew up close by. One of the most important towns was San Antonio.

Moses Austin liked southeastern Texas. It got plenty of rain. Its mild climate and rich soil seemed just right for growing cotton and other crops.

"This is a fine place for pioneers to settle!" declared Austin. "There is room for thousands of families. I must bring people here."

Austin talked the Mexican government into giving him a large grant of land. Soon after his return to the United States, Austin became ill. He asked his son Stephen to carry on his work.

Stephen Austin urged many pioneers to settle in Texas. He made speeches and wrote letters praising this land. He boasted that it was the finest region in the whole world. He said that good land was cheap. People could buy eight acres for a dollar.

Many people moved to Texas. Austin himself led hundreds of families to the new frontier. He named his first settlement Austin. Find Austin on the map (page 125). Today Austin is the capital of Texas.

Thousands of people set out in covered wagons for Texas. Some left signs on their homes. There were signs like "Gone to Texas" and "Starting from Scratch in the Southwest."

By 1835 almost 30,000 people had come from nearly every state. The largest number came from the South. They planned to grow cotton, rice, and sugar.

Some Texas pioneers had a hard life. Here is a letter that might have been written by a settler to her brother in Virginia.

Dear Brother George,

At last we are settled in Texas! It was a long journey. We came through the Cumberland Gap to Kentucky. At the Ohio River, we hired a flatboat to bring our covered wagon and horses down the Mississippi.

We took the wheels off the wagon and braced it so that it would not fall into the river. North of New Orleans, we left the flatboat and traveled across the plains by wagon.

We are many miles from a village. Once every two or three months I go to the general store in the village to get supplies. This trip takes several days. I hurry back as soon as I can. There's so much work to do!

We have built a comfortable cabin and planted vegetables and corn. But farming is hard, slow work.

Of late, we have had plenty of wild honey and corn bread. We crush our corn into meal with a hammer and stones.

We do not have schools yet, so I will teach the children their "three R's."

My regards.

Your sister,
Jenny

The Alamo became a symbol of the Texan fight against Mexico. What happened at the Alamo?

The pioneers worked hard. Besides farm work they had to get meats and fruit ready for storage. They had to grind corn into meal and churn butter. They had to make their own soap and candles. They had to spin yarn and weave it into cloth. They sewed their own clothes. They cared for sick people and animals. And always they lived with the dangers of the frontier.

Texas gains independence

The pioneers in Texas were governed by Mexico. People here did not have the same rights as they had in the United States. For example, they were not allowed to set up their own churches.

The pioneers were not happy with Mexico's rule. Still, more and more settlers came to Texas. So many came that Mexico feared it would not be able to control them. To prevent this, the Mexican government passed more laws for the colonists. One law would not allow new pioneers to come into Texas. Another increased taxes.

Stephen Austin went to Mexico to talk over the pioneers' problems with General Santa Anna, the new president. But Austin was put in jail. When he was set free, he went back to Texas.

It was the year 1835. Fights between Texans and Mexican troops had already started. That year the Texans formed their own government.

The Texans fought a battle with Santa Anna's soldiers at the Alamo. The Alamo was San Antonio's old Spanish mission.

Santa Anna led about 5000 soldiers against 187 Texans at the Alamo. Santa Anna ordered the Texans to give up. They told Santa Anna that they would not give up as long as one person still lived.

Santa Anna thought he would win in hours. Day after day, though, the Texans held the fort. One soldier was James Bowie, inventor of the Bowie hunting knife. Another was Davy Crockett, the famous frontier scout from Tennessee.

147

When Texas became a state, Sam Houston was one of the first two senators.

Sam Houston was chosen commander-in-chief of the Texas army. Houston was born in Virginia. When he was fourteen, he moved with his family to Tennessee. Though he disliked school, he liked to read. When Sam was sixteen, he went to work in a store. Then he ran away to live with nearby Cherokee people.

Sam stayed with the Cherokees for nearly three years. He learned their language and way of life. Later he told people they should treat Native Americans fairly.

In 1832 the President of the United States sent Houston to Texas. Houston's job was to make treaties with the Native Americans who lived on the borders of the United States. He stayed on in Texas. He became one of the main leaders in the settlers' fight against Mexico.

Houston's soldiers tracked down Santa Anna's troops. The Texans attacked Santa Anna's soldiers, shouting "Remember the Alamo!" The Mexican troops were taken by surprise. The Texans won with ease. General Santa Anna was taken prisoner. He was forced to sign the paper that gave Texas its freedom from Mexico.

Texas became an independent nation in 1836. It formed a government much like that of the United States. Sam Houston was chosen to be the first president of Texas. Because its flag had one star, Texas was called the "Lone Star Republic."

The Republic of Texas was larger than the state of Texas is today. As the map shows, it went north over lands that are now part of Oklahoma, Kansas, Colorado, and New Mexico.

Texas was a republic for more than nine years. Many Texans, though, wanted to be citizens of the United States.

The Texans held the Alamo for twelve days. At last the fight grew hopeless. Storming the walls, Santa Anna's troops broke into the fort. Only Mrs. Dickinson, her daughter, and three others were still alive. They were captured by Santa Anna.

The Battle of the Alamo was a loss for the Texans. Yet it led to final success. While it was being fought, other Texans were forming an army. Farmers, stock raisers, and adventurers were joined by the slogan "Remember the Alamo." They were more set than ever to fight for freedom. Their leader was Sam Houston.

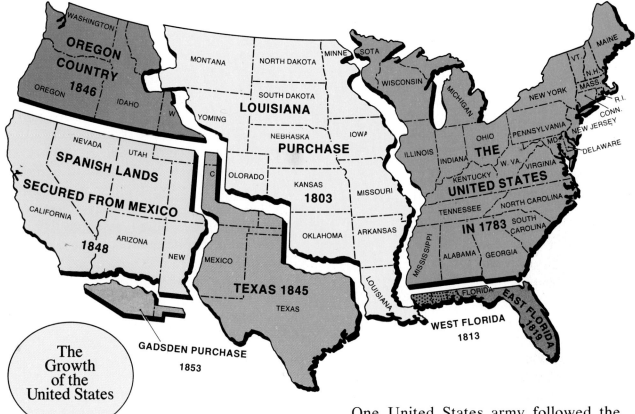

The Growth of the United States

(Map labels:)

WASHINGTON

OREGON COUNTRY 1846
OREGON
IDAHO
W
YOMING

MONTANA | NORTH DAKOTA | MINNESOTA
SOUTH DAKOTA
LOUISIANA
NEBRASKA | IOWA
PURCHASE
1803
KANSAS | MISSOURI
COLORADO
OKLAHOMA | ARKANSAS

NEVADA | UTAH
SPANISH LANDS
SECURED FROM MEXICO
CALIFORNIA
ARIZONA
NEW | MEXICO
1848

TEXAS 1845
TEXAS

LOUISIANA

WISCONSIN | MICHIGAN
ILLINOIS | INDIANA | OHIO | PENNSYLVANIA
THE
UNITED STATES
KENTUCKY | W. VA. | VIRGINIA
TENNESSEE | NORTH CAROLINA
IN 1783 | SOUTH CAROLINA
MISSISSIPPI | ALABAMA | GEORGIA

MAINE
VT | N.H.
MASS.
NEW YORK
R.I.
CONN.
NEW JERSEY
MD.
DELAWARE

FLORIDA
WEST FLORIDA 1813
EAST FLORIDA 1819

GADSDEN PURCHASE 1853

The United States adds the Southwest

In 1845 Texas became the twenty-eighth state. This caused hard feelings in Mexico. Mexico thought that the United States had taken over a lot of land that did not belong to it.

War between the United States and Mexico broke out in 1846. One reason was that the countries could not agree on the southern boundary of Texas. Another reason was that the United States wanted more land. The leaders thought it could be won from Mexico.

One United States army followed the Santa Fe Trail and took control of New Mexico. Then other United States soldiers won California.

After two years the United States had won the war with Mexico. A peace treaty was signed between the two countries. Mexico gave up the vast Southwest for the sum of $15,000,000. This pushed the borders of the United States south to the Rio Grande and west to the Pacific Ocean.

In 1853 the United States bought a strip of land from Mexico. This was called the Gadsden Purchase. Locate the Gadsden Purchase on the map above. The land of the Gadsden Purchase became part of which two states?

Many Mexicans who were living in the Southwest stayed on. They became citizens of the United States.

Do you remember?

1. Who was Oñate? What did he do?
2. When was Santa Fe founded? What is its most famous building? What kind of architecture does it have? Why?
3. Who was Pike? What did he learn about the Southwest?
4. Who was Stephen Austin? Who was Sam Houston? Why were these two men important?
5. Why was the fight at the Alamo important?
6. How did the United States get the Spanish Southwest?

What do you think?

1. What is the land of the Southwest like? How do its climate and land affect plant and animal life?
2. What is a republic? Do you think that the United States is a republic? Why?

Things to do

1. Use an encyclopedia to find information about one of these topics.

   Oñate   Alamo
   Santa Fe Texas as a republic
   Pueblos   Sam Houston
   Navajos   Apaches

2. Use the map on page 149. Find what states or parts of states were once a part of Mexico. Then find a larger map of one or more of these states. Make a list of Spanish place names that appear on this map.

The Mormons settle Utah

The Mormons were organized by Joseph Smith in 1830. The members of this religious group first lived in New York State. But because of their beliefs and ways of living, they were treated badly. At last they were forced to leave New York.

The Mormons moved west to Ohio. After a time, they went to Missouri and still later they went to Illinois. They were trying to find a place where they could live in peace. Joseph Smith and his brother were killed in Illinois.

Finally some of the Mormons set out for Utah. It was part of the land that the United States got from Mexico. Led by Brigham Young, 143 pioneers crossed the plains and mountains. They guided carts and covered wagons. They took cows, horses, mules, dogs, and chickens.

One hot summer day in 1847, the travelers stopped to rest. They had reached the western side of the Wasatch Mountains, a range of the Rockies. The tired people looked down on a broad sun-baked land. They saw the shining waters of Great Salt Lake. Then Young said, ''This is the place! Here we shall build our homes.''

The new land did not look inviting. Mountains and sage-covered hills were all around. It was a dry, brown desert. One Mormon wrote in her diary.

I had hoped we would settle in a peaceful green valley. But our good leader says we will build our homes on this dry land. He tells us we can bring water from the mountains for our crops. We shall! With hard work we shall make this a green land.

As the years passed, the hard-working pioneers changed their dry lands into fine

Notice that when this Mormon handcart brigade made a rest stop, everyone had a chore to do.

farms. Little rain fell. So the farmers had to irrigate their fields. They built dams on the streams that rushed down from the high mountains.

The Mormons had many hopeless times. One spring the new crops had just come up. Then millions of hungry locusts swept in. They began to eat every green thing they could find. Men, women, and children fought the swarms of insects. But their work seemed useless.

Then all at once there was a rush of wings. Thousands of seagulls swooped down and gobbled up the crickets. The pioneers were thankful. In honor of the seagulls, they put up two handsome monuments.

After the Mexican War, Utah became a United States territory. The Oregon Trail passed through Utah. Hundreds of families traveled over the Oregon Trail on their way to California.

Many people came to Utah to stay. By 1860 there were 150 towns. The most important one was Salt Lake City. It was named for the large salty lake nearby. Within a short time several thousand Mormons had settled in Salt Lake City. Today it is the capital of Utah. Find the city on the map on page 125.

Pioneers settle in California

California was far to the west along the Pacific coast. Find California on the map on page 149. It extended more than a thousand miles along the coast. For nearly

151

three hundred years, California belonged to Spain. In 1821 Mexico won its independence from Spain. Then California was Mexican territory. After the Mexican War was over, California became a part of the United States.

Juan Rodríguez Cabrillo discovered California in 1542. He sailed into San Diego Bay and claimed the land for Spain. As the years passed, other Spaniards explored California. They named some of its bays and islands. At the same time Russian fur traders were moving down the Pacific coast from Alaska.

In 1769 pioneers from Mexico started the first mission in California. Father Junípero Serra was in charge of the work. The next year, a soldier named Gaspar de Portola set up a military post.

The first mission was at San Diego. In time, Father Serra and others built twenty more missions. They went from San Diego as far north as Sonoma. Find these two cities on the map on page 341. The missions were about a day's trip apart. They were joined by a trail. It was called El Camino Real, which means "The King's Highway."

Most missions in Spanish California were built around a central courtyard. One building was a church with a high bell tower. Another was the place where the *friars*, or priests, lived. Still another was a workshop. In the workshop Native Americans learned how to spin, weave, and make soap and candles. They also learned to make furniture, boots, and saddles. They were closely watched by priests and Spanish soldiers.

The walls of the mission buildings were made of thick adobe and stone. They had red tile roofs.

Some Native Americans cared for the mission's vegetable gardens and fields of grain. The seeds for these crops had been brought from Spain and Mexico. So had seeds and cuttings of orange, lemon, and olive trees.

The large farms owned by the missions were called *ranchos*. The English word *ranch* comes from this Spanish word.

In time, many of the mission ranchos were given to Mexican leaders. Other Mexicans started new ranchos. Most families on ranchos lived in low, one-story adobe houses. Native Americans worked on the ranchos and raised the crops. They took care of the cattle and sheep that roamed the hills.

It was a happy time when a rodeo was held. The word *rodeo* is Spanish and means "to drive into a circle." At rodeo time the people of nearby ranchos gathered to round up the cattle. The workers drove the calves into a circle to be branded, or marked. Each rancho had its own special brand, or mark. After the hot, dusty work, the families enjoyed feasting, dancing, and talking.

In the mid-1800s other people began to come to California. There were traders who came by ship. There were trappers, mountain guides, and a few settlers.

Jedediah Smith was a trader and trapper. He was a strong man who loved the outdoors. He lived through many dangers. One of these dangers was a fight with a grizzly bear. He became a famous trailblazer and guide.

Kit Carson was another trapper and guide who explored California. He had worked as a mule driver on the Santa Fe

Spanish missions could be found throughout the Spanish lands. This picture shows the Mission St. Stephen in Acoma, New Mexico. Notice the "beehive" oven which was used for baking.

Trail. He had made friends with several groups of Native Americans and could speak their languages. Carson also worked for the United States army. He helped drive the Navajos from their homeland to a fort in eastern New Mexico.

James Beckwourth, whose mother had been a slave, was a trapper. He discovered an important pass through the Sierra Nevada. It is called Beckwourth Pass.

John Sutter, a trader and settler, was given a land grant. Captain Sutter's 97,000 acres of land lay in the Sacramento Valley. His land stretched to the wooded slopes of the Sierra Nevada. Point to these mountains on the map on page 125.

153

The *Helena* races another ship around Cape Horn on the way to the California gold fields.

Sutter's ranch was a rich one. It had wide grasslands where thousands of cattle grazed. Fine crops grew in the rich soil. Hidden unknown in its stream beds was a fortune in gold.

In 1848 gold was discovered on Sutter's ranch. Sutter had hired James Marshall and other workers. They were to build a sawmill on a stream in a wooded canyon. One morning Marshall saw bits of yellow gravel shining in the stream bed. He picked up some of the bright pebbles. "These look like gold," he said to himself. The next day Marshall rode through a pouring rain to show Captain Sutter the bits of yellow gravel that he had found.

"Captain Sutter!" he called out as he stopped beside the ranch house.

"Yes?" Sutter answered. "Oh! It's you, Marshall! Come in! You're wet and out of breath! What's happened?"

"I've special news! But keep it a secret!" replied Marshall as he gave Sutter a

bottle. "Look what's in there! It's gold! I'm sure!"

"Gold!" exclaimed Sutter, looking at the soft, heavy bits of rock. "We must be certain!"

The two men tested the metal. At last Sutter said, "You're right! This is gold! Where did you find it?"

"It's from the stream near the sawmill," answered Marshall.

The two men agreed to keep their news a secret. But it leaked out. Soon farm workers stopped their plowing. Stock raisers left their cattle to hurry to "the magic stream bed."

One day a man ran down the muddy streets of San Francisco. Waving a bottle of fine gold sand, he shouted, "This is gold! Gold! Sutter's ranch is rich with gold!"

When the news spread over the town, strange things began to happen. Owners of businesses locked their offices. Merchants closed their stores. Sailors left the ships in the harbor. Soon only a few people were left in San Francisco. Hundreds set off for the new gold fields.

News of the gold fields traveled across the United States. Newspapers printed glowing tales of how much gold a person could find in a day. Everywhere people talked of making a fortune out west. By 1849, thousands of people were heading for the gold fields. They were known as "Forty-Niners."

Some Forty-Niners who lived along the Atlantic crowded on ships bound for California. The ships sailed south around South America and then north along the Pacific coast. Sometimes this voyage took six months. There were many days of

154

During the Gold Rush, San Francisco's Telegraph Hill was covered with miners' tents.

stormy weather. There was sickness. Sometimes supplies of fresh food and drinking water ran low. But what did hardships matter if you could reach the gold fields?

Some Forty-Niners traveled overland. They painted their covered wagons with signs that said, "Californy or Bust." They followed the long California Trail. Find it on the map on page 125.

Many Mexican miners were hired at first. They had worked in mines in Mexico. They knew how to use water to wash gold away from the rock.

The fortune hunters found many hardships in the gold fields. There were no comfortable houses. So people set up tents or built rough shacks. Prices were high. A loaf of bread cost a dollar, and eggs sold for three dollars each. Sugar cost three dollars a pound, and a chicken cost about ten dollars.

Sending mail was costly, too. There was no mail service to or from California. People sent letters by boat or with travelers. It cost as much as five dollars to send one letter.

More and more people moved west to California. Many came to hunt for gold. Only a few made fortunes. Soon the easy riches were gone. Then people had to find other ways of making a living. Some became ranchers. Other people found jobs in the towns. Many Chinese people came to work in the mines and then later to help build railroads.

Most people who came to California stayed. Within a year California had enough people to become a state. It was made a state in 1850.

155

These Forty-Niners stock up on supplies to prepare for their long journey to the California gold fields.

San Francisco grew rapidly with the arrival of the settlers from the East. By 1851 it was an important city.

Mexican ways influence the Southwest

Mexican ways of living influenced the settlers. Many of the settlers in the Southwest built Spanish-style houses. The houses had stucco walls and tile floors and roofs. They had arched doorways, deep porches, and flower-filled courtyards. This style of architecture is still used today in the Southwest.

The settlers learned to cook Spanish and Mexican foods. They learned to grow and use lemons, oranges, and olives. They copied the Mexican ways of raising sheep and cattle.

The settlers kept the Mexican custom of having rodeos. Rodeos are still held today. They are shows in which riders and ropers compete for prizes.

Thousands of Spanish place names are used in the Southwest. For example, *Colorado* is a Spanish word meaning red. It was given to the Colorado River, which flows in part along red cliffs. The word California is the name of a treasure land in an old Spanish tale.

157

Which are partners?

Write the items in List A in a column on paper. After each one, write the correct "partner" from List B. You will have twelve sentences, each of which tells a fact.

List A

Zebulon Pike	Father Serra
Sam Houston	Santa Fe Trail
Santa Fe	Juan Rodríguez Cabrillo
Mormons	Stephen Austin
Irrigation	Forty-Niners
Brigham Young	James Marshall

List B

led Mormons to Utah.

discovered California.

discovered gold on Sutter's ranch.

led Texas' fight for independence.

built the first California missions.

explored the Spanish Southwest.

led many settlers to Texas.

is a system of watering lands.

is a city built by Spaniards in the Southwest.

settled Utah.

went to California during the Gold Rush.

was the chief route to the Southwest.

Put these in order

On paper, copy the following events in the order in which they happened. Before each one write on your paper the date it happened.

The California Gold Rush began.

Texas became a republic.

Mexican settlers founded Santa Fe.

Brigham Young led Mormons to Utah.

Oñate led Mexicans to New Mexico.

United States obtained Southwest from Mexico.

Can you read map symbols?

Copy on paper the numbers in Column 1. Find in Column 2 the meaning for each symbol in Column 1. Write it after the correct number.

Column 1		Column 2
1.	▬ ▬ ▬	branches of a river
2.	▲	state boundary line
3.	▬▬▬	mountain peak
4.	•	future state boundary
5.	︾	route
6.	••••	international boundary line
7.	▬·▬·▬	city

Things to do

1. Use an encyclopedia to learn more about one of these people.

Joseph Smith	Brigham Young
John Sutter	Kit Carson
Davy Crockett	Father Junípero Serra

2. Imagine that it is 1849. You have decided to leave your home in Tennessee to search for gold in California. Write a letter to a friend. Try to convince your friend to go to California with you.

3. Act out a short play about something that happened to the Mormons who settled in Utah. If you need information, read about the Mormons in an encyclopedia or a library book.

4

How our country changed

159

12

Fighting a war between the North and the South

Colonists bring Africans to America

A Dutch ship brought the first African workers to the English colonies. The ship arrived at Jamestown, Virginia, in 1619.

The settlers wondered why the ship had come. Soon they found out. The Dutch captain had some Africans on his ship. He wished to trade them for supplies.

The trade was made, and twenty Africans were brought ashore. In time these people were freed. Some became landowners.

American plantations grew in number and size. More workers were needed, but they were hard to find. Planters said that slaves might be the answer. Ships began bringing more Africans to the colonies.

The captured Africans suffered on the trip across the Atlantic. They were packed in the bottom part of a ship. Often they were chained to one place. They were given only a little food and water. Even this was sometimes spoiled. Many Africans died during the voyage.

The Africans were sold to owners of southern plantations. Most of them became house slaves or field slaves. House slaves had to clean, polish, cook, and serve meals. They cared for the planter's children. They also had to sew, wash, iron, make soap and candles, churn butter, and weave cloth. The house slaves took care of the lawns and gardens. The children born to house slaves were slaves, too. They did jobs such as running errands. They also helped in the kitchen and yard and with some of the garden chores.

Field slaves did the hard farm work. These men, women, and children cleared the land and plowed. They planted and cared for the fields. They picked and cleaned the cotton and tied it into bales.

A few slaves became skilled workers. They were sent by their owners to work in factories, mills, and mines. Some became brickmasons, carpenters, or workers in iron. They built bridges, houses, docks, and railroads. Some worked on ship crews or as blacksmiths. Their owners got the money these slaves earned.

Plantation slaves worked sixteen hours a day, six days a week. They lived in small one-room cabins with dirt floors. Many slept on beds of corn husks. They ate mostly cornmeal, pork, and molasses.

Slaves could not leave a plantation without the owner's permission. They could not visit with friends or have church services without a white person there. They could not go to school or speak in court.

An owner could hurt a slave without being punished. An owner could sell a slave's children or separate a family at any time. Slaves had no choice about where they would live and work.

There were three ways that slaves could become free. They could escape, be freed by an owner, or buy freedom. Otherwise they were slaves for life.

Differences grow between the North and the South

The Northern states could get along without slaves. Find these Northern states on the map on page 167. Most farms in the North were quite small. Farmers could do most of their own work. The growing season was short. During the long,

Fibers

Seeds

In this picture, workers use a cotton gin to remove the seeds from the cotton fibers. The clean cotton will be shipped to mills where it will be made into cotton cloth.

cold winters, no work was done in the fields. So owning slaves did not pay.

Farming was just one way to make a living in the North. Some people were in the lumber, fishing, and shipbuilding businesses. Others were shopkeepers and merchants. Thousands of women and men worked in businesses or in factories and mills. Farm girls were hired in textile mills in Lowell, Massachusetts.

Many of the people who took jobs in factories were immigrants. *Immigrants* are people who come into another country to live. Many immigrants moved to the United States in the early 1800s. Many were poor and eager for jobs. Some went west to start farms. Most found jobs in the mines and mills.

The immigrants gave the North a good supply of labor. The North did not need slaves. By 1804 all of the states north of Maryland had passed laws against slavery.

Farming was the main industry in the Southern states. The South's climate was just right for growing tobacco, sugar cane, rice, and cotton. Find the Southern states on the map.

Cotton became the main crop of the South. Planters sold their cotton to mills both in the United States and in England. These mills hardly were able to weave

161

cloth fast enough to supply all of their customers.

Growing the cotton was not the hard part. Getting it ready for the mills was. When cotton is picked, it has many small seeds. The seeds must be removed before the cotton goes to the mill. At first this had been done by hand. It took about eight hours to clean a single pound (450 grams) of cotton. Many workers were needed to get the cotton ready for the mills.

Catherine Littlefield Greene encouraged a young teacher to find a faster way to remove the seeds. He was Eli Whitney.

Whitney invented a machine which he called the cotton engine. It became known as the cotton gin. It could comb the seeds from fifty pounds (22.5 kg) of cotton in a day. In time the cotton gin was improved. Then it could clean a thousand pounds (450 kg) of cotton a day. Now planters wanted to raise more cotton.

After the early 1800s, many planters moved farther west to a broad fertile plain. This rich land reached across Alabama, Mississippi, Louisiana and into Texas. It was a good area for raising cotton. There was a long growing season with hot summers and plenty of rain.

The South grew so much cotton that it was called the "Cotton Kingdom." Cotton brought in so much money that people said it "ruled" the South.

Planters began raising more cotton than ever. So they needed thousands of workers. The number of slaves in the South grew. By 1850 the South had more than three million slaves. This is a large number. But only about one in four white southern families owned slaves. Three out of four did not.

Many people in our country opposed slavery. Some people had been speaking out against it for a long time. In 1775 Quakers had started the first anti-slavery society in America.

After the War for Independence, some Americans said that the words "all men are created equal" meant slaves, too. They thought that the freedom they had won should belong also to slaves.

Benjamin Franklin spoke out against slavery. Thomas Jefferson urged Congress to forbid the slave trade with Africa. George Washington said that his own slaves should be set free after his death.

Many Americans hoped that slavery would die out. This did not happen. So some people began to work to abolish, or do away with, slavery. They were called *Abolitionists* (ab′ə lish′ə nists).

Some Abolitionists published newspapers. One of the best known was the *Liberator*. It was published by William Lloyd Garrison. Abolitionists such as Lucretia Mott helped slaves to escape. Lucy Stone and others helped runaway slaves to read and write. They found places for them to live and work.

The Abolitionists formed a number of anti-slavery groups. These groups then sent people throughout the country to speak against slavery. The Grimké sisters, Angelina and Sarah, were famous anti-slavery speakers.

Many Abolitionists suffered because of their ideas. Their houses were burned. Their newspaper presses were wrecked. Mobs shouted and threw stones when they spoke.

Some people caught reading Abolitionist newspapers in the South were whipped.

Sojourner Truth *(above left)*, Frederick Douglass *(above right)*, and Harriet Tubman *(right)* worked for abolition in different ways. Truth made speeches. Douglass edited an abolitionist newspaper. Tubman became a conductor on the Underground Railroad and led runaway slaves to freedom in the North.

There were rewards for the capture of people who helped slaves escape.

Some Abolitionists had been slaves at one time. Sojourner Truth, for example, had been a slave for thirty years. After she gained her freedom, she took the name ''Sojourner Truth.'' She spent the rest of her long life traveling across the country. She preached against slavery and helped freed slaves.

Frederick Douglass was another leading Abolitionist. As a slave he was not allowed to attend school. But he learned to read and write anyway. He became a fine speaker and writer. He worked full time against the slave system.

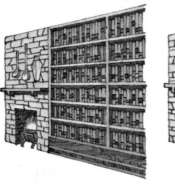

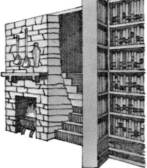

Many Underground Railroad stations had secret hiding places large enough for several escaped slaves. Safely hidden from the slave catchers, the escapees could rest for a while.

Harriet Tubman had been a field slave. She had run away to the North. She became one of the most daring workers on the *Underground Railroad*.

The Underground Railroad was the system of secret escape routes. These routes were used by slaves to escape from the South. Some of the routes led to Canada. "Conductors" along the Underground Railroad showed the slaves the routes to follow. They gave them food and clothing. They brought them to "stations" where they would find shelter. The stations were homes and barns along the way.

Runaway slaves moved northward at night. They slept during the day, hidden in stations, in the woods, or in caves.

The Underground Railroad helped many slaves escape. Harriet Tubman alone made about twenty trips to guide slaves to freedom. She led more than 300 slaves out of the South. Her own parents were included among them.

Some slaves did not use the Underground Railroad. They ran to swamps, forests, or mountains near where they lived. There they lived in small groups with other runaways.

Other slaves fixed papers that said they had been set free. They then took jobs in factories or on ships.

The Creeks and Seminoles in Georgia and Florida helped slaves to escape. Many runaways stayed to live in the villages of those Native Americans.

From time to time groups of slaves revolted. There had been revolts on slave ships from the start. In 1800 Gabriel Prosser, a Virginia slave, made plans to attack Richmond. Almost all of the slaves living nearby agreed to help him. His plan failed and he was hanged. In 1822 Denmark Vesey planned a huge slave revolt. He, too, failed.

In 1831 Nat Turner, a field slave whose father had escaped to freedom, led a revolt in Virginia. Nearly sixty people were killed before the revolt was ended by the state soldiers.

One of the most famous revolts was led by John Brown. But it failed also.

Many Southerners blamed northern Abolitionists for their problems. The Abolitionists, on the other hand, became even more set on ending slavery.

The states quarrel about slavery

The North and the South could not agree about slavery in new states. The Western territories were being settled. One by one they asked to become a state. But there was a problem. Would the new states be slave-holding states or free states? A *free state* was one which did not allow slavery.

Most people in the North wanted Congress to forbid slavery in all new states. Many people in the South thought each new state should decide for itself about slavery.

Each state sent two senators to Congress. For a time there were as many slave states as free ones. The North and the South then had the same number of senators. One group in the Senate could not pass laws harmful to the other side.

In 1850 California asked to join the United States as a free state. Senators from the South opposed this. It would have made 16 free states to 15 slave states. Members of Congress quarreled bitterly over this matter.

A few Southerners were already hoping their states would leave the United States. They thought that a state had the right to do this if there was a good reason. They thought a citizen should be loyal first to the state, then to the nation.

Many Northerners did not agree. They felt that a citizen's first loyalty should be to the nation.

Daniel Webster and Henry Clay were working for peace. These able leaders had been members of Congress for many years.

When he was elected to the presidency, Abraham Lincoln left his home and law practice in Springfield, Illinois, to move to Washington.

Webster was a senator from Massachusetts. He was famous for his stirring speeches. Often he spoke out about the Constitution of the United States.

Clay was a senator from Kentucky. His friendly smile and quiet manner helped to stop many quarrels in Congress. He tried to end the trouble over California.

Clay worked out a plan called the Compromise of 1850. In a compromise, each side gets part of what it wants. But each side also gives up some things. By Clay's compromise, California was to be a free state. This pleased the North. Certain other new states were to decide for themselves about slavery. That pleased the South. Another thing that the South liked was that runaway slaves were to be caught and returned.

Many leaders did not like this compromise. But Webster made a strong

speech in favor of it. The compromise became law. The United States, or the Union, was saved for a time.

The Compromise of 1850 did not work very well. Many Northerners would not return runaway slaves. In fact, they were helping more slaves to escape.

After 1850 the North and the South became more angry with each other.

In 1860 Abraham Lincoln was elected President. But there was trouble ahead. Lincoln wanted all new states to be free states. The South knew that. Some of its leaders had warned that if Lincoln became President, their states would leave the United States.

Lincoln was born in Kentucky on February 12, 1809. His home was a one-room log cabin. His parents were poor farmers. They cleared the land and raised crops between the tree stumps. When Abe

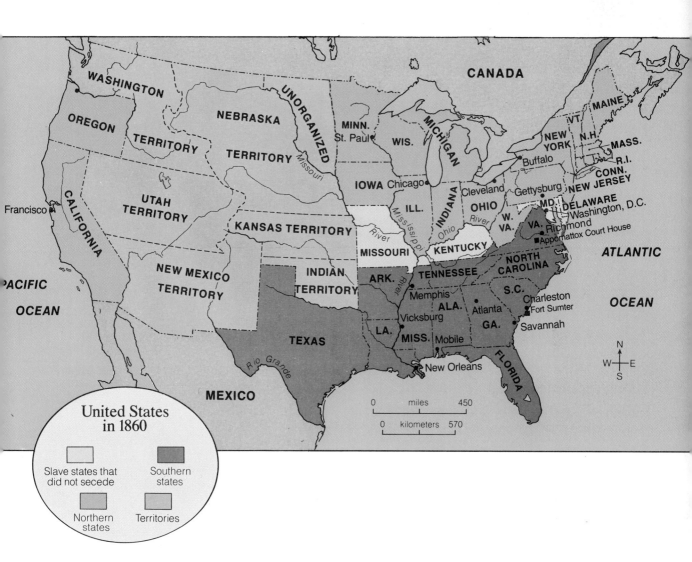

United States
in 1860

Slave states that did not secede

Southern states

Northern states

Territories

was 7 years old, his family moved to Indiana. Fourteen years later they moved to Illinois.

While Lincoln was growing up, he worked at many kinds of jobs. For a time he was a clerk in a country store. He was also a rail splitter. When he was 19, he worked on a riverboat on the Mississippi. In New Orleans he saw people buy and sell slaves.

Lincoln had always dreamed of becoming a lawyer. With part of his earnings, he bought books and studied law. In 1836 his dream came true.

Lincoln settled in Springfield, Illinois. There he practiced law. He also held office in the state government.

In November 1860, Abraham Lincoln was elected President of the United States. The South was unhappy about that.

After the election some states left the union. South Carolina was first to act. Its people said that they were no longer a part of the United States. Within a few weeks, six other states also left the United States. They set up a government of their own. They called it the *Confederate States of America,* or the *Confederacy.* Soon four more states joined the Confederacy. That made a total of eleven Confederate states. Jefferson Davis was elected President of the Confederacy. The states that remained part of the United States were called the Union.

167

Some study questions

1. Why was slavery more important in the South than in the North?
2. How did the cotton gin make slavery more important in the South?
3. Who were the Abolitionists? How did they help slaves.
4. What was the Underground Railroad?
5. What eleven Southern states left the United States? Why?
6. What slave holding states stayed in the Union?

Using a political map

Turn to the map of the United States in 1860 on page 167. Use it to help you answer these questions.

1. Notice that color is used to show three groups of states. What are these groups? What part of the map tells you what the colors mean? Why is part of the map shown in gray?
2. Why is this called a political map?
3. Does this map show relief or not?
4. Does it have an inset map?

The names of some states on this map are written in abbreviated, or shortened, form. Point to Massachusetts. Notice that its abbreviation is "Mass." Vermont's is "Vt."

On a piece of paper, copy the names of the states below. Then write the correct abbreviation after each one. If you need help, refer to page 435 in the Tables for Reference.

California	Illinois	Michigan
Connecticut	Wisconsin	Ohio

What do you think?

1. Why do you think the Abolitionists risked their lives to work against slavery?
2. What do you think caused slave revolts?
3. Many Southerners did not believe their states should withdraw from the United States. What are some reasons they might have had for believing this?

Review note-taking

As you have learned, note-taking helps a person remember important facts. Here are some points to review. Keep them in mind as you take notes.

1. Read each paragraph carefully.
2. Write the important facts.
3. Keep notes as brief as you can.
4. Use abbreviations when possible.
5. Organize notes.

Things to do

1. Read in another book about one of these leaders.

   Daniel Webster   Lucretia Mott
   Harriet Tubman   Frederick Douglass

   Take notes on what you read. Keep in mind the points about note-taking which you just reviewed. Be ready to share what you learn.
2. Evaluate your note-taking. On a piece of paper write 1 to 5 in a column. Read again the points for note-taking. Write "yes" for each one you followed.

Abraham Lincoln, accompanied by President Buchanan, rides to the Capitol for his inauguration.

The North and the South at war

In 1861 Lincoln became the President of a divided United States. He took the oath of office on a high platform in front of the Capitol in Washington, D.C. He was dressed in a black suit, a stiff white shirt, and a high silk hat. He carried a cane with a gold handle.

Lincoln stepped forward and placed his left hand on a Bible. Raising his right hand, he promised to "preserve, protect, and defend the Constitution of the United States." People wondered how he would do this. Seven states had already left the United States. Would Lincoln try to punish them? What would he say about slavery?

Lincoln did not answer all of these questions in his Inaugural Address. He said that no state had the right to leave the United States. He warned that he would protect the forts and buildings which belonged to the United States government.

War broke out only a few weeks after Lincoln became President. It became known as the Civil War.

The war began at Fort Sumter in South Carolina. Fort Sumter was on a small island in Charleston harbor. Find it on the map. It belonged to the United States government. Union soldiers from the North held the fort. South Carolina, now a part of the Confederacy, ordered Fort Sumter to surrender. When the commander of the fort refused, the food supply was cut off.

Lincoln had food shipped to Fort Sumter. This made Confederate leaders angry. Southern soldiers fired on the fort. North-

169

ern soldiers fired back. A fierce battle took place. At last the Northern soldiers had to give up. This was the first battle of the Civil War.

Thousands offered to serve in the Union Army. Thousands rushed to join the Confederate forces, too. Everyone hoped the war would be over soon. But it wasn't. It dragged on for four years.

During the second year of the war, both sides ran short of troops. They then drafted, or ordered, people into the armies. This was the first time in United States history that soldiers were drafted.

Both sides needed money, supplies, and troops. Money-raising events were held in the Union and in the Confederacy. Groups were formed to help the families of soldiers.

Women who had never worked outside their homes went to work in offices and factories. Some women ran the family farms and businesses for the first time. Others knitted and sewed uniforms and made bandages to use in hospitals.

Doctors and nurses went to serve on the battlefield. Mary Walker was one of the doctors. At first she was allowed to work only as a nurse. Later, though, she became an Army officer and worked as a doctor.

Clara Barton was called the "Angel of the Battlefield." She was born on a Massachusetts farm on Christmas Day, 1821. For a while, she taught school near her home. Later she moved to Washington, D.C. She was a clerk in one of the government offices.

When the Civil War began, Clara Barton carried medicines and food to injured soldiers. The officers ordered her away. They said the battlefield was no place for a

woman. But she did not give up. In fact, she got other women to join her. After a time, she ran a large hospital for wounded soldiers.

Clara Barton served suffering people the rest of her long life. She helped to find missing Union soldiers. She took care of the victims of wars in other parts of the world. She helped people who had lost homes in fires, floods, and storms. She founded the American Red Cross.

Dorothea Dix was another nurse during the Civil War. She had spent years trying to make life better for people in prisons and poorhouses. During the Civil War, though, she took time out from her work to care for wounded soldiers. She was in charge of all the nurses for the Union Army.

The North blockaded, or blocked, the South's ports. Northern ships guarded the coasts. They blocked the South's harbors from Virginia to Texas. The South

The Union victory at Gettysburg was a turning point in the war.

had few factories. The South had to buy clothing, shoes, and guns from Europe. The blockade by the North kept most of the ships from reaching Southern ports.

The North also won control of the Mississippi River. One by one, Northern troops took the main cities along the river. The last big one to fall was Vicksburg. Find this city on the map on page 167.

This cut the South into two parts. Now the states east of the Mississippi could not get food from Texas, Louisiana, and Arkansas.

One key battle of the war was fought near Gettysburg. It is a town in Pennsylvania. Find Gettysburg on the map. The Battle of Gettysburg lasted three days. At last, the Union forces drove the Confederate troops back. Because more than 50,000 soldiers fell there, Gettysburg was made a national cemetery. A national cemetery is a place where many people who have served in the armed forces are buried.

A special service was held at the cemetery. Two great leaders came to speak. One was Edward Everett, who was famous for his fine speeches. The other speaker was President Lincoln.

Edward Everett talked for two hours. When he finished, people clapped loudly. But only a few could recall what he had said.

Then Abraham Lincoln stood before the solemn crowds. He began his speech like this:

Four score and seven years ago our fathers brought forth on this continent a new nation, conceived in Liberty, and dedicated to the proposition that all men are created equal.

Lincoln's speech had only about three hundred words. It lasted less than five minutes. But today Lincoln's Gettysburg Address is remembered and loved by millions of Americans.

On April 9, 1865, General Lee *(right)* surrendered to General Grant *(left)* at Appomattox Courthouse.

On January 1, 1863, Lincoln made an important announcement. He declared that the slaves in the Confederacy were *emancipated,* or freed. This order was called the Emancipation Proclamation.

The Emancipation Proclamation said that blacks could join the Union forces as soldiers. Until this time they had served only as cooks, drivers, and laborers.

About 180,000 blacks joined the Union forces. Some had never been slaves. Others were former slaves who had escaped. Thousands had been freed when Union troops captured their owners' lands.

Slave owners in the Confederacy did not obey the Emancipation Proclamation. Many slaves kept on serving their owners. Some even went to war with them.

Two great generals led the armies toward the end of the war. Ulysses S. Grant was the leader of the Union troops. He had served as an officer in the United States army. After Grant captured Vicksburg, he took charge of all of the Union forces. Later, Grant became President of the United States.

General Robert E. Lee served as leader of the Confederate troops. He was a kind, brave man. He was honored and loved by many.

When the Civil War began, Lee had a hard time deciding what to do. He had been an officer in the United States army for 36

172

years. He thought slavery was wrong. He had already freed his own slaves. He did not want any states to leave the Union. Yet Lee felt a strong loyalty to his state of Virginia. He stayed with his family and friends and served Virginia.

In 1865, General Lee surrendered to General Grant. The Confederacy had one defeat after another. Over half of its soldiers had been killed or wounded. Many of its soldiers were barefooted. Most of its ammunition and food were gone. Confederate leaders knew it was no use to fight on.

One April morning General Lee rode to see General Grant. They met in a little town called Appomattox (ap′ə mat′əks) Courthouse, in Virginia. They shook hands and then sat down to talk. After a time General Grant agreed that the Confederate officers could keep their swords. He also said that the soldiers could keep their horses and mules.

Grant arranged to send food to Lee's hungry army. Northern soldiers had cut the South's food supply.

Lee thanked Grant. Then he got on his horse and rode back to talk to his troops. As he left, Union soldiers began to cheer and fire their guns. But Grant stopped them. He told them that the war was over and that the Southern soldiers were once again their fellow Americans.

When Lee talked to his soldiers, tears filled his eyes. He praised them for their courage. He said that their cause was lost and that he had surrendered. He told them that they would not be put in prison. They could keep their swords and their horses. He asked them to go back to their homes and do their best to make the country strong and united again.

Abraham Lincoln was attending a performance of *Our American Cousin* the night he was shot.

Lee set a good example. He became the president of a university. He did much to win friendship between the North and the South. He proved himself to be as great an American in defeat as he had been in victory.

In 1864 Abraham Lincoln had been re-elected President. The war was not yet over. But Lincoln was at work making plans to bring the North and the South together again. He wanted the Confederate states to be treated as though they had never left the Union. But he was not able to carry out his plans.

A few days after the war ended, Lincoln was shot. President and Mrs. Lincoln had gone to a theater in Washington. The play had just begun when shots were fired.

Friends carried the wounded President to a nearby house. Doctors rushed to his bedside and did what they could. But Lincoln died early the next morning.

Fredericksburg, Virginia, was only one of many towns damaged during the war.

Many problems come with peace

Some very unhappy years followed the Civil War. President Lincoln was dead. Andrew Johnson became the next President. Johnson had served as Vice-President while Lincoln was President. If a President dies, the Vice-President becomes the new President.

President Johnson wanted to carry out Lincoln's plans not to punish the South. He hoped that leaders of the North and South would work together to rebuild the country.

But some Northern leaders in Congress would not agree. They wanted the South to be punished.

Living conditions in the South at the end of the war were tragic. Some Confederate soldiers found their homes empty or burned to the ground. Furniture had been stolen or ruined. Tools and livestock were gone. Weeds covered the fields. Bridges, roads, and railroads were destroyed. Cities such as Richmond and Atlanta were in ruins. Families were scattered. Thousands

had died from diseases that swept through the South.

The people needed to rebuild their homes and plant crops. They had to build new railroads and bridges. A lot of money was needed. But most Southerners were now very poor. They did not know where to get help.

Freedom brought new problems to the former slaves. At first freedom had seemed wonderful. Many black people had left plantations to look for a better life. But even after one day's travel, they knew that they had no place to go. They had no way to earn money for food and clothing.

The former slaves had no jobs. They had no land, no tools, and no one to help them. They lacked training. And now they had to support themselves.

After the war many Northerners went to the South. Some were Union soldiers who were sent to set up new governments and to keep order. Others were teachers and missionaries. They started schools for freed slaves and gave them other help. Laura Towne was one of these workers. She left Massachusetts to help black people in South Carolina. She started the Penn School to train former slaves for jobs.

Another was M. J. R. Richards. She was a black woman who came to help teach. During the war she had been in the secret service of the Union army.

Some Northerners came into the South to help the freed slaves learn to vote and to hold public office. Others wanted public offices for themselves. Some bought farms and started new businesses.

Many of these Northerners were honest. Others, though, were very greedy and dishonest. They bribed people to vote for them. They then gave these people government jobs, even if they were not able to do them.

Southerners called most of the Northerners in the South "carpetbaggers." Carpetbaggers got their name because their suitcases were made of carpet fabric.

Some Southerners, too, were greedy and dishonest. These "scalawags," as they were called, tried to get ahead by hurting other people.

Some freed slaves went North to look for jobs in cities. Many went to Washington, D.C. There an Abolitionist named Josephine Griffing set up a program to find homes and jobs for freed slaves.

Many freed slaves had no choice but to work for their former masters or for other landowners. They worked as sharecroppers. That is, they got a share of the crops grown on the owner's land. They got a cabin, food, a mule, a plow and other tools.

The landowners also gave them seed and the use of the land.

But the food and supplies were not free. The sharecropper went into debt to buy what the family needed. Most of the families were always in debt to the landowner. The share of the crop that the family got had to be used to help pay off the debt. Then the family had to borrow money all during the next year. This happened year after year.

Some freed slaves became tenant farmers. They rented land. Some tenant farmers saved enough money to buy small farms.

Carpetbaggers arrived in the defeated South after the war.

Former slaves went to school to learn practical skills as well as how to read and write. What is being taught in this school?

Training and education helped former slaves improve their lives. Many wanted other kinds of jobs. They wanted to become mechanics, government workers, doctors, and teachers. They needed education for such jobs. Schools and colleges were started to educate former slaves. Howard University in Washington, D.C., was one of these new schools.

Whenever possible, former slaves went to school. Many made better lives for themselves through education and hard work.

For most former slaves, though, life was not much better. White Southerners were elected to state offices. They passed laws that took away the freedoms of the black people. Some of the laws set up rules about voting. Other laws kept them from traveling and from starting businesses.

The North and the South began to work together again. In time, the army and the carpetbaggers left the South. Southerners rebuilt their homes, businesses, bridges, railroads, and roads. They began to raise larger crops of tobacco, cotton, and sugar cane. They began to grow other crops. They started factories and mills. In fact, so many changes took place they called it "The New South."

Slowly the North and the South learned to be friends again. Together they looked ahead to a happier future.

176

Complete these sentences

Write 1 through 6 on a paper. Read each incomplete sentence below. Then, from the list, choose the word or group of words that completes each sentence correctly. Write the answer after the number of the sentence.

1. The first battle of the Civil War was fought at Fort ____.
2. The ____ freed slaves in Confederate territory.
3. ____ was the leading general of the Union forces.
4. Robert E. Lee was the commander of the ____ army.
5. The Civil War started in the year ____.
6. ____ was head of the nurses in the Union army.

List

Henry Clay	Confederate
Emancipation	1861
Proclamation	Sumter
Vicksburg	Ulysses S. Grant
Dorothea Dix	Robert E. Lee
Union	1756
Mary Walker	

Put these events in order

Below are some events you read about in chapter 12. Write these events in a column on paper. Write them in the order in which they happened. Then write after each event the year it took place.

The war ended.

Lincoln was born.

Lincoln freed the slaves.

Lincoln died.

Lincoln was elected President for the first time.

Things to do

1. In an encyclopedia read about one of the people listed below. Be ready to share what you learn.

Abraham Lincoln	Robert E. Lee
Ulysses S. Grant	Clara Barton
Frederick Douglass	Harriet Tubman
Dorothea Dix	Lucretia Mott

2. Dramatize an event in the life of the person you read about.

3. Review the paragraphs about taking notes, on page 112. Read in another book about the Underground Railroad. Take notes on the main facts.

4. Find out all you can about how Dorothea Dix worked to help prisoners and people with mental illness. List ways in which her work helps people today.

Changing farms and growing cities

Inventors help the farmers

It was time to harvest the wheat. Will Turner was cutting his wheat by hand. That was slow, hard work. He was glad to stop and chat with Walter Evans, a neighbor who had ridden up.

"What's new?" asked Turner.

"Haven't you heard? Tomorrow young Cyrus McCormick will show how his reaper works. Aren't you coming to watch?"

"That odd contraption?" exclaimed Turner. "No! It didn't work the last time he tested it."

"But he's been tinkering with it," said Walter. "He says he's fixed the problem. You'd better come!"

"Can't waste my time!" said Will. "I have more wheat to cut, and I can't get help. If I could, I'd raise more."

"Sure! So would I," agreed Walter. "If this machine works, though, it might be just the help we need. Factories might be making reapers by the hundreds before long."

That hot day in July 1831 Cyrus McCormick's reaper worked. It rattled, but it worked. It cut six acres of grain. That was many times as fast as a farmer could do it by hand. You can imagine, then, how the people cheered.

McCormick's reaper was pulled by horses. It was strange looking. Someone called it "a mixture of a chariot, a wheelbarrow, and a flying machine."

Cyrus McCormick grew up on a farm in Virginia. One job he did not like was cutting grain. It had to be done by hand. He often wished that there was a better, faster way to do this job.

Cyrus's father had tried for years to make a reaper. Cyrus had worked with him. But they had failed, again and again. At last his father had given up. Young Cyrus kept trying to make the dream of inventing a reaper come true. It did. He was only 22 years old when his reaper worked that July day.

A few years later, young McCormick and his wife Nettie went to Chicago to start a reaper factory. They knew that Chicago was a good place. It was near the plains in the middle of the United States. They knew that many farmers were moving to the plains. The reaper could help them with their farming.

Cyrus and Nettie McCormick came to Chicago with only $60. But, before long, their factory was making a thousand reapers a year. The reaper was slowly improved. Farmers could then harvest huge amounts of grain.

Nettie Fowler McCormick shared equally in the running of the factory. It burned down in a great Chicago fire. Nettie pushed to rebuild the plant and make it larger. She gave her time and money to many schools, churches, and hospitals.

Other farm machines were invented, too. One was the threshing machine. After grain is cut, it must be threshed, or separated, from the stalk. Doing this by hand was another slow, hard job. But about the time the McCormicks sold their first reaper, a threshing machine was made.

Later the reaper and the thresher were combined to make one machine. This was called a combine. The early combines were pulled by as many as twenty or thirty horses.

In the 1830s John Deere, a blacksmith in Illinois, invented a new and stronger plow. It made plowing much easier.

The first farm machines were pulled by horses. After the 1860s some farm machines were run by steam. Later, tractors and other types of machinery were run by gas-powered engines.

Cyrus McCormick and his helper, Jo Anderson, built the first successful reaper. Later the reaper was combined with a thresher to make a combine. Today's combine looks very different from the first reaper. What differences can you see in these pictures?

Farmers today use machines to pick tomatoes, cut corn, and harvest soybeans. Such machines enable fewer farmers to feed more people.

Today, on farms in the United States, machines do many things. Machines plant seeds and bale hay. They pick corn, cotton, soybeans, and potatoes. Often a single machine does many things. For example, a beet picker takes the tops off the beets, digs them out of the ground, cleans them, then puts them into a wagon.

Electric power is now used to run some farm machines. It is used to milk cows and cool the milk. Electric power runs grain dryers, egg sorters, and other machines.

New machines are still being made. A tomato picker was made in the early 1960s. It now takes half as long to pick tomatoes as it did before.

Other inventions have helped farmers. Trucks have taken the place of horse-drawn wagons. A big farm might use an airplane to spray crops for insects or to drop food to animals after a snow storm.

180

Discoveries by scientists have helped farmers. Men and women in science have found ways to improve soil, plants, and animals. At first, scientists showed farmers how to use natural materials like ground bones to improve soil. Next, they developed chemical fertilizers. These plant foods help farmers grow larger crops.

Scientists made poisons to kill insects that hurt crops and animals. They found cures for plant and animal diseases. Some scientists brought plants from other countries. Soybeans were brought from China many years ago. They were brought here for animal food. Then people found out that soybeans are good food for people. Soybeans are also used in making many products.

George Washington Carver was a scientist. He found many uses for soybeans. He also worked with sweet potatoes and peanuts. He found how to make more than 300 products from peanuts.

Farm machines and science brought changes. Farmers could own larger farms. They could produce more crops on the land they had. They lost fewer crops and animals to disease.

Not long ago, a farm family could grow enough food for themselves and four others. Now a farm family can produce enough to feed themselves and 96 other people.

Farmers in 1900 had to work about 38 hours to produce 26 bushels of corn on an acre of land. Today they have to work only four to six hours and grow three times as much corn!

Each farm family could grow more and more farm products. So fewer and fewer farmers were needed. Gradually farm

George Washington Carver
helped southern farmers
become less dependent on cotton.

families left their farms. They moved to the cities. In 1820 about 75 out of every 100 American workers had been farmers. By 1890 fewer than 4 out of every 100 workers were farmers.

Today many farm families grow some food for their own use. But most farm products are sold. And farm families buy most of the things they need. What a change from long ago!

Imagine what farm life was like in 1840. Farm families made nearly all the things they needed. Families baked their own bread and churned butter. They canned fruit, made soap, and dipped candles. They made most of their own clothes.

Neighboring families worked together to build the houses and barns. Some crops were sold. But much food was raised for a family's own use.

181

Americans move to cities

By 1900 most Americans lived in towns and cities. In 1800 only about 125,000 people lived in the five largest cities in the United States. By 1860 New York City alone had 800,000 people. In those days New York was a city of narrow, winding streets. The streets were filled with people selling everything from silk to vegetables. They were crowded with horse-drawn carriages and wagons.

Older cities, such as Boston, Philadelphia, and Baltimore, were also growing larger. So were southern cities like Charleston and New Orleans.

Many factories and mills were built in the cities. A *factory* is a building where products are manufactured, or made by machines. Sometimes factories are known as mills.

The earliest factories made yarn and cloth. Spinning yarn and weaving cloth by hand took a long time. In colonial days most of this work was done at home. This work is now done in large textile mills. The machines in the mills do the work much faster. Many women work on the spinning and weaving machines. At first they were members of farm families who had moved to town. Other women worked to help pay for the family farm.

Lucy Larcom worked at a mill in Lowell, Massachusetts. She and other women would meet in the evenings to listen to speeches and read things they had written. Lucy became well known as a poet. She wrote a story of her early life. It is called *A New England Girlhood*.

Many things made in the factories were new kinds of products. They included telephones, typewriters, phonographs, electric lights, and cash registers.

The sewing machine was invented by Elias Howe and Isaac Singer. More and more clothes were then made in factories.

Tin cans and the machines to make them were invented. Before long, food was being canned in factories.

In 1913 Henry Ford started making cars on an assembly line. On an *assembly line* each person has a small part in making a product. Each person does a job. Then the product goes to the next person, and the next person, until the product is finished. Assembly lines in factories meant that goods could be made faster and cheaper.

Power was needed to run the machines in the factories. The early textile mills ran on water power. The mills were built on the banks of rivers.

Then the steam engine came along. It was invented in England. Steam was made by making water boil. In the earliest days, wood fires kept the water boiling. Later, coal was used as fuel. With steam power, factories no longer had to be built beside rivers. Today electric power is used in place of steam.

Raw materials were needed for the new factories. Raw materials are things that are used to make products. Raw materials come from plants, animals, and minerals. Cotton, for example, is a raw material. It is made into cotton thread at a spinning mill.

Transportation is needed to bring raw materials to factories. It is needed, too, to carry products from farms and factories.

Railroads became a chief means of transportation. In the years before the

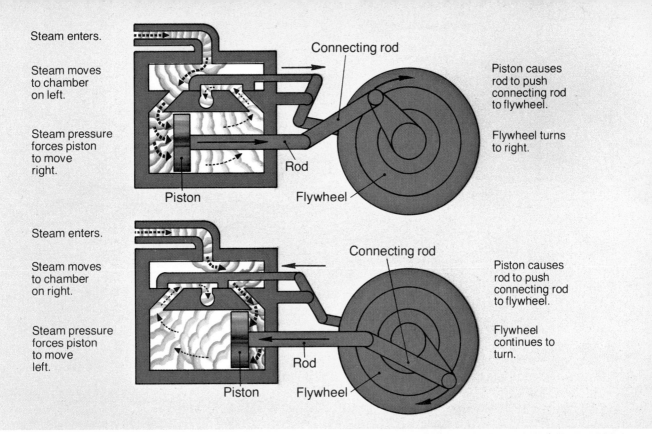

Steam enters.

Steam moves to chamber on left.

Steam pressure forces piston to move right.

Connecting rod

Rod

Piston

Flywheel

Piston causes rod to push connecting rod to flywheel.

Flywheel turns to right.

Steam enters.

Steam moves to chamber on right.

Steam pressure forces piston to move left.

Connecting rod

Rod

Piston

Flywheel

Piston causes rod to push connecting rod to flywheel.

Flywheel continues to turn.

The steam engine made modern industry possible. People no longer had to depend on the power of muscles, water, or wind to run machines.

Civil War, railroads were built between the cities of the East coast and the Midwest. Shorter routes linked cities in the South and East. A railway to the West coast was finished in 1869.

Rivers continued to be used. Barges carried goods to cities on the coast. From there, the goods were shipped to other countries.

After 1900 trucks were used more and more. Today cargo planes are used to carry goods that must reach buyers in a hurry.

By 1900 people in all parts of the country were buying goods from factories. People were shopping in small-town general stores and in the new city department stores. They were also buying through mail-order catalogs. The catalogs were a big help to people in rural areas.

Using assembly-line methods, Henry Ford was able to produce cars the average family could afford.

Arriving immigrants often crowded on deck to get their first view of the Statue of Liberty.

Workers were needed for the many jobs in factories. They were needed to run the machines and to inspect the final products. Some were hired to find ways to make products better and to draw the plans for new ones. Workers were needed to load and unload materials, to fix machines, and to supervise workers. Office workers and sales people were needed.

People came from other countries to work in American cities. Between 1820 and 1865 about four million immigrants came to the United States. Nearly half of them were from Ireland. Others came from England, Germany, Norway, Sweden, and Denmark. Some of these people settled on farms in the Middle West. Many went to work in factories.

Chinese men who came to America during these years mined gold in California. They also did much of the work of building the western railroads. San Francisco was home for many Chinese Americans. Both men and women came from most countries. But Chinese immigrants were mostly men until the 1900s.

After the Civil War, millions more people came to the United States. In the early 1900s nearly 15,000 immigrants poured into New York City each day. They had left homelands in Italy, Greece, Poland, Austria, Hungary, Russia, and Turkey. They were hoping to find both jobs and freedom. Many people were still coming from Ireland. Many Jewish people were among those who came.

Many European immigrants found their first homes in the slums. In the big cities they crowded into *tenements*. These were apartment buildings. They were often firetraps. An entire family might live in one room. They shared cooking space and the bathroom with other families.

The immigrants went to work in the steel mills, coal mines, and garment factories. Many women and girls worked as housemaids. In those days, even the finest home did not have an automatic washer, vacuum cleaner, or other labor savers.

Many of these immigrants or their children finally left the slums. In the meantime millions of black people from the rural areas of the South were moving to northern cities. They were part of the movement of people from farms to cities.

Later many people came to large cities from Mexico, Puerto Rico, and Cuba. Many of these people, too, had lived in rural areas in their homelands.

Many new jobs opened up as American cities grew. Big offices were built. Here people worked for banks, insurance companies, mail-order houses, and big firms of all kinds. These businesses hired women and men to deal with customers. They hired workers to write and type letters, to order supplies, and to do hundreds of other jobs.

There were offices for government workers, too. These men and women kept records, handled taxes, and provided many kinds of public services.

As cities grew, so did the number of service jobs. These are jobs that provide help, rather than goods, to other people. Doctors, nurses, librarians, lawyers, cleaners, and bus drivers are service workers. People who do repair work have service jobs.

New York's Hester Street became the center of a large Jewish immigrant community.

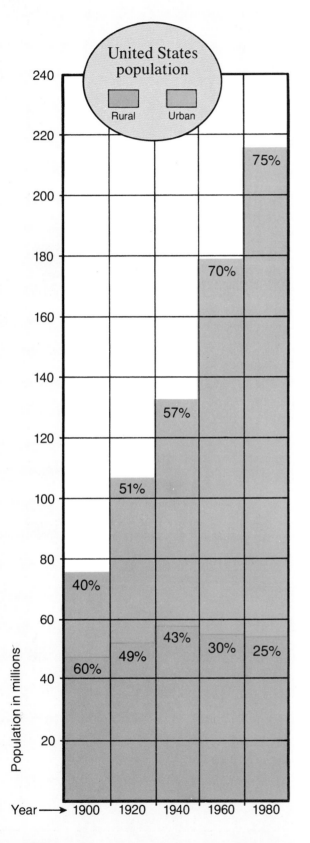

United States population

Rural   Urban

Population in millions

240

220

75%

200

180

70%

160

140

57%

120

51%

100

80

40%

60

43%   30%   25%

49%

40

60%

20

Year → 1900   1920   1940   1960   1980

Today over three-fourths of Americans live in urban areas. Urban areas are made up of cities and the suburbs, the smaller towns, that surround them. This is shown on the population map of the United States. *Population* means the number of people living in a region. A region where few people live is said to be sparsely, or thinly, populated. A region where many people live is said to be densely populated.

Study the map key and the explanation below it. How are the most sparsely populated areas shown on the map? How are the most densely populated areas shown? Where are they? Where are the most densely populated areas in the United States? Why are they densely populated?

The crowding in urban areas brings many problems. You know how trouble can happen in a crowded school or on a crowded playground. Crowding brings problems in the city, too. Noise pollution, for example, comes in part from so many people moving about. They ride in cars, buses, trucks, trains, and planes. There is much noise in the building and repair of streets and buildings, too.

Air pollution is another problem. Gases, smoke, and other wastes from cars and trucks enter the air. Other wastes come from factories and power plants.

Cities also face problems of water pollution. Costly sewage-treatment plants must be built. Factories may have to put in equipment to clean the water emptied into rivers or lakes.

People in many city neighborhoods work to solve problems. Some people form block clubs. Block clubs might work on clean-up campaigns. The clubs might help neighbors who are in trouble.

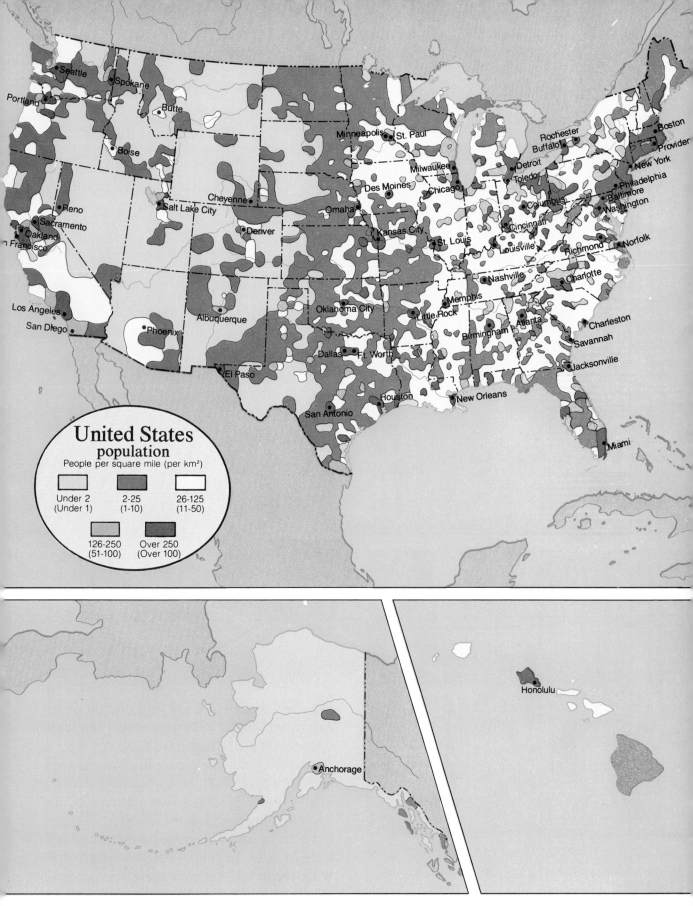

United States
population
People per square mile (per km²)

Under 2
(Under 1)

2-25
(1-10)

26-125
(11-50)

126-250
(51-100)

Over 250
(Over 100)

Seattle
Spokane
Portland
Butte
Boise
Reno
Sacramento
Oakland
San Francisco
Los Angeles
San Diego
Salt Lake City
Cheyenne
Denver
Albuquerque
Phoenix
El Paso
Dallas
Ft. Worth
San Antonio
Houston
Oklahoma City
Little Rock
Minneapolis
St. Paul
Milwaukee
Des Moines
Chicago
Omaha
Kansas City
St. Louis
Memphis
Nashville
Birmingham
Atlanta
New Orleans
Detroit
Toledo
Columbus
Cincinnati
Louisville
Rochester
Buffalo
Boston
Provider
New York
Philadelphia
Baltimore
Washington
Richmond
Norfolk
Charlotte
Charleston
Savannah
Jacksonville
Miami

Anchorage

Honolulu

187

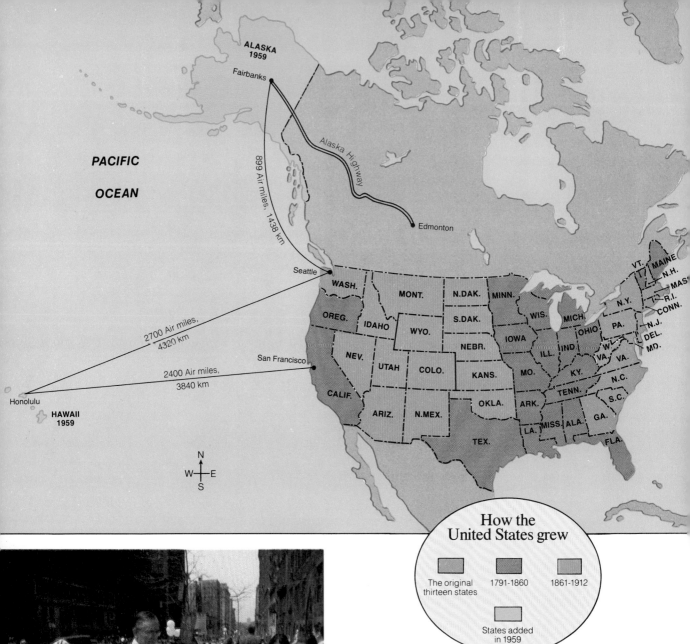

PACIFIC

OCEAN

ALASKA
1959

Fairbanks

899 Air miles, 1438 km

Alaska Highway

Edmonton

Seattle

2700 Air miles,
4320 km

San Francisco

2400 Air miles,
3840 km

Honolulu

HAWAII
1959

WASH.
OREG.
IDAHO
MONT.
WYO.
N.DAK.
S.DAK.
NEBR.
MINN.
WIS.
IOWA
MICH.
ILL.
IND.
OHIO
PA.
N.Y.
VT.
MAINE
N.H.
MASS
R.I.
CONN.
N.J.
DEL.
MD.
NEV.
UTAH
COLO.
KANS.
MO.
KY.
W.
VA.
VA.
N.C.
CALIF.
ARIZ.
N.MEX.
OKLA.
ARK.
TENN.
S.C.
LA.
MISS.
ALA.
GA.
TEX.
FLA.

N
W E
S

How the
United States grew

The original
thirteen states

1791-1860

1861-1912

States added
in 1959

People held block parties to help
solve urban problems.

Other kinds of groups organize to improve city living. Many groups work on city-wide problems, not just one block or neighborhood. They may save fine old homes and office buildings from being torn down. They may help people plant gardens in empty lots. They clean up the banks of local rivers. Some groups have set up summer programs for children. Others have set up adopt-a-grandparent programs to help older people. These are just some ways that city people are working together. Working together is the American way.

Hawaiians and Alaskans celebrate their new statehood. Now they, too, could vote in presidential elections.

The United States grew steadily from 13 states to 50 states. By 1860 our country had 33 states. But most of the West was still made up of territories. Year after year, people from other parts of the country and many immigrants settled these lands. They built farms and towns, businesses and factories. By 1912 these western territories had become states. In 1959 Alaska and Hawaii became states.

All of the states are shown on the map on page 188. In which state do you live? Find it on the map. Did it become a state before or after 1860? Study the map to find out. Locate Alaska and Hawaii. You will learn about all of the states in later chapters.

How? Why? What?

1. How did machines change farming? What were some of these machines?
2. What are some ways in which scientists have helped farmers?
3. Why did so many people move to cities?
4. How did factories change over the years?
5. What kinds of jobs were people able to get in the cities?

What do you think?

1. Name an invention that you think has made life better for people. How has it done this?
2. How have people in your community joined to solve problems or to help the community? Why do people need to join together to solve community problems?
3. Why do immigrants come to the United States?

Things to do

1. Have you wondered how you will earn your living when you grow up? Many types of jobs were named in this chapter. Do any of them sound interesting to you? Choose one and find out more about it. If you can, watch people working at this job. Talk to them about it, if possible. Read about it. Find out what training you would need for such a job. Discuss what you learn with your class.
2. Use reference books to find out more about jobs for women in early factories in our country. Take notes on what you read. Organize them and be ready to share what you learned with your class.
3. Find out what raw materials are used in making jeans, nylons, and plastics.

14

Becoming a world power

Americans are traders

Linda and Bob were on a tugboat heading for New Orleans. The tug was pushing five barges loaded with wheat down the Mississippi River.

Near New Orleans the boat passed long rows of docks and warehouses. Along the docks were freighters and barges of all sizes and shapes.

The tugboat captain explained, "Every year many tons of wheat are shipped out of this port of New Orleans. The wheat is bought from farmers in the middle of the country. Barges carry it down the Mississippi to New Orleans. From there it is sent to countries all over the world."

"Look at those barges," said Linda. "They're carrying oil."

"They are going to an oil refinery. There the oil will be separated into gasoline and other products," explained the captain.

"Where does the oil come from?" asked Bob.

"It may come from oil fields in the United States," answered the captain. "Or maybe from oil fields in other countries. We buy much oil from other lands."

"Look at that freighter over there," said Linda. "It's unloading bananas."

"We buy bananas and many products from the countries of Central America and South America," said the captain. "This is one of the busiest ports in the world. About

5000 freighters from at least 60 countries come here each year. They bring products that we buy. They carry away goods that we sell. The United States is a busy world trader.''

Trade is the exchange of one thing for another. Trade has two parts, getting and giving in exchange. You may do some trading every day. Once in a while, you may *barter,* or make a direct trade. You could barter, or trade, an apple for an orange. You might trade a pair of skates for a ball and bat. What are some things you have bartered?

Most of the time, people use money to make a trade. For example, you might sell a pair of used skates. You would get money for them. Then you might use the money to buy a ball and bat. A bakery owner sells a cake. She may use the money to buy flour.

Most people sell their services for money. You might earn $2 by taking care of a young child. You could use the money for a movie ticket. You have traded some work time for a movie. The movie owner may use the $2 to buy popcorn. A factory worker might trade 40 hours of her time and skill for $200. Then she could trade her $200 for food, clothes, rent, or other things.

There are a number of reasons that we use money for making trades. Let's look at two reasons. First, it is hard to barter, or make direct trades of things. Let's say you want a skateboard. But it's hard to find someone who will trade one for your old ice skates. A farmer can't trade a load of corn for the electric bill. It's better to use money to make these trades.

A second reason for using money is that it is easy to send or to carry with us. Let's say that you have corn to trade. And suppose you could find a doctor who would take your corn. It is much easier to send money than corn to the doctor. Money is easier to send or carry for trade than almost anything you can think of.

To trade means to exchange one thing for another. This girl is exchanging her labor in mowing the lawn for money. For what does she exchange the money?

The United States trades with the world

Our country began its world trade long ago. World trade is the exchange of goods and services between countries. We buy goods from France. In turn, French people use the money to buy goods from us or from other countries. We trade with people in every country.

The Thirteen Colonies traded with Britain and other countries in Europe. They also traded with islands in the West Indies.

Then the colonists won independence and formed the United States. Our trade with other countries went up.

In those days the United States exported mostly raw materials, such as timber, cotton, and tobacco. *Exports* are goods that are sent out of a country for use in another country.

In early days the United States had only a few factories. It imported many manufactured goods. *Imports* are goods that are brought into a country.

In time, American farms turned out more products than Americans needed. These products were exported. As American factories made more goods, some of these were exported, too.

At the same time, many people in the United States could afford to buy more goods. They wanted more sugar than could be grown in the United States. They drank more tea and coffee. They needed raw materials for factories. The United States began to import more and more goods.

World trade helps the United States. About one-fourth of our farm products are exported. About one-tenth of all American workers depend on exports for their living.

American manufacturers need imports. Most tin comes from other lands. Imports are needed to produce aluminum and steel. Fifteen raw materials must be imported to make telephones. Autos need many imported raw materials.

As time goes by, exports and imports change. At one time the United States exported large amounts of oil. But we are using more oil every year. In 1978 nearly half of the oil was imported.

The United States becomes a world power

By 1900 the United States was a world power. That means that the United States was looked upon as a leader by people in other countries.

Trade helped the United States to become a world power. Other things helped, too. In its early years, other nations left the United States alone. We were able to develop and become strong.

Also, America was rich in natural resources. It had plenty of land for growing crops. We had water for irrigation and power. We had forests and minerals. We

had raw materials for use in manufacturing. We had eager and able workers. A large number of them were immigrants.

Most immigrants wanted better lives. They were willing to work hard. Also, they felt they were free to reach their goals. They brought many special skills with them. They were free to invent things and to improve ways of doing things.

World War I broke out in Europe in 1914. In this war Germany and other countries fought against the Allies (al′īz). The Allies were England, France, Russia, Belgium, and other countries. They were called Allies because they were allied, or joined together, against Germany.

In April 1917 the United States sent troops to fight on the side of the Allies. The United States sent ships and supplies. A year and a half after we entered the war, it was over. American help had made a great difference to the Allies. The war ended on November 11, 1918. On this day the Germans asked that fighting be stopped.

The Allies were happy that the long war was over. They were saddened, too, by the ruin caused by the war. Over 5 million soldiers had been killed. Over 21 million had been wounded. A fortune in ships and

In a surprise attack on the morning of December 7, 1941, the Japanese bombed the naval base at Pearl Harbor. The attack forced the United States to enter World War II.

cargoes had been lost. In Europe, towns and farms were in ruins. Disease had swept the land. People were starving.

In 1939 a second world war broke out in Europe. Germany marched into Poland. Great Britain and France declared war on Germany. Italy and then Japan joined Germany. Then later, the Soviet Union, or Russia, declared war on Germany.

Germany at this time was ruled by the Nazi (nä′tsē) party. It was headed by Adolf Hitler. The Nazis seemed to be set on taking control in Europe. They treated the Jewish people harshly. Millions of them were put to death.

For two years the United States sent food and other goods to Great Britain and the other Allies. Then in December 1941, Japanese planes bombed American ships and buildings at Pearl Harbor in Hawaii. They also attacked some other military bases of the United States. The United States entered the war.

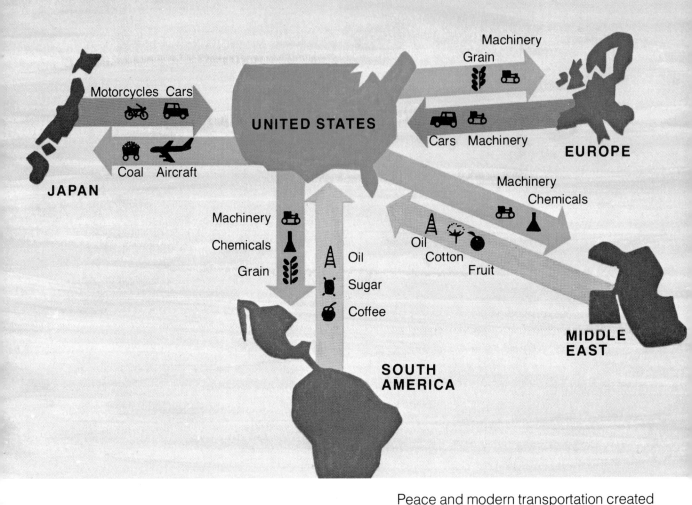

Motorcycles Cars

Coal Aircraft

JAPAN

UNITED STATES

Machinery
Grain

Cars Machinery

EUROPE

Machinery
Chemicals

Machinery

Chemicals

Grain

Oil

Sugar

Coffee

Oil
Cotton
Fruit

Machinery
Chemicals

MIDDLE
EAST

SOUTH
AMERICA

Peace and modern transportation created
trade with new nations and for new goods.

World War II went on for four more years. Bitter battles were fought in Europe, in the Atlantic and Pacific oceans, and in North Africa and Asia.

It was a war of machines as well as of soldiers. For the first time, bombs dropped from airplanes were a main weapon. The Nazis bombed the cities of Great Britain. British and American fliers bombed German and Japanese cities. Millions of people were killed, wounded, or left homeless.

After more than six years, World War II ended in 1945. More than 35 million soldiers and civilians had been killed. Millions were left scarred and crippled. The war ruined homes, farms, factories, and cities. It cost billions of dollars.

The Allies had won the war. But many countries were in ruins. People said that such a war must not take place again.

World leaders met in 1945 to set up the United Nations. The leaders talked over ways to work together for peace. They planned for an organization called the United Nations. The United Nations is often called the UN. Today most countries of the world are members. Meetings are held at the UN headquarters in New York City.

The chief goal of the UN is to keep peace. The UN has other goals, too. One is to cut down air and ocean pollution around the world. Another is to help needy people all over the world raise more food and improve their living conditions. The UN works to prevent the spread of diseases like smallpox.

People are working for peace in other ways, too. Some countries have student-exchange programs. Students live and study in another land for a period of time.

Rich countries send experts to help poor countries grow more food. Some countries carry on joint science projects. For example, in 1975 the Soviet Union and the United States joined in a space flight.

In spite of people working for peace, wars have broken out. The United States has had a part in two wars—one in Korea and one in Vietnam in Asia. Other fighting has occurred in Africa and in the Middle East. Much work is still needed to insure world peace.

United Nations staff members vaccinate this Iranian boy against diphtheria, whooping cough, and tetanus.

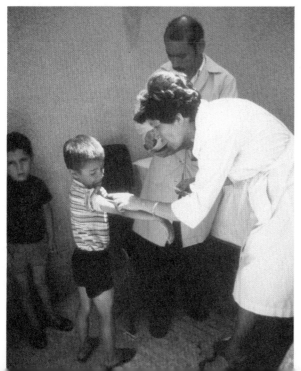

Using a world map

Use the world map on pages 196-197 to help you answer the questions below.

1. What ocean is nearest your state?
2. Do you live near another large body of water? If so, point to it and name it.
3. What continent lies southeast of the United States?
4. What continents are shown on the map?

Can you answer these questions?

1. What does it mean to trade? Describe some ways in which you and your friends trade.
2. How does money help people trade?
3. What does export mean? What does import mean? What are some products that the United States imports?
4. What helped the United States to become a world power?
5. What types of damage were caused by World War I and World War II?

Summarizing

A *summary* is a very short "story" of the main facts. A summary may be written or told. When you give briefly the main facts about a topic, you are *summarizing.*

Summarizing is useful. It helps us keep in mind the main facts that we have read or heard.

The Peace Corps was set up to bring help to other countries. Read in a reference book about the Peace Corps. Take notes on what you read. Summarize them in a report to the class.

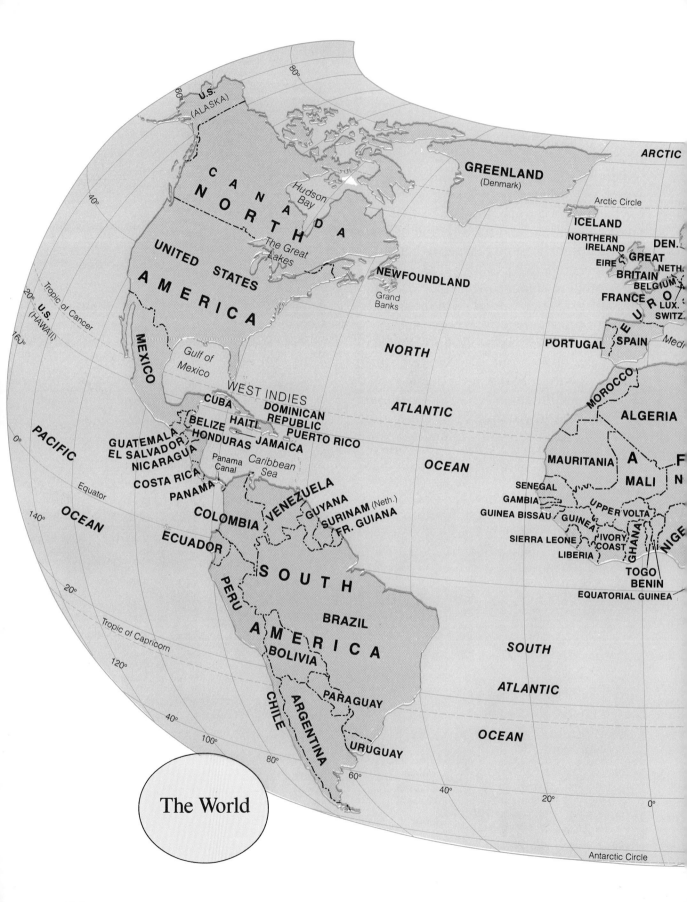

The World

OCEAN

NORWAY
SWEDEN
FINLAND

GERMANY
E. POLAND   AUSTRIA
CZECH.
HUNGARY
ITALY YUGO. ROMANIA
ALB. GREECE   BULGARIA
TURKEY
Terranean   LEBANON
Sea   ISRAEL   SYRIA
IRAQ
JORDAN   KUWAIT
QATAR
UNISIA   LIBYA   EGYPT
(U.A.R.)
YEMEN ARAB
REPUBLIC   OMAN
PEOPLES DEMOCRATIC
REPUBLIC OF YEMEN
DJIBOUTI

RICA   NGER   CHAD   SUDAN
CAMEROON   CENTRAL
AFRICAN EMPIRE   ETHIOPIA   SOMALIA
UGANDA
CONGO   RWANDA   KENYA
GABON   BURUNDI
ZAIRE   TANZANIA
ANGOLA   MALAWI
ZAMBIA   MOZAMBIQUE
RHODESIA
NAMIBIA   BOTSWANA
(S. Africa)   SWAZILAND
SOUTH   LESOTHO
AFRICA

Black Sea
Caspian
Sea

UNION OF SOVIET SOCIALIST REPUBLICS

A   S   I   A

Red Sea   Arabian Sea

AFGHAN-
ISTAN   PAKISTAN

SAUDI
ARABIA

IRAN

INDIA

NEPAL   BHUTAN

BANGLADESH

Bay of
Bengal

SRI LANKA

MADAGASCAR

INDIAN

OCEAN

Equator

Tropic of Capricorn

MONGOLIA

CHINA

N.KOREA
S.KOREA   JAPAN

BURMA   LAOS
THAILAND   VIETNAM

CAMBODIA

MALAYSIA

Sumatra

Java

Borneo

Celebes

Timor

80°

Bering Sea

40°

PACIFIC

TAIWAN
(FORMOSA)   MARIANA
ISLANDS

PHILIPPINES   OCEAN

CAROLINE ISLANDS

WEST IRIAN   PAPUA
NEW GUINEA

INDONESIA   SOLOMON
ISLANDS

AUSTRALIA   NEW ZEALAND

20°
180°

160°

140°   0°

20°

120°   40°

100°

80°

60°

40°

20°

60°

197

15
The struggle for human rights

A fighter for human rights

The phone rang.

The President of the United States was on the line. A conversation like this may have followed.

"Good morning, Mrs. Roosevelt. This is Harry Truman."

"What a pleasant surprise, Mr. President," said Mrs. Roosevelt. "What can I do for you?"

"Quite a lot, Mrs. Roosevelt," replied the President. "I want you to be a delegate to the United Nations. You would represent the United States very well. I hope you will do it."

"This would be a great honor, Mr. President," said Mrs. Roosevelt. "Please let me think about the matter a day or so. Then I'll call you back."

That December day in 1945, Eleanor Roosevelt agreed to be a delegate to the United Nations. She served in the United Nations for several years. She was also chosen as the leader of the Human Rights Committee.

The Human Rights Committee studied many problems of people around the world. Then the Committee wrote a Declaration of Human Rights. It was about the rights that all people should have.

The Declaration was read in a UN meeting. Each of its parts was discussed. At last, the delegates were ready to vote. The delegates from the Communist countries would not vote. But the other delegates did, and it passed.

After the vote, many delegates stood up and cheered Mrs. Roosevelt. She had worked hardest of all for the Declaration of Human Rights.

Eleanor Roosevelt had long been interested in people and their rights. She'd had a lonely childhood. Her mother died when she was eight years old. A few months later, one of her brothers died, and then her father. She was broken-hearted.

The young girl was sent to Europe to a private school. She was far from home and friends. But she often filled her lonely hours by helping other people.

When Eleanor was twenty-one, she married Franklin D. Roosevelt. In time, he became the President of the United States. She was First Lady. In fact, she was the First Lady for more than twelve years.

During those years, Mrs. Roosevelt found many ways to work for human rights. She was concerned about the poor. She encouraged clean-up work in slums. She tried to find jobs for people who were out of work.

President Roosevelt died in April 1945. Then the Vice President, Harry Truman, became the President of our country.

Mrs. Roosevelt returned to her home in New York. She expected to live a quiet life there. Instead she began her duties at the UN. She spent the rest of her life working for human rights.

Some early struggles

The struggle for human rights has gone on since early times. Probably people have always needed to speak out for their rights.

The Pilgrims came to America to have more rights. So did the Puritans and the Quakers. Thousands of other colonists also came because they had few rights in their homelands.

Eleanor Roosevelt worked actively for human rights. In 1946 she helped write the Universal Declaration of Human Rights.

The War for Independence was fought to gain an important right. The colonists wanted the right to govern themselves.

Finally the war ended. Then the colonies became states. They had won the right to govern themselves. A Constitution was written for the new United States. But many Americans were not satisfied with it. They said it did not protect the rights of the people.

The Bill of Rights was added to the Constitution in 1791. The Bill of Rights is the first ten amendments, or added parts of the Constitution. The first eight amendments give certain rights and freedoms to every American citizen. One of these rights is freedom of religion. Many people had come to America for the right to worship as they chose.

Another important right is freedom of speech and press. The colonists had enjoyed this freedom. They spoke out boldly at their town meetings. They felt free to say what they thought. They wrote pamphlets and put out newspapers. They had used this right to speak out when the English government was unfair.

Other parts of the Bill of Rights protect people who are accused of crimes. They must not be jailed and held a long time without a trial. They must be told why they have been arrested. They must be told that they have the right to keep silent. All people have the right to be helped by a lawyer. And they can't be forced to talk to the police if they do not have a lawyer with them.

Since 1791, other amendments have been added to the Constitution. Every state also has a Bill of Rights in its Constitution. Virginia's Bill of Rights was written in 1776.

Many people used freedom of speech and press to fight slavery. One of them, Frederick Douglass, was a slave until he escaped to New York. Then he moved to Boston. He began to speak against slavery. He became well known. Douglass went to

199

England to speak about slavery. After two years he came back to the United States. He had raised some money in England. He used it to buy his freedom.

Frederick Douglass held positions in government. Among them were Minister to Haiti and United States Marshal for the District of Columbia. He owned a newspaper. He wrote in his paper about the evils of slavery.

During the Civil War, Douglass worked with President Lincoln to solve the problems of black soldiers in the Union Army.

Sarah and Angelina Grimké grew up on a plantation in South Carolina. Their parents owned slaves. The sisters hated the slave system. They left home and went north to speak against slavery. But many people were for slavery. Others thought women should not speak out in public. People were often rude to the sisters. The Grimké sisters also began to work for women's rights.

Freedom from slavery is a basic human right. But the fight for this freedom took many years. At last, in 1865, the Thirteenth Amendment stopped slavery in the United States.

Women demand equal rights

Women worked as hard as men did to settle our country. They shared the same dangers. They cared for large families, their homes, and gardens. They took care of the sick people. Women could do just about anything and everything. And did!

Some women worked with their husbands as innkeepers. Some women set up bakeries in their homes. Some had dressmaking shops at home.

Outside their homes, though, few jobs were open to women. Some worked in textile mills. Others taught in small schools. Still others were nurses. But their wages were small. There was little chance to get ahead.

Most girls did not go to high school. They were not supposed to study such things as algebra and history.

Women were not allowed to vote. Many people said they should not speak in public, either. They grew tired of being held down. Some leaders decided to work to change things.

The first Women's Rights Convention was held in 1848. It was held in Seneca Falls, New York. Lucretia Mott and a friend, Elizabeth Stanton, planned it. A hundred people gathered for the meetings. Some were men who thought women should have more rights. The newspapers wrote about the convention. Many other women read about what had been done at these meetings.

Two years later, Lucy Stone set up a Women's Rights Convention in Worcester, Massachusetts. Some men came to this convention, too.

Then meetings were held in many parts of the country. Women wrote to government leaders about getting the vote. Some went on trips through the country to make speeches. One leader who became famous was Susan B. Anthony. You will read about her in chapter 18. Carrie Chapman Catt was a strong leader in the later years of this fight for women's rights.

In 1920, women finally won the right to vote. This right was made a part of the Constitution. It was given to them by the Nineteenth Amendment.

The 1899 International Council for Women supported the fight for the vote for women. Then women began to work for an equal rights amendment. Today women continue to work for the ERA.

As late as the 1920s, many kinds of jobs were not open to women. Even if they were, men were usually hired first. And a man was paid more than a woman in the same job.

Congress talked about many laws for equal rights. A few were passed. These laws say that employers must not refuse to hire people just because they are women. They say that women who do the same work as men must be paid the same.

In the 1960s Martha W. Griffiths worked hard for an Equal Rights Amendment to the Constitution. She was serving in Congress from the state of Michigan. This amendment is known as ERA. It says that men and women shall have the same legal rights. Congress passed it. Next it had to be passed by at least three-fourths of the states. Many states agreed on it very soon. But ERA met defeat in several states. If passed, it will be the Twenty-seventh Amendment.

Other groups seek equal rights

The Constitution calls for equal justice under the law. This is stated in the Fourteenth Amendment. All people have the right to be treated as equals under the law. It does not matter whether they are rich or poor. People of minority groups also have this right. A *minority group* is one that is less than half of a large group.

There are many minority groups in the United States. All Americans belong to some minority group. Black Americans do, and so do Jewish people. Mexican Americans and Native Americans do. Japanese Americans and Chinese Americans do, too. The groups of Polish Americans, Swedish Americans, German Americans are all minority groups.

Senior citizens are a kind of minority group. They are older Americans, perhaps sixty-five years of age or older. Many have left their jobs and retired. Thousands of senior citizens are giving their time and know-how to help others.

Handicapped people are another kind of minority group. These are disabled persons. Perhaps they cannot use their arms or legs as other people can. Or they may be blind or deaf. They may be mentally retarded. There are many kinds of handicaps. Many handicapped people have special training. Many handicapped persons have good jobs.

These people are all members of minority groups. What other minorities can you name?

Our country is proud of all of its people. All of our people work together. Working together makes our democracy strong.

Black people have carried on a long fight for equal rights. Equal rights for most black people did not come with the end of slavery. Some businesses would not serve them. Certain states made it hard for black people to vote. In some states there were separate schools for black children.

Black leaders said that laws that treated black people differently from whites were wrong. Such laws did not agree with the Constitution. And the United States Supreme Court can set aside a law that does not agree with the Constitution. So from time to time black people took their cases to court.

Black people won a big fight for equal rights in 1954. The Supreme Court ruled that all children must be allowed to attend the same schools.

Soon black people began to win other rights. One was the right to equal treatment on public buses. In some places, buses had signs inside. The signs might say, "Whites in front; Coloreds go to the rear." Black people were not allowed to sit in front seats.

In 1955 Mrs. Rosa Parks took a bus home from work. Mrs. Parks was tired. She went to the back of the bus and sat down. But when the front part of the bus was full, Mrs. Parks was told to give her seat to a white man. She refused to do this, was put off the bus, and arrested.

The black people in that city had had enough. They boycotted the bus company. When you *boycott* something, you refuse to use or buy it. The boycott was led by Martin Luther King, Jr. Dr. King was the minister of one of the city's churches. He had spoken out against the bus system for a long time. But nothing had been done.

Mrs. Rosa Parks is fingerprinted after her arrest for refusing to give up her seat on a bus.

More than 200,000 people marched to Washington, D.C., in 1963 to demand equal rights for all citizens. Dr. King helped organize the march.

Now all of the black people stopped using the buses. The boycott worked. The bus company lost a lot of money. Soon the company agreed that blacks could sit anywhere on a bus.

King led marches and demonstrations to win more rights for blacks. His life was often in danger, but he would not give up the fight. Finally he was shot and killed while on a speaking trip in Tennessee.

Laws were passed to give equal rights to black people and other minorities. In a few years many laws began to be changed. Congress passed a major Civil Rights Act in 1964. One part of it said that eating places, hotels, and some other kinds of businesses must serve all people who want service. Another part of the law was about giving people equal job rights.

Other laws have made it easier for people to live wherever they choose. Some people want to live with those of their own minority group. But they don't want to stay in just certain neighborhoods. Some black people have been turned away by people selling or renting homes. Now the laws try to stop such treatment.

Handicapped people are working for more rights. They want cities to have ramps instead of curbs at street crossings. They have asked builders to put ramps as well as steps on buildings. Ramps help people who can't climb steps to enter buildings. The disabled people want buses that are easier to enter and leave. They are backing laws to gain more rights.

A recent law tries to help handicapped persons get and hold suitable jobs. Companies that do business with the United States government must help. They must show that they are treating handicapped workers and jobseekers fairly.

With modern voting machines, election results can be tallied more rapidly than in the past.

Political rights

Human rights include the chance to take an active part in government. A chief way to take part is by voting. Over the years the right to vote was given to more and more people. Today all citizens may vote when they reach age 18. So young people can also help to choose our leaders.

But having the right to vote is not enough. Laws must make it easy, not hard, to vote. In the past the laws in some states made it hard for people to become voters. Now most states make it fairly easy for citizens to *register*, or sign up, to vote.

Serving in public office is another political right. Frances Perkins was the first woman to serve in a President's Cabinet. In 1933 President Franklin D. Roosevelt chose her to be the Secretary of Labor.

Shirley Chisholm was the first black woman to serve in Congress. She was elected as a representative from New York. Barbara Jordan, a black woman, was elected to the House of Representatives by the people of Texas in 1972. She has been an active civil rights leader.

Nellie Tayloe Ross became the governor of Wyoming in 1924. She was the first woman governor to be elected. Her husband had been the governor. He died during his term. A special election was held, and Mrs. Ross was elected in his place.

In 1974 Ella Grasso was elected governor of Connecticut. Mrs. Grasso had been a member of the state legislature. Other women state governors had followed or replaced their husbands. Mrs. Grasso was the first woman elected on her own.

Thurgood Marshall is a justice of the United States Supreme Court. He was the first black appointed to the highest court. Justice Marshall graduated from college and then from law school. He worked as a lawyer and a judge for many years. He has helped many blacks gain more rights.

Hiram Fong was the first Chinese American to serve in the United States Senate. His parents moved from China to Hawaii many years ago. They found jobs on a sugar plantation. Hiram Fong was one of eleven children. He helped his family in the fields. But his parents urged their children to go through school. Fong worked his way through college and law school. He chose to serve in government.

Max Cleland was picked by President Carter to head the Veterans Administration. It handles benefits that Congress has voted to give to former members of the armed services. Cleland was crippled in the Vietnam war. He lost both of his legs and one hand. He then had to use a wheel chair to get around.

Americans have the right to protest about things they don't like. The right to protest is another political right. It is one way in which people can tell their leaders what

Millions of Americans took part in antipollution protests and clean-up projects on Earth Day.

they want. Speaking out is just one way to *protest*, or disagree, about a matter. Sometimes people protest by gathering at meetings. Or they may march in parades. Workers may go on strike. People may find other ways to protest, too.

Daniel K. Inouye protested by joining the United States Army. He served in World War II. Inouye is a Japanese American. He and his family have always been proud of being Americans.

When planes from Japan bombed Pearl Harbor, the Inouye family was shocked. They tried to think of ways to protest the bombing and loss of life. Many other young Japanese Americans felt the same way. They decided to join the American army. At first they were turned down.

But then word came that Japanese Americans could serve in the armed forces. Daniel and his friends ran the three miles to a place where they could sign up. They served bravely in Europe. Daniel was wounded and lost his right arm. After the war Inouye went to college. Later the people of Hawaii elected him to the United States Senate.

Many people in our land protested the Vietnam war. At first only military advisers were sent to Vietnam. Then thousands of soldiers were sent to fight. They were drafted by the United States armed forces.

Many people said that this was not fair. They said that the armed forces were not defending our own country. Some young men refused to go. They fled the country to avoid being drafted. Many people met to protest. They had protest marches and spoke at meetings. Finally, in 1973, United States troops were pulled out of Vietnam.

Someone has to decide what is to be done about a protest. Often people protest at a baseball game. They don't like the umpire's decision. They may argue with the umpire. In the end, though, they know they must accept the decision.

That is the way it works in other kinds of protests. We may speak out. But in the end, we must accept the "umpire's call." In government a judge may be the umpire. The courts make decisions. The highest court is the United States Supreme Court. Its judges decide on many questions of rights.

Economic rights and freedoms

Americans have much freedom to choose jobs and engage in business. We can choose our work. The government doesn't tell us what jobs we must take.

Today all kinds of jobs are open to both men and women. Some women are engineers and contractors. Some are bus and truck drivers. Some are on the police force and work for fire departments.

Companies are hiring many members of minority groups. They are also employing more handicapped people. Training programs help workers learn more about their jobs.

People may own their own businesses. We call this system "free enterprise." In Communist countries most businesses are owned and run by the government. In free enterprise the owners must earn a profit to stay in business. So the company must produce goods or services that people are willing to buy. Success in business also depends on having special knowledge and skills.

More and more women own and run businesses today. Katherine Graham publishes a leading newspaper in the East. Banks, stores, and factories have been started by women.

Government makes many kinds of rules for business. People can run their own businesses. But they must do so within a set of rules. Eating places must obey health rules, for example. Factories may have to put in equipment to stop air and water pollution. Employers must pay the workers at least a certain wage and make jobs as safe as possible.

There are many laws and rules to protect consumers, who are buyers of goods and services. Auto makers must install safety devices. Food processors must not add harmful chemicals to foods. Labels must give the buyer needed information. Companies must not make untrue claims in their ads. There are many other rules.

Many people in government have jobs that deal with consumer protection. Some of them make rules. Some of them see that rules are obeyed. President Carter chose Esther Peterson to take charge of some consumer affairs.

Workers have the right to belong to a labor union. Unions were started in earlier years to protect workers. Employers often treated workers unfairly. Wages were low. The working day was often 10 or 12 hours. Often the job was unsafe.

Labor unions at times could get a company to make changes that would help workers. Many times the unions did not succeed at first. Then they might call a strike. During a strike, workers did not go to their jobs.

Then labor leaders and company managers sat down to talk things over. They tried to settle the strike. Sometimes they compromised—each side got a part of what it wanted.

Laws now require a company to deal with a union if a majority of the workers want it that way. Many men and women have worked hard to get workers to join a union.

Cesar Chavez is a Mexican American farm workers' leader. He was born on a small farm in Yuma, Arizona. Every fall he and his family went to California to help harvest the crops.

By joining together, workers can bargain more effectively for better working conditions and wages. About 25 per cent of all American workers belong to unions.

The work was hard. Life in tents or rough shacks was hard, too. The workers earned very little money for their tiresome work. Chavez saw that the workers did not have many rights. He spent many years trying to make things better for these workers.

Our country works for freedom from want in old age. Workers try to save money for the time when they retire from work. They put their savings in banks. They buy insurance. Some people buy property with their savings. But often the savings are not enough to live on when they retire.

In 1935 Congress set up the Social Security System to help people save money for their old age. The system is a kind of big insurance company run by the federal government.

Part of each worker's pay goes into the Social Security fund. The employer pays as much for each worker as the worker pays. When people retire, they receive checks each month from the fund.

Social Security helps retired people pay hospital and medical bills. It makes payments to families when the wage earner dies before retirement. Such payments go for the care of children under age 18.

Our governments—local, state, and national—run other programs to help needy people of all ages.

Rights and responsibilities

All rights carry responsibilities with them. Having rights does not mean that we can do exactly as we please. One big *responsibility*, or duty, is to respect the rights of other persons. Other persons must be treated fairly, too. Rights are for everyone. It is up to us to make "rights" work.

The right to vote carries with it the duty to learn about the people running for office. In some elections there are big issues, or questions, to be decided. A good voter will study the issues.

Freedom of speech carries with it the duty to speak the truth. And the right to protest means peaceful protest, not fighting or stopping traffic.

Can you think of other duties that go along with the rights that you have read about in this chapter?

207

Make the correct choice

In each sentence, one of the three choices will make it correct. Copy each sentence so that it is correct.

1. One economic right is that of (voting) (holding a job) (going to school).
2. A minority group is (most) (all) (less than half) of the population.
3. (The Nineteenth Amendment) (Social Security) (ERA) helps retired persons with their living expenses.
4. (All) (A few) (Most) Americans are equal under the law.
5. American citizens have the right to vote after they become (21) (18) (25) years of age.
6. Consumers (buy) (sell) (manufacture) products.

What do you think?

1. What can be done to help handicapped people get jobs? What is being done in your community to help handicapped people?
2. We live in a free country. We have many rights. But we may not do entirely as we please. Why? Why do we say that responsibilities go along with rights?

Things to do

1. Find out what is being done in your community about one of the following.
   - a job-training program in some industry
   - hiring handicapped persons
   - equal pay for equal work
   - protecting consumers
2. Pretend that you are on a Human Rights Committee in your community. Make a list of things you would try to learn. Be ready to tell your class which one you think is most important and why.
3. Read in another book about one of the people listed below.

   Frances Perkins
   Thurgood Marshall
   Barbara Jordan
   Hiram Fong
   Shirley Chisholm
   Martin Luther King, Jr.
   Ella T. Grasso
   Cesar Chavez
   Jesse Jackson
   Martha W. Griffiths
   Andrew Young
   Lucy Stone
   Eleanor Roosevelt
   Daniel K. Inouye
   Carrie Chapman Catt
   Esther Peterson

   Take and organize notes on what you read. Be ready to share what you learn.
4. Find out if there is a Better Business Bureau in or near your community. If there is, write a letter to this group asking what its main work is. Help your class choose one letter to mail to the Better Business Bureau.

5
Binding the nation together

16
Transportation: traveling and carrying goods

Two young brothers were trying out a "flying machine" toy. Their father was with them.

"What makes it fly?" Orville asked his father. Wilbur asked other questions. The two boys were always curious about how things worked.

When the toy was worn out, the boys took it apart. Then they built a little "flying machine" of their own. When they sent it into the air, though, it fell to the ground. Their "machine" had failed.

The boys were sad. But they found out what was wrong. They corrected the problem in their next "machine," and the "machine" flew.

Years later Wilbur and Orville Wright set up a workshop. They fixed bicycles to earn money to buy tools. They built new bicycles, too. The two brothers were good workers. Their repair business grew quickly. But Wilbur and Orville liked their spare-time job best. It was planning a large "flying machine."

In time the Wright brothers built a glider 16 feet (5 m) long. It looked like a large box kite. It had no engine or power of its own. Only air currents kept it flying.

The Wrights took their glider to the sand dunes near Kitty Hawk, North Carolina. They tested it by guiding it off a sandy hill. The glider "flew." So did larger ones that the two brothers built and tested later.

Then Wilbur and Orville Wright decided to build a machine with an engine. An engine would spin a propeller to move the glider. The two young inventors built and tested. At last they had an airplane made of wood, wire, and cloth. It was powered by a gasoline motor. The pilot had to lie on the lower wing near the engine.

The Wright brothers went back to Kitty Hawk. They asked people to come to watch them fly. Most people thought this just a stunt. So only a few people came to see them.

On that December day in 1903 the Wright brothers made history. Orville flew their plane 120 feet (36 m). He stayed in the air 12 seconds. This was the first flight of a motor-driven plane in the United States. On a fourth flight that same day, Wilbur flew the plane 852 feet (260 m) in 59 seconds. The Wright brothers had proved that people can fly.

Today, except for spaceships, airplanes are the fastest kind of transportation. *Transportation* is the means that people use to travel and carry goods.

Fast ways of transportation are very important. We can't do without them today. People did, though, in earlier days.

Americans build roads

The first roads in America were narrow trails. At first only Native Americans used them. Then early settlers walked or rode horses along these trails. Sarah Knight wrote about the hardships of travel from Boston to New York in 1704.

In time, trails linked towns and farms. By 1775 there was a road from Boston to Charleston, South Carolina. New York and Philadelphia were along this road. Many of the delegates to the Continental Congress rode to Philadelphia along this road.

This main road was rough and narrow. In rainy weather it was dotted with mud puddles. In dry weather the road was dusty and bumpy with deep holes.

Some colonists had horse-drawn carriages. Many settlers owned some kind of cart or buggy.

By 1776 large carriages, or coaches, were carrying passengers between some cities. One coach line ran between New York and Philadelphia. In good weather drivers made the 90-mile (145 km) trip in two days. They stopped at inns along the way. These stops were called stages. So the coach became known as a stagecoach.

Riders were not comfortable on the early stagecoaches. At times the trip was exciting. Here is what one traveler might have written in a diary.

We left New York in a bright red-and-blue coach pulled by two teams. The coach had hard benches without backs. Some of us sat on our bundles. Two of our party

Riding in a slowly moving coach along narrow, deeply rutted roads, travelers had an uncomfortable ride from Trenton to Philadelphia.

rode high up on the outside with the driver. Some baggage and mail were carried on top of the coach.

We rode only by daylight. We stopped at inns at night. There we were served good meals and plenty of hot tea.

It rained during most of the trip. Those who rode with the driver got soaked and spattered with mud.

Twice our coach got stuck in the mud. The driver asked us all to get out. We pushed and pulled to get the coach moving again.

How glad we were when we reached Boston. That trip took ten days!

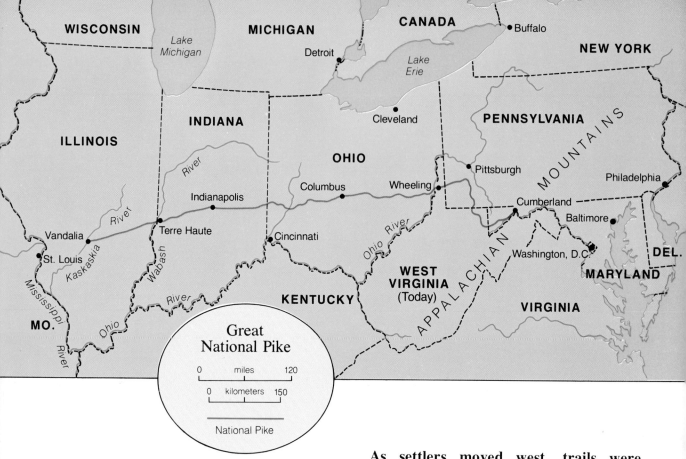

Great
National Pike

```
0        miles      120

0      kilometers   150
```

National Pike

After the War for Independence, more
roads were built. Some were *toll* roads
built by companies to earn profits. To use a
toll road, travelers paid a small amount of
money, or toll. They paid to cross toll
bridges, too.

Low places in the roads stayed muddy
long after a rain. Often logs were laid
across the road at these places. The logs
kept coaches and wagons from getting
stuck. A ride over a "corduroy road" like
this was rough and bumpy.

Later, some macadam roads were built.
They were named after their inventor,
John McAdam, a Scottish surveyor. They
were built higher in the center to let rain
and snow drain off. Early macadam roads
were made with layers of broken stone
topped with sand. Heavy rollers pressed
these layers into a hard solid road.

As settlers moved west, trails were
blazed. Daniel Boone blazed the Wilderness Road through the Appalachians. This
and other early roads west followed the
routes of Native American trails.

Later the Oregon Trail and the Santa Fe
Trail led west. These are shown on the map
on page 125. Hundreds of thousands of
settlers moved west of the Mississippi
along these trails. As towns grew, roads
were built to connect them. The western
towns were far apart. Stagecoach drivers
changed horses and picked up mail and
passengers at these stops. At other stops
along the way, they rested and ate. Some
of these stops grew into towns.

The first highway built in the United
States was started in 1811. It was built by
the United States government. It led west
across the Appalachians. The road went
from Cumberland, Maryland, on the
Potomac River to Wheeling on the Ohio
River. It was called the Great National
Pike. Later it became known as the Cum-

Today's superhighways use different road levels to keep traffic flowing smoothly.

berland Road. Later this road was built to Vandalia, Illinois. Find this road on the map.

The National Pike at first was a macadam road, made with crushed rock. Pioneers in covered wagons used it on their way west. Stagecoach drivers used it. Farmers and ranchers drove cattle, sheep, and hogs over it to markets in the East.

In time workers built miles and miles of macadam roads. By the early 1900s, Americans were driving cars on the roads. As the number of cars grew, drivers wanted smoother, wider roads.

Engineers began to use concrete and other improved materials for the newer highways. And they had to design stronger bridges.

Today the United States has millions of miles of fine highways. Some are superhighways, freeways, or expressways. In some places they are wide enough for six or eight lanes of cars. Those that charge tolls are known as turnpikes, toll roads, or tollways.

Freeways often lead around towns or cities. Some cut through large cities. For long distances there are no traffic lights.

Americans travel by water

For hundreds of years ships carried the heaviest loads. Transportation by water was the best way to carry goods long distances.

In early times people used oars, poles, and paddles to move their boats. They also used sails when the wind blew in the right direction. Then sailors learned how to tack, or sail against the wind. This meant that ships could sail to distant places without using oars.

The earliest American colonists used water transportation. They settled along the coast and near rivers. They used rafts and flatboats to travel on the rivers. Ships brought goods and mail to the colonists and carried their crops to markets.

Native Americans taught some colonists how to use canoes. They showed them usable waterways. They pointed out places where canoes could be carried between bodies of water.

Small sailing ships made trips along the coast from one seaport to another. These trips could be full of danger. In some places sharp rocks and sand bars caused shipwrecks. The trips were slow. Ships had to depend on the wind. When it died down,

John Fitch used steam-driven wheels to move the oars on his steamboat. Fitch's invention was only one of many changes that were taking place in transportation.

vessels drifted about helplessly. Still, going by water seemed safer than risking the dangers of the wilderness by land.

When the steam engine was invented, people began to dream of making it drive ships. Two American inventors who worked on this idea were John Fitch and Robert Fulton.

John Fitch built the first usable steamboat in the United States. Fitch was a Philadelphia watchmaker. His steamboat had six paddles on each side and a steam engine to work them. In 1787 he tested his boat on the Delaware River.

Many people watched Fitch's strange boat. Some were members of the Constitutional Convention. People could hardly believe their eyes. They saw the steamboat slowly churn up and down the Delaware.

"An interesting toy," said some. "But steam won't move a boat very far."

Later, Fitch's strange boat began regular runs from Philadelphia to Trenton, New Jersey. It made this short trip of about 25 miles (40 km) many times. But one day it was wrecked. Sad Mr. Fitch did not have enough money to build a new boat.

Robert Fulton built a better steamboat, the *Clermont*. In August 1807 Fulton's *Clermont* was ready to move up the Hudson River. The trip was from New York City to Albany. This was a distance of about 150 miles (240 km).

A large crowd came to watch the *Clermont* leave. The big paddle wheels began to turn. The *Clermont* moved slowly away from the docks. Soon it was chugging along at about five miles (8 km) an hour. Some onlookers cheered. Others laughed and called the boat "Fulton's Folly." Folly means something that is very foolish. Many people thought it was foolish to go on a long boat trip without sails.

214

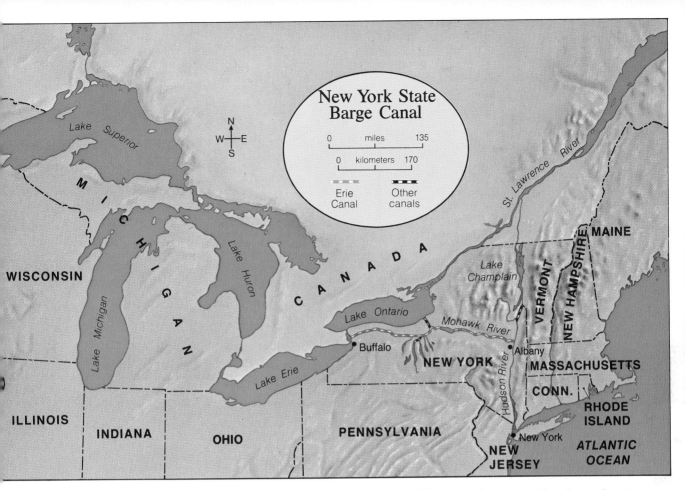

New York State Barge Canal

0   miles   135

0   kilometers   170

Erie Canal   Other canals

What two important bodies of water did the canals connect?

The *Clermont* reached Albany in thirty-two hours. Fulton had proved that steam can drive boats long distances. This success led to the building of other steamboats.

Soon many steamboats were chugging up and down rivers. Some went on the Hudson River. Others steamed up and down the Mississippi and Ohio rivers. Others were used on the Great Lakes. People, crops, lumber, and coal could now be moved at low cost.

But there was no river linking the Great Lakes region with eastern cities. Farmers needed such a water route to send their crops to market. People in New York City wanted a water route to the Midwest. So leaders decided to make the needed "river." They would build a canal. A *canal* is a waterway made by people. It often connects two other bodies of water.

Building the Erie Canal began in 1817 and was completed in 1825. It joined the Hudson River with Lake Erie. The Erie Canal was more than 360 miles (580 km) long. Find it on the map. What two cities did it connect?

The new canal was a good east-west route for the lands around the Great Lakes. Boats used it to carry tons of crops to markets. The canal brought new business to New York. It helped New York become the largest city in the United States. Many other towns and cities on the canal route also grew rapidly.

Today the Erie Canal is a part of the New York State Barge Canal System. This waterway is used by barges hauling

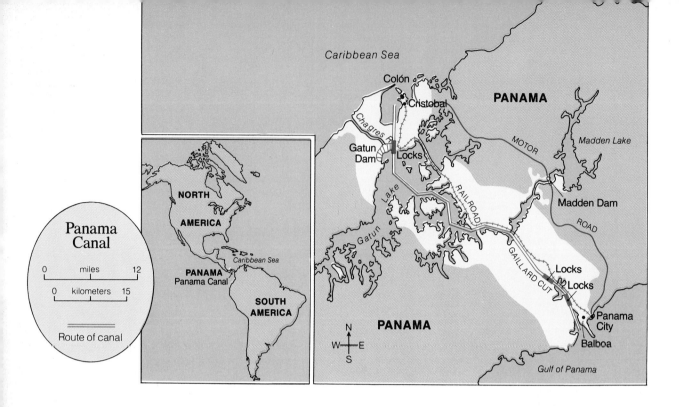

Panama Canal

0 — miles — 12
0 — kilometers — 15

Route of canal

Caribbean Sea

Colón
Cristobal
PANAMA

Chagres R.
Gatun Dam
Locks
MOTOR
Madden Lake

NORTH
AMERICA

Caribbean Sea

PANAMA
Panama Canal

SOUTH
AMERICA

Lake
Gatun

RAILROAD

Madden Dam
ROAD

GAILLARD CUT

Locks
Locks

N
W—E
S

PANAMA

Panama City
Balboa

Gulf of Panama

thousands of tons of products. Pleasure boats also move along it.

Handsome American sailing ships were crossing the oceans. Some were called packet ships. They hauled many letters and packets, or small packages. Packet ships carried freight and some passengers.

The most famous American sailing ships were the *clippers*. They got this name because they sailed at a fast clip. They were long and graceful. Clipper ships had large crews to handle the huge sails.

Many clipper ships went back and forth to Europe. Some made the long trip around South America and up the Pacific coast. Clipper ships carried gold seekers to California during the Gold Rush. Clippers sailed to China and other distant lands in Asia.

By 1840 another kind of ship was being built. Steamboats worked well on the rivers. Next they were tried on the sea. As early as 1819, a kind of "steam" ship had crossed the Atlantic. It was the *Savannah*.

It had sails as well as a steam engine. The *Savannah,* though, needed its sails most of the way across the ocean. People doubted that steam would ever work on the ocean.

About twenty years later, an improved steamship crossed the Atlantic. From that time on, iron steamships began to replace wooden sailing ships. Later, steel and plastics were used in shipbuilding. Since 1965 some ships have been made of concrete.

Some ships are known as freighters. Freighters carry American products to nearly all the seaports of the world. They bring back imports from other lands.

Container ships hold containers the size of truck trailers. Huge cranes unload the containers from the ships and load them on railroad cars and trucks.

Tankers are ships that are divided into tanks. They are usually used to transport liquids, such as oil.

Some ships carry many passengers. These large ocean liners and cruisers are like big floating hotels.

216

Seattle, Washington, is one of the world's great seaports. Ships from all over the world load and unload their cargoes along its 50 miles (80 km) of wharves.

Ferryboats carry cars and passengers short distances. Hydrofoils, too, have been used. They are made to rise up in the water and speed just above the surface.

Many ships carry products through the Panama Canal. This canal links the Caribbean Sea and the Pacific Ocean. It cuts through the Isthmus of Panama. An *isthmus* is a narrow strip of land that connects two larger bodies of land. Why can we say that the Panama Canal connects the Atlantic Ocean and the Pacific Ocean?

The Isthmus of Panama connects the continents of North America and South America. Find this isthmus on the map of North and South America. Notice what a narrow bridge of land it is.

For many years, people dreamed of digging a waterway through this isthmus. Ships had to sail around South America to go from the Atlantic to the Pacific. Ships sailing from New York to San Francisco had to go more than 11,000 miles (17,600 km). The trip took many weeks and was full of danger. No wonder, then, that people wanted a shorter route.

In 1914 the United States completed the Panama Canal. It crossed the middle of the isthmus. Locate the Panama Canal on the map.

Building the canal was a big job. It took years of planning and hard work.

Ships from many nations pass through the Panama Canal every year. Each ship is charged a toll. The cost depends on the size of the ship. A large ship may pay several thousand dollars toll.

The Panama Canal has meant much to the countries of North America and South America. Perhaps it has helped the United States most of all. It provides for low-cost shipping from one coast to the other.

Your answer, please

1. How did Native American trails help the early colonial road builders?
2. What were the first roads like in the American colonies?
3. What are corduroy roads? toll roads? macadam roads?
4. What was the first highway built in the United States? How are today's highways different?
5. Why did people call the *Clermont* "Fulton's Folly"?
6. What types of ships sail the seas today?
7. Why was the flight of the Wright brothers important?
8. Where was the Panama Canal built? Why was it built?

Put these in order

Below are listed some main events. On paper write them in the order in which they happened. Show the order by writing the numbers 1 through 6 before the sentences you copy.

The Panama Canal was completed.

The first highway in the United States was started.

Fulton's *Clermont* reached Albany.

The Wright brothers made their flight at Kitty Hawk.

Fitch's steamboat was tested.

The *Savannah* crossed the Atlantic.

Some other things to do

1. Use an encyclopedia or other book to learn more about one of the topics listed below. If you use a book, remember to look first in the index for the topic.

   steamboats   clipper ships
   canoes   Erie Canal
   stagecoaches   Panama Canal

   Write a summary of what you learn. Share your summary with the class.

2. Use a highway map of your state to answer the following questions.

   How far is your community from the largest city in your state?

   On what road or roads would you travel to get there?

   What towns would you pass through on your way?

   What symbol is used to show the capital of your state?

   Pick a city in the northeast section of your state and one in the southwest. What directions would you give a person for traveling between these two cities? Write them on paper.

The first American steam locomotive lost a race to a horse-drawn carriage in 1830.

Americans travel by rail

People used rails long before the steam engine was invented. There is a story about some English workers in the late 1500s. They were digging stones from a hillside. One worker said, "This is going to be heavy. Let's put down rails for the wagons to travel on. Then the horses can pull larger loads."

The idea of using rails spread. Rails were laid in shipyards and coal mines. They were put in quarries where blocks of stone were being cut and moved.

The first trains were introduced in the early 1800s. They were pulled by steam engines called locomotives. Behind the locomotive were little box-like cars. These cars carried the wood or coal to be burned in the engines.

The passenger cars looked like stage-coaches. They had no cushions on the seats or glass in the windows. Smoke and red-hot cinders blew in on the riders. The cinders burned holes in their clothes. The black smoke covered them with grime. Hats were often blown out the windows. On rainy days leather curtains were pulled. This made the unlighted cars dark and stuffy.

Many people were afraid to ride in the first trains. They were noisy and had clumsy brakes. When they jerked to a stop, passengers were often thrown to the floor.

The first trains had no regular schedules. They did not travel at night. They had no conductors, so engineers took the fares.

One famous early steam engine was the *Tom Thumb*. It ran a race with a horse-drawn coach. At first the *Tom Thumb* was far ahead. But it broke down, and the horse won.

219

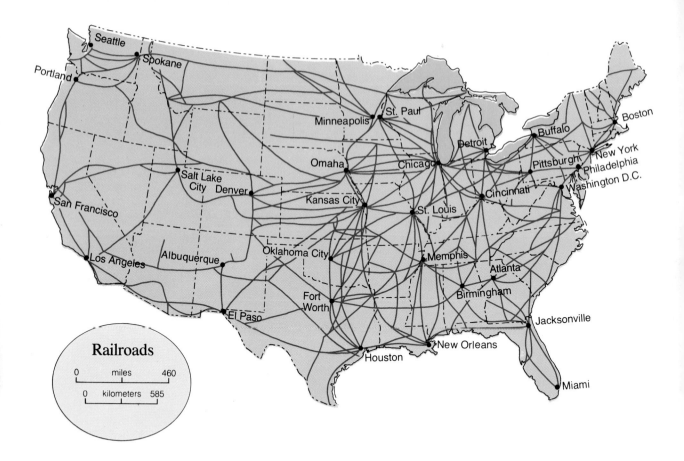

Railroads

```
0          miles          460
|------------------------------|

0      kilometers      585
|------------------------------|
```

By 1830 railroads were becoming a chief means of transportation. More miles of track had been laid. Trains had regular schedules. Some traveled at night. They had shelves covered with hay where riders could sleep. Larger trains pulled by stronger engines were built later. They were safer and more comfortable.

By 1860 railroads served the eastern United States. Some went west to St. Louis. None, though, went to the Pacific coast.

In 1863 two companies started a railroad across the West. One began to lay tracks west from Omaha, Nebraska. Another started building to the east from Sacramento, California.

Some workers on the railroad came from eastern cities. Others came from China and countries in Europe.

In 1869 the two parts of the railroad met at Promontory, Utah. There an excited

crowd watched a train from the East chug toward a train from the West. The two trains stopped close to each other. Then spikes were driven into the last rail. One spike was silver and one was gold. At last a railroad went across the United States.

More and more railroad tracks were put down. Trains were improved. Diesel engines took the place of steam locomotives. Some trains moved with electric power. Automatic safety signals were developed. Later, computers were used to keep track of the trains and railroad cars.

By the 1950s, freight trains were hauling huge loads of coal, grain, ore, lumber, oil, autos, and other products.

The railroads faced more and more problems, though. Barges, trucks, pipelines, and cargo planes got more of the freight business. Cars, buses, and planes took most of the long-distance passenger business. Government rules kept the railroads

Commuters travel every day from their suburban homes to jobs in the city.

from dropping costly services. Main railroads began to lose money.

In 1970 the federal government formed a company called Amtrak. "Amtrak" is made up of parts of the words "American," "travel," and "track." Amtrak now runs most of the passenger trains between cities. One of its goals is to improve services. Another goal is to help the railroads by taking over a part of the business that doesn't earn a profit.

Railroads are part of the mass transit systems of big cities. *Mass transit* is a way of moving large numbers of people within urban areas.

Commuter trains carry riders from suburbs to jobs in the city. They are part of the mass transit system. *Subways* are electric trains in underground tunnels. Subways are part of some mass transit systems. So are *elevated trains* that run on tracks built above the streets. Buses are a big part of mass transit, too.

Most mass transit systems were built in the late 1800s. Many people used them until about the 1950s. Then more people began to own cars. By the 1970s only about one-tenth of the people in urban areas were using mass transit.

The drop in the use of mass transit became a matter of deep concern. Fares and taxes had to rise to keep the systems running. Also mass transit was an energy saver. A bus, subway, or commuter train uses a third to a half less fuel per rider than does a car with one person. And cars create more air pollution.

Leaders discussed ways to improve mass transit. Then more people might use it. Some cities such as San Francisco, Washington, and Atlanta began building new systems. Denver, Seattle, and other cities improved their bus systems. Many places cut fares for older citizens. Some cities fixed the stations and buses so that disabled persons could use them more easily.

Bicycle riding was as popular in the 1890s as it is today. How did these bicycles differ from today's?

Americans travel on roads

Today more bicycles than automobiles are made. In the United States, about 100 million people ride bicycles. Some city streets are now marked with bikeways. Parks also have bike trails.

The bicycle was invented in Europe. Early bicycles were heavy and clumsy. They had iron tires and no springs. They were so hard on the rider that they were called ''boneshakers.''

Later there was a bicycle with a big front wheel and a small back wheel. The rider's seat was high over the front wheel. It took real skill to ride it.

Later the ''safety'' bicycle came along. It had good brakes and rubber tires. It also had a spring ''saddle'' seat. The bicycles of today are improved ''safety'' bicycles.

222

In the late 1800s, inventors began to build the ''horseless carriage.'' It was an ancestor of the modern auto. Some early cars were run by steam power. But the gasoline engine soon took over. Early in the 1900s Henry Ford and others began to build and sell motor cars.

At first each car was put together by a small group of workers. In 1913 it took 12 hours to put a car together at the Ford Motor Company. Cars were very expensive. Only a few people could buy them.

Later, though, Henry Ford found a better and cheaper way to make them. Parts for the cars were made by machines. Workers put the parts together on an assembly line. So, in 1914, eight cars came off the line in a little over 12 hours. This output kept rising higher and higher.

Riding in an early motor car was a real adventure. The car was started by turning a crank at the front of the car. The engine coughed and wheezed. The driver jumped into the car and moved handles and pedals. This sent the roaring car along with a jerk. It might reach the frightening speed of twenty miles (32 km) an hour.

At times the car broke down. Then people would shout, ''Get a horse! A horse will go when you want it to.''

In those days, cars had no windshields or windows. Many had no tops. The roads were often rough and dusty. People had to protect themselves as best they could. Drivers often wore caps and goggles.

Motor vehicles use huge amounts of gasoline. Large cars may need a gallon of it for every eight or ten miles (13 to 16 km) of travel. Small cars may go twenty miles (32 km) or more on a gallon.

More people drive cars each year—and

drive them farther. So more gasoline is needed. In recent years we have had to import about half the petroleum needed to make gasoline. These imports are costly to our country. And foreign countries can shut off the supply. That happened for a few months in 1973–1974.

Lawmakers have worked on the problem. New laws said that auto makers must make cars that use less gas. Auto companies are making more smaller cars. This is the best way to meet the new rules. Also, gas prices rose fast in the 1970s. This led some people to want cars that use less gas.

The truck was developed about the same time as the car. Today there are trucks for all kinds of hauling jobs. There are refrigerated trucks for carrying food. There are moving vans, cattle trucks, and gasoline tankers. There are dump trucks to haul rock and gravel.

Trucks have taken a growing share of the freight business. Some of it has been taken away from the railroads. One reason is that trucks can give door-to-door service. A truck can take goods from a factory and bring it right to the buyer. Trucks can go anywhere there are roads.

Trucks have another edge on the railroads. Trucking firms don't have to build

The automobile changed the way people traveled. Today, as more and more cars crowd our highways, concern about air pollution and conserving energy is growing.

and repair their own roads. Trucks use public roads and streets. Trucking firms do pay a lot of taxes for the use of the roads. But railroads have a heavy tax bill, too. And their other costs are very high.

Buses provide another chief means of transportation. They play a big part in mass transit. Also, buses carry school children in rural and urban areas. Buses carry riders between cities. They take sightseers on tours. In recent years the rising use of cars has led to some drop in bus travel.

Pipelines transport great amounts of oil and natural gas. They are a cheap way to carry a liquid or gas from where it is produced to where it is used. Some pipelines are buried in the ground. Others are under water or above ground.

The first pipelines were built in the 1920s. They were about 200 miles (320 km) long. Later, longer pipelines were built. One was built to carry gas from Texas to New York City and other places on the East coast. Pipelines now form a vast network across the United States.

Air travel has changed since Orville Wright piloted the first successful flight. Today millions of people travel by air each year. What are the advantages of air travel?

Americans travel by air

The Wright brothers got aviation off to a good start. You have read about their flights in 1903. Other flights followed. But many people still felt that flying was a crazy dream that would fade away.

The Wright brothers and others were excited by this dream. They worked to build better planes. Companies were started to make airplanes. Daring men and women learned to fly and test them. Before long, airlines started mail and passenger service.

Thus the big aviation (ā′ vē ā′shən) industry was born. *Aviation* is the business of making and flying all kinds of aircraft.

Many brave persons proved the airplane could do many useful things. Glenn Curtiss built and flew the first successful seaplane. He had designed the country's first lightweight plane engine. He used it in his plane. He added a pontoon, or float, as landing gear. In 1911 he took off and landed on the water near San Diego, California.

Charles Lindbergh thrilled the world in 1927. He flew, alone, nonstop from New York to Paris, France. His small plane was named the *Spirit of St. Louis*. In later years, he explored and mapped many new air routes.

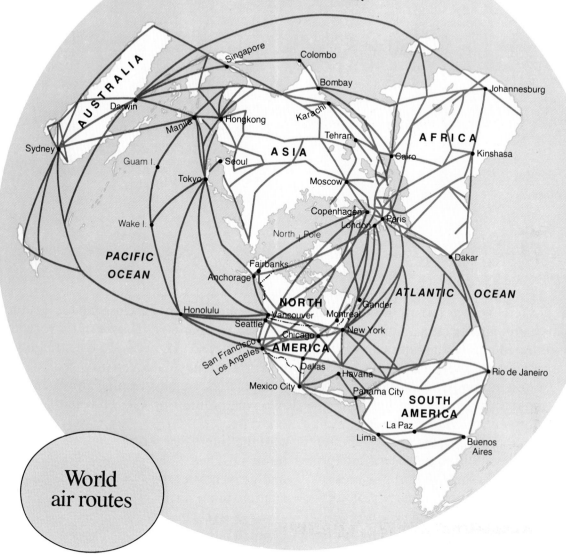

INDIAN OCEAN

AUSTRALIA

Singapore
Colombo
Bombay
Johannesburg
Darwin
Karachi
Manila
Hongkong
AFRICA
Tehran
Kinshasa
Sydney
ASIA
Cairo
Guam I.
Seoul
Moscow
Tokyo
Copenhagen
London
Paris
Wake I.
North Pole
Dakar
PACIFIC
OCEAN
Fairbanks
Anchorage
ATLANTIC OCEAN
Honolulu
NORTH
Gander
Vancouver
Montreal
Seattle
New York
Chicago
San Francisco
AMERICA
Los Angeles
Dallas
Havana
Rio de Janeiro
Mexico City
Panama City
SOUTH
AMERICA
La Paz
Lima
Buenos
Aires

World
air routes

In 1932 Amelia Earhart flew alone across the Atlantic. Three years later she became the first person to make the even longer flight from Hawaii to California. Earhart was lost in the South Pacific in 1937 trying to fly around the world.

Jacqueline Cochran was another pioneer pilot. She broke many speed, distance, and altitude records. In World War II, she started the Women's Airforce Service Pilots (WASP).

During World War II, jet airplanes were developed. They were much faster than any other planes at that time. They could also take off on shorter runways.

Today large jets carry hundreds of people. There are hundreds of regular flights between cities. Each flight has an expert crew. The pilot is the person in charge. A co-pilot and navigator help in the cockpit. Flight attendants help passengers in the cabin.

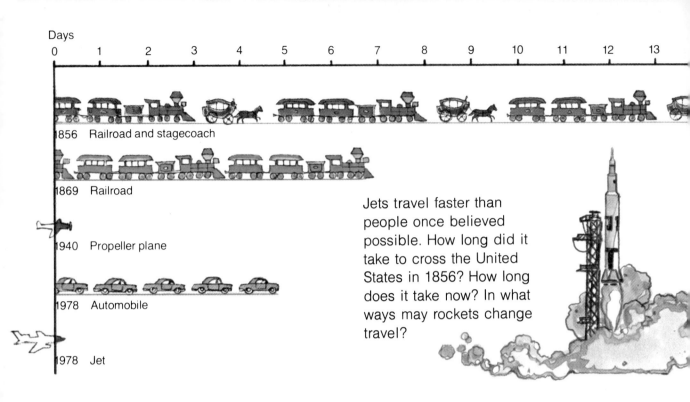

Days
0 1 2 3 4 5 6 7 8 9 10 11 12 13

1856   Railroad and stagecoach

1869   Railroad

1940   Propeller plane

1978   Automobile

1978   Jet

Jets travel faster than people once believed possible. How long did it take to cross the United States in 1856? How long does it take now? In what ways may rockets change travel?

The United States has thousands of airports and landing fields. One or more can be found in nearly all American cities.

Air traffic controllers direct all plane traffic around an airport. They use radio, radar, signal lights, and special instruments to do their job. A pilot coming in for a landing calls the control tower on the radio. The pilot is told when to land and on what runway. At a busy airport in Chicago a small group directs nearly 700,000 takeoffs and landings a year.

There are planes for doing many kinds of jobs. Cargo planes carry freight. People use air cargo when the goods must move fast. Cargo planes fly fresh flowers from Hawaii, lobsters from Maine, and early strawberries from California. Cargo planes have extra large doors and no seats. They have built-in elevators that speed up loading and unloading.

Some farmers use planes to dust and spray crops. Cattle ranchers fly in small planes to check on their herds. Firefighters fly to burning forests. Foresters use planes to spray trees to control insects.

Helicopters can fly close to the ground to do special jobs. They can fly forward and backward. They can move straight up and down. They can even hover, or stay in one place, for a short time. They can land in a vacant lot or on the flat roof of a large building.

Helicopters are used to report on traffic tie-ups. They may be used to rescue people. They carry riders on short trips, such as to an airport.

Air travel has made the world seem much smaller. People and cargo can move faster by plane than by any other way. Planes can fly over mountains and oceans. They can take the shortest routes between places.

Air routes connect all the large cities in the United States and many of the smaller ones. A person can fly from New York City to Los Angeles in a few hours.

Large jets fly nonstop to many cities in other countries. Distances seem to have shrunk. Today all the countries of the world are neighbors because of fast air transportation.

226

A matching game

Write the items in List B on paper. After each item write the correct name from List A.

List A

Amelia Earhart John Fitch
Robert Fulton Erie Canal
Pipeline Charles Lindbergh
Panama Canal Promontory, Utah
Amtrak Henry Ford
Wright brothers Clippers

List B

Built the first usable steamboat in the United States

Waterway that connects the Hudson River with Lake Erie

Famous American sailing ships

Where the cross-country railroad was joined in 1869

System of railroad passenger service

First to fly from Hawaii to California

First to use the assembly-line method for making motor cars

Used to carry liquid products over long distances

Made the first successful plane flight in the United States

Flew nonstop from New York to Paris in 1927

Using a map

What does the map on page 220 show? Use the scale of kilometers on this map to measure the distance by railroad from

Cincinnati to Memphis.
Denver to Fort Worth.
Houston to Albuquerque.
Salt Lake City to Los Angeles.
San Francisco to Portland.

Things to do

There are many careers in transportation. Just a few of them are listed below.

Roads
construction engineer
highway maintenance worker
toll collector
safety expert
truck inspector
heavy equipment operator

Railroading
computer expert
conductor
engineer
ticket seller
track worker
subway driver

Motor Vehicles
truck driver
car designer
test driver
dealer
assembly-line worker
gas-station manager

Shipping
tugboat captain
dock worker
canal locks operator
sailor

Aviation
helicopter pilot
flight attendant
baggage handler

Choose one of these, and find out as much as you can about it. Make a poster showing some part of the work.

What do you think?

1. Why are good roads important to a country?

2. Why do we say that airplanes make the world seem smaller?

3. Suppose you had to send a box of pineapples, 50 tons (45 metric tons) of wheat, and 20 head of cattle from California to New York. What means of transportation would you use for each? Why?

4. Compare the first motor cars with cars today. How are they alike? How are they different?

227

17

Communication: keeping in touch

Colonists create a postal system

"My patience has worn thin," complained Benjamin Franklin one day in 1736. "I'm still waiting for a letter I expected six weeks ago."

"That's bad news," replied Franklin's friend.

"Indeed it is," said Franklin. "Mail from New York should reach us here in Philadelphia in three weeks. Our mail system in the colonies is much too slow. We can't depend on it. I'll write about this in my newspaper!"

"You should," said the friend. "But, Ben, our mail system won't change until someone like you is in charge of it."

"Come now!" Franklin said with a chuckle. "I'm a printer, not an expert on mail."

"You could be, Ben," the friend replied. "You have good ideas, and you get things done."

In a few months Benjamin Franklin was the postmaster of Philadelphia. He made many improvements in that city's mail system. Some of his ideas were used in other places.

The earliest colonists sent mail any way they could. Ships brought letters from England. But there was no good way to send mail from one colony to another colony or even to send mail from one town to another.

At times travelers and hunters carried mail. A traveler would take a letter as far as he was going. He would leave it at an inn. It might be at the inn for weeks before another traveler carried it on. Two or three copies of important letters were made and

228

sent at different times. Then surely one copy would arrive.

In those days there were no postage stamps. Letters were sent "collect." That is, a traveler might collect a small amount of money from a person getting a letter. This was "pay" for carrying the letter, of course.

By 1700 some colonies had started mail service. They hired riders to carry mail from one city to another. Riders went through thick forests along lonely trails. They put up with the rain, icy winds, snowstorms, and summer heat. They left the mail at a central place called the post or post office. Often a post office was in a corner of an inn or home. The riders became known as postriders.

There were not enough postriders to carry mail to and from small towns. So travelers helped with this service.

In time, some leaders said that the colonies must have a better mail system. One of these leaders was Benjamin Franklin.

In 1753 Franklin became the postmaster general for all the colonies. He was picked by the English government. Franklin held the position until 1774. He did much to improve mail service in the colonies. He set up three mail trips a week between Philadelphia and New York. He worked to get faster handling of the mail between Boston and Philadelphia. He also started the plan of mailing newspapers. He found ways to help pay for sending mail.

In those days the cost of sending a letter depended on its weight and how far it was going. It cost about 40 cents to send a letter from Boston to Philadelphia. About 18 cents was charged to send a letter from New York to Philadelphia. Why was there

The Pony Express advertised for young, skinny riders. The less weight a horse had to carry, the faster it could travel.

this difference? If you locate these cities on a map, you will have some idea. Which two are farther apart?

In 1775 the Continental Congress set up a postal service. By this time the colonies were at war with England. The Congress chose Benjamin Franklin as the Postmaster General. He held that office only a short time. But he kept on finding ways to improve mail service.

Slow transportation made carrying the mail a huge job. There were few good roads. Also thousands of people had moved west. The frontier was hard to reach by mail.

In time, stagecoaches carried a lot of mail over the Cumberland Road. Steamboats hauled some on the rivers and on the Great Lakes. By 1840 railroads were carrying a large share.

Sending mail west of the Mississippi was a big problem for a long time. No railroad reached that vast part of the country until 1869. Ships and stagecoaches hauled the mail. Neither way worked very well.

Most sailing ships took six months or more to make the long trip around South America. There was no Panama Canal yet. Clipper ships might make the voyage in three months. But they charged high prices.

The trip overland had to be made by stagecoach. The route was long and risky. It took about 25 days to go from Missouri to California. Some stagecoaches didn't finish the trip at all. Others were held up by bad weather, robberies, or broken axles.

In 1860 the Pony Express began a route to the West Coast. It was about 2000 miles (3200 km) long. It started at St. Joseph, Missouri, and ended in San Francisco. Eighty riders and five hundred ponies were used.

The Pony Express was like a relay race. It was run from one stop to the next. The stations were from 10 to 15 miles (16 km to 24 km) apart. A rider galloped to a station. There he got on a fresh pony and tossed the mail bags over its back. Each rider covered several stops for a distance of about 75

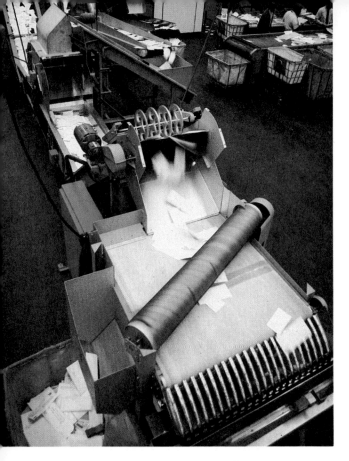

Machines help sort the 80 billion pieces of mail the Post Office handles each year.

service began. Each new way to move goods helped to speed up mail service.

During the 1960s many changes took place in post offices. More and more of the work was done by machines. The Zone Improvement Plan (ZIP) began. A ZIP code number was given to each small part of the country. A large city might have a dozen or more ZIP code areas. Now mail without a ZIP code must be sorted by hand. It may be delayed as much as a day.

Today the United States Postal Service has about 700,000 workers. They work in the 31,000 post offices throughout the country. They handle over 80 billion pieces of mail each year.

Each letter mailed must have stamps on it for the correct postage. The United States government has been printing postage stamps since 1847. Some stamps have a picture of a great person. Others may show a great event in history or a scenic area.

Americans print newspapers

Town criers "broadcast" the news in some early colonial villages. They walked about ringing bells and shouting some news. After dark they served as a kind of guard, singing out, for example, "Ten o'clock and all's well."

During the War for Independence there was much to announce. The happiest news of all was called out by a crier at three o'clock one morning. The crier shouted, "Cornwallis has surrendered to General Washington and all is well."

In those days, town criers took the place of daily papers. But as towns grew into cities, newspapers were published.

miles (120 km). At the end of a run, the weary rider stopped to rest. A fresh rider raced on.

The long trip took about ten days. The fastest trip ever made took about eight days. That time the riders carried a copy of Lincoln's First Inaugural Address as well as letters.

Sending a letter by Pony Express was costly. Even the lightest one cost about five dollars. Still the Pony Express lost money for its owners. It was given up in 1861 after only about eighteen months of service. In that same year California was linked to the East by the telegraph. Eight years later the railroad began to carry mail west.

The early 1900s brought many changes. Trucks were being built. They began to carry mail short distances. In 1918 airmail

230

Benjamin Franklin's *Pennsylvania Gazette* was the first American newspaper to carry a cartoon. Franklin published the *Gazette* for more than 35 years.

The first successful newspaper was the *Boston News Letter*. It began in 1704. It had four pages of articles in small print. Later another paper was started by Benjamin Franklin's brother. Young Ben worked in his brother's print shop. In those days, printing was not easy. The press was worked by hand. Printing the paper took a long time.

Franklin liked being a printer but enjoyed writing for the paper even more. He wanted to keep this fact a secret. So he signed his articles with a pen name, Mrs. Silence Dogood.

Some years later, Franklin published a paper of his own in Philadelphia. In it he wrote many articles about the city's problems. He often used a pen name. Then he could complain freely about the rough streets. He could speak out about fire dangers and the poor mail system. He brought out ways to solve problems, too. Through his paper Franklin did much to improve life in Philadelphia.

The first *daily* newspaper in America was started in Philadelphia in 1775. Like Franklin's paper it ran more articles about problems than news stories. News traveled very slowly in those days.

Many daily newspapers are printed in the United States today. A daily paper in a large city may have fifty or more pages. Its front page gives important local, state, and national news. It may also have news about other countries.

Inside the paper are more news stories, sports news, comics, radio and TV news, and special articles. Newspaper editorials often deal with big problems.

Every newspaper fills much space with ads. Business firms pay well to advertise goods and services.

A daily paper employs many women and men. Some work in its business office. Others set type or run presses. Some people sell ads. Artists and layout experts put together the pages. Other workers deliver the papers.

Reporters and photographers gather and write news stories and take pictures. Some travel over the world to get news. Editors work in the newsroom. They write headlines and rewrite stories. They decide what stories and pictures should be used.

The reporters in the city room check information and write the stories for the next day's paper. Some newspapers are printed in Braille, a system of small raised dots that can be read by touch.

Publishing has become big business

Books were published in the United States before newspapers. The first books came out in the middle 1600s. Soon Boston, New York, and Philadelphia had presses. There were law books, religious books, almanacs, and school books. One popular book in the 1700s was Ben Franklin's *Poor Richard's Almanack*. It was a collection of advice and wise sayings. Franklin published it for more than 30 years.

Today many types of books are printed. There are fiction, or "story" books, and nonfiction books. There are "how-to-do-it" books about nearly everything. Millions of books come out as paperbacks each year.

There are books for people with special needs. Some are large-print books. Books are printed in Braille for blind people.

The first United States magazine came out in the middle 1700s. By 1800 about 100 magazines had been started. Most didn't last very long.

During the 1900s many magazines of all types became a success. One was *The Saturday Evening Post*. It was published from 1821 to 1969. There seemed to be a magazine for everyone. There were some for children, too.

Advertising pays much of the costs of producing most magazines. In recent years magazines have had a hard time. They cost more to print. Postage costs have gone up. Ads are harder to sell. TV has taken some of their advertising. Many magazines have gone out of business.

Cities open public libraries

Our first public libraries opened in the 1800s. Before that time all libraries had been owned by persons, schools, or groups. They were not open to everyone.

Today public libraries contain books, newspapers, magazines, pamphlets, records, tapes, and films.

Many libraries store copies of old newspapers on microfilm. A *microfilm* copy is a page-by-page photo of printed material. It is projected on a screen to be read. Some libraries store microfiche copies of things. A *microfiche* (mī′krō fesh′) copy is the same as a microfilm copy only much smaller. A microfiche of a newspaper page, for example, is about the size of the period at the end of this sentence.

The Library of Congress in Washington is a great national library. It is the largest one in the world. It contains millions of books. In recent years it has been adding about one million books each year.

The Library of Congress has more than 5000 books that were published before 1501. It has famous collections of music, prints, maps, and movies. It has many books and tapes for blind people.

When?

1. When was the Pony Express started?
2. When did airmail service begin?
3. When were postage stamps first printed?
4. When did the Continental Congress start postal service in the colonies?
5. When was the first successful newspaper published?

   Make a timeline to show the dates and events listed above.

Other things to do

1. Make a chart about our mail system. At the top of your paper write, "Some ways our mail system has changed." Then draw a line down your paper. Write at the top of the first column "Long Ago." Write "Today" at the top of the second column.

   Think of as many differences as you can. Then write them across from each other in the two columns. Be ready to share your lists with the class.

2. Read in another book about one of these topics.

   The United States Postal System
   Book Publishing
   Libraries

   Which one did you choose? Find out what are five kinds of jobs in it. Which job interests you the most? Be ready to tell your class about it.

The Library of Congress, a storehouse of valuable information, is one of the world's busiest research centers.

When Samuel Morse sent Annie Ellsworth's message from Washington to Baltimore, Dolly Madison and Henry Clay were among the observers.

Inventors learn to send messages by wire

The telegraph was invented by Samuel Morse. He was already a famous American artist. He had sailed to Europe for further study. While in Europe he became interested in electricity. One day as he was coming home on board ship, he and some friends began to discuss electricity. Morse told them that messages might be sent over wires by means of an electric current.

"Impossible!" one friend said.

"Not at all!" Morse insisted. "I'll show you how it could be done." Then he made drawings of a telegraph machine.

When Morse got home, he began to build his telegraph. In 1838 the telegraph was finished. Morse had also worked out signals for each letter of the alphabet. These signals became known as the Morse Code.

Morse asked a friend to help test his telegraph. Together the two strung a long wire through the shop. They placed the sending set in one corner. The receiving set was moved as far away as possible. Then Morse tapped out a message. The signals traveled over the long wire. The message came through clearly.

Morse showed his invention to many friends. He took it to Washington, D.C., to show to government leaders. He hoped that Congress would build a telegraph line from Washington to Baltimore. This was a distance of about 40 miles (64 km). Messages sent over such a line surely would prove how useful the telegraph could be.

Some government leaders listened with interest. But others made fun of the odd equipment. Then one day Morse heard that Congress was ready to discuss his telegraph. He hurried to Washington with high hopes. Then he learned that Congress had turned to other matters. Months passed, and Morse made plans to go home.

The next morning, though, a knock at his door brought good news. At Morse's door stood young Annie Ellsworth, the daughter of a friend.

"Father has sent me to tell you something wonderful," she said. "Late last night, at Congress's last meeting, it agreed to build a telegraph line. Father was there and heard about it."

Morse could hardly believe what she said. It was the most thrilling news he had ever heard. Morse asked Annie to choose

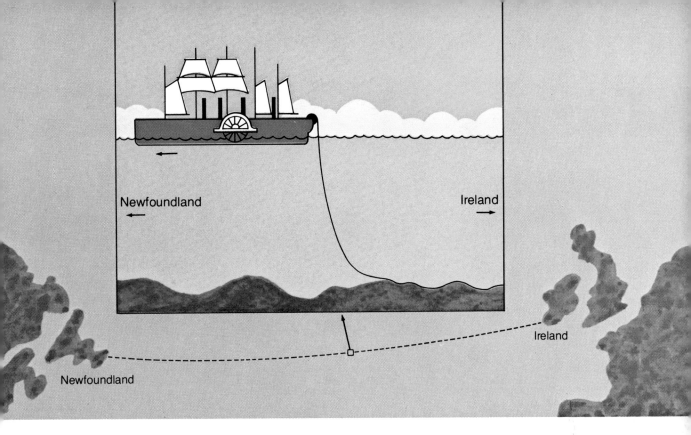

Newfoundland

Ireland

Ireland

Newfoundland

the first message he would send over the wires. She chose words from the Bible, "What hath God wrought!"

In May 1844 crowds gathered at the Capitol in Washington. Morse was at the Washington end of a wire that stretched to Baltimore. An electric current went through the wire between Washington and Baltimore. The crowd watched Morse tap on his key. His tapping caused a bar at the other end to make a clicking sound. Using his special code, Morse tapped out the message, "What hath God wrought!"

Morse's helper in Baltimore changed the tapped code into letters. Then he spelled out the words "What hath God wrought!" The telegraph had worked.

Later, Morse and others improved the telegraph. Telegraph wires were strung from city to city in the eastern part of the country. By 1861 a line reached all the way to the Pacific coast. Morse lived to see his invention serving people in many ways.

Although Cyrus Field's first undersea cable broke four weeks after it was completed, it was the beginning of fast communication between America and Europe.

Cyrus Field arranged to lay a big telegraph cable across the ocean. Field was a wealthy paper manufacturer. In 1857 he made plans to lay a heavy telegraph *cable,* or line, across the floor of the Atlantic Ocean. It was to connect Newfoundland and Ireland. Find these places on the map of the world.

Field and his crew began to lay the cable from Ireland. Sailing slowly west, they dropped the cable to the ocean floor. As the picture shows, the ocean floor has plains, mountains, and valleys.

At first the laying of the cable went well. But four hundred miles (640 km) out at sea, the cable broke and sank. Field tried again, but there were more failures. Still he did not give up. At last, after nine years, the job was done.

Delighted at the success of the first telephone message, Watson ran upstairs to give Bell the good news.

The cable across the Atlantic was more than 2000 miles (3200 km) long. Copper wires were woven together for it. They had been soaked in oil, pitch, and wax. They were covered with waterproof material.

This was the first cable laid across an ocean. There are now more than 400,000 miles (640,000 km) of such cables. They connect the United States with the world's chief seaports. Businesses use them each day to carry on buying and selling in other lands.

Today machines are used to send and receive "telegraphed" messages. One is the teleprinter. It looks a lot like a type-writer. A special circuit links it with a print-ing machine at the other end of the line. A message is typed on a teleprinter. It is printed by a machine where it is received. Groups such as United Press International (UPI) send news stories to newspapers in this way.

Alexander Graham Bell invented the telephone. Bell was born in Scotland. There his father taught deaf people how to speak. Bell became a teacher of the deaf in Boston, Massachusetts. He learned how the voice forms sounds and how the ears hear. These studies led him to think about making a special instrument. It could send a voice by wire across distances. This in-strument became known as the telephone. Telephone means "speak from afar."

Bell and Thomas Watson spent many months working on their telephone. Wat-son was a mechanic and model maker. At last the telephone was ready to test. They strung wire from Watson's workbench in the basement to Bell's study, two floors above. Then Bell talked over the tele-phone. But Watson could not understand the words. Bell and Watson were disap-pointed. But now they worked harder than ever.

One day when Watson was busy in the basement, Bell spoke over the transmitter, "Mr. Watson, come here! I want you!"

The surprised Watson ran up the stairs, shouting, "I heard you! I heard you!" On that March evening in 1876, Watson had heard and understood the first telephone message.

Later that year Bell took his invention to Philadelphia to a World's Fair. This fair was celebrating one hundred years of United States independence. Bell thought that many visitors would want to hear about his telephone. At first most people did not.

Then one day a stranger stepped up. He was the emperor of Brazil, a country in South America. "What is this?" he asked Bell.

"A telephone, sir," answered Bell. Then he told how it worked. "If you will listen, I'll speak into the transmitter."

When the emperor heard Bell's voice over the telephone, he was amazed. "It talks! It talks!" he exclaimed. Then others crowded around. From then on, people asked questions. Soon there were reports in newspapers about the telephone.

Bell and other inventors continued to improve the telephone. He and some partners formed a telephone company. It began to make telephones and build telephone lines. Before long, workers began to put phones in homes and offices.

There have been many improvements in telephone service. Automatic dialers help people who often call the same numbers. A card or a tape is put into a kind of phone. The phone then "dials" the number.

One pair of phone cables can carry more than 3500 phone messages at a time. But each cable is only about the size of a pencil.

Communications satellites are used to carry phone calls over long distances. A *satellite* is a body that moves in space around another body such as the earth. A communications satellite can pick up phone calls from one place on earth. Then it sends them back down to another place.

Directory assistance operators use computers to provide customer information.

Nearly a million people work in the telephone industry. Some make the phones. Others are operators and installers. Scientists work in research laboratories to improve telephone service and equipment.

Messages can be sent without wires

Guglielmo Marconi found a way to send messages without using wires. In the 1890s this young Italian flashed the dots and dashes of the Morse Code through the air. He called his invention the wireless telegraph. Marconi soon learned to flash wireless messages across the Atlantic. He sent them from England to Newfoundland.

The wireless telegraph proved valuable to ships at sea. Ships could use the wireless to send SOS, or distress signals.

Many other inventors worked to make a wireless telephone. One was Lee de Forest. He invented a special kind of tube. It could send a voice or music long distances without using wires.

237

Guglielmo Marconi *(left)* used this station in Eastham, Massachusetts *(right)* to send the first transatlantic wireless message from the United States.

The wireless telephone is called a *radiophone*. It sends messages through the air by means of electrical, or radio, waves. The radiophone can be used to talk to people on moving trains. It is used to phone people on ships at sea and pilots on airplanes. It can connect us with people on other continents.

Wireless telegraph and radiophone led to the radio. Lee de Forest's special kind of tube made it possible to broadcast voices and music. But no one person invented the radio. Many scientists and inventors worked on it.

By 1920 the radio was coming into use. The first radios looked like little boxes. Each one had a long wire attached to it. There was a headphone which the listener clamped over the ears to hear a program.

Today there are more than 400 million radios in the United States. Nearly 60 million radios are bought each year. Most American cars have radios. Many radios are small and lightweight and are run by batteries. They can be carried just about everywhere.

Around 6500 radio stations broadcast programs. Most stations provide entertainment, especially music. Stations also provide news programs and interviews. There are call-in shows and sports events.

Putting on a radio show takes the skills of many people. They include writers, announcers, and sound technicians. They also include program planners, advertising salespeople, and disk jockeys.

Some people use a two-way radio on the job or as a hobby. Two-way radios are installed on fire engines, in police cars, and in taxis. They can be used to send messages and to receive them. For example, the police can call their stations or be called by them.

Citizens' band (CB) radio is a special two-way system that also can be used for short distances. Truck drivers often use CB radios to talk with other truck drivers on the highway. Some farmers depend on CB radios to keep in touch with helpers in the fields.

Many people use CB radios as a hobby. They install the radios in their cars and

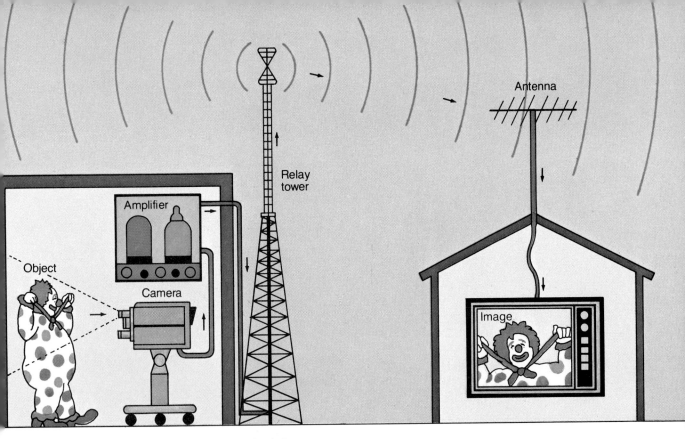

Trace the path of the television picture from the studio to your home. Separate amplifiers are used for the sound and the video signals.

homes. They can then talk with other CB radio owners.

A very tiny radio is used in medicine. A patient swallows a radio pill. The radio then sends out signals that give information about the person's health.

Radar uses radio waves to locate some objects that cannot be seen. Radar can tell where an object is. Radar can tell whether it is moving, how fast it is going, and in what direction.

Radar was tested and developed during the 1920s and 1930s. It was first used widely in World War II to spot enemy planes. Today radar has many uses. It is used by the police to detect speeders and by ship navigators to "see" other ships. It is used by pilots to help them fly around storms.

Television is an important way to communicate

Inventors dreamed of television when they began working with electricity. The work of Thomas Edison and Lee de Forest helped later inventors develop TV. One was Philip T. Farnsworth, a high school student. In 1922 in his physics class he found a way to improve a TV picture.

The word "television" means "to see far." TV makes it possible to see and hear programs from "far" places. TV combines sight and sound.

The first regular TV broadcasts in the United States began in 1941. By 1949 there were a million TV sets in the country. Two years later there were 10 million. By the early 1970s there were 93 million sets. About 95 out of every 100 homes had TV sets. A growing number of them had color television.

Communications satellites, like this one, enable us to send messages from one part of the world to another instantly.

Commercial television stations broadcast mainly entertainment, news, and educational programs. Sponsors buy broadcast time. They use it to advertise their products.

Public television is not paid for by advertisers. Programs are paid for by money from individuals, business firms, and the government. Public TV stations give much time to programs for children.

Both commercial and public television stations try to meet the needs of their large audiences. For example, some stations provide programs in languages other than English. Some have news programs trans-

lated into American Sign Language for deaf viewers.

Cable TV is brought into the home through a wire rather than through the air. Some cable systems show programs that are not carried on regular channels. Others bring TV to areas of the country that cannot pick up signals from the air.

Closed circuit television is meant for special small groups. It is used by the people who own the systems. Some school districts, for example, put closed circuit TV sets in each classroom. One teacher or group of teachers can then give a lesson for hundreds of children.

The Big Top Show at Circus World Museum is popular with visitors of all ages.

Large apartment buildings can be "guarded" by closed circuit TV cameras. People who live in the buildings can turn their TV sets to a special channel and see who is in the lobby.

Communications satellites bring us TV from all over the world. In 1962 *Telstar* was sent into space. It was a kind of radio and TV station in space. It could receive and send messages and pictures thousands of miles using powerful ground stations.

Telstar's first program was sent from the United States to Europe. It showed pictures of Americans at work and a minute of a Chicago baseball game. It included a short visit with the President.

This program lasted only seventeen minutes. It proved, though, that satellites could flash clear sounds and pictures long distances. Today communications satellites link the United States with about 65 countries.

Communities establish museums

Our country's first museum was set up in Charleston, South Carolina. The year was 1773. Today there are thousands of museums in the country. Workers in these museums collect, study, and exhibit, or show, objects.

There are three main types of museums. Art museums have such items as paintings, sculpture, pottery, and sometimes films and music. Historical museums contain objects from the past. A historical museum might be a whole village. Greenfield Village in Michigan is this type of museum. So is Sturbridge Village in Massachusetts.

Museums of science and technology can be different types. Zoos and gardens are two types. Natural history museums contain plants, rocks, animals, and other things from nature. Some museums specialize in one thing. For example, the Circus World Museum in Baraboo, Wisconsin, has circus wagons and other circus items.

This model of a lunar module is a prized exhibit at the National Aeronautics and Space Museum. Lunar modules were designed to land on the moon.

The Smithsonian Institution is a very famous museum in Washington, D.C. It is really many museums. It contains art, objects from the past, a zoo, and a theater. One of its buildings is the National Air and Space Museum. It has the Wright brothers' first airplane. It also has the plane used by Charles Lindbergh to fly across the Atlantic. Visitors can see all kinds of spacecraft, too.

Museums offer special services to their communities. They arrange for tours, art festivals, concerts, and research projects. In recent years museums have made it easier for more people to use them. Some have fixed the buildings for use by disabled people. Some provide directions in different languages.

Review some chapter highlights

Each of the following sentences has a missing word or date. These missing items are shown in the list below the ten sentences. Copy each sentence. Write the correct missing word or date in the sentence. You will not use all the items in the list.

1. By ____ many colonies had begun to hire postriders to carry the mail.
2. Railroads, planes, and ____ carry mail in the United States.
3. The Pony Express carried mail from St. Joseph to ____.
4. ____ invented the telegraph.
5. ____ laid the first cable to span an ocean and connect continents.
6. ____ invented the telephone.
7. ____ discovered how to send messages by wireless.
8. ____ makes it possible to hear and see programs at the same time.
9. Some television programs are sent by communications ____.
10. The ____ Institution is a famous museum in Washington, D.C.

List

Field	1860	Massachusetts
continents	1847	airplanes
San Francisco	Morse	expensive
television	Marconi	satellites
trucks	Bell	Smithsonian
1700		

Reporting news items

Think of an event that has happened in your town or neighborhood recently. Be prepared to make a news report about it to your class.

Here are some ideas to keep in mind when you share your news item with your class.

1. Practice telling your news before giving it to the class.
2. Understand it well enough to give it briefly and in an interesting way.
3. Try to show pictures related to it.
4. Show on a map where it took place.

What do you think?

1. It has been said that "communication has conquered distance." What do you think this means?
2. Many of the inventors named in this chapter worked a long time before they succeeded. Tell about a time that you worked at something that was difficult.
3. What kinds of information can you get from radio and TV programs?
4. What TV programs should young children watch? Which ones should they not watch? Why?

Things to do

1. There are many careers in communication. Some are listed below. Choose one. Find out as much as you can about it. Then make a report on the career you chose to the class.

    photographer (newspaper, magazine)
    newspaper reporter
    typesetter
    magazine illustrator
    editor (magazine, book)
    teleprinter operator
    telephone operator
    ship radio operator
    radio announcer
    TV game show emcee
    sound technician
    TV weather forecaster
    repair person (radio, TV)
    scriptwriter (radio, TV)

2. TV shows are rated by how many people watch them. You might want to do your own class ratings. Using a TV guide, make a list of the programs that are shown between 7:00 and 9:00 pm, Monday through Thursday, during the next week. On Friday check to see how many people in the class watched each program.

3. Look in an encyclopedia or another book for more information about one of these inventors.

    Alexander Graham Bell   Cyrus Field
    Guglielmo Marconi   Samuel Morse

    Dramatize a scene from the life of one you read about.

4. If you collect stamps, bring your stamp album and show it to the class. Tell your class about several interesting stamps.

18
Governing the United States

Women struggle for the right to vote

It was election day in November 1872. The voters were choosing the next President. Four women came up to one voting place. The man in charge asked, "What are you doing here? "You know women can't vote. It's against the law!"

"So it is," declared the leader, Susan B. Anthony. "But that law is unfair! It must be changed, and women will see that it is!"

Then she and her three friends voted and marched off.

The man in charge was furious. So were many other people. The four women were arrested for what they had done.

Susan B. Anthony did not give up. She knew that women lacked many rights. She was set on changing things.

Miss Anthony and her friends worked hard. They wrote newspaper articles. They sent letters to state and national leaders. The women gave speeches in dozens of towns and cities. Often people laughed or shouted at them. But they kept on, year after year. Their first success was in 1869. That year women were allowed to vote in Wyoming.

Miss Anthony gave her last speech when she was 86 years old. By that time she was frail and her voice was weak. She inspired her listeners just the same. When she finished, they cheered her for ten minutes. They promised to carry on the struggle for which she had spent her life. Miss Anthony did not live to see her dream of the vote for women come true. Finally, though, it did.

In 1920 women won the right to vote in all states. This law was the 19th Amendment to the Constitution of the United States. An *amendment* is a law that has been added to the Constitution.

Susan B. Anthony was active in many causes before she devoted all her energy to the fight for women's rights.

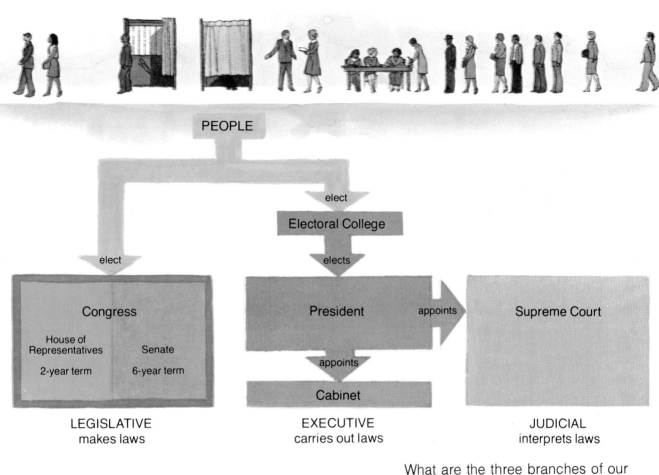

PEOPLE

elect

Electoral College

elect

elects

Congress

House of Representatives

Senate

2-year term

6-year term

President — appoints → **Supreme Court**

appoints

Cabinet

LEGISLATIVE
makes laws

EXECUTIVE
carries out laws

JUDICIAL
interprets laws

What are the three branches of our government? Which national leaders do the people elect? Which are appointed?

We have a national government

The Constitution is our country's plan of government. You read in chapter 6 about how it began. The planners of the Constitution wanted a system that would last ages. They also wanted one that planned for future changes.

Their plan has proven to be a wise one. The Constitution has worked for nearly 200 years. It has been suited to the needs of the growing nation. When changes have come about, amendments have been passed.

The first ten amendments are known as the *Bill of Rights*. The 13th Amendment did away with slavery in the United States.

The 19th Amendment gave women the right to vote. The 22nd Amendment limited the President to two terms. The 26th Amendment gave the vote to 18-year-olds.

The Constitution divided the powers of government. It set up three branches. They are the executive branch, the legislative branch, and the judicial branch.

The President is the head of the executive branch. Our Chief Executive is in charge of enforcing the laws, of making treaties, and of dealing with other nations. The President also is the Commander-in-Chief of the Armed Forces. These include the Army, Navy, and Air Force.

245

The President is elected for a term of four years and may be re-elected for a second term. Margaret Chase Smith and Shirley Chisholm were among the first women to seek the job.

The job of President is a huge one. So the President needs many "helpers." Some, called secretaries, serve as members of the President's Cabinet. Each secretary heads a special department. For example, the Secretary of State heads the Department of State. It is in charge of foreign affairs, our business with other countries.

Often a President's wife has gone to other countries to try to improve relations with them. Pat Nixon, Betty Ford, and Rosalynn Carter all did this. They also have carried out projects of their own. Jacqueline Kennedy, for example, restored some rooms in the White House. "Lady Bird" Johnson worked on a program of beautifying the country. Mrs. Carter took a strong interest in mental health.

The second branch of government is the legislative branch. It is the Congress, which is made up of the Senate and the House of Representatives. The citizens in each state send two Senators to the Senate. They are elected by the people and hold office for six years. They may be re-elected.

Representatives are also elected. The number of Representatives that a state sends to Congress depends on the state's population. Some states like California and New York have large populations. So they send many Representatives to Congress. A few small states elect only one or two Representatives. Representatives serve for a term of two years. They may be re-elected to any number of additional terms.

The Constitution gives Congress the power to make laws. Congress can pass tax laws, can declare war, and can borrow money. All treaties made by the President must be approved by the Senate.

Members of Congress serve on committees to study problems. The committees work on the proposed laws. Then all members of Congress may discuss and vote on the laws.

The third branch of government is the judicial branch. The Supreme Court heads the judicial branch. It is the highest court in the country. It has nine justices, or judges. These justices are chosen for life by the President with the consent of the Senate.

The Supreme Court decides questions about laws that have been passed. There may be a dispute about what the words in a law mean. The Supreme Court *interprets* the law, or decides what the law means. The justices may decide whether or not a law agrees with the Constitution. If they decide that it does not, it is unconstitutional. It is then no longer a law.

The city of Washington is the center of the national government. Find Washington on a map of the United States. What symbol is used to show that it is the capital of the nation?

Washington is not a part of any state. It is located in an area of its own, the District of Columbia. That is why the letters D.C. are added to its name.

Washington, D.C., is located on the winding Potomac River. At its center is the Capitol Building. Its white dome rises 300 feet (90 m) above the round center of the building. On each side is a large wing. In the right wing an entrance leads to the

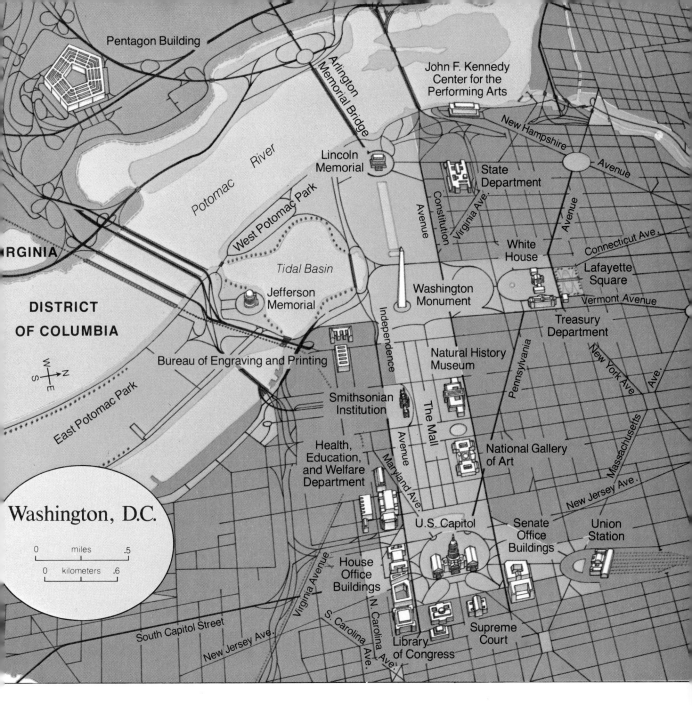

Washington, D.C.

| 0 | miles | .5 |
| 0 | kilometers | .6 |

chamber where the Senate meets. The entrance in the left wing leads to the chamber where the Representatives gather. There are 540 rooms in the Capitol. These rooms include committee rooms, offices, and rooms where visitors can watch Congress at work.

Look at the map of Washington. Notice how the Capitol faces a long mall. This green, park-like mall leads to the tall Washington Monument. It is 555 feet (170 m) high. It is covered with white marble that is 7 inches (18 cm) thick. The inside of the monument is hollow. It has an elevator to carry visitors to the top.

Beyond the Washington Monument is a long pool, then the handsome Lincoln Memorial. It holds a statue of Abraham Lincoln. Nearby is the memorial to Thomas Jefferson.

More than one and one half
million tourists visit the
White House each year.

The White House is the official home of the President. Locate it on the map. This stately mansion has gardens, lawns, and trees around it.

The White House is almost as old as the nation. It was started in 1792. George Washington chose its location, and he watched some of it being built. But it was not completed in time for the Washingtons to live there. The second President, John Adams, and his family lived in the White House.

The White House has 132 rooms. Five of these are open to the public. Special dinners and receptions are held in them. The State Dining Room can hold as many as 140 people for dinner. The Blue Room is where the President greets guests. The walls of the Green Room are covered with light green silk. This room is used as a sitting room. So is the Red Room. The largest room in the White House is the East Room. It is 79 feet (24 m) long and 37 feet (11 m) wide.

The President and staff work in offices in the White House. The President's family lives in private rooms on the second floor.

The Capitol and the White House are the center of Washington. Main streets extend out from these buildings. Many of the streets are named after states. Find some of these streets on the map.

George Washington laid the cornerstone for the Capitol building in 1793.

Millions of people visit Washington, D.C. each year. Some are leaders of foreign countries. But most of the visitors are American sightseers.

There are hundreds of places you can see in Washington. For example, you can walk or ride past beautiful buildings. One is the Supreme Court Building. It is made of gleaming white marble. You can look at more than 300 memorials and statues in the city.

You can visit the National Gallery of Art or other art galleries. You can walk through the gardens at Dumbarton Oaks. Georgetown is an old and interesting part of the city. You can visit the zoo in Rock Creek Park. This park is one of the largest within any city in the world.

In Washington you can visit the Bureau of Engraving and Printing to watch money being made. You can see the Constitution and the Declaration of Independence. They are preserved in the National Archives.

The House of Representatives (top) meets in the south wing of the Capitol, the Senate (above) in the north.

The Supreme Court justices hand down their decisions in this room (below).

We choose our state and city leaders

Each state has its own constitution for a framework of government. Most states used the Constitution of the United States as a pattern. Each state constitution contains a Bill of Rights. Each one provides for three main divisions of government. They are the executive, the legislative, and the judicial.

The governor is the chief executive officer of the state. The governor is elected by the people for a term of two or four years, depending on the state's plan of government. It is the governor's duty to see that the state laws are enforced. The governor tries to keep the affairs of the state running smoothly. Who is the governor of your state?

Each state has a lawmaking body elected by the people. It is the legislative branch. In many states it is called the legislature. What is it called in your state?

This group makes some laws that may be especially interesting to you. Some are about the use of automobiles. The laws of most states require that a person pass certain tests to get a driver's license. Others require that each auto have license plates. Some laws are made to make auto travel safer. State governments also make laws about schools.

States employ engineers, planners, and construction workers to build highways and bridges. They pay workers to cut grass along highways, to shovel snow, and to repair roads. They hire nurses, doctors, and aides for state hospitals. They hire people to take care of parks and camping areas.

State inspectors test milk and other foods. State employees give tests and issue licenses for many jobs and businesses. Social workers help the disabled and those who can't get jobs.

Cities and towns have their own local governments. These local governments provide for schools. They hire people for the police force. They hire fire fighters. They arrange for the care of streets and city parks and for garbage pickup.

Do you live in a town or city? If so, what services does the local government provide for the people?

Certain officials are in charge of a city's affairs. One is the mayor, or executive. The legislative group is often known as the council, or the city council. It makes the ordinances, or laws, for a city. It is the mayor's duty to see that the laws are enforced. The mayor and the council members are elected by the people.

Some cities are run by a group of elected people called commissioners. Each commissioner is the head of a city department. The mayor is the chief commissioner.

Many cities are run partly by a city manager. Such a manager has special training in handling city business. A city manager is hired by the city council and must make sure that its ideas are carried out.

Cities hire many other women and men to give services to the citizens. Some plan parks and gardens. Assessors help in setting taxes. Sanitation workers collect the garbage, repair sewers, and run street sweepers. Inspectors check the water supply, restaurants, and elevators. Teachers, police officers, fire fighters, and some bus drivers are city employees.

Sometimes young people visit their local

City Hall. There they can learn some things about how city business is carried on. They may attend some meetings that are open to the public. Such a visit helps to show how local government works.

Students take part in government

Perhaps you help with "government" at your school. You do if you suggest some of the rules, or "laws," that are made for your school. You also help if you have a part in seeing that the rules are enforced.

Some classes help govern themselves. They elect officers. They talk over problems that develop on the school grounds and in the halls and classrooms. They try to solve the problems. These classrooms

Each major political party selects its candidate for President at a national meeting called a convention.

have a kind of democracy. Democracy means that people govern themselves.

When you become 18 years old, you will be able to vote. Then you will have a part in choosing local, state, and national leaders. In time you may even be elected to an office. You may hold an office in your city. You may become a state or national government leader. Or you may be appointed to a job in government.

You can start now to be a good citizen. You can work to keep democracy strong by taking part in school government. Democracy is an important part of the American way.

Choose the correct ending

Copy on paper each of the following sentences with the correct ending.

1. The United States plan of government is called (the Bill of Rights.) (the Constitution.) (the National Archives.)
2. The purpose of the legislative branch is (to make laws.) (to carry out laws.) (to interpret laws.)
3. The purpose of the executive branch is (to make laws.) (to carry out laws.) (to interpret laws.)
4. The purpose of the judicial branch is (to make laws.) (to carry out laws.) (to interpret laws.)
5. The lawmaking body in most states is called (the Supreme Court.) (the executive body.) (the legislature.)
6. The number of Representatives a state sends to Congress depends on (population.) (location.) (wealth.)
7. The official home of the President is (the Mall.) (the White House.) (the Capitol.)
8. The plan of government for each state is (a constitution.) (a legislature.) (a democracy.)
9. Each state has a (manager.) (governor.) (president.)

What do you think?

1. What is a democracy? What rights do the people of a democracy enjoy? What responsibilities must they take to keep their government a democracy? What are some advantages of living in a democracy?
2. What does it mean for a person to have a political career? Would you like to plan for this kind of career? If so, why?

Things to do

1. Learn more about your state and its early settlers. Use the Tables for Reference at the end of the book to find out when your state entered the Union. Find out all you can about your state's flag. Locate your state capital on the map on pages 254-255. Learn who your governor is. Find out how many Representatives and Senators your state sends to Washington. What are the names of your Senators? What is the name of the Representative from your area?
2. Use library books and travel pamphlets to find out more about Washington, D.C. Then choose five places you would like to visit there. Tell why you would like to visit each one. If you have visited Washington, tell the class about five of your favorite places.
3. Many people are hired by the national, state, and local governments. They are in hundreds of types of jobs. A few are listed below. Choose one and find out as much as you can about it. Then write a job-wanted ad for that job. Maybe you can find such ads in your local newspaper.

presidential aide	driver's license examiner
secretary	milk inspector
Supreme Court Justice	city manager
White House gardener	zoo keeper
White House chef	assistant to the mayor
White House guide	chief of police
employee at state tourist information center	tax assessor
	elevator inspector

Looking at our great nation

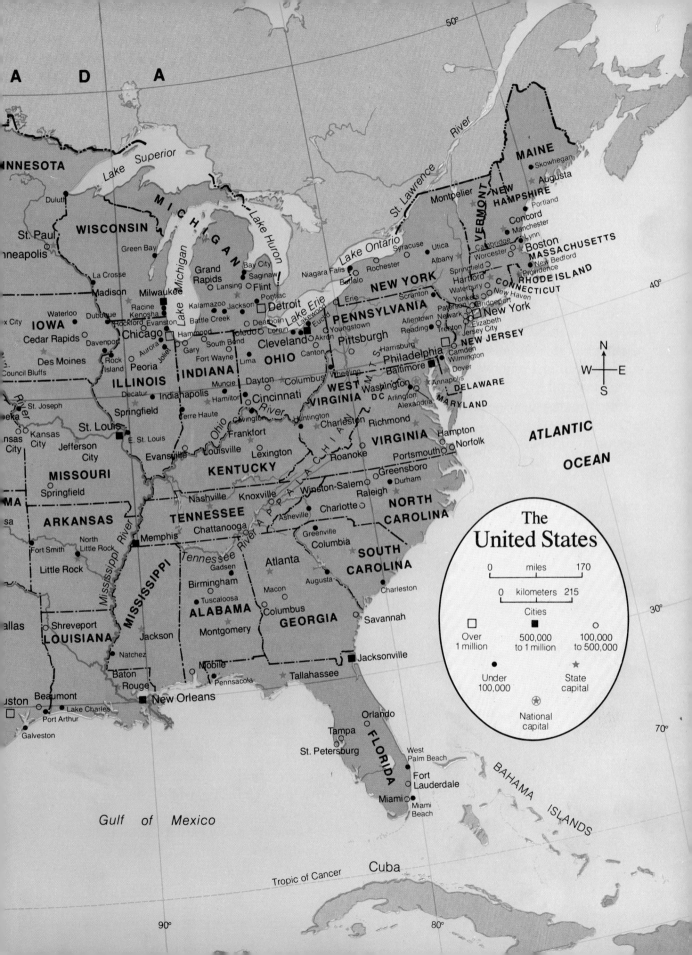

CAN A D A

MINNESOTA

Lake Superior

Duluth

St. Paul
nneapolis

WISCONSIN

MICHIGAN

Lake Huron

Green Bay

La Crosse

Madison
Milwaukee

Racine
Kenosha

Grand
Rapids

Bay City
Saginaw

Lansing

Flint

Pontiac

Detroit

Lake Michigan

IOWA
x City

Cedar Rapids

Waterloo

Dubuque

Rockford Evanston

Davenport

Rock
Island

Des Moines

Council Bluffs

Chicago

Aurora

Joliet

Peoria

Gary

South Bend

Hammond

Kalamazoo

Jackson

Battle Creek

Dearborn

Lorain

Toledo

Lakewood

Euclid

Cleveland

Akron

Canton

Youngstown

OHIO

Fort Wayne

Lima

INDIANA

Muncie

Dayton

Columbus

Wheeling

ILLINOIS

Decatur

Indianapolis

Hamilton

Cincinnati

WEST
VIRGINIA

Springfield

Terre Haute

St. Joseph
eka

Kansas
City
as City

St. Louis

E. St. Louis

Covington

Ohio

River

Frankfort

Huntington

Charleston

Jefferson
City

Evansville

Louisville

Lexington

KENTUCKY

Richmond

Roanoke

VIRGINIA

MISSOURI

Springfield

Nashville

Knoxville

Winston-Salem

Greensboro

Durham

Raleigh

NORTH
CAROLINA

Portsmouth

Hampton

Norfolk

MA
a

ARKANSAS

TENNESSEE

Chattanooga

Asheville

Charlotte

Memphis

Tennessee

River

Greenville

Columbia

SOUTH
CAROLINA

Fort Smith

North
Little Rock

Little Rock

MISSISSIPPI

Gadsen

Atlanta

Macon

Augusta

Charleston

Birmingham

Tuscaloosa

ALABAMA

Columbus

GEORGIA

Savannah

Mississippi River

Jackson

Montgomery

allas

Shreveport

LOUISIANA

Natchez

Mobile

Pennsacola

Tallahassee

Jacksonville

Baton
Rouge

uston

Beaumont

Lake Charles

New Orleans

Port Arthur

Galveston

Orlando

Tampa

St. Petersburg

FLORIDA

West
Palm Beach

Fort
Lauderdale

Miami

Miami
Beach

Gulf   of   Mexico

BAHAMA

ISLANDS

Tropic of Cancer

Cuba

St. Lawrence

River

MAINE

Skowhegan

Augusta

Montpelier

VERMONT

NEW
HAMPSHIRE

Portland

Concord

Manchester

Lynn

Cambridge

Boston

MASSACHUSETTS

Worcester

New Bedford

Springfield

Providence

Syracuse

Utica

Rochester

Albany

Hartford

RHODE ISLAND

CONNECTICUT

Niagara Falls

Buffalo

NEW YORK

Erie

Scranton

Waterbury

New Haven

Bridgeport

New York

PENNSYLVANIA

Allentown

Paterson

Newark

Elizabeth

Reading

Trenton

Jersey City

Harrisburg

Pittsburgh

NEW JERSEY

Philadelphia

Camden

Baltimore

Wilmington

Dover

DELAWARE

Washington

Annapolis

D C

Arlington

Alexandria

MARYLAND

APPALACHIAN MTS.

ATLANTIC

OCEAN

N
W   E
S

50°

40°

30°

70°

80°

90°

The United States

0	miles	170

0	kilometers	215

Cities

Over 1 million	500,000 to 1 million	100,000 to 500,000
□	■	○

Under 100,000	State capital
•	★

National capital ⊛

19

New England: from textiles to electronics

An exciting new industry: electronics

John and his parents were visiting his aunt in Boston. She was Dr. Roberts. She runs her own business. They were talking about careers.

"I don't know what I want to be," said John.

"Most fifth graders don't know," answered his aunt. "Even if you did, you might change your mind. Later on, you might choose a career that isn't even thought of today."

John looked surprised.

Dr. Roberts continued. "New kinds of jobs open up every year, John. Hundreds of them! When I was in fifth grade, my company didn't exist. It makes computers to help explore space."

"Computers!" said John. "I'm interested in them. They work like magic, don't they?"

"Yes, they do!" replied Dr. Roberts. "They are the magicians of our modern industry."

The computer, an electronic wonder, can do many jobs. Much work is being done to find new uses for electric energy. This work has made the electronics industry. Computers are a part of this industry.

A computer can work hard math problems in a flash. It can add thousands of numbers in a second.

Computers are used in stores, banks, offices, and factories. Computers help run our schools and libraries. Some work for airlines and railroads. Computers help prepare weather news for radio and TV. They guide spaceships. Some set type for printing books and newspapers.

Some amazing computers can "tell" other machines what to do. At a bakery, for example, a special kind of computer may be used. It will "tell" a machine to measure milk, butter, and eggs to be put in a mixing machine.

Computers can't think, however. No, indeed! Trained experts must tell them what to do. Experts must feed much information into the machine before it can go to work. Thousands of skilled people are needed.

There are many careers in the electronics industry. If you like math, a job with computers may interest you. A person may start to work with computers in high

Airlines use computers to help make passenger reservations.

school. But many jobs call for a college education. One kind of job is called computer programing. The worker writes directions for the computer to follow in solving problems. These could be problems about pollution, population growth, or space travel.

The making of electronic products is a booming business today. The Boston area turns out millions of dollars worth each year. So there are also many factory jobs. There are jobs in making and assembling the parts needed in electronic products.

A look at New England

New England's six states make up a small region. Its area is a little less than the state of Washington.

New England has a long coast on the Atlantic Ocean. This coast is a ragged one, as the map shows. It has many harbors, large and small.

Much of this coast is rocky. It is dotted with lighthouses that warn ships away from danger spots. The oldest lighthouse was built just two years after George Washington became the first President of the United States.

Most of New England is mountainous or hilly. The relief map on pages 90–91 shows this. Along the New England coast are low hills. Some have rocky cliffs that border the sea. Inland, the hills become much higher.

Western New England has many low mountains. They stretch in long chains from north to south. What ranges do you see on the map? New England's hills and mountains are a part of the Appalachian Mountains.

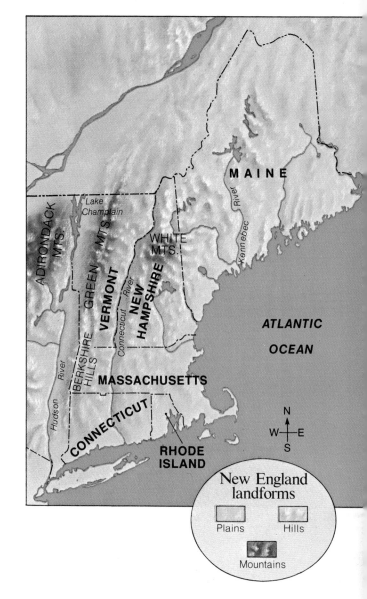

New England landforms

Plains   Hills

Mountains

New England has hundreds of lakes and streams. Lake Champlain (sham-plān′) between Vermont and New York, is the largest lake. It is named for a French explorer who visited Vermont in the 1600s.

The lakes are fed by small streams that flow from the hills and mountains. From the lakes flow other streams that meet to form rivers. In New England the rivers don't have to go far to reach the ocean. As they rush down through the hilly lands, they form rapids and falls. The winding Connecticut is the largest river in this region.

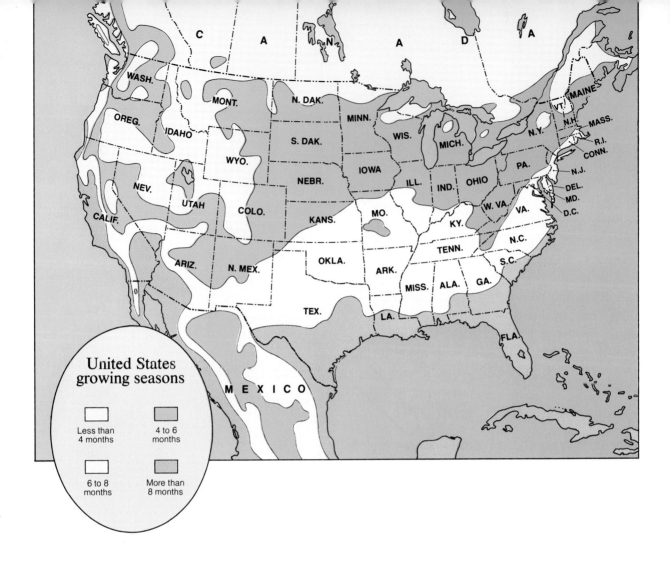

United States
growing seasons

Less than 4 months

4 to 6 months

6 to 8 months

More than 8 months

What do the maps show about climate in New England? Climate is the kind of weather a place has over a long period of time. The map above shows the length of the growing season.

You know that as a rule the lands to the north have a cooler climate than those near the equator have. And highlands have a cooler climate than lowlands have in the same area.

The *growing season* is the length of time crops can grow because of weather. It begins when the spring frosts have ended. It lasts until the fall frosts come.

Northern New England has a growing season of less than four months. We know, then, that its winters are long and cold.

About how long can plants grow in southern New England?

Snow may fall in early November in New England. This region can expect icy winds and snowstorms from December to March or April.

New England's summers are pleasantly warm. But generally the weather is not as hot as in many other parts of the United States. For one thing, New England is located quite far north. Also, it is often cooled by ocean breezes and cool air from Canada.

Now look at the rainfall map. How much rain does most of New England get in a year? New England gets plenty of rain for growing crops.

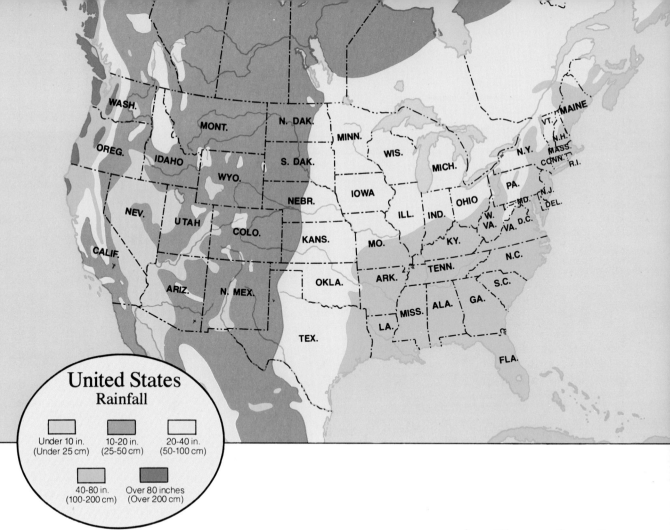

United States
Rainfall

Under 10 in. (Under 25 cm)	10-20 in. (25-50 cm)	20-40 in. (50-100 cm)
40-80 in. (100-200 cm)	Over 80 inches (Over 200 cm)	

Earning a living from soil and sea

New England produces a variety of farm crops. Some farmers supply city markets with chickens, turkeys, and ducks, as well as eggs. Other farmers grow vegetables. Vermont has many dairy farms. Milk companies buy the milk and sell it to stores. Some milk is used for making butter, cheese, and ice cream.

Berries and other kinds of fruit are raised. Many hillsides are lined with rows of apple trees. Apples grow well in the cool climate.

Certain sections of New England are famous for special crops. Vermont has many sugar maples. The sap from these trees is used to make maple syrup and sugar.

Northeastern Maine produces many potatoes. Tobacco grows in the Connecticut River Valley. Some of Cape Cod's lowlands produce cranberries.

Many river valleys and lowlands in New England have deep rich soil. But most of New England is not suited for farming.

Many early New Englanders tried to farm. They cut down trees and planted crops between the stumps. But much of the land was too hilly to plow and the soil was full of stones.

Settlers cleared stones from their farms. The stones were piled up in "walls" at the edge of the fields. Miles of low stone walls can still be seen.

The farmers worked hard and raised

259

New England fishing fleets have made villages like this one their home base since colonial times.

enough food for the people of New England. But many people found other ways to make a living.

Some early New Englanders turned to fishing. They learned that the waters off their coast were rich with cod. Settlers soon depended on fish for a part of their food. As time passed, some New Englanders earned their living at fishing.

For a time, catching whales was a major activity. The whales were hunted for their oil. In those days whale oil was used in many lamps.

Fishing is still an important industry in New England. It is carried on chiefly along the *banks*. A shelf of sunken land lies off the east coast. Large parts of this shelf rise to form underwater hills and plateaus known as banks. The waters are quite shallow here. They are good places for fish to find food.

Today most of the fishing boats are trawlers. They drag nets through the sea and catch many fish at one time. A trawler may be back with a full load of fish a week after it sets out.

Other fishing takes place near the shores. Lobsters are caught in wooden traps sunk in the water. Clams are dug from the mud when the tide is low.

The fishing industry gives work to thousands of people. Some make and repair nets. Many work in the fish canneries and freezing plants. The chief fishing ports are Gloucester (glos′tər), Boston, New Bedford, and Portland. Locate these cities on the map of the New England states.

CANADA

NEW
BRUNSWICK

QUEBEC

Moosehead
Lake

MAINE

Penobscot River

• Bangor

Rangeley
Lakes

Kennebec River

Androscoggin River

Lake
Champlain

VERMONT

• Burlington

Montpelier •
• Barre

WHITE

▲ Mt. Washington
6,288 ft., 1917 m

Auburn •
• Lewiston

Augusta

MOUNTAINS

NEW

Lake
George

MOUNTAINS

HAMPSHIRE

Portland

ATLANTIC

• Rutland

Connecticut River

Lake
Winnipesaukee

• Biddeford

NEW

Concord ✪

OCEAN

YORK

GREEN

Manchester •
• Portsmouth

Bennington
• Brattleboro

Nashua •

• Lawrence

BERKSHIRE

Lowell •
Lexington •

• Gloucester

Merrimack River

Concord ••
Somerville ○
Boston

• Lynn

HILLS

MASSACHUSETTS

Worcester ○

Newton ○

Cambridge

Springfield ○

Plymouth
Pawtucket •

Cape
Cod
Bay

Cape
Cod

CONNECTICUT

Providence •

RHODE

Hartford ✪
• New Britain

• Fall River
• New Bedford

ISLAND

Hudson River

Waterbury ○

New Haven •

Martha's Vineyard

Bridgeport •
Norwalk ○
Stamford ○

Sound

Island

Nantucket Island

Long

Long Island

☐
New York

New
England states

0   miles   145

0   kilometers   185

Cities

☐
Over 1
million

○
100,000
to 1,000,000

●
Under
100,000

★
State capital

New England was an early center for the textile industry. This woman is working at a spinning frame.

Forest products provide jobs and income

New England has about five times as much land in forests as in farms. More than half of this land is in Maine.

In colonial times lumbering was a major industry of New England. In the early 1700s one small river in New Hampshire supplied water for 70 sawmills. They turned out six million feet of lumber a year.

Much lumber was sent to England. And much was used for building ships in New England. Some workers who were skillful

with tools built ships and fishing boats. In time, New England became famous for its strong, handsome sailing ships.

Today lumber and wood pulp for paper-making bring in money. The many fine forests also help to attract tourists.

Manufacturing in New England

New England's manufacturing began in colonial days. The first "factory" was built in Rhode Island about ten years after the War for Independence. It was a mill that had machines for spinning cotton into thread.

The British had invented spinning and weaving machines. They started the first textile mills. These mills could make cloth very cheaply. So cloth making became a big business in Britain. Laws were passed to protect this business. No one could send machines or drawings of them out of Britain. Trained workers were not allowed to leave the country. But one did. His name was Samuel Slater.

Slater had worked in a cotton mill in Britain. He tended a wonderful new machine. It could spin as much thread in a day as a person could in three months. He learned all he could and became the manager of the mill.

Young Slater wanted to come to America. He knew that New Englanders wanted to start cotton mills. Some business people could pay well to have spinning machines built. They had money from fishing and trade.

Sam Slater pretended to be a farm worker. Then he slipped on board ship. When he got to New York, he heard of

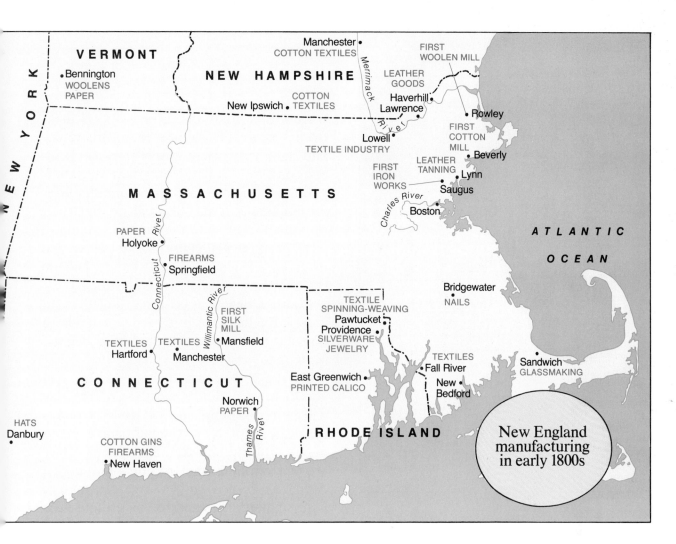

Map labels:

VERMONT

NEW YORK

NEW HAMPSHIRE

Manchester
COTTON TEXTILES

• Bennington
WOOLENS
PAPER

FIRST
WOOLEN MILL

LEATHER
GOODS

New Ipswich • COTTON
TEXTILES

Haverhill
Lawrence

• Rowley

Merrimack River

Lowell
TEXTILE INDUSTRY

FIRST
COTTON
MILL

• Beverly

MASSACHUSETTS

FIRST
IRON
WORKS

LEATHER
TANNING

• Lynn
Saugus

Charles River

Boston

ATLANTIC

OCEAN

PAPER
Holyoke •

Connecticut River

FIREARMS
Springfield •

Bridgewater
NAILS

Willimantic River

FIRST
SILK
MILL

TEXTILE
SPINNING-WEAVING
Pawtucket •
Providence
SILVERWARE
JEWELRY

TEXTILES
Hartford •

TEXTILES
• Manchester

• Mansfield

TEXTILES
• Fall River

CONNECTICUT

East Greenwich •
PRINTED CALICO

New •
Bedford

Sandwich
GLASSMAKING

Norwich •
PAPER

Thames River

RHODE ISLAND

New England
manufacturing
in early 1800s

HATS
Danbury
•

COTTON GINS
FIREARMS
• New Haven

someone who wanted spinning machines built. Slater wrote a letter offering to build such machines from memory.

Slater's memory served him well. Within a few months he had set up his machines in a spinning mill beside a river.

Water power ran the machines. Falling water turned the mill's big wheel. As the wheel turned round and round, it ran the machines that spun the thread.

Business people were pleased that the thread could be made so fast. Soon, weaving machines were built. Then spinning and weaving mills sprang up all over New England.

In time, New England had more textile factories than any other part of our country. That is not true today. Many textile mills are now located in the South.

As time passed, factories of many kinds were started. The map shows the many products made in New England in the early 1800s. By 1860 New England was the leading manufacturing area of our country. It had much water power. It had a long coast with many good harbors. Ships could bring in raw materials and carry away finished goods. Also, New England had many workers. Quite a number had recently come from Ireland.

In the years that followed, people from many countries came to work in New England. Italians and French Canadians arrived. So did people from Poland, Germany, and Russia. Many of these people were Jews. Portuguese newcomers settled

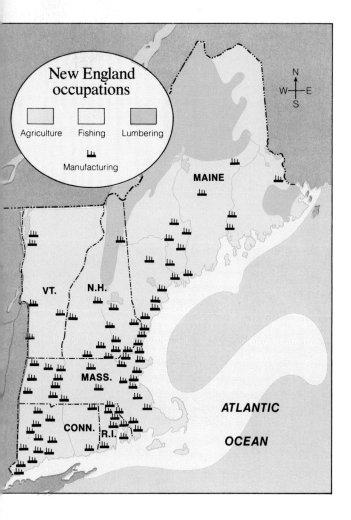

New England occupations

Agriculture Fishing Lumbering

Manufacturing

MAINE

VT.   N.H.

MASS.

CONN.   R.I.

ATLANTIC

OCEAN

The Boston area is famous for its electronic products. Among them are X-ray and radar equipment, computers, and calculators.

Calculators belong to the computer family. A calculator may be small enough to fit in your pocket. Even so, it can calculate, or work, math problems quickly. Have you used one? The map at the left shows where the different kinds of work are done.

Many cities are crowded together in New England. So it is hard to tell where one city ends and the next one begins. Many people live here.

What does the map on page 187 tell you about New England's population? The key will help you find out. The thickly populated areas of New England have many manufacturing and trading centers. They are metropolitan (met'rə pol'ə tən) areas. A *metropolitan area* is a large central city with smaller cities and towns around it.

Boston is New England's largest metropolitan area. More than 70 cities and towns make up metropolitan Boston. Find Boston on the map on page 261. Notice that it is a seaport on Massachusetts Bay. It also is a land and air transportation center. Railroads, highways, and air routes connect it with other parts of our country.

A manufacturing and trading center needs banks. Boston has dozens of them. Business firms need a bank for borrowing money. A business also must have a safe place to keep its money. Can you think of other ways that a business uses a bank?

Boston also has many *wholesale* businesses. They buy raw materials and finished products from producers. Then the wholesalers sell these products to *retail* stores or other business firms. Retail

in seaports. The men were expert at fishing. Many Portuguese women were skilled workers in plants that processed fish.

Manufacturing is the leader in New England today. Thousands of people earn their living working in factories and mills.

New England is known for the production of shoes and other leather goods. Tableware, jewelry, sports trophies, and fine silverware are made here. Workers also make cameras and medical instruments. There are other products from pins and needles to jet engines and nuclear submarines.

New England makes paper goods. And it publishes books. This book you are reading was published there.

264

Among the historic sights of Boston are "Old Ironsides" and the Old State House. "Old Ironsides" is the nickname of the *Constitution,* a famous ship of Revolutionary War days. The Old State House was the center of colonial Boston.

stores sell to all people who come to buy. There are many careers in the banking and wholesale fields.

Boston is a government and educational center. Boston is the capital of Massachusetts. Much of the state government's business is carried on there. Many people work there for the United States government and for the city of Boston too.

Metropolitan Boston is a famous educational area. There are many colleges and universities here. They provide career training and jobs for people in business, science, trades, and education.

Like every city, Boston offers jobs for people who provide services. They include taxi drivers, mechanics, dentists, reporters, lawyers, barbers, plumbers, and many others.

Another industry: caring for tourists

Caring for tourists is another main way of earning a living. Many people from other parts of the country vacation in New England. This means jobs in providing food, places to stay, and other services.

Some tourists enjoy camping and fishing. Others like the seashore. In the winter, tourists go to New England to ski. Boston attracts many sightseers.

Boston is a fascinating old and new city to visit. Some of its buildings date back to the days of the colonies. On one narrow street is Old North Church. In its belfry

Boston's historic Faneuil Hall and Quincy Market are now part of a very popular shopping center.

Paul Revere's friend hung a lantern to warn that the British were coming.

The Boston Common was once a pasture set aside for cattle. It is hard to imagine that now. Today it is a fine park. Under part of the Boston Common is a huge underground parking garage.

Boston has some old and narrow streets, and some broad new avenues. It has fine new buildings. Some old ones have been rebuilt into homes, shops, and offices. Part of this *urban renewal* has been sponsored by the Christian Science Church. Its main offices are in Boston. This church was started by Mary Baker Eddy in 1879.

Near Boston are exciting reminders of our country's past. As a tourist you can visit Plymouth, where the Pilgrims landed in 1620. At Cambridge you can see the grounds and buildings of Harvard University. Nearby is the home of William Wadsworth Longfellow, the poet who wrote "The Midnight Ride of Paul Revere."

If you drive northwest of Boston, you soon reach Lexington and then Concord. There the first shots of the War for Independence were fired. Louisa May Alcott lived in Concord. She wrote *Little Women* and other books for children.

Many tourists take a boat from Cape Cod to Nantucket Island. They see houses where some of the daring New England sea captains lived in the 1800s. Here, as a child, Maria Mitchell started to study the stars and planets. She won a gold medal from the king of Denmark for discovering a comet.

Choose the correct ending

On paper, write each of the following sentences with its correct ending.

1. Most of New England is (hilly.) (plains country.) (lowlands.)
2. The largest New England state is (Massachusetts.) (Maine.) (Vermont.)
3. Some farmers in Maine grow large quantities of (potatoes.) (wheat.) (corn.)
4. Some lowlands on Cape Cod produce many (cranberries.) (potatoes.) (vegetables.)
5. Vermont is famous for its (codfish.) (maple sugar.) (sugar beets.)
6. The largest river in New England is (the Ohio.) (the Connecticut.) (the Hudson.)
7. New England is noted for its (electronic goods.) (steel.) (glass.)
8. A central city together with nearby cities and suburbs is (a rural area.) (a metropolitan area.) (a seaport area.)

Some other things to do

1. List some things that are manufactured near your home today.
2. See if your class can visit a factory. Be ready to discuss what you see.
3. Use an encyclopedia or other reference materials to learn more about the electronics industry. Summarize what you learn and share it.
4. Turn to the map on page 258. Study the key. Tell what part of New England has the shortest growing season. Tell which has the longer growing season, southern Maine or the area in which you live.

Interviewing

One way to get more information about a topic is to *interview,* or talk, to an expert.

Plan for your interview by reading about the topic first. Learn all you can about it. Then make a list of questions to ask during your interview.

Begin your interview by introducing yourself. Then you will want to tell what your class is studying. Be ready to ask the questions you have prepared. Listen carefully without taking notes. You cannot write as fast as a person talks. After the interview, write the main facts you learned and be ready to share them with the class.

Find out all you can about one kind of career suggested in this chapter. Read in another book to get helpful information. Also interview someone who is working in the field that interests you. Organize your notes in outline form. Be ready to talk over what you learn with your class.

How, what, and why?

1. How is New England different from the part of our country where you live?
2. What is the most important industry in your community? Why did it become important?
3. Why are computers used today? How and where are calculators used?
4. If you could go on vacation to New England, how would you travel? What would you take along? What places would you visit?

20

The Middle Atlantic states

New York is an important part of the megalopolis that spreads across the northeastern part of our country.

Meeting a megalopolis

Jean was taking her first airplane trip. The family was flying from Maine to Philadelphia. Her parents made sure that she had a seat by the window.

At first the plane flew over forests and lakes. Once in a while, Jean saw a town.

Then the scenes began to change. There were more towns and cities, but thin clouds nearly hid them. Then Jean saw a giant city that spread out in every direction. You can share her view by looking at the photo on this page.

"How different this is from Maine!" Jean said. "What a huge city! It seems to go on and on!"

"You're looking at a megalopolis," replied her mother.

"A what?" asked Jean.

"A meg-a-lop-o-lis," her mother repeated. "*Megalopolis* means great city. This one extends from southern New Hampshire to southern Virginia. It is about 500 miles long."

Look at the population map on page 187. See how thickly settled the area is from southern New Hampshire to southern Virginia. Some big cities are shown: Boston, Providence, New York, Philadelphia, Baltimore, Washington, Richmond, and Norfolk. But there are far more towns and cities than the map can show.

A megalopolis is not a single city, however. There are towns and cities, one after another. They are joined by railroads and highways.

For years, these towns and cities were separated by countryside. Between them were farms and patches of "woods." This is still true of some. But many towns and cities have grown close together. They seem to be one great city.

This megalopolis extends long distances through the Middle Atlantic states.

What are these states like?

There are seven states in the Middle Atlantic region. Find them on the map on page 269. Notice that they are New York, Pennsylvania, New Jersey, Delaware, Maryland, Virginia, and West Virginia.

Middle Atlantic States

miles 0 — 80
kilometers 0 — 100

Cities

□ Over 1 million ■ 500,000 to 1 million ○ 100,000 to 500,000 ● Under 100,000

★ State capital ☆ National capital 〰 Barge canal

CANADA

Lake Huron

Lake Ontario

Lake Erie

Niagara R.
Niagara Falls
Niagara Falls
Buffalo

Rochester

New York State Barge Canal

Syracuse
Utica
Schenectady
Albany
Troy

Mohawk R.

St. Lawrence River

Lake Champlain

VT.

N.H.

MASS.

Connecticut R.

CONN.

NEW YORK

Hudson R.

Watertown

Erie

Elmira
Binghamton

Poughkeepsie

OHIO

Allegheny River

PENNSYLVANIA

Susquehanna River

Scranton
Wilkes-Barre

Delaware R.

Mount Vernon
Paterson
Jersey City
Newark
Bayonne

New York City

New York Bay

Long Island Sound
Long Island

Pittsburgh
McKeesport

Altoona
Johnstown

Harrisburg
Lancaster
York

Easton
Bethlehem
Allentown

Reading

NEW JERSEY

Trenton

Philadelphia

Chester
Camden
Wilmington

Atlantic City

Wheeling

Monongahela River

Ohio River

Clarksburg

Cumberland

Hagerstown

Potomac River

MARYLAND

Baltimore

Dover

DELAWARE

Delaware Bay

COASTAL PLAIN

WEST VIRGINIA

Huntington
Charleston

APPALACHIAN

GREAT VALLEY

CENTRAL
BLUE RIDGE

Shenandoah River

Arlington
Alexandria

Annapolis
Washington

Chesapeake Bay

ATLANTIC OCEAN

KY.

James River

Roanoke

VIRGINIA

PIEDMONT

Richmond

Williamsburg
Petersburg

Portsmouth
Norfolk

Danville

NORTH CAROLINA

N
W—E
S

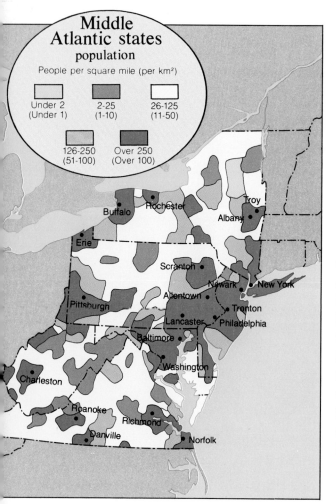

Middle Atlantic states
population

People per square mile (per km²)

Under 2 (Under 1)	2-25 (1-10)	26-125 (11-50)
126-250 (51-100)	Over 250 (Over 100)	

Buffalo · Rochester · Troy · Albany
Erie
Scranton · Newark · New York · Allentown · Trenton · Lancaster · Philadelphia
Pittsburgh · Baltimore · Washington
Charleston · Roanoke · Richmond · Danville · Norfolk

Population maps show how thickly settled various areas are. Trace the Washington, Baltimore, Philadelphia, New York megalopolis on this population map of the Middle Atlantic states. How many people are there per square mile in this megalopolis? How many are there per square kilometer?

The District of Columbia is also in this Middle Atlantic region. It is not in a state. It is between Maryland and Virginia.

The Middle Atlantic region has hundreds of cities and towns. It has almost one-fourth of the people of the United States. The map above shows how thickly settled it is. It has many factories and other businesses that provide millions of jobs.

This part of our country has large bays along the coast. One is New York Bay. Find it on the map on page 269 of the Middle Atlantic States. What large city is on it? Locate Delaware Bay and see how it is the gateway to Philadelphia. Now find Chesapeake Bay. It is the largest bay on the Atlantic coast from Maine to Florida.

Point to the long piece of land between Delaware Bay and Chesapeake Bay. It is a peninsula. Its lands are low and flat and have many farms.

Sandy beaches extend along the seacoast. In the summer thousands of people go to the beaches.

The Middle Atlantic region has some important plains and mountains. Find the Atlantic Coastal Plain on the map on pages 90-91. It is almost as flat as a table. This plain is quite narrow near New York City. But it widens toward the south. It has deep soils and a fairly mild climate, so many crops can be grown.

Plains also follow along Lake Ontario and Lake Erie. Find them on the same map. There are many farms there.

West of the coastal plain is the hilly Piedmont. On the same map see how the Piedmont lies between the Atlantic Coastal

Plain and the Appalachians. The word Piedmont means "at the foot of the mountains." The Piedmont is a belt of hilly lands. There are green valleys, wooded slopes, and many farms in this region.

Between the Piedmont and the coastal plain is the fall line. On the map notice that the *fall line* marks the end of the coastal plain. At this place are the first waterfalls as you go up the rivers. Imagine that you are on a boat going up a river from the coast. The water would be smooth through the coastal plain. But then you would reach some waterfalls, and the boat could go no farther. This is the fall line.

The fall line of the James River in Virginia is at Richmond. This was a good place to start a town. There, cargo from farms and forests could be loaded on boats for the coast. And boats carrying cargo inland had to stop here for unloading. It is one reason that fall-line towns grew into trading centers. Notice some other fall-line cities: Washington, Baltimore, Wilmington, Philadelphia, and Trenton.

Towns on the fall line grew for another main reason. The falls provided water power. You know how the colonists in New England put the power of rushing water to work. It was used to run grain and textile mills. This was also true in the Middle Atlantic region. Many mills and factories were built beside the falls. Water power helped the towns on the fall line to grow into busy manufacturing cities. Busy highways and railroads follow along this fall line to connect the cities.

The Appalachian Mountains rise west of the Piedmont. Notice on the map on pages 90-91 how the mountains run southwestward. They stretch from New Eng-

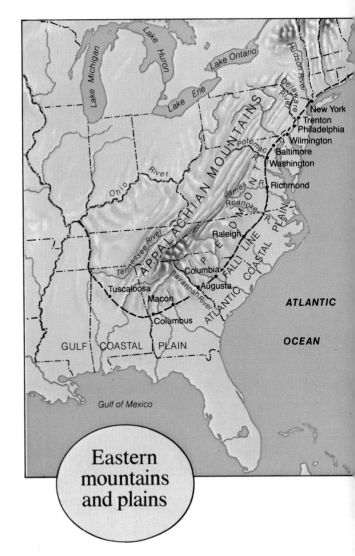

Eastern mountains and plains

land to Alabama. They include many ranges of rounded, worn-down mountains.

The highest peaks are about 6000 feet (1800 m) high. They rise in long ranges, one after another. Their slopes are covered with forests. There are few low passes in the ridges. Between the long ridges are deep valleys. One of these valleys is called the Great Valley.

The Great Valley extends through the Appalachians for many miles. It begins in southeastern New York and continues to the middle of Alabama. It is one of the longest valleys in the world.

The Great Valley has fertile soil. Its farms produce fine crops. Coal and limestone are found in some parts of this valley.

271

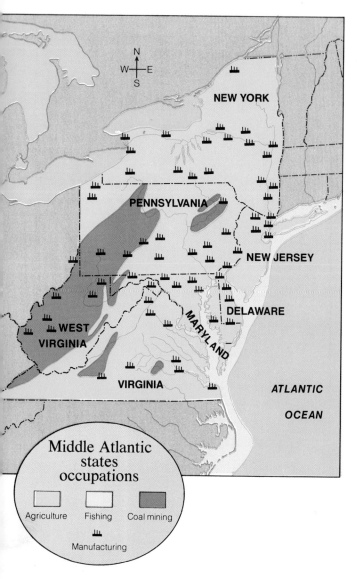

N
W–E
S

NEW YORK

PENNSYLVANIA

NEW JERSEY

DELAWARE

WEST VIRGINIA

MARYLAND

VIRGINIA

ATLANTIC OCEAN

Middle Atlantic states occupations

| Agriculture | Fishing | Coal mining |

Manufacturing

The map of occupations in these states shows where the different kinds of work are done. Why is each kind of work done where it is?

Important rivers flow through the Middle Atlantic states. You found several on the map when you looked at the fall line. The largest rivers are the Hudson, the Delaware, and the Susquehanna (sus′kwə-han′ə). Locate them on the map. Notice how each enters the Atlantic Ocean through a large bay. Each one serves as a main water highway.

The Hudson begins in the mountains. It flows south through hills and plains and ends at New York Bay.

Pioneers pushed north on the Hudson and west on the Mohawk River to settle new lands. On the map you can see that the Mohawk is a branch of the Hudson. Together, the Hudson and the Mohawk valleys form a pathway through the Appalachians. The Erie Canal cuts through the Mohawk Valley.

South of the Hudson is the Delaware River. William Penn and his Quaker friends sailed up the Delaware to start the city of Philadelphia. Today many freighters follow this river to Philadelphia. Some bring raw materials for factories. They carry away manufactured goods.

The Susquehanna River winds through Pennsylvania. This river flows into Chesapeake Bay.

Two great lakes and Niagara Falls face this region. The lakes, Ontario and Erie, are a part of the Great Lakes inland waterway. Large freighters travel across the lakes and through connecting rivers and canals. They carry raw materials, such as iron ore and wheat. They go to Buffalo,

Some iron ore is also mined. Iron ore, coal, and limestone are used in making steel.

Highways and railroads lead through the Great Valley. Trucks and railroads haul farm and mine products to factories and markets.

West of the mountains are more highland areas. Find them on the map on page 271. Through what states do they extend?

These highlands have many rich farms. But coal mining is one of the main industries. Large stores of coal are buried beneath the surface of this region. Many people earn their living as coal miners.

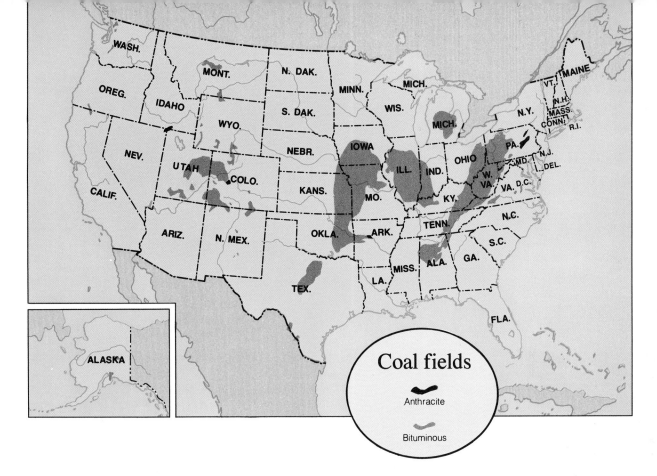

Coal fields

Anthracite

Bituminous

Cleveland, Erie, and other busy lake ports.

By working together, Canada and the United States made this useful waterway still more valuable. Parts of the St. Lawrence River were deepened. Also, canals between the lakes were improved. Ships can now travel from the Atlantic Ocean to any of the Great Lakes on this St. Lawrence Seaway.

The map of the Middle Atlantic states on page 269 shows that the Niagara River links Lake Erie and Lake Ontario. But the mighty Niagara Falls keeps ships from using this river route.

What kind of climate is found in the Middle Atlantic states? Let's refer to the maps on pages 258 and 259. The rainfall map shows that these states get plenty of rain. The growing season map shows that the coastal plain and the Piedmont have quite a long growing season. How long is it? Is it longer or shorter than New England's growing season?

Coal mining and steel manufacturing

Much coal is mined in the Appalachian region. The coal is found in layers under the ground. A large area of coal deposits is called a *coal field*. Find the coal fields on the map above. Large fields stretch across most of western Pennsylvania and West Virginia.

There are two main kinds of coal. One is *bituminous,* or soft coal. When it is burned, a heavy black smoke pours out. The other kind is *anthracite,* or hard coal. It burns with less smoke. Which kind of coal is more plentiful in our country? Look at the map to find out.

Some coal lies deep below the earth's surface. To mine it, *shafts* are usually cut

273

straight down to the layers of coal. Then tunnels are dug out from this shaft. The miners dig coal in these tunnels. An elevator carries the miners to and from their place of work. Elevators also carry the coal to the surface.

In some soft-coal mines a tunnel is cut into the layers of coal from the side of a hill. The coal is loaded on small railroad cars and brought to the tunnel entrance.

When coal deposits are close to the surface of the earth, strip mining is used. Giant machines remove the earth that covers the coal. Then the coal is broken up and loaded onto trucks. Strip mining damages the land. Laws now require mining companies to level the land and plant trees or ground cover.

Coal, limestone, and iron ore are used in making iron and steel. You learned that this region has deposits of coal and limestone. The early settlers also found some iron ore in Pennsylvania.

One of the largest iron-ore deposits in the world is located along the shores of Lake Superior. Much of our iron ore comes from this deposit. Boats haul the iron ore across the Great Lakes. Its ore will be unloaded and used at the steel mills.

Strip mining and deep mining are two ways of mining for coal. Strip mining is used when coal deposits lie near the surface. Deep mining is used when they are deep within the earth. Compare the pictures. Why do you think strip mining might be faster and less expensive than deep mining?

To make iron and steel, first the iron ore is melted. This is done in tall round blast furnaces. The furnace must be very hot to melt the iron from the ore. So a fuel called coke is burned. Coke is made from coal.

Iron ore, limestone, and coke pour into the red-hot blast furnace. Limestone helps to separate the iron from the waste rock. As the iron ore and the limestone melt, the heavy iron settles to the bottom. The limestone mixes with the waste rock and rises to the top.

From the bottom of the furnace comes a hot liquid called *molten iron*. Some of it is cooled in molds. It is known as *pig iron*. This may be shipped to many distant places.

Today, however, most molten iron is used to make steel. It is rushed to nearby steel mills. There it is mixed with scrap metal in hot furnaces. It becomes the strong, tough metal called steel.

Thousands of people work in the steel industry. Some of them run giant cranes. Others carry materials from place to place on lift trucks. There are many jobs for machine operators. Some run giant machines that roll the steel into sheets or bars.

The steel is checked to see that it is just right. Engineers figure out the right mix of materials for the kind of steel needed.

Office workers handle orders for raw materials and the finished products. Other people in the office prepare the paychecks. Some keep health and accident records. Some officials make safety rules and see that they are obeyed.

Steel companies employ doctors, nurses, watchmen, plumbers, carpenters, and dozens of other kinds of workers.

Many important cities

Most Middle Atlantic cities are manufacturing centers. Buffalo has flour and feed mills and a huge cereal-packing plant. Some factories make iron and steel products. The wheat and iron ore are brought in by boats.

In Schenectady (skə nek′tə dē), locomotives, washing machines, refrigerators, and many kinds of electrical goods are made. It has been called the City of Magic. Amazing new electrical discoveries are being made in laboratories. Rochester is known for its cameras, film, and copying machines. Troy produces clothing, steel, and paper. Utica makes many metal products, including parts for autos and planes.

These cities are in New York State. The map on page 269 shows you that they are all on waterways. How has this helped them grow?

Allentown, Pennsylvania, manufactures cement, trucks, and buses. Some cities in eastern Pennsylvania have textile mills.

Trenton, Camden, and Newark are three busy manufacturing cities in New Jersey. They make all kinds of products. Notice on the map that they are all port cities.

The five largest cities in this region are New York, Philadelphia, Pittsburgh, Washington, D.C., and Baltimore.

New York is the largest city in our country. New York City is made up of five sections called *boroughs*. But metropolitan New York extends far beyond them.

Manhattan is the heart of the city and the chief business center. The four other boroughs connect with Manhattan by huge bridges and by tunnels under the rivers.

New York City has famous museums and art and educational centers. Columbia University was started in colonial times. New York also is widely known for its theaters and music halls. Plays, ballets, and concerts are presented. It is a leading magazine and book publishing center. And, of course, it has thousands of factories and other businesses.

New York City is a fascinating place to visit. Let's go sightseeing. We'll take the route shown in red on the map across the page.

This tour starts on the southern tip of Manhattan Island. Across the bay on a small island is an inspiring sight. There, rising over 300 feet above the sea, is the Statue of Liberty. It was given to us by France. This statue stands at the entrance to New York harbor. The Goddess of Liberty holds her torch of freedom high.

The first stop is Wall Street. Find it on the map. This narrow street was named long ago when the Dutch built a wall there. Now, skyscrapers almost wall in this district. In them are large banks and other business firms that deal in money and trade.

We ride up Broadway. It is crowded with traffic! Everywhere we see skyscrapers. After the city used up its land on the island, it kept on growing. It grew "up" as taller and taller buildings were built.

In the distance are the tallest skyscrapers in New York. These are the twin towers of the World Trade Center. Business firms that carry on the world trade of the city have offices here.

The next stop is at the famous Empire State Building. It rises 102 stories from the street. About 25,000 people work in its offices. Fast elevators speed tourists to its top. There they have a fine view of New York City and its great harbor.

Back on Broadway, we ride through part of New York's big garment district. Much of the clothing worn in our country is made in this area.

Across Times Square is New York's theater section. At night, electric signs glow above every theater, restaurant, and shop.

On our way north up Broadway we drive past the New York Coliseum. It is a building where many trade shows are held. One big show every year features the new model cars. Also buyers for stores look at products here. Next we turn east across Central Park to Fifth Avenue. Locate Central Park on the map. It stretches for blocks between two very busy streets. It has lawns, trees, a zoo, an outdoor theater, and playgrounds.

On Fifth Avenue there are many shops. Rockefeller Center is a group of skyscrapers. Its RCA Building holds about forty broadcasting studios. Some distance away are the United Nations buildings. Find them on the map. What river do they face?

New York is our country's greatest seaport. It includes Upper New York Bay and parts of Newark Bay. It also includes the lower parts of the Hudson and East rivers. New York has more than 600 miles (960 km) of busy docks and wharves.

Hundreds of ships can tie up at these docks at one time. More than 10,000 ships from many different nations enter or leave the port every year. They bring many kinds of raw materials and finished goods from other lands. Ships bring such imports as oil, sugar, coffee, tea, and bananas.

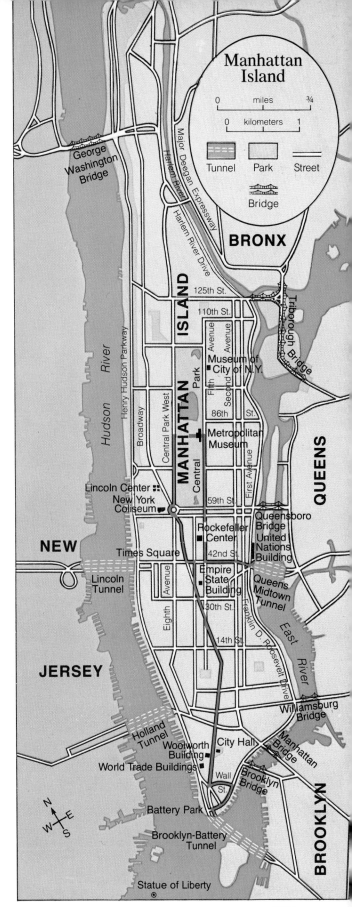

Philadelphia *(left)*, Pittsburgh *(above)*, and Baltimore *(right)* are all located on bodies of water. How did such a location help them become important trading centers?

Ships carry to other countries the goods we export. Wheat and other crops from our farms are exported. So are machinery, tools, textiles, and other products from our factories.

About 300 trucking firms and a dozen railroads serve the port. They bring products to be exported. They haul away the imports.

New York's location has helped it to become a giant city. You know about its fine harbor. It is at the end of an inland water route from the Great Lakes.

Railways, highways, and airlines connect New York with every part of our country. They move huge amounts of raw materials and finished products to and from the city. New York, therefore, has become a great manufacturing, trade, and business center.

Philadelphia is another busy port and manufacturing city. Find it on the map of the Middle Atlantic states (page 269). It faces the Delaware River. Ships from the Atlantic Ocean sail up this broad river to the piers and docks. The waterfront extends for about 32 miles (52 km).

Philadelphia is a key transportation center. Railways, highways, and airways connect it with other parts of our country. Factories turn out machinery, electronic equipment, textiles, and other products.

Philadelphia is an exciting city, partly old and partly new. It was founded in 1682 by the Quaker, William Penn. Stately Independence Hall is in this city. Here colonial leaders signed the Declaration of Independence. Thousands of tourists visit the hall and other famous places nearby.

Downtown Philadelphia has large buildings with stores and offices. But there are no towering skyscrapers. No building is higher than City Hall, which is topped by a tall statue of William Penn.

Philadelphia never forgets Benjamin Franklin. Several places bear his name. One is a wide, tree-lined avenue, the Benjamin Franklin Parkway.

Some older parts of Philadelphia became rundown. So *urban renewal* work was begun. It was a program to improve city

areas. Whole blocks of buildings were replaced. Many well-built but rundown houses have been restored.

Metropolitan Philadelphia spreads out far beyond the city itself. It has fine universities, libraries, and art and music centers.

Pittsburgh is a city of iron and steel manufacturing. This river port grew up on the point of land where the Allegheny and Monongahela rivers meet. They join to form the Ohio River, as the map shows.

Barges crawl up and down these rivers. They haul coal, iron ore, and other materials to Pittsburgh's factories and mills. Freight trains chug along the banks of the rivers. Some cars are loaded with limestone, coal, and iron ore for Pittsburgh's steel mills. Pittsburgh is well-known for its steel mills and for factories making products from steel. Other plants produce glass products, chemicals, electrical equipment, and food products.

Not long ago, waste materials of the mills and factories were polluting the air.

Also, the center of the city was old and rundown. So people worked together to improve conditions.

People studied how to keep factories from polluting the air. Then laws were passed to stop the pollution. Many old buildings were torn down and replaced by new buildings and parks.

Baltimore is a large port and factory city on Chesapeake Bay. This city is about 200 miles (320 km) from the ocean. It is located on the fall line on a river that flows into Chesapeake Bay. Baltimore has a fine harbor, and its port does much business. Industrial and business districts are both near the harbor.

Baltimore's many factories make hundreds of articles, from pins and bottle caps to airplanes. The city is noted for its iron and steel goods.

Automation and other major changes in industry affect jobs. The factories and offices of the Middle Atlantic region employ millions of workers. From week to week many people get new jobs. But many others lose jobs, too.

Some workers lose jobs because of *automation,* the use of highly automatic machinery. Machines run, or control, other machines. Dial telephones are an example of automation. At one time an operator had to connect the wires for every phone call. Now electronic machinery does the job for most calls. Automation exists in many industries.

Many changes are taking place in factories and offices. It is now harder for a person to learn just one job for a lifetime. More and more job training is needed to help people shift to a new line of work.

Farms and foods in these states

Many farms are scattered through the Middle Atlantic states. There are truck, or vegetable, gardens. Dairy and poultry farms are near the cities. Farther away, mixed farming is carried on. Mixed farming means the raising of several kinds of crops and livestock.

New York and Pennsylvania are noted for their dairy farms and fruit orchards. Large areas are hilly. But they have fine orchards. And the hills have pastures where cattle graze. Hay fields produce winter feed for the cattle. The farms supply city dwellers with dairy products and fruit.

The fertile Lake Ontario plain in western New York grows vegetables and fruit. Some of these are apples, grapes, cherries, pears, and plums.

Truck, dairy, and poultry farms spread across New Jersey and Delaware. This is one of the chief truck-farming areas in our country. Farmers raise many kinds of vegetables. Some are sold fresh, but tons of them are canned or frozen. Farmers in these states also raise melons, strawberries, peaches, pears, and apples.

Maryland and Virginia are rich farming states. Fruit orchards are very large. There are also fields of berries, tomatoes, and vegetables.

Maryland has its "oyster farms" in Chesapeake Bay. Farmers drop millions of tiny oysters in the small protected inlets. The oysters stick to rocks on the floor of the bay. After they grow for three or four years, they are ready to harvest. They are loosened with long-handled tongs and gathered into boats. Some oysters are sold fresh, some are frozen, and many are canned.

On Virginia's sandy coastal plain, peanuts are raised. The plants have whitish-yellow blossoms. After the blossoms fall, the flower stalks bend over and push their heads into the soil. Then the peanuts begin to grow. In the fall the plants are dug up and dried. The peanuts are then torn from the plants by a threshing machine.

Southern Virginia farmers, or planters, raise lots of tobacco, mainly in the Piedmont section. The large tobacco leaves are hung in curing barns to dry. These barns are found on most tobacco farms. Some farms have as many as fifteen. The dried, or cured, tobacco is sold to factories to be made into tobacco products.

Many tourists visit the Middle Atlantic states. Caring for tourists is an important way of earning a living in this region. You have read in this chapter about some places tourists like to see.

280

Which belongs where?

On paper write 1 through 9. For each number, write the word or words needed to complete the following sentences correctly. Use the list of words that follows the sentences.

1. A large group of cities extending one after another is called a _____.
2. The four largest cities of the Middle Atlantic region are _____, _____, _____, and _____.
3. Lakes _____ and _____ border the Middle Atlantic region.
4. Ocean-going vessels can travel from the Atlantic to Lake Superior on the _____.
5. New York is our largest _____.
6. Much tobacco is raised in _____.
7. _____ has many oyster farms.
8. Iron ore and limestone are used in making _____.
9. Great coal fields lie in _____ and _____.

List of words

Pittsburgh	farms
Maryland	dairy
megalopolis	Baltimore
Ontario	Virginia
West Virginia	Pennsylvania
New York City	Philadelphia
plain	St. Lawrence Seaway
Chicago	Erie
steel	Atlantic Coastal Plain
Huron	seaport

Check on your reading

1. What are the Middle Atlantic states?
2. What is the fall line? Why have cities grown up along it?
3. Describe the Great Valley. In what ways do people earn a living there?
4. What are two kinds of coal? How do they differ?
5. What natural resources are used in making steel?
6. Why is the steel industry so important?
7. Why is steelmaking a main industry in the Middle Atlantic states?
8. What are some jobs in the steel industry?
9. Why does strip mining damage the land? How can the damage be corrected?

Learning about cities on a map

The Middle Atlantic states have many cities. The larger ones are named on the political map on page 265. The map key gives you a general idea of their size. Let's use it.

Locate Pittsburgh, PA. Is it about the size of New York City or of Baltimore? Look at the key and decide. What other cities have a population about the size of Pittsburgh?

Table 5 in the Tables for Reference shows how many people live in a metropolitan area. A metropolitan area is bigger than a city. It includes a large central city plus surrounding urban areas. Turn to Table 5 on page 437. Find out how many people live in the Pittsburgh metropolitan area.

On the map, find Syracuse in New York State. What does the map tell about its size? How many cities in the Middle Atlantic states have more than 100,000 people? Use Table 5, and count them.

21

The Southern states

Skylab and its space pioneers

It was May 1973. Excitement filled the air at Cape Canaveral, Florida. A spaceship sat high on a huge rocket, ready for countdown. It was Skylab, a roomy workshop or laboratory.

Skylab was a giant compared to earlier spaceships—30 feet by 22 feet (9 m by 7 m). It had a place for cooking and eating, one for sleeping, a bathroom, and work sections.

Skylab was packed with supplies! It had food, water, oxygen, and some medicines. There were cameras, computers, and telescopes.

The countdown was perfect. Then the powerful rocket roared upward. It pushed Skylab 270 miles (430 km) into space. Then Skylab went into orbit around Earth.

Cape Canaveral, Florida, is an important center for space research.

Sometime later, the astronauts were launched in another spaceship. They caught up with Skylab. With much skill they joined the two spaceships. Then they moved into their space home to stay four weeks.

From then on, Skylab was directed by scientists at the Space Center near Houston, Texas. Engineers at this center had planned the design and the building of Skylab.

The astronauts followed a daily plan of eating, sleeping, working, and resting. Some time was spent in exercising.

The space pioneers worked about eight hours a day. They studied and took photos of the sun and other bodies in space. They

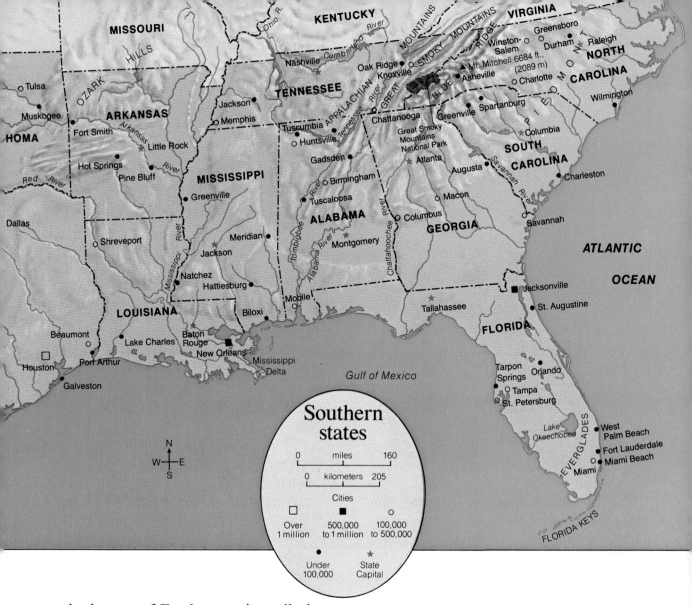

Southern states

0 miles 160

0 kilometers 205

Cities

□ Over 1 million ■ 500,000 to 1 million ○ 100,000 to 500,000

○ Under 100,000 ★ State Capital

took pictures of Earth, even its pollution. They had ways of "hunting" for new sources of mineral resources, perhaps oil. They also learned much about health problems in space.

Several weeks later, these astronauts returned. Others were sent to work in the space laboratory. The second group stayed for 59 days.

In early winter a third group of space pioneers worked in Skylab. All these Skylab crews proved that people can live and work in space for weeks at a time.

Cape Canaveral, Florida, and the Space Center near Houston are in the huge part of our country known as the South.

Looking at the South

The South is a region made up of eleven states. Look at the map of the Southern states. Notice that the region stretches from the Atlantic Ocean to the dry plains of western Texas. It reaches from the Gulf of Mexico north through Oklahoma, Arkansas, Tennessee, and North Carolina.

Name the eleven Southern states. Which is largest? Point to the peninsula state. Find the states that face the Gulf of Mexico. Which ones border the Atlantic Ocean? Name the states that have no coast line.

283

Because of its location at the mouth of the Mississippi River, New Orleans has long been an important shipping and trading center.

The Mississippi River flows through the Southern states. Notice how the river is part of the boundary line for several states.

More than 250 rivers flow into the Mississippi. The largest branch is from the east, the Ohio River. The largest branches from the west are the Missouri and the Arkansas.

In the spring the Mississippi's waters are often very high. Then, its branches carry much water from melting snow. At times the Mississippi spills over its banks and floods the lowlands. To help prevent floods, the government has built miles of strong walls, or levees, along the banks. Dams have been built on some rivers. The dams hold back part of the water. It is stored in reservoirs until it is needed.

The Mississippi is a muddy river. Its branches carry soil down mountain slopes and across plains. The giant river carries some soil even to the Gulf of Mexico.

The Mississippi widens as it flows south. It slows down as it winds through the flat plains along the Gulf of Mexico. At its mouth the Mississippi divides into several branches. The *mouth* of a river is the place where it empties into a large body of water. When the mouth of a river has several branches, it is called a *delta*. Find the delta of the Mississippi on the map of the Southern states.

Broad plains cover much of the southern region. Locate them on the map on pages 90–91. Find the *Atlantic Coastal Plain*. It continues all the way south to Florida.

In Florida the Atlantic Coastal Plain joins the *Gulf Coastal Plain*. Look on the map and see how this plain reaches west along the Gulf of Mexico. Much of it has deep rich soil.

In some places the Gulf Coastal Plain is low and flat. The water cannot drain easily. These low, wet places are swamps. One huge swamp in southern Florida is called the Everglades.

The map shows that plains also cover most of Texas and Oklahoma. Along the Gulf of Mexico they are a part of the Gulf

National Parks

ALASKA
Mount McKinley

HAWAII

Coastal Plain. But the inland plains are much higher than those along the coast.

The southern region has mountains and hills. Find them on the map on pages 90–91. Notice how far south the Piedmont extends. It goes through North Carolina, South Carolina, Georgia, and west into Alabama.

West of the Piedmont are the Appalachians. Several ranges of mountains stretch through these highlands. On the east are the Blue Ridge Mountains. Farther west are the Great Smokies.

The Great Smoky Mountains National Park is a favorite vacation spot. A *national park* is land set aside by the government for visitors to enjoy. What other national parks are located in the South? Look on the map above to find them. The Appalachians reach into Kentucky and farther north into Tennessee and Alabama. More highlands rise in Missouri and Arkansas and extend into Oklahoma.

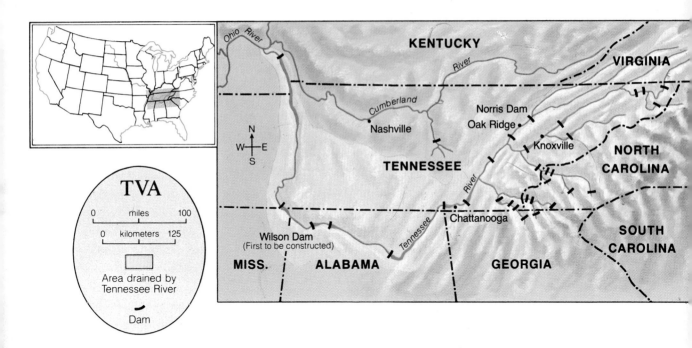

TVA

0   miles   100

0   kilometers   125

Area drained by
Tennessee River

Dam

The Tennessee Valley includes parts of seven states. It is the area drained by the Tennessee River and its branches. Find this valley on the map above.

This large valley gets much rain. Long ago, forests covered the floor of the valley and the nearby hills and mountains. The roots of the trees and shrubs held the soil. But through the years, farmers and town builders chopped down the trees. When the rains fell, the water raced down the slopes. Bad floods damaged farmlands and towns.

The racing water washed away the soil. Such loss of soil is called *erosion*. Only poor crops would grow in the thin soil that was left.

In 1913 the Norris Dam was built to *conserve*, or protect, this valley's rich natural resources. This dam did its job well. In 1933 the government began building more dams on the rivers of the Tennessee Valley. The Tennessee Valley Authority, or TVA, was in charge of this work.

Today there are about 50 dams. They can store much water. They have pre-

vented many floods. New forests have been planted. Farmers are using ways of farming to prevent erosion. They plow around the hillsides so that rain is trapped in the furrows. This method is called *contour plowing*.

The TVA dams also supply electric power. It comes from power plants built below the dams. Low-cost power has led to the growth of industry in the Tennessee Valley.

The TVA has also helped shipping. The Tennessee River was deepened. Now boats can travel on it as far as Knoxville. Many boats move along the Tennessee carrying grain, coal, iron, and steel. Some haul forest and petroleum products.

The Southern states have a generally mild climate. Warm moist winds blow across these states from the Gulf of Mexico. They help to keep the winters mild.

The northern edge of this region is colder than the lands along the Gulf. It gets some snow. But freezing weather may occur as far south as Florida when cold winds sweep south from Canada.

Citrus fruit *(left)* and rice *(above)* are important cash crops in the South. Both crops need a lot of water to grow. Irrigation is used to provide enough water.

Summers in some regions of the South are usually hot and damp. The warm weather begins in the early spring and lasts until late in the fall. So the South has a long growing season. Study the map on page 258. What parts have a growing season of more than eight months?

This long growing season and plentiful rains help the South to grow many crops. Let's look at the rainfall map on page 259 and see what it tells us.

Notice that the western parts of Texas and Oklahoma get little rain. Cattle and sheep are raised on these lands. Most of the South gets enough rain to grow crops. What areas get more than 40 inches a year? They can raise such crops as cotton, tobacco, sugar cane, rice, and peanuts.

Agriculture is a leading industry

Cotton is the main crop in the southern region. Farmers grow much cotton. Texas grows more cotton than any other state. But cotton is the chief money crop all over the Cotton Belt. Look at the Cotton Belt on the map on page 288. Notice that this belt is sprinkled with tiny black dots. Each little dot stands for 10,000 acres of cotton. In some places the dots are very close together. What does that tell you?

Many farmers in the cotton belt are growing soy beans in place of cotton. Some of them think soy beans will take the place of cotton as the main crop.

The Cotton Belt does not include Florida or certain lowlands along the Gulf coast. They get too much rain for growing cotton. Nor is cotton grown in some parts of dry west Texas.

Cotton is planted in the spring after the fields are plowed. Many farmers use planting machines pulled by tractors. Large machines can plant six or eight rows of cotton at once. They do several other jobs, one after another. They drop the

287

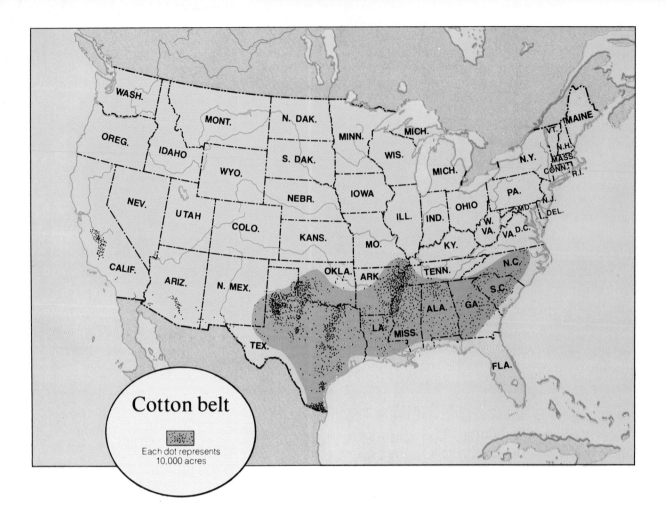

Cotton belt

Each dot represents
10,000 acres

seeds in the furrows, add fertilizer, and cover the seeds. Then they tap down the soil. Later on, the fields are cultivated to keep down the weeds.

When the cotton plant is about a foot tall, it bears white blossoms. Within a few days they turn a reddish color. Then they drop off, leaving small green seed pods called *bolls*. The cotton fibers grow in these bolls. The bolls grow larger and larger. By September they begin to ripen and turn brown. Soon they burst open. Then they look something like snowballs.

Cotton picking begins not later than September. Today most cotton is picked by machine. The raw cotton is hauled to the gins for cleaning. There machines comb out the seeds. The cleaned cotton is pressed into huge bales. Much of the cotton goes to the textile mills of the South.

What other major crops are grown in the South? Georgia and South Carolina are famous for peaches. Peanuts and pecans are raised in many sections of the Cotton Belt. But Georgia raises more than any other state.

Florida and southwest Texas are noted for grapefruit and oranges. These fruits are called citrus fruits. Water from the Rio Grande in Texas is used to grow large groves of orange and grapefruit trees. Settlers from Mexico brought the first citrus trees to Texas long ago.

Citrus trees have shiny dark-green leaves and sweet-smelling white blossoms. When the trees are in bloom, the air around them is fragrant. Citrus fruits grow well only where there is little frost.

Rice is raised on the wet lowlands of the Mississippi Delta and the Gulf coast of

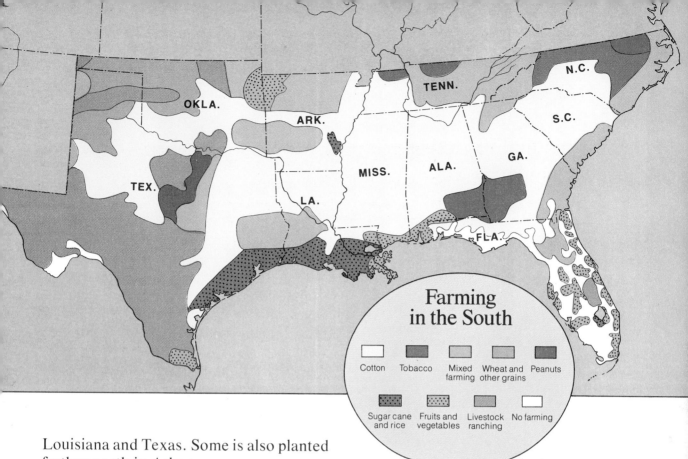

Farming in the South

Legend:
- ☐ Cotton
- ■ Tobacco
- ▨ Mixed farming
- ▩ Wheat and other grains
- ■ Peanuts
- ▦ Sugar cane and rice
- ▤ Fruits and vegetables
- ▨ Livestock ranching
- ☐ No farming

Louisiana and Texas. Some is also planted farther north in Arkansas.

When the rice plants are a few inches high, the fields are flooded. The roots are usually kept under water until just before harvest time. When the grain begins to ripen, the fields are drained. Soon, combines move in to cut and thresh the grain.

Louisiana has huge fields of sugar cane. This area is often called the Sugar Bowl of the South. Find it on the "Farming in the South" map. Some sugar cane is raised in Florida.

Tobacco is the main crop in a large part of North Carolina. What other states grow tobacco? Other important crops include corn, soybeans, watermelons, and sweet potatoes.

The Southern states raise many vegetables. Some are sold in southern cities. But many truck farmers in North Carolina, South Carolina, Georgia, Florida, and Texas grow winter vegetables to sell in the North. Because of the mild climate, they can grow vegetables most of the year.

The South does much mixed farming. Find some mixed farming areas on the map. Dairy farming is important near the cities.

Large wheat ranches spread across the plains of Oklahoma and northern Texas.

Western Texas and Oklahoma raise many beef cattle. This industry began on the plains of Texas long ago. These western plains are too dry to farm without irrigation. But their grass feeds large herds of cattle.

Beef calves are usually born during the spring. They remain on the grazing lands with their mothers for about six months. In the fall most of them are sold to farmers who have feed lots. There they are fattened for market.

Huge fenced cattle ranches spread over Texas. The King Ranch is larger than the state of Rhode Island. Oklahoma also has large cattle ranches.

Other natural resources of the South

Lumbering is another major industry in the South. The South supplies more than one fourth of our lumber. But only a little of the early southern forests remain. Most of the forests in the South today have been planted.

Many pine trees are raised as a crop. They are grown on hilly lands that can't be farmed. The South has a mild climate, long growing season, and heavy rainfall. So these trees grow rapidly.

Loggers are busy winter and summer cutting down trees. Many logs go to sawmills to be made into lumber. Hardwoods, such as oak and maple, are used for making furniture and for woodwork in buildings.

Much pine is used for building. Also, many pine logs are ground into pulpwood for making paper and rayon goods. The South's woodlands furnish much of the nation's pulpwood.

Many pine trees are tapped for their sticky *resin*, or sap. The resin oozes out from cuts in the tree trunk. Resin is used to make paints, varnishes, linoleum, and some soaps.

The South has many mills and factories that use the raw materials from the forests.

Some southern workers earn their living at fishing. Oysters are plentiful in the warm, shallow coastal waters of the Gulf of Mexico. Shrimps are caught in the Gulf waters. Fishing boats bring in menhaden, mackerel, flounder, sea trout, and red snappers. Menhaden are caught mainly for their oil. The oil is used in soap and paints.

Thousands of people work in the South's oil industry. Crude oil, or petroleum, is a thick greenish-black liquid. In some parts of the world, oil is found deep in the ground in layers of rock. So it is called petroleum, which means "rock oil."

The first oil wells in the United States were dug in Pennsylvania more than a hundred years ago. At that time some

Large petroleum deposits lie off the coast of Texas and Louisiana. Portable drilling platforms like these are used to bring the oil to the surface.

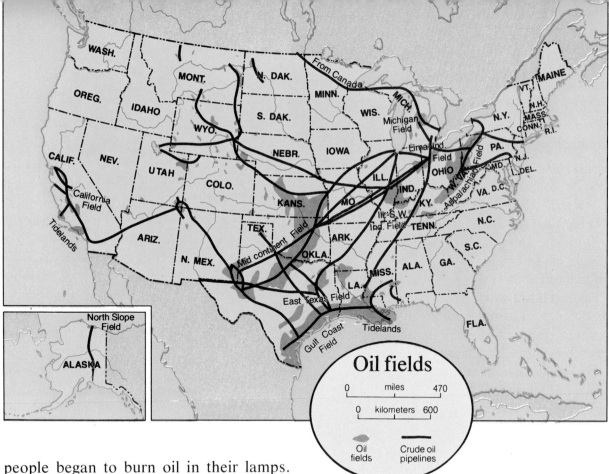

Oil fields

0	miles	470
0	kilometers	600

Oil fields — Crude oil pipelines

people began to burn oil in their lamps. Today we make many products from crude oil.

The South has several large oil fields. Find each one on the map. Notice how the Gulf Coast Field goes from the coast of Texas into Louisiana. Another is the East Texas Field. A third, the Mid-Continent Field, runs from northern Texas through Oklahoma into Kansas. Another is under water off the coast. It is called the Tidelands Field.

This oil is found deep in the ground. To get it, workers drill holes deep into the earth. Tall derricks hold the drilling machinery.

Crude oil is pumped into huge storage tanks. Then it is sent to refineries. Much goes by pipeline. Some is hauled by truck or railroad tank cars. Some is shipped in tankers. At the refineries the crude oil is heated. This separates it into gasoline, kerosene, fuel oil, lubricating oil, and other useful products.

We need oil as fuel for autos, trucks, buses, airplanes, and farm equipment. Some is turned into heating oil. Some is used for making electricity. Oil is also used to make synthetic fabrics and many plastic products.

But we produce only about half of what we need. When oil is pumped from the earth, it cannot be replaced. We need to use this chief source of *energy,* or power, wisely.

Natural gas is found in Texas, Louisiana, and Oklahoma. It is used for cooking and for heating homes and other buildings. Natural gas is used as the chief fuel in some factories.

In many oil fields, natural gas comes from the wells along with petroleum. In some places it is found without oil. Pipelines carry gas to such distant cities as Los Angeles, New York, and Boston.

291

Tennessee and Georgia have quarries of marble and granite. A quarry is a large pit, or hole in the earth, from which stone is taken. Marble and granite, which are taken from quarries, are used in buildings.

Florida and Tennessee have rich deposits of phosphate, a mineral used in making fertilizer.

Texas and Louisiana mine sulfur. It is a yellowish material found far under the ground. Sulfur is needed in making paper, matches, tires, and many other products.

In Arkansas a clay called *bauxite* is found. This is the ore from which aluminum comes. Aluminum is used for making pots and pans, auto and airplane parts, and many other useful things.

Alabama has deposits of coal, iron ore, and limestone.

Manufacturing, trade, and cities

Manufacturing is a main industry in the South. The farms, forests, and mines of this region provide many raw materials. There is plenty of electric power to run the factories. The South also has the skilled workers that the factories need.

Southern mills and factories produce textiles, clothing, paper, and furniture. Aluminum, iron, and metal articles are turned out. Dozens of products are made from cottonseed oil, soybeans, and peanuts. Large amounts of chemical products are produced.

The busy farms and factories produce goods that must be sold, or traded. And trade leads to the growth of cities. Far more than half of all southerners now live in cities and towns.

A megalopolis has developed in the Piedmont part of the South. A megalopolis, you know, takes in many cities and towns. They are strung together by roads and railways.

Look at the map on page 187. Find the megalopolis that extends through the Piedmont. Follow the areas shown in red. The megalopolis stretches from North Carolina through South Carolina and Georgia into Alabama. It has many cities with factories and mills. One is Birmingham, Alabama's largest city.

Birmingham and Atlanta are large cities in the Southeast. Birmingham is a big iron and steel center. It is located near coal, iron ore, and limestone deposits. Recall that these are the chief materials for making steel. Birmingham is also noted for its colleges and a famous museum.

Atlanta is one of the largest cities in the South. Metropolitan Atlanta has more than a million people. Atlanta is a leading transportation center. This has helped its mills and factories grow. Many textiles and other products are made here.

There are many other manufacturing cities in this region. Some in Georgia and the Carolinas have textile mills. For example, cloth, textile machinery, and fine furniture are made in Charlotte, North Carolina.

Some cities in North Carolina and Florida manufacture tobacco products. Several in Tennessee have aluminum plants. Many cities in the South have lumber and paper mills. Some also have aircraft and electronic plants.

Memphis is the largest city in Tennessee. This busy Mississippi River port has many industries. Some of them make cottonseed products, textiles, machinery, and chemicals.

Two cities with new industries are in the South. Oak Ridge is a young city in the Tennessee Valley. It has laboratories for developing peaceful uses of atomic power.

Huntsville, Alabama, has been called "the Space Capital of the World." Here many scientists worked together to develop guided missiles. Huntsville has huge laboratories. Workers in its factories plan and produce engines for giant rockets. Rockets from Huntsville launched the spacecraft that landed on the moon.

Scientific research is an important industry in the South. At Huntsville (left), scientists work with rocket research, while those in Oak Ridge (above) work to find new and peaceful uses for atomic energy.

Houston is a busy inland seaport in Texas. A ship channel connects Houston with the Gulf of Mexico. The city's fine location for shipping has helped it grow very fast.

Houston is a business and shipping center for cotton, livestock, wheat, and oil. You remember that Texas is the leading cotton state. It also has huge cattle ranches. Oil and natural gas fields are found here. Metropolitan Houston has many kinds of manufacturing industries.

Houston is an exciting city. Like many other cities in the South, it has universities, museums, and art and music centers.

Remember, too, that a major Spacecraft Center is in this area. The astronauts trained here.

Many Texas coastal cities share the "Golden Crescent." The crescent is shaped like a new moon. This "Golden Crescent" is about 370 miles (590 km)

293

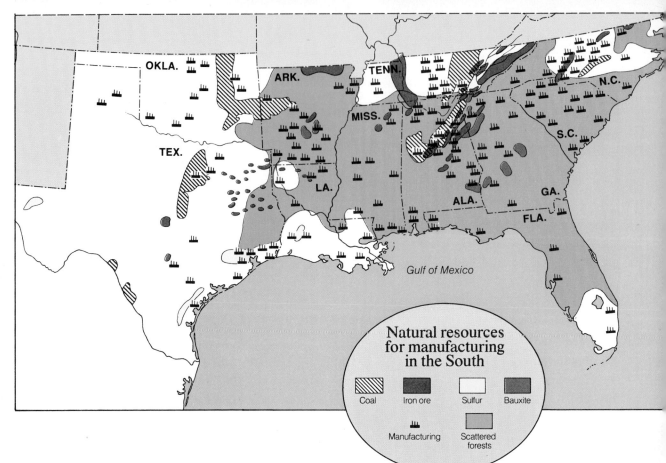

Natural resources
for manufacturing
in the South

▨ Coal	◼ Iron ore
☐ Sulfur	◼ Bauxite
⯃ Manufacturing	▦ Scattered forests

long. It runs along the state's coast from Beaumont to Brownsville. Find this area on the population map on pages 262-263.

Once much land on this coast was used to raise sugar and rice. Today much of this same land is used by oil refineries, chemical plants, and factories. This long, curved area is so rich with industry that it is called the "Golden Crescent."

Dallas and Fort Worth are two other important Texas cities. In Dallas are branches of many large business firms. They employ many skilled workers.

Fort Worth is a leading business center for oil, grain, and livestock. Meat packers and farmers gather here to buy and sell cattle.

New Orleans is another of the South's many busy ports. It has long stretches of wharves and warehouses. Ships bring in goods like coffee and bananas. They carry away goods such as corn, wheat, cotton, gasoline, and steel products.

New Orleans is a major manufacturing center. Rice and sugar are prepared for market. Oil refineries and giant chemical plants are located near New Orleans.

The South has many other busy ports. On or near the Gulf of Mexico are Corpus Christi, Port Arthur, Galveston, Mobile, and Tampa. Locate them on the map. Charleston, Savannah, and Jacksonville are thriving ports along the Atlantic coast.

Laredo and El Paso are busy trading cities on the Rio Grande. Much of our trade with Mexico takes place in these two Texas border cities. Imports must be checked by officials of the United States Bureau of Customs. They see that import taxes, or *customs duties*, are paid. Most big import centers are on the seacoast. Laredo is the largest United States import center that is not on a coast.

These gardens are in Mobile, Alabama, and the houses are in Charleston, South Carolina.

The tourist business

Many people earn a living caring for tourists. Let's think again about some services tourists want. They eat at restaurants and need places to stay. They use buses, planes, and trains. Or they buy gasoline for their cars. They may rent boats and take sightseeing tours. Caring for tourists is a big business in the South.

Some cities in the South attract many tourists. One example is Miami, Florida. It is one of the most famous winter resorts in the United States. People flock to it and other resorts nearby. They like Florida's mild winter climate. And they enjoy swimming, fishing, and sailing.

Miami is a busy city the whole year round, however. It is a transportation center. Airways connect it with cities in the West Indies and South America.

Mobile, Alabama, has a long azalea "trail." Every March when these plants bloom, crowds of sightseers visit the city. New Orleans is widely known for its old French quarter. There are many interesting homes and restaurants there. Its Mardi Gras (mär′dē grä) is a festival held every year in late winter. In South Carolina, Charleston's handsome old homes and fine gardens draw visitors.

The South has many vacation lands and historic sites. Among them are some national parks. One unusual area is the Florida Keys. This is a series of tiny

The Florida Everglades are one of the few subtropical areas in our country. In 1947 the southern part of these swamplands was set aside as a national park.

islands in south Florida. A highway with many bridges connects these islands. One can drive over it to Key West at the end.

The Great Smoky National Park is visited by people from all states. It is a leading park in number of visitors.

Tourists can visit many Civil War battle sites. Fine houses built before the Civil War are open to visitors in Natchez, Mississippi, and other places. Helen Keller's childhood home is at Tuscumbia, Alabama. Miss Keller helped to show that blind and deaf children can be educated.

Do you remember Ponce de León? You can visit the Fountain of Youth Park at St. Augustine, Florida. Would you like to see the Cowboy Hall of Fame at Oklahoma City? At Ponca City, Oklahoma, you can see a monument that honors pioneer women.

A matching game

The words in List A describe places or things that are mentioned in this chapter. Write the numbers of these items in a column on your paper. Beside each number write the matching item from List B.

List A

1. A leading space center
2. Strong walls to hold back a river
3. Low lands along the Gulf of Mexico
4. A scenic playground in the Appalachians
5. A large Florida swampland
6. An iron and steel center
7. Texas' new coastal industrial area
8. A main industry in western Texas
9. Trees tapped for resin
10. An important crop in southern and central Louisiana
11. Grain grown in flooded fields
12. Ore used in making aluminum

List B

Birmingham	bauxite
Great Smoky Mountains	soybeans
National Park	maple
Cape Canaveral	rice
Everglades	sugar cane
levees	pine
Alabama	peanuts
hickory	Golden Crescent
Gulf Coastal Plain	raising cattle

Using numbers and letters on a map

A road map shows highways, cities, and other important places. To help people locate such places, letters and numbers are often placed at the edge of a map.

Look at the picture map below. It shows one section of a community. Notice the numbers and letters shown along the edges of the map. Use them to locate places in this section.

Locate the school at C 3. First find C at the northern and southern edges of the map. Then find 3 on the eastern and western edges. Now move one finger down or up from the C in a straight line. Move another finger straight across from 3. Notice that your two fingers meet where a line from 3 crosses a line from C. The school is located there, as you can see.

Use the letters and numbers on the map below to help you answer these questions:

1. What is at A 1?
2. Where is the church located?
3. What do you find at C 1?
4. What is at A 2?
5. Where is the fire department located?
6. What is at D 2?
7. Which direction is the church from the fire department?

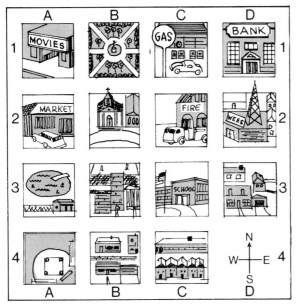

Some other things to do

1. List the South's main industries. Arrange pictures of some on your bulletin board. Find out which ones are carried on in your state.

2. Read in another book about one of the natural resources found in the South.

3. Find out about career opportunities in the South. Among them may be working as a logger, salesperson, mechanic, or farmer. There are jobs for computer operators, chemists, oil drillers, tourist guides, and florists. Talk over with your class what you learn.

4. Help your class plan a "Cotton Products" exhibit. Choose committees to bring, label, and arrange a variety of products made from cotton.

5. Turn to the map of the Southern states. Use the scale of kilometers to measure the distance from

   Houston to New Orleans.
   Dallas to Little Rock, Ark.
   Miami to Birmingham, Ala.
   Atlanta to Nashville, Tenn.
   Houston to Raleigh, N.C.
   Tulsa, Okla. to Jacksonville, Fla.

Try to remember

1. Name and locate the Southern states. Which is the largest? Which is a peninsula? Which border the Mississippi?

2. What are the leading crops of the South? Why can such a variety be grown?

3. What is the TVA? How has it helped the South?

22

The Central states

Many large fields of corn, wheat, and other crops are raised in the Midwest. Dairy farming is also an important activity. Often this region is called the "food basket" of our country.

Farmers and fields

Fred and Jill Henkel chose farming careers. They live on an Iowa farm and raise corn, soybeans, and hay. They feed most of their crops to their livestock. They fatten hogs and beef cattle for market.

"I like farming," Mrs. Henkel told a visitor. "It's great to work with growing things. I take care of the garden."

"Both of us help with the livestock," continued Mr. Henkel. "We keep records on each animal from the time we buy it until it is sold. We grow most of their food. So there's plenty of work in the fields."

"Especially at planting time," said Jill Henkel. "We both drive the tractors. So we work in the fields together at the busiest times."

"We certainly do," agreed Fred. "And Jill is our bookkeeper. She keeps our accounts."

"During the winter, we have time to read and study about new ways of farming. We attend farm meetings, too," said Jill.

"Successful farmers are always looking for better ways of doing things," said Fred.

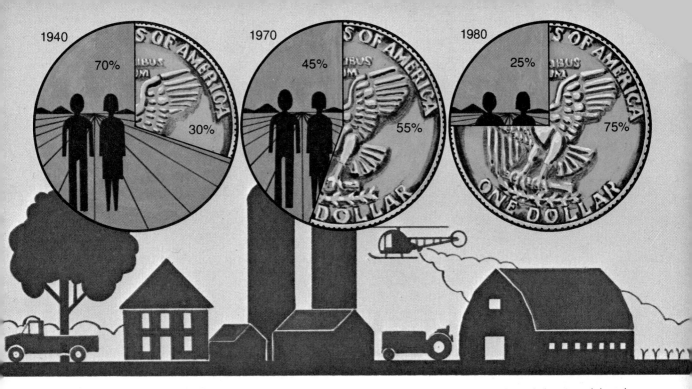

Farmers need to be all-around experts in their career. They must decide what crops are best for their soil and climate. They must care for their fields wisely. They must know how and when to plant. They need to choose the best safe ways to control weeds and harmful insects.

Farmers depend on radio and TV for weather news. If winter storms continue into spring, planting must be delayed. If heavy spring rains come, fields may be too wet to plant. Farmers must decide what to do in all kinds of weather.

Farming is a business operation, but a risky one. Farmers do much buying and selling. But they do not get regular paychecks. Their *income,* or pay, depends on what they receive for what they sell.

If crops or livestock do well, sales may bring a good profit. But the selling prices of most farm products change from day to day. A farmer must decide when is the best time to sell.

Farmers have heavy expenses. They must buy seed and fertilizers. They must

Farming requires labor and land, shown by the orange colored slices in the diagram. But farming also requires equipment and other things that are paid for by money. As the years went by, which became more important: labor and land or money? Why do you think this is true?

buy or rent special equipment. They need many kinds of costly machines. Young animals cost money to buy, feed, and prepare for market.

Farmers want to be sure their income will pay the bills and pay for the family's work. They also hope to earn a profit. A *profit* is money left after all expenses are paid and the owners have paid themselves a wage for their own work. Farmers try to know what crops may make a profit. They try to figure the total cost of raising each animal. They decide whether certain machines are worth their cost or whether to rent them. They figure when to buy new equipment. Many farmers live in the Central states.

299

Looking at the Central states

The Central states spread across the middle of our country. This region is often called the Middle West. Thirteen states share this fertile central region. Locate each one on the map on pages 300–301. Which states reach farthest north? Which are farthest west?

Rolling plains sweep across most of the central region. The lands east of the Missouri River are called the Central Plains. They were settled first. These plains begin just west of the Appalachians. They have fertile croplands. Their rivers can be used as water highways.

The eastern part of the Central Plains was once covered with forests. The first settlers had to cut down trees and clear the land to plant crops. But west of the Mississippi there were only patches of forest. Farther west were prairies of tall grass.

For a time, few settlers lived on the prairies. Farmers feared that if trees would not grow, neither would crops. Later they found that the prairies had deep rich soil.

The Great Plains stretch west to meet the Rockies. The Great Plains are higher and drier than the Central Plains.

Hills and mountains frame parts of the central region. On the east the Appalachians reach down through Ohio and Kentucky. On the west are the high Rockies.

The wooded Ozark Hills spread over southern Missouri. Other areas of hills reach through parts of Wisconsin and Michigan. The Black Hills rise on the western edge of South Dakota. Locate the hilly regions on the map.

Valuable waterways cut into the central region. There are many important rivers in this region. Most join the Mississippi.

The United States government has deepened the channels of the Mississippi River. Boats can travel far upstream. They

can dock at Minneapolis and St. Paul in Minnesota. They can go up the Ohio River to Pittsburgh. Strings of low, flat barges are the freight cars of the river. They are pushed by powerful tugboats. Barges carry heavy loads such as coal and automobiles.

The map of the Central states shows that the Great Lakes are in this region. The Great Lakes and the St. Lawrence River are an important inland waterway.

The Great Lakes and the Mississippi and its branches have helped the region. They

301

The Corn Belt's climate and gently rolling land are ideal for growing corn. Farmers use machines, called combines, to harvest the corn.

have provided cheap transportation for goods. Notice how many cities are either on a river or on one of the Great Lakes.

The central region has several kinds of climates. The winters in the northern parts are long and cold. Minnesota and Wisconsin often have heavy snowstorms. The snow remains on the ground much longer than in Kentucky or Missouri.

Summers are hot and often humid, or damp. On some hot nights, the air scarcely stirs. Still, the farmers seldom complain. Hot days and nights are good for their crops.

Use the growing season map on page 258. Notice that most of this region has a shorter growing season than the South. In general it lasts from four to six months. This is long enough to grow many food crops.

Summers are longest and hottest in the southern part of the region. Crops can grow for a longer time in Kentucky than they can in northern Michigan, for example. Killing frosts may come to northern Michigan early in the fall.

Most areas in the Middle West receive twenty inches or more of rain each year. Much rain comes in the late spring and early summer when the growing crops need it most.

The western section of the region is the driest part. Notice this on the rainfall map. Farmers in this western section grow crops that need less rain. One is wheat. Farther east, the leading crop is corn.

The Middle West is the Corn Belt

Native Americans taught the colonists how to grow corn. Soon corn became an important crop in all the colonies. The pioneers carried precious seed corn when they journeyed to settle western lands.

This early kind of corn often had small ears and poor kernels. Farmers and scientists worked hard to produce better kinds. They have had success. Also, ways have been found to destroy enemy insects and worms.

Corn is our biggest and most valuable crop. More land is used for producing corn than for any other crop. Some corn is raised in nearly every state. But the main corn-growing area is the Corn Belt. Locate it on the Corn Belt map. Notice that it extends from eastern Ohio to the edge of Colorado. The leading corn-producing states are Iowa, Illinois, and Indiana.

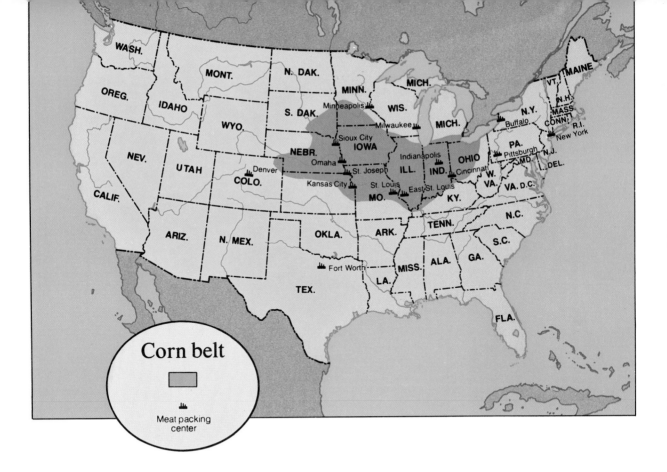

Corn belt

Meat packing center

Spring is a busy time of year on a Corn Belt farm. Farmers work long hours during the planting season. After the fields are plowed and prepared, planting begins. A tractor pulls a machine that can plant four or more rows of corn at once. This same machine may spray on fertilizer and a weed-killer.

The tender young corn plants push through the soil. Hot sunshine, warm nights, and frequent rain help the corn to grow very fast. Before long, the sturdy green stalks begin to show golden tasseled heads. By August, the stalks may be very tall.

In autumn, the corn is ready to harvest. A huge machine moves down the rows. It is called a combine. It pulls the ears of corn from a few rows of stalks at one time. The combine husks the corn and removes the kernels from the cobs. The shelled corn is loaded on to wagons or trucks.

Most of the corn is used as feed for hogs and other livestock. Hogs eat about half of the total crop. Much corn also goes into feed for cattle and poultry.

Some food products are made from corn. Among them are cereals, corn meal, syrup, cooking oil, and margarine. Sweet corn is a favorite food.

Corn is also used in making paint and other non-food products.

Mixed farming and feedlots are found in the Corn Belt. Its farms also grow oats, barley, wheat, soybeans, and hay. Many farms have feedlots where meat animals are fattened for market. Thousands of calves are bought from ranches in Texas, Montana, or other parts of the west. They are fed corn, soybeans, and other foods for six months. Then they are ready to sell.

The Corn Belt has our leading hog-producing states. Hogs provide bacon, ham, and other kinds of pork.

303

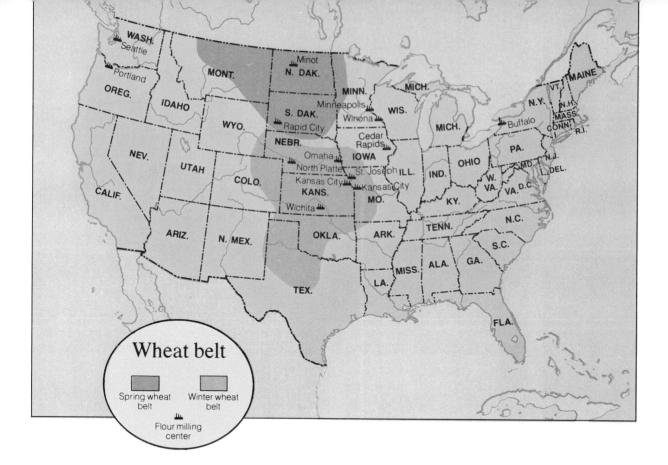

Wheat belt

Spring wheat belt
Winter wheat belt
Flour milling center

Many meat animals are sent to market from the Corn Belt. They are loaded on trucks or on the stock cars of a freight train. Then they are rushed to stockyards.

Large stockyards in the region are found in Kansas City, St. Louis, Milwaukee, and Omaha. Each of these cities is in the heart of a busy farming area. There are also smaller stockyards in many cities in the Corn Belt.

From the stockyards, the cattle and hogs are driven into packing plants. There they are prepared for market. Some meat is canned. Ham and bacon are preserved in other ways. But most of the meat is sold fresh. Refrigerator trucks and railroad cars carry the meat to all parts of the nation.

Many people work in the meat industry. Every part of the animal is used. Many people earn their living making useful goods from hides, bones, and fat. Hides are made into leather for shoes, belts, suitcases, and other leather goods. Bones are ground up into fertilizer. Much fat is used for making soap.

The Corn Belt is the Soybean Belt, too. Every part of the soybean is useful. Some stalks are fed to farm animals. Some plants are cut and plowed into the soil to enrich it. But most of this crop is harvested for its beans.

At the factory the oil is pressed from the beans. Soybean oil is used in margarine and cooking oil. Some oil is used in making paints and soap. One product from soybeans is added to candy and breads. After the oil is removed, the rest of the bean is ground into meal. Soybean meal is a good cattle food.

Our "bread basket"

The western Central states raise large quantities of wheat. These states make up a large part of our country's Wheat Belt. It has been called our nation's "bread basket." This belt's fertile soil and fairly dry climate are well suited to growing wheat. Two main kinds of wheat are grown.

Winter wheat grows in the southern part of the Wheat Belt. Kansas is a leading winter-wheat state. Farmers prepare their fields in the late summer and sow the seeds in the fall. Within a few weeks the fields are green. The plants are several inches tall.

Cold weather stops growth, and snow covers the wheat. The snow protects the roots of the plants. When the warm spring days come, the plants grow very fast. By June this winter wheat is ready to be cut and gathered.

Spring wheat is raised in the Dakotas and Montana. Find this area on the Wheat Belt map. In these states the winters are too long and cold for young wheat. Here, the wheat must be planted in the spring. It is ready to be harvested in the late summer.

Wheat farmers must use much costly equipment. Tractors pull the plows, harrows, and planters. After the fields are plowed, they are harrowed. Harrows have sharp blades that break up and rake the lumpy soil. Then fertilizer is spread. Later the farmer drives the tractor that pulls the planter.

At harvest, the farmer goes to the field with a huge combine. It cuts the grain from the stalks and shakes the grain loose. Trucks haul it to a grain elevator.

Elevators store the wheat after the grain is harvested. They have equipment for unloading, cleaning, and storing grain. They store the grain until it is hauled to the mills. Find the chief centers for flour milling on the Wheat Belt map.

Some other foods

Many farmers in the central region raise vegetables and fruits. Some farms grow such vegetables as peas, tomatoes, sweet corn, beans, and potatoes. A part of this fresh produce is sold in city markets. But much of it is canned or frozen.

Other farms specialize in growing fruits and berries. Along the shores of Lake Michigan are many fruit orchards. Apples, peaches, grapes, plums, and pears are grown.

Fruit-picking time brings the busy canning season. Large canneries hum long hours canning fruit to sell in markets.

Some people grow vegetables, berries, and fruit for the quick-freezing industry. These crops are rushed to plants, prepared, and quickly frozen to preserve them. Frozen foods can be bought in markets all year. When they are thawed and ready to eat, they taste fresh.

Clarence Birdseye helped to start the quick-freeze industry. In 1915 this Massachusetts inventor visited Labrador. This is a part of Canada. While there, he learned that the people often preserved fish by freezing it quickly. When thawed and prepared, it tasted like fresh fish. After Birdseye returned home, he worked with quick-freezing methods. His processes have been improved steadily. Today many people work in this industry.

A wide Dairy Belt reaches across the northeast. It extends from North Dakota through New England. The Dairy Belt has long cold winters and rather short rainy summers. Such lands are not well suited to many kinds of farming. But there are green pastures and good hay crops. So this is a

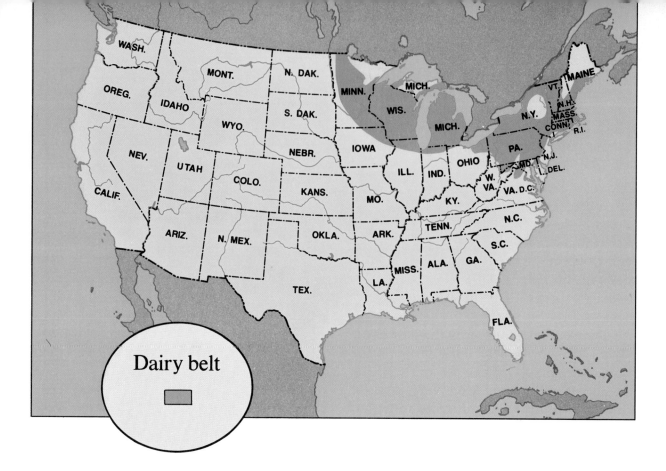

Dairy belt

good area for dairy farming. Which Central States are in the Dairy Belt? Use the Dairy Belt map.

Dairy farmers are busy people. In the summer they raise hay and some corn for winter feed for their cattle. The green hay is cut, dried, and put in bales. They are stored in the haylofts of huge barns. Much corn is cut while still green. Its stalks, leaves, and ears are fed into a chopping machine. The chopped corn is blown through huge pipes into a silo. This corn feed is called silage. It stays fresh stored in the silo. Silage and hay are used to feed dairy cattle all winter long when pastures are not green.

Winter and summer, the cattle must be tended. They must be fed each day. Every morning and evening they must be milked.

Dairy farmers keep the milking barn clean. They wash it down often. Cows are brushed before they enter the milking

room. The dairy inspectors make sure that the milk will be pure. Impure milk can cause disease.

Most milking is done by machine. The milk flows through pipes to a cooling room. At the dairy plants, milk is pasteurized, or heated, to destroy germs. Then it is cooled and sealed in cartons.

Much fresh milk is turned into other food products. At milk canneries the milk is poured into tanks and heated. Milk is partly water. The heat makes much of the water evaporate, or steam off. The milk that is left is thick and creamy evaporated milk. It is also called canned milk.

Cream, butter, and cheese are other dairy products. Milk is poured into the tanks of separator machines. As the milk whirls around, the cream separates from the rest of the milk. The cream comes out of one spout. The skimmed milk flows out of another.

Milk is used to make cheese *(left)* and ice cream *(right)*. What other dairy products can you name?

Much cream is churned into butter. Some churns are so large that they can make as much as a ton of butter at one time. Minnesota is the leading butter-producing state in our country.

Much milk is used to make cheese. Wisconsin is the leading cheese-making state. It has hundreds of plants making all kinds of cheese.

Mining in the central region

Certain parts of the region are rich in iron ore. About four-fifths of our iron ore comes from near Lake Superior. There are ore deposits from eastern Minnesota through northern Wisconsin and into Michigan.

Some ore is near the top of the ground. Miners scoop it out of open pits with large power shovels. Most of the rich ore has been mined. Today most ore comes from low-grade deposits. This taconite iron ore is refined near the mines. The refining produces rich ore in the form of pellets.

Freight cars haul the ore and taconite pellets to ports on Lake Superior. Long ore boats haul their cargo to large steel centers such as Gary, Chicago, Detroit, Cleveland, and Buffalo. Some is then sent on freight cars to inland steel centers like Pittsburgh.

Other mineral resources are found in the central region. Coal is mined in Illinois, Indiana, and eastern Kentucky. What other Central states have coal deposits?

Deposits of limestone are found in Michigan, Ohio, Indiana, Illinois, and other states. Some limestone is used as building material.

Much salt lies beneath the ground in Michigan, Ohio, and Kansas. You know how useful salt is. Animals need salt, too. Farmers supply large chunks of salt for their livestock. Salt is also used in some industries.

Some large cities

There are dozens of busy cities in the Middle West. Most of them are manufacturing centers. Which ones are a part of a megalopolis? Look on the map on page 187 and see.

Millions of autos are made in Michigan's cities. Some cities in Illinois make farm machinery, railway cars, and other iron

307

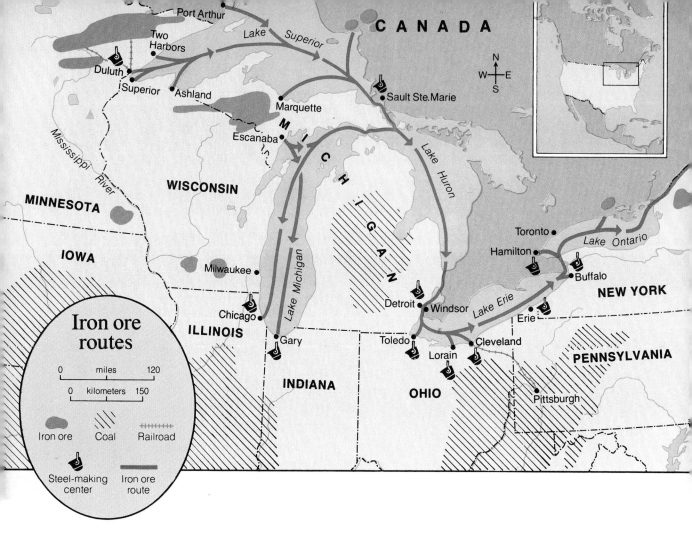

Iron ore
routes

0   miles   120

0   kilometers   150

Iron ore   Coal   Railroad

Steel-making
center

Iron ore
route

and steel products. Akron, Ohio, is called the rubber capital. It turns out more rubber tires than any other city in our country.

Some cities in Ohio have steel mills. Milwaukee, Wisconsin, is a busy lake port. It manufactures many kinds of goods, including farm machinery. Minneapolis has huge meat-packing plants and flour mills. So do Omaha, St. Louis, and Kansas City. St. Louis makes shoes, clothing, and electrical products.

The three largest cities in this region are Chicago, Detroit, and Cleveland.

Chicago is the second largest city in our country. Nearly seven million people live and work in the Chicago metropolitan area.

Chicago is on the southwestern shore of Lake Michigan. It has a fine location and is

a leading transportation center. It is a center for railroads, highways, and airways.

Chicago is a lake port as the map above shows. Boats bring in raw materials from other lake ports. The boats carry away manufactured products, grain, and meat.

Ocean-going ships move along the St. Lawrence Seaway to reach Chicago. A canal and river link the city with the Mississippi. Chicago is in the heart of the Corn Belt. So it is a busy grain-trading center.

Chicago is a leading producer of iron and steel. It makes food products, transportation equipment, farm machines, and many other products. This city is well-known for its research laboratories. In one, experts study weather. Another has people who work on ways to improve food.

Many tourists visit Chicago to attend

This arch in St. Louis reminds
people of the important role St.
Louis played in settling the west.

conventions and to sight-see. People enjoy concerts, art exhibits, and museums.

Detroit is the automobile capital of the world. It produces more autos and trucks than any other city. Its giant auto industry began in the early 1900s. Henry Ford and others started to build "horseless carriages." Today, many plants make auto parts. At an assembly plant you can see an automobile "grow."

The car's "skeleton" moves slowly on a belt through a huge room. Workers and special machines add parts to the auto frame as it travels along. At the end of the long line, out comes a shiny new car.

Detroit also makes machinery and tools. It makes chemicals and other goods.

Like Chicago, Detroit has a good location. It is near steel mills and coal mines. It

is on the waterway between Lake Erie and Lake Huron. So it is linked to many other cities by the St. Lawrence Seaway. Ships can sail to and from Detroit with raw materials and manufactured goods.

Cleveland is a busy port on Lake Erie. Notice on the map that Cleveland has a fine location for trade and manufacturing. It is a leading city in the manufacture of iron and steel products.

Pollution has harmed some of the Great Lakes. Fast-growing cities and their many factories caused most of the pollution. Cities poured sewage into the lakes. Factories dumped their wastes. Lake Superior has been polluted with waste from taconite ore refineries.

But today many people are working to clean the waters. Cities are treating sewage. Companies are putting in equipment to cut down pollution. This clean-up job costs much money. But people know that the job must be done.

The Middle West has many places for tourists to visit. Michigan, Wisconsin, and Minnesota are dotted with hundreds of lakes. The Ozarks attract campers and hikers.

Canton, Ohio, has the Pro Football Hall of Fame. About 100 old-time buildings have been moved to Greenfield Village at Dearborn, Michigan. They are a kind of museum. One building is "a little red schoolhouse." Other cities in the region have museums and historic sites.

Visit Mount Rushmore in the Black Hills of South Dakota. There you can see giant stone carvings of four great Presidents. The graves of Wild Bill Hickok and Calamity Jane are in Deadwood, South Dakota.

In Watertown, Wisconsin, is the building that had the first kindergarten in America. It was started by Margaretha Schurz in 1856.

Ohio was the birthplace of seven Presidents. Lincoln lived in Kentucky, Indiana, and Illinois.

Two famous women who worked to stop the sale of liquor are remembered in this region. Frances E. Willard started a national society at Evanston, Illinois. Carry Nation worked to shut down saloons in Kansas. Her tiny stone house at Medicine Lodge, Kansas, is now a museum.

Which are partners?

In List A are beginnings of sentences. The endings are in List B. Write the complete sentences on your paper.

List A

1. The Central states
2. The drier parts of the Central states are
3. Corn is our country's
4. Native Americans taught the settlers
5. A silo stores
6. Machines such as tractors and combines
7. The western Central states raise enormous
8. Wisconsin makes
9. Most of our corn is
10. Parts of Michigan, Wisconsin, and Minnesota
11. Chicago is
12. Detroit is called

List B

a. quantities of wheat.
b. how to grow corn.
c. cattle feed.
d. have rich deposits of iron ore.
e. many kinds of cheese.
f. the automobile city.
g. are a rich agricultural region.
h. the second largest city in the United States.
i. biggest crop.
j. the western lands of Kansas, Nebraska, and the Dakotas.
k. fed to cattle, hogs, and poultry.
l. help many of the wheat farmers.
m. have few cities.

Some review questions

1. What states make up the Dairy Belt?
2. What important minerals are found in the Central states? Which of these have helped to develop the automobile industry?
3. Why are so many iron and steel centers found in the central region?
4. Why has Chicago become a large city?

Fun with maps

Use the map of the Central states (pages 300-301) to help you do these things.

1. Tell two main ideas which the inset map shows about the central region.
2. Tell in what direction
   a. St. Louis is from Chicago.
   b. Minneapolis is from Detroit.
   c. Cleveland is from Milwaukee.
3. Measure the distance between
   a. Chicago and Detroit.
   b. Kansas City and Cincinnati.
4. Study the key and the map. Then name the cities that have a population of more than one million. Name those that have 500,000 to one million.

Reporting news items

Here are some ideas to keep in mind when you share news items with your class.

1. Practice telling your news before giving it to your class.
2. Know it well enough to give it briefly and in an interesting way.
3. Try to show pictures related to it.
4. Show on a map where it took place.

Find and share a news item about one of the industries discussed in this chapter. Try to keep in mind the ideas you just read about giving a news item.

Think it over

1. If you do not live in the central region, how does this region differ from your part of the country?
2. How has climate influenced ways of making a living in the central region?
3. What do you think this saying means, "Don't put all of your eggs in one basket"? What might this mean to a farm family in the Corn Belt?
4. Wise planning and looking ahead are keys to success. Why is this true, do you suppose? What kinds of planning do farmers need to do?

Some other things to do

1. Locate the central region on the map on pages 90-91. Use the elevation sketch to tell which is higher.

   The Central Plains or the Great Plains.
   The Central Plains or the Ozark Hills.

2. Read in an encyclopedia to learn more about the uses of one of the following.

   soybeans   corn
   alfalfa   oats

3. Draw a mural of a farm scene.
4. Read more about one of these cities in a reference book.

   Chicago   Akron
   St. Louis   Detroit
   Kansas City   Cleveland
   Des Moines   Gary

23

The Rocky Mountain states

An explorer finds a wonderland

John Colter was a trapper. He went west with the Lewis and Clark party. You know that these brave people explored the huge Louisiana Territory.

On the way back, Colter asked to leave the party. He wanted to trap beaver. He also planned to trade with groups of Native Americans.

Colter tramped off alone through the rugged wilderness. One day he came to a place where strange things were happening. The earth was trembling under his feet. There were many pools of mud boiling up. They seemed to be cooking on a hidden stove.

Great fountains of hot water were bursting out of the earth. They were *geysers*. But Colter did not know that. He had never heard of geysers.

Colter wandered through the wilderness for six years. Then he returned to St. Louis.

The trapper told stories to his friends about the strange sights he had seen. "Nonsense!" they exclaimed. "You're just dreaming up tall tales!"

Some years later, another explorer visited the western land. He too brought back surprising tales. People shook their heads when they heard them.

One young man believed the reports. He decided to go west and find out for himself. In 1870 he led some explorers to the land of strange sights.

The explorers found the wonders that Colter had talked about. They watched huge geysers shoot plumes of water and steam toward the sky. They saw a great waterfall that poured into a yellowish stone canyon.

One night the group sat by a campfire. Someone spoke up. "This land is thrilling! Someone should buy it and charge to let people see it. A person could make a big fortune."

"No!" someone said. "It would be wrong to do that. I think this beautiful area should be a park. A national park could be saved for all the people to enjoy!"

"A great idea!" others agreed. Then they talked about ways to make this dream come true.

In time, some of these people went over the country telling people about the Yellowstone region. More and more interest was stirred up. In 1872 Congress passed a law that made the Yellowstone region our first national park.

One of the first peoples to live here were the Shoshoni. They hunted bear, mountain sheep, buffalo, elk, and deer. Other Native Americans came to hunt at certain times of the year. One tribe called the area "Mi-tsi-da-ze," or "Yellow Rock." This is how the area came to be called "Yellowstone."

The Rocky Mountain states

The Rocky Mountain states are "out West." They make up a large region that begins just west of the Central states. Look at the map of the Rocky Mountain states. It stretches from Canada to Mexico, about 1200 miles (1900 km). The Rocky Mountains are in the six states of this region. They are Idaho, Montana, Wyoming, Colorado, Utah, and New Mexico.

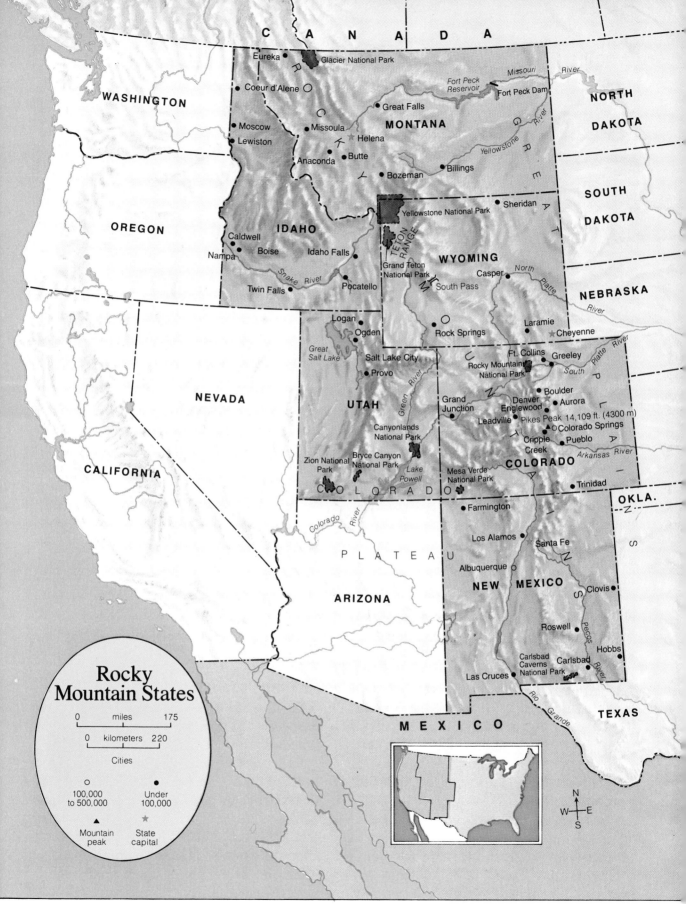

Rocky Mountain States

CANADA

WASHINGTON

Eureka
Glacier National Park
Coeur d'Alene
Great Falls
Fort Peck
Reservoir
Missouri
River
Fort Peck Dam

NORTH
DAKOTA

Moscow
Missoula
MONTANA
Yellowstone
River

Lewiston
Helena
Butte
Anaconda
Bozeman
Billings

OREGON

IDAHO

Caldwell
Boise
Idaho Falls
Nampa
Twin Falls
Snake River
Pocatello

Yellowstone National Park
Sheridan

SOUTH
DAKOTA

TETON RANGE
Grand Teton
National Park
South Pass

WYOMING

Casper
North Platte River

NEBRASKA

Logan
Ogden
Rock Springs
Laramie
Cheyenne

NEVADA

Great
Salt Lake
Salt Lake City
Provo

Ft. Collins
Greeley
Rocky Mountain
National Park
South Platte River

UTAH

Green River

Grand
Junction

Boulder
Denver
Englewood
Aurora
Leadville
Pikes Peak 14,109 ft. (4300 m)
Colorado Springs
Cripple
Creek
Pueblo
Arkansas River

CALIFORNIA

Canyonlands
National Park

Zion National
Park
Bryce Canyon
National Park
Lake
Powell
Mesa Verde
National Park
COLORADO
Trinidad

COLORADO

OKLA.

Farmington

PLATEAU

Los Alamos
Santa Fe
Albuquerque
NEW MEXICO
Clovis

ARIZONA

Roswell
Pecos River
Hobbs

Carlsbad
Caverns
National Park
Carlsbad
Las Cruces
Rio Grande

TEXAS

MEXICO

Rocky Mountain States

0 miles 175
0 kilometers 220

Cities

○ 100,000 to 500,000
● Under 100,000
▲ Mountain peak
★ State capital

N
W E
S

In Colorado, the western part of the Great Plains rises gently towards the Rocky Mountains.

Four Rocky Mountain states share the Great Plains. These plains go from the Central states into Montana, Wyoming, Colorado, and New Mexico. Long ago, Native Americans lived here. They hunted buffalo. Explorers and hunters crossed the Great Plains and so did long wagon trains.

These plains are covered with short grass except where they have been plowed. They look nearly as level as a floor, but they aren't. They rise as they go west to the mountains. Notice this on the elevation sketch at the bottom of the map on pages 90–91.

The snow-capped Rockies rise high above the Great Plains. They extend all the way through this region. The Rockies, you know, have many mountain ranges.

West of the Rocky Mountains lies plateau country. A plateau, you know, is a highland that is usually not as level as a plain. The Rocky Mountain region has a part of the huge Columbia and Colorado plateaus. Find them on the map on pages 90–91. They have rolling lands, deep valleys, and ranges of mountains.

Idaho has part of the Columbia Plateau. The Colorado Plateau goes through parts of Colorado, Utah, and New Mexico.

Two Rocky Mountain states share the Great Basin. The Great Basin extends through western Utah and north into Idaho. It has mountains, valleys, and large deserts.

The Great Basin also has sloping sides. Since higher lands are all around its floor, water can't run out. Streams that flow into the Great Basin do not reach the ocean.

"What happens to this water?" you may ask.

Some of it dries up in the hot summer sunshine. Some sinks into the ground. And some flows into Great Salt Lake.

Great Salt Lake is in Utah on the eastern side of the Great Basin. It is the largest body of water in the Rocky Mountain region. But it is shrinking. Less water flows into it because so much goes to water crops. Also, some water dries up in the long hot summers.

Great Salt Lake is too salty to be of much use. It is now five or six times more salty than the ocean. You see, all fresh water has a little salt in it. This is true of the streams that feed the lake. When the lake water evaporates, the salt is left behind. Because no streams flow out of the lake, the salt is never washed away.

314

Some large rivers begin in the Rocky Mountain region. Among them are the Colorado, Missouri, Arkansas, and Snake rivers and the Rio Grande. Locate them on the map on pages 90–91. Find where each one starts. Which river empties into the Columbia? Name the river which joins the Mississippi. Which one empties into the Gulf of Mexico?

These rivers are far more valuable than all the gold and silver found in this region. Dams on the rivers hold back much water. It is used by towns and cities and for irrigation of farms. Dams also provide water power to make electricity.

There are several dams on the Missouri River. The largest one is Fort Peck Dam. Find it on the map of the Rocky Mountain states. The reservoir, or lake, back of it is 189 miles long (305 km). It furnishes much irrigation water. Below the dam is a powerhouse to make electric power. Dams on the Snake River supply water for the farmlands of southern Idaho.

The Grand Teton Mountains in Wyoming *(top)* and Bryce Canyon in Utah *(above)* are among the scenic wonders of the Rocky Mountain states.

Vast areas in the Rocky Mountain region are dry. The map on page 317 shows this. Study the caption and key. What color shows the driest lands? Locate them. A much larger part of the region gets just 10 to 20 inches (25 to 50 cm) of rain a year. This is not enough to grow most crops.

This region is dry because the clouds from the Pacific drop most of their rain before they get to this area. Only a little rain falls on the Great Basin and most of the plateau lands.

Climate is varied in the Rocky Mountain states. This is not strange. Notice how far these states extend from north to south. Also plains, plateaus, and valleys have a warmer climate than mountains have.

The northern lands often have long cold winters. Icy winds sweep across the plateaus and plains. They bring blinding snowstorms called blizzards. It is not safe to be out in a blizzard. The air is so full of whirling snow that people can't see. Animals can get covered by snow, and die.

The high mountains stay very cold from fall to late spring. In many places they are half buried under heavy snows. When warm weather comes, much snow melts. But some peaks have snow on them all year.

The mountains have nice summers with cooler weather than the lower lands nearby. But the summers are short. You can see this if you turn to the Growing Season Map on page 258.

Where in the Rocky Mountain region can crops grow the longest? Where can they grow from 4 to 6 months? In these areas, summer temperatures may climb to 100° F (38° C), or more. Some weeks, it is just as hot on the plains and plateaus in the north as it is in the south. Day after day the burning sun beats down. Cooling showers come only once in a while. But even in these dry lands, farming is important.

Farming and ranching

Some farmers carry on dry farming on the plains. Dry farming tries to make use of all the rain and snow that falls. Farm families plant only one part of their land each year. The rest of the fields are left unplanted, or fallow. But the unplanted fields are cultivated. This loosens the soil so that rain can sink in. It also kills the weeds that use up moisture. Fallow fields are plowed so the furrows can catch and save the water. The moisture stored in the ground will help the next crop.

In dry farming, only crops are raised that can grow well with little rain. Wheat and some other grains are grown by dry farming. Wheat is the main crop. Look at the map on page 304 and find the chief wheat-growing areas in the Rocky Mountain states.

People who came from eastern Europe taught Americans the secrets of dry farming. They came from lands where dry farming was carried on. They knew how to grow some kinds of wheat where only a little rain falls.

Irrigated farming is also important in this region. Find the irrigated regions in the Rocky Mountain states on the map on page 319. What symbol is used to show the irrigated regions?

Rivers flowing down the mountains provide water for irrigation. It is stored in reservoirs behind dams. Canals carry the water from the reservoirs to the farmlands.

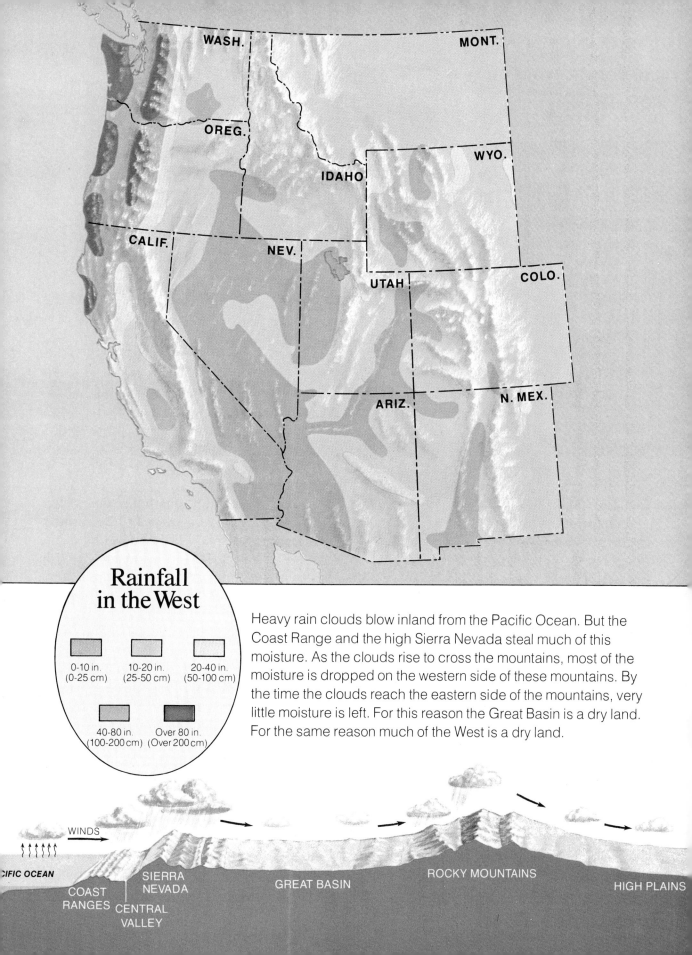

Rainfall in the West

Legend:
- 0-10 in. (0-25 cm)
- 10-20 in. (25-50 cm)
- 20-40 in. (50-100 cm)
- 40-80 in. (100-200 cm)
- Over 80 in. (Over 200 cm)

Heavy rain clouds blow inland from the Pacific Ocean. But the Coast Range and the high Sierra Nevada steal much of this moisture. As the clouds rise to cross the mountains, most of the moisture is dropped on the western side of these mountains. By the time the clouds reach the eastern side of the mountains, very little moisture is left. For this reason the Great Basin is a dry land. For the same reason much of the West is a dry land.

WASH.
MONT.
OREG.
IDAHO
WYO.
CALIF.
NEV.
UTAH
COLO.
ARIZ.
N. MEX.

WINDS

PACIFIC OCEAN
COAST RANGES
CENTRAL VALLEY
SIERRA NEVADA
GREAT BASIN
ROCKY MOUNTAINS
HIGH PLAINS

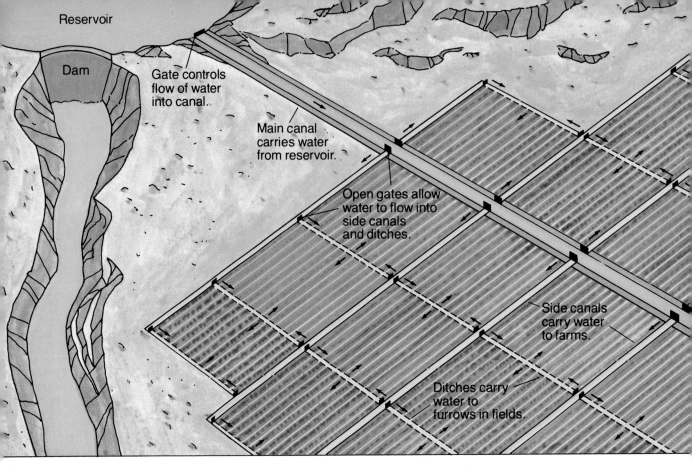

Reservoir

Dam

Gate controls flow of water into canal.

Main canal carries water from reservoir.

Open gates allow water to flow into side canals and ditches.

Side canals carry water to farms.

Ditches carry water to furrows in fields.

Through irrigation, desert land is turned into productive farmland. Canals carry water to the fields from reservoirs high in the mountains.

Large dams have been built by the United States government. Farmers pay for the water they use.

Many small irrigation projects have been built by groups of farmers. They share the cost of the work and the water.

What are some irrigated crops grown in this region? Potatoes and peas are grown in Idaho and Utah. One part of Colorado is known for its melons.

The only cotton in this region is grown in New Mexico. What kind of weather does cotton need to grow?

Several states grow sugar beets. Look at the same map and name them. The sugar beet is related to the red beets we eat. But the sugar beet has a whitish root.

Sugar beets are planted from seeds. They are ready to harvest in late summer or early fall. This work is done by a machine, a beet harvester. It loosens the soil, pulls the beets, and cuts off their tops. Then it dumps them on a moving belt that carries them to a truck. The tops are used for cattle feed. The beets are hauled to a sugar refinery.

At the refinery a large machine washes and cleans the beets. They are sliced in thin strips. The strips are treated to remove the "juice." It is boiled, made pure, and finally comes out as sugar.

Farmers raise alfalfa in each of the Rocky Mountain states. It is a main crop in Idaho. Alfalfa is an important food for livestock and a good soil builder. It helps to put certain plant foods back into the soil. Alfalfa can grow in quite dry soil. Its roots grow as far as 25 feet into the ground. It finds water better than short-rooted plants.

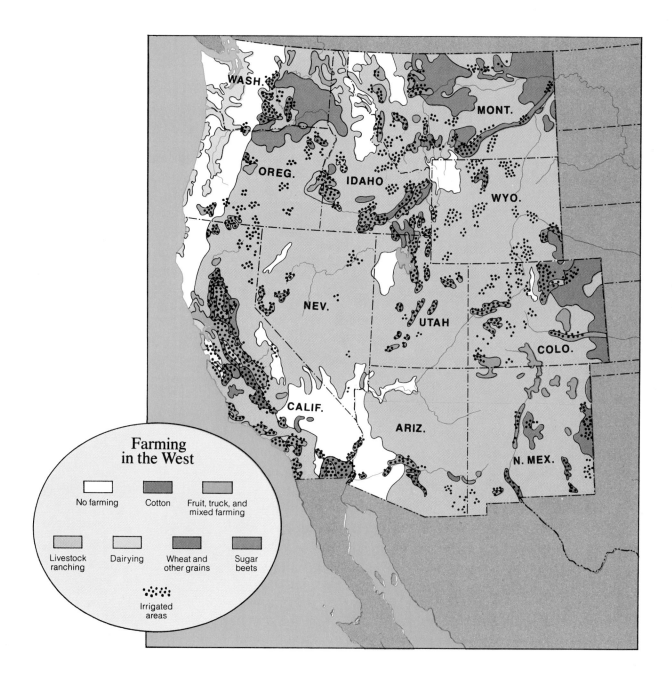

**Farming
in the West**

- No farming
- Cotton
- Fruit, truck, and mixed farming
- Livestock ranching
- Dairying
- Wheat and other grains
- Sugar beets
- Irrigated areas

Many ranchers in this region raise beef cattle. The map above shows the areas where livestock ranching is carried on. The grasslands are used for grazing cattle and sheep.

The cattle industry began long ago. In early days a rancher could let the cattle roam. There were no fences. The land was owned by the government and was called the *open range*.

Cowhands were hired to tend the cattle. Some were Mexicans and some were blacks. They often wore bright woolen shirts, tight pants, and high-heeled boots with spurs. Their broad-brimmed hats shaded them from the burning summer sun. Large handkerchiefs kept the wind and sun off their necks.

On the open range a rancher's herd mixed with other herds. Still it was easy to

319

tell the cattle apart, for they had been branded, or marked. For instance, Dobsons' cattle bore a mark which looked like a circle with an X in it. Their ranch was known as the Circle-X ranch. Each ranch had its own brand.

In the spring the cowhands rounded up the cattle. Then each calf was branded with its mother's brand.

Today these lands have fences. One ranch may have several thousand acres. Cattle ranches have to be large. The grass is so thin that many acres are needed for each cow.

No longer do the cowhands ride the open range to follow the cattle. They do other work. They make sure the animals are getting enough grass and water. From time to time they drive the cattle to fresh pastures. Cowhands must check the fences and keep them mended.

In the fall or early winter the cowhands round up some cattle. These are shipped by truck or railroad to feed lots in the Corn Belt to be fattened.

Some ranchers own large flocks of sheep. Sheep can live where the land is too dry or rough to raise cattle. They can feed on shorter and poorer grass.

Each flock is tended by a sheep herder and several dogs. The herder may live in a truck-drawn "covered wagon," or trailer, and move from place to place. In the early summer the herder may drive the animals to mountain meadows. Here they find greener grass and more water than on the hot, dry plains. But when fall comes, the sheep are driven back to their ranches.

Sheep are raised for meat and wool. Most of those in this region and other parts of the West are raised for their wool.

Mining and lumbering

Miners opened up part of the Rocky Mountain region. Gold was found in present-day Colorado, Montana, and Idaho about a hundred years ago. Silver was also found in some areas.

Many fortune hunters came to the new treasure fields. Mining towns sprang up overnight. They grew so fast that they were called "boom towns." Some had names like *Last Chance* and *Rabbit Hole*.

For a while, gold and silver were easy to find. But when the supply ran out, people moved away. The empty boom towns were so quiet they were called ghost towns.

Now most mining is done by large companies using machinery.

Today this region mines many kinds of treasure. Among them are gold and silver. Idaho has the largest silver mine in the United States. But the main "mining" industries are concerned with uranium and coal. The state is rich in oil shale. The high price of oil is causing oil companies to consider the oil in oil shale.

Some miners in Utah and Montana work in the copper mines. Utah has a giant open-pit copper mine.

Butte (byüt), Montana, is the center of another copper-mining area. The copper is blasted from rock deep in the earth beneath the city. The ore is hauled to the surface by small electric cars. It is taken to a smelter to be melted and refined.

Butte and some other areas produce zinc. It is a bluish-white metal that has many uses. It is melted with copper to make brass. A thin coat of zinc is often used on other metals to protect them from rust.

Geiger counters are used to detect the presence of uranium in the ground. Uranium is the major source of nuclear energy. The richest deposits of uranium in our country are in New Mexico, Wyoming, Colorado, and Utah.

Much lead is mined in Idaho and Utah. Lead is a soft metal but a very useful one. It is used to cover electric cables and to protect works from X rays and uranium. Leadville, Colorado, has been the center of one lead-mining area. It is located at an elevation of more than 10,000 feet (3050 m). It is now a center of mining for molybdenum (mə lib′də nəm). Look at the map on page 273. Which of these states have big coal fields?

Miners are finding "new" minerals. One is the metal molybdenum. Molybdenum is used to make the hard, tough steel needed in cutting tools. It is also used in airplane motors. The world's largest molybdenum mine is also near Leadville.

Colorado and some other Rocky Mountain states mine uranium. It is used in producing atomic energy.

Five states in this region have important oil fields. They are New Mexico, Wyoming, Colorado, Montana, and Utah.

Look on the map on page 291 to see where these oil fields are. This map also shows the main pipelines that carry the crude oil from the fields to refineries.

Thick forests grow in some parts of the Rocky Mountain states. They grow well in northern Idaho and western Montana. And with good reason. Trees grow best where there is plenty of rain. Look on the map on page 317 and see how much rain these northern highlands get.

Lumbering has many kinds of jobs for people who live near the forests. Some people are loggers. Others work in the sawmills and in factories which make wood products. Some earn their living growing Christmas trees.

Cities in the Rocky Mountain states

The Rocky Mountain region is thinly populated. The map on page 187 shows this. Then look at the map on page 313 to see how far apart the cities are. Towns too small to show on this political map are scattered here and there. But one can ride for miles and miles and not see a town.

The towns and cities are trading centers. They serve the farms, ranches, and mines near them. Some have become busy manufacturing centers. Their factories and mills change crops, minerals, and other raw materials into useful products.

Denver is the largest city in the Rocky Mountain region. It is in the heart of Colorado "where the mountains meet the plains."

Denver, the capital of Colorado, is called the "Mile High City." The words "one mile above sea level" appear on the fifteenth step of the Capitol. From its dome, one can see a thrilling view of the Rockies that rise nearby.

Denver is one of the leading cattle and sheep markets of the world. Meat animals from the Great Plains are shipped to its huge stockyards. Some people work in its packing plants getting meat ready for market. Some earn a living in the flour mills and beet-sugar refineries. Others work in factories that produce leather goods or machinery. A lot of mining business goes on here. The tourist business is important, too.

Many tourists come to Denver. Because of its elevation, it has pleasant summer weather. Denver is the gateway to vacation lands in the Rockies. Many people have jobs in the tourist industry. Some are mountain guides. Others teach people how to ski.

This city is the gateway to other parts of the Rocky Mountain region and to the states farther west. Railways, highways, and airways connect it with other cities. One is Salt Lake City just west of the Rocky Mountains.

Salt Lake City is called the "Crossroads of the West." It is the second largest city in the region and is the capital of Utah. Salt Lake City spreads over a wide dry basin at the foot of high mountains. Water for the city and nearby farms comes from these snow-capped mountains.

The Mormons founded Salt Lake City. They laid out wide, straight streets and built some fine buildings that are in use today. One is the Mormon Temple. Another is the Tabernacle in which the famous Mormon Tabernacle Choir sings. You may have seen and heard this choir on television.

Salt Lake City was first called "The Crossroads of the West" during the days of the pioneers. The main trails to the Far West led through or near it. Today, railroads and highways follow these same routes.

Salt Lake City is the chief trading center for miles around. It has canneries, dairies, flour mills, and beet-sugar refineries. Some plants prepare salt for market. Like Denver, it has the main offices of some mining companies.

Other cities serve the Rocky Mountain region. Pueblo, Colorado, is widely known for its steel mills. Cheyenne (shī an′) is a transportation center and Wyoming's capital. On the grounds of the

State Capitol is a statue of Esther Hobart Morris. She worked to get a woman's equal rights law passed in Wyoming in 1869.

Helena (hel′ə nə), Montana's capital, began when gold was found nearby in a mining area called Last Chance. Helena is a busy trading center for mines and farms.

Albuquerque (al′bə kėr′kē) is New Mexico's largest city. It was started by the Spanish in 1706. Many Spanish buildings can still be seen in old sections of the city. Today Albuquerque is an important center of trade and industry. The University of New Mexico is in Albuquerque. Because of its dry, warm climate, many people come to Albuquerque for health reasons.

New Mexico has one of our youngest cities. It also has a very old one. Los Alamos was started in 1943 on a windy *mesa,* or high flat area. It was the place where scientists did secret work on the first atomic bomb. Santa Fe began in 1610 as a Spanish city. It is the capital of New Mexico.

Famous natural wonders

Beautiful wonderlands are scattered through this region. Tourists can see towering mountains crowned with snow. There are shining lakes, tumbling falls, and clear cold streams. In some deserts the giant rocks look like towers and castles.

Some of these wonderlands are national parks. The map on page 285 shows most of our national parks. Which ones are in the Rocky Mountain region? Have you visited any of them?

Yellowstone is the oldest national park. It was made a park in 1872. It is more than

There are six main geyser areas in Yellowstone National Park. The buffalo are grazing in the Upper Geyser Basin. The cross country skier has stopped to admire Castle Geyser.

Hikers enjoy the natural beauty of Olympic National Park in Washington. This trail leads to the High Divide.

twice the size of Rhode Island. Tourists can travel on fine highways which wind through this park. They can stay at hotels or cabins or in camping areas.

At Yellowstone, you may see many sights besides the amazing geysers. One is the Grand Canyon of the Yellowstone. It was carved out by a river that now flows hundreds of feet below.

Yellowstone has many kinds of wildlife. There are bears in the back country. There are fenced meadows where shaggy buffalo feed. In the forests are deer, elk, and moose. Bighorn sheep feed high on the cliffs.

Several other national parks are in the Rockies. In Wyoming there is Grand Teton with its sharp, high peaks. Glacier National Park is in the mountains of western Montana. It has interesting trails and some fine roads. Its "Going-to-the-Sun Highway" is well-known. Much snow falls in the mountains of this park. It collects year after year, layer upon layer. Some of it never melts. The lower layers have changed to ice. These huge masses of ice are glaciers. They creep ever so slowly down the mountain slopes. Some of the snow melts and runs into streams and lakes.

Rocky Mountain National Park is in Colorado. It has 65 peaks that are more than 10,000 feet high (16,000 m). The tallest have snow on them all summer. This park is dotted with deep sparkling lakes and threaded with silvery streams. Camping areas and miles of trails attract many visitors.

Bryce Canyon and Zion Canyon are in southwestern Utah. Bryce Canyon is filled with bright, strangely shaped rocks. Some rise hundreds of feet above the floor of the canyon.

Zion Canyon is also full of color. A river has carved this deep narrow canyon, leaving high walls and towers of stone.

Southwestern New Mexico has Carlsbad Caverns National Park. It is a chain of huge caves. Each one is like a large room. One cave, called Big Room, is about six-tenths of a mile (1 km) long. Amazing stone "icicles" hang from the ceilings of these caves. Other strange column-like rocks rise from the floors.

Questions to help you review

1. What are the Rocky Mountain states? Which ones share the Great Plains? Which ones have some plateau country?

2. Why are rivers so important to this region? How are they used?

3. What are the main industries in the Rocky Mountain states?

4. What are the leading crops? What are some chief natural resources?

5. Why is this region famous as a vacationland? What national parks are located in it?

Fun with maps

Use the map on page 187 to help you tell which has fewer people.

Colorado or Wyoming?
New Mexico or Texas?
Utah or Illinois?

Why is the Rocky Mountain region thinly populated? The map on pages 90-91 can give us some clues. Turn to it.

Which will you choose?

Find the ending that makes each of the following sentences true. On paper, write the correct letter of the word or words after each sentence number.

1. The Rocky Mountain region lies just west of (New England.) (the Central states.) (the Middle Atlantic states.)

2. Dry farming is used to raise (wheat.) (corn.) (sugar cane.)

3. A main industry in this region is (fishing.) (stock raising.) (shipping.)

4. Many ranches raise large numbers of (horses.) (dairy cattle.) (beef cattle.)

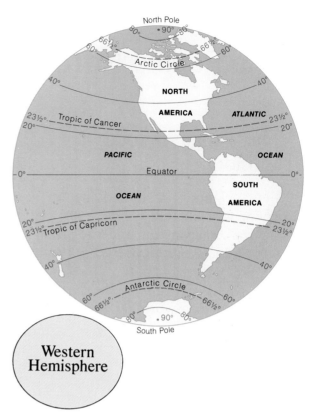

Western Hemisphere

Learning about east-west lines, or latitude

On page 297 you learned how to use letters and numbers to locate places on a map. Many maps have north-south lines and east-west lines.

East-west lines run east to west on a globe or map. Look at the picture of the globe. Find the equator. It is a line from east to west on a globe or map of the earth. It shows the place around the earth that is halfway between the North Pole and South Pole. Now turn to the map of the United States on pages 254-255. Notice the east-west lines. Find the east-west line that runs south of New York City. Is Denver just north or south of an east-west line shown on the map? What city in Nevada is located almost on an east-west line?

The line that runs through northern Florida is numbered 30°. 30° means 30 degrees. The city of Salt Lake City, Utah, is a little north of the east-west line numbered 40°. Find Salt Lake City. An east-west line is called *latitude,* or line of latitude.

24
The Pacific Northwest

The Tlingits—today and long ago

New neighbors were moving in, and Lorraine was excited. "Hello," she called as she walked up to a girl and a boy beside a moving van. "I'm Lorraine. I live next door. Welcome."

"Thank you," replied the girl. "I'm Sue, and this is my brother Ron."

"Hi," said Ron. "We're moving here from Portland, Oregon."

"You'll like Anchorage," answered Lorraine, "and you will like living in Alaska."

"That's wonderful!" answered Sue. "Have you lived in Alaska very long?"

"Oh, yes, forever," Lorraine replied proudly. "I mean my people have. We've lived in Alaska for thousands of years. We're Native Americans. We're Tlingits."

The Tlingits (tling′əts) are part of the 50,000 Native Americans in Alaska. Others include Eskimo, Aleut, Athabascan, and Haida people. They do all kinds of work. Some own or work in fish canneries. Some are plane mechanics and pilots. Some are teachers, road builders, carpenters, and lawyers. They are an important part of Alaska today.

The Tlingits lived along the coast of southern Alaska. They settled there long before the first people came to America from Europe. Their land extended along the Pacific for hundreds of miles.

This is a mountainous land covered with thick forests. Rivers flow from the mountains to the Pacific.

Many fish swam in the rivers and ocean. Seals, otters, and whales were found in the ocean. Deer, bear, and other large and small animals lived in the forests.

The Tlingits collected fish, animals, and berries from spring to fall. They prepared and stored much of this food for winter. In winter they lived in villages. Several related families lived in each house.

In winter the Tlingits made beautiful and useful objects from wood, stone, and bone. They wove blankets and clothing from the wool of mountain sheep and from cedar bark. They made fine baskets. They also held feasts and celebrations.

The families in a house had a crest. It stood for an animal or bird that was a part of their history. It was put on articles owned by the families. The crest was also woven into blankets. It was carved on totem poles and canoes or painted on the house.

The Tlingits no longer live in groups of families in handsome wooden houses. Many live in cities. But they are proud of their past. They still hold some of their old celebrations. They work to help each other. Some Tlingit artists keep alive the beautiful art of their people.

Our Northwest

Oregon, Washington, and Alaska are the states of our Northwest. Point to each one on the map. Alaska is our largest state. It is in the northwestern part of North America. It is about one-fifth the size of the rest of the United States.

Oregon was the first to become a state in the Northwest. It was once a part of the Oregon Country. Oregon became a state more than a hundred years ago. You read how pioneers went over the Oregon Trail to settle on its rich lands.

U.S.S.R.

Bering Strait

Bering Sea

Barrow • Point Barrow

ARCTIC COASTAL PLAIN

Beaufort Sea

BROOKS RANGE

Prudhoe Bay

• Nome

ALASKA

Yukon River

Alaska Pipeline

PRIBILOF ISLANDS

YUKON PLATEAU

Mt. McKinley National Park

Tanana

RANGE

Fairbanks

Yukon

Alaska River

Highway

YUKON TERRITORY

NORTHWEST

ALASKA RANGE
Mt. McKinley 20,320 ft. (6194 m)

ALEUTIAN ISLANDS

Matanuska Valley

Anchorage

Dutch Harbor

ALASKA PENINSULA

Cook Inlet

KENAI PENINSULA

Seward

Valdez

Mt. St. Elias 18,008 ft. (5489 m)

TERRITORY

ROCKY

CANADA

• Kodiak
Kodiak Island

Gulf of Alaska

Skagway

Juneau

PANHANDLE

MOUNTAINS

Sitka

Wrangell

Ketchikan

BRITISH

Dawson Creek

PACIFIC

OCEAN

COLUMBIA

Vancouver Island

Inside Passage

Northwest States

| 0 | miles | 175 |
| 0 | kilometers | 220 |

Cities

■ 500,000 to 1 million   ○ 100,000 to 500,000   • Under 100,000

★ State capital

N
W E
S

Puget Sound

Bellingham

North Cascades National Park

RANGE

Grand Coulee Dam

Olympic National Park

• Everett

■ Seattle

• Spokane ○

Tacoma

WASHINGTON

Olympia

Mt. Rainier National Park

River

IDAHO

COLUMBIA

• Yakima

Vancouver

Mt. Rainier 14,410 ft. (4392 m)

Portland

Columbia

Bonneville Dam

Whitman Mission

COAST

RANGE

Salem

CASCADE

Mt. Hood 11,245 ft. (3427 m)

Snake River

PLATEAU

Eugene

OREGON

Willamette River

Crater Lake

Crater Lake National Park

Medford •

• Klamath Falls

CALIFORNIA

Fishing is a major industry in Alaska. These king crabs were caught in the lower part of Cook Inlet.

Washington was named in honor of our first President. George Washington's picture appears on its flag. Washington's first pioneers were Marcus and Narcissa Whitman. You read about these missionaries earlier. George Bush, a black pioneer, is not as well-known. But he helped many newcomers get a start. He gave them food from his farm.

Alaska became the forty-ninth state in 1959. But it had become a part of our country nearly ninety years earlier.

The first European to see Alaska probably was a Danish sea captain, Vitus Bering. He claimed it for Russia, the country that had hired him. The map on page 327 shows how close Alaska is to Russia.

Both the Bering Sea and the Bering Strait are named for this explorer. A *strait* is a narrow channel of water that connects two larger bodies of water.

The Russians built fur-trading posts in Alaska. But they were not very successful.

Russia lost interest and offered to sell Alaska to the United States. Our country bought it for $7,200,000. In 1867 the American flag was raised above Sitka, Alaska's first capital.

Oregon, Washington, and Alaska have miles of seacoast. Oregon's rugged coast is famous for its beauty. Travelers on the coastal highway enjoy grand views of the Pacific and the rocky cliffs.

Washington's western coast also faces the Pacific. Its northern shores look out on a long strait. This waterway leads to Puget (pyü′jit) Sound. It is the "front porch" of a number of Washington's cities. Find Puget Sound on the map of the Northwest states.

Alaska has a very long seacoast, since Alaska is a giant peninsula. The icy Arctic Ocean lies north of this huge land. To the west are the Bering Strait and the Bering Sea.

Southern Alaska has a long tongue of land known as the Alaskan Peninsula. It leads southwestward to the Aleutian Islands. This chain of islands curves across the Pacific for more than a thousand miles (1600 km). Many Aleuts (al′ēütz) live here.

Southeastern Alaska is bordered by a ragged coastline. It is known as the Panhandle. It has more inlets than the map can show. They reach deep into the mainland. They were made by glaciers long ago.

Hundreds of forest islands are scattered off the shores of the Panhandle. Between them and the mainland is a natural waterway. It is the Inside Passage. The islands shelter it from storms that sweep across the open sea. Many ships sail this sheltered route. Some carry tourists to Alaska. Other ships carry on trade between ports in the Northwest.

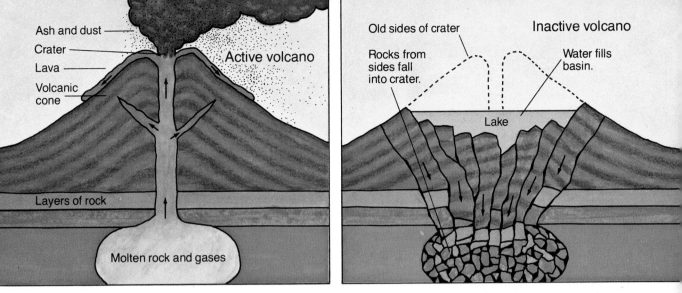

Ash and dust
Crater
Lava
Volcanic cone

Active volcano

Layers of rock

Molten rock and gases

Old sides of crater

Rocks from sides fall into crater.

Inactive volcano

Water fills basin.

Lake

Sides of inactive volcanos often crumble and fall into the crater. If water fills the crater basin, a lake is formed.

Washington and Oregon share the Coast Ranges. They are chains of hills and mountains that extend along the Pacific.

Trees grow close together on the western slopes. They thrive in the rainy climate. The western slopes may receive as much as 150 inches (380 cm) of rain a year. This is some of the wettest land in our country as the map on page 317 shows.

East of the Coast Ranges are fertile lowlands and the Cascades. Find the areas that extend back from Puget Sound in Washington (page 327). Now locate the long Willamette River Valley in Oregon.

The Cascades are high mountains that usually have long cold winters. One snowstorm follows another. In places, the snow may pile up about forty feet (10 m).

The tallest peak, Mount Rainier, is in Washington. Its thick cloak of snow and glaciers makes it look like a huge frosted cake. This grand peak is part of Mount Rainier National Park.

Mount Hood is Oregon's highest peak. It, too, is a well-known vacation land. Skiing is popular on its glacier-clad slopes summer and winter.

Many peaks in the Cascades were formed by volcanoes. A *volcano* is an opening in the earth's surface. Steam, ashes, and lava are forced out of it. *Lava* is rock that has been melted into red-hot liquid by heat deep in the earth.

When a volcano is pushing out materials, it is *erupting*. It may pour out so much lava that it builds up a high mountain. Study the drawing at the top of the page to find out how this happens. Notice that some lava piles up around the mouth of the volcano. When it cools, it becomes hard and rocklike. When the volcano erupts again, more lava piles up and the mound grows taller.

Volcanoes that erupt are *active* volcanoes. Mount Rainier and Mount Hood are quiet now. They have not been active for a long, long time. Scientists have been watching Mt. Baker in Washington. This volcanic mountain has been releasing steam. It may erupt some day.

The Cascades in southern Oregon are also volcanic lands. Beautiful Crater Lake is at the top of one quiet volcano. Many ages ago a volcano caved in. This left a giant bowl-like crater about six miles across. Gradually it filled with water, to form Crater Lake.

Crater Lake seems to be dark blue in color. From a plane it looks like a large

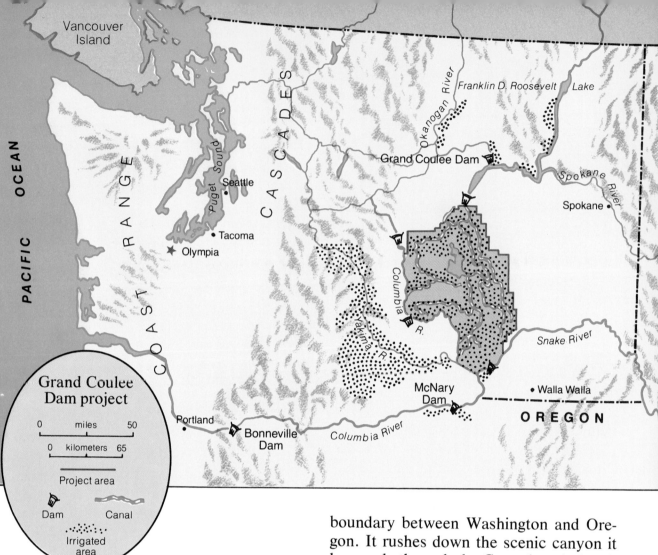

Map labels

Vancouver Island

PACIFIC OCEAN

COAST RANGE

Puget Sound

Seattle

Tacoma

Olympia

CASCADES

Okanogan River

Franklin D. Roosevelt Lake

Grand Coulee Dam

Spokane River

Spokane

Columbia R.

Yakima R.

Snake River

McNary Dam

Walla Walla

Portland

Bonneville Dam

Columbia River

OREGON

Grand Coulee Dam project

| 0 | miles | 50 |
| 0 | kilometers | 65 |

Project area

Dam   Canal

Irrigated area

---

blue jewel. Around the lake, reddish lava cliffs rise about a thousand feet (1600 m) above the water. This is part of Crater Lake National Park.

The Columbia Plateau begins east of the Cascades. Find it on the map (page 327). It covers much of eastern Washington and eastern Oregon. Only a little rain falls on this rolling, sun-baked land. But parts of it produce very good crops and grass for livestock.

The Columbia is the most important river in the Northwest. Find it on the map above. It tumbles swiftly down mountains to the plateau which bears its name. Then it zigzags west and south. Just after the Snake River joins it, the Columbia flows westward. From then on, it marks the

boundary between Washington and Oregon. It rushes down the scenic canyon it has made through the Cascades. At last it empties into the Pacific.

In the past the Columbia caused bad floods. But now dams control its flow. One is Bonneville Dam, just west of the Cascades. Its electric plant makes power for many farms and cities in the area.

Grand Coulee is the largest dam on the Columbia. It holds back a lake 150 miles long (241 km). It provides water for irrigating many farms. From the dam, electric power goes to plants and homes near and far.

Mountains cover more than one third of Alaska. In the Panhandle, forested mountains rise above the ocean. The islands off this coast are the tops of mountains resting in the sea. Glaciers fill the high valleys of the mountains on the coast.

The long, narrow Alaska Peninsula has a range of mountains with some active volcanoes.

The Alaska Range is part of the Rocky Mountains. Locate the Alaska Range (page 327). Mount McKinley is its highest peak. It is also the highest mountain in North America. It soars to a height of 20,320 feet (6190 m). It is almost four miles above sea level.

This towering peak is part of Mount McKinley National Park. There you might see caribou, moose, bears, and many other wild animals.

To the north is the Brooks Range. In what direction does it extend?

Alaska also has valleys, flat lands, and rolling hills. On page 327 find the Yukon Plateau in middle Alaska. Through it flows Alaska's largest river, the Yukon. It begins in Canada, the country to the east. During the summer the Yukon is a useful waterway for boats that deliver supplies to villages. But this river is frozen during the cold winters.

North of the Brooks Range are rolling uplands and flat coastal plains. The Arctic Coastal Plain lies north of the Arctic Circle. Here, the very cold winter lasts about nine months.

Much of the land is *tundra,* or frozen plain, where no trees grow. The tundra is frozen solid many feet below the surface. It thaws some in summer but not enough for trees to thrive. But grasses, moss, and wildflowers do grow here.

The Northwest states have a range of climates. The Alaska tundra has the coldest winters. The sun shines very little during midwinter. For about two months, days are almost as dark as nights.

Summers in the far north are short but sunny. For weeks the sun shines both day and night. A person can read a newspaper by daylight all night long.

In Fairbanks, farther south, the people get ready for long, cold winters. But often the weather is quite like that in North Dakota and Montana. Fairbanks has long hours of summer daylight. People here greet the longest day of the year, June 21, with a baseball game. It is played at midnight with no lights.

Southeastern Alaska has a climate much like that of western Oregon and Washington. Summers are most often cool with some showers and fog. The winters, except for the highlands, are mild. Almost no snow falls. Yet some of these lands are farther north than New England. You read about New England's long winters with heavy snows.

What protects this coastal Northwest? The Pacific Ocean helps. The ocean water stays about the same temperature all year long. So winds blowing from off the ocean cool these lands in summer and warm them in winter. The Cascades and other ranges also play a part. They shut out the icy winds that sweep down from the Arctic.

The areas west of the mountains have rainy winters. In fact, people in some places keep raincoats handy about 200 days of the year.

East of the Cascades the rainfall story is different. Little rain falls on the plateau lands. Why? Study the diagram below the map on page 317 to find out.

These inland areas have winter temperatures that dip far below freezing. They are too far inland for ocean breezes to help. The mountains cut off the ocean breezes.

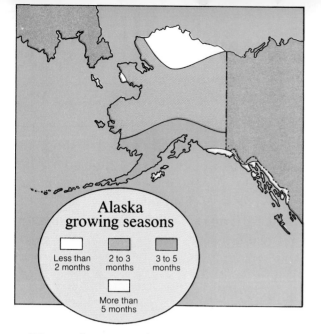

Alaska
growing seasons

Less than 2 months
2 to 3 months
3 to 5 months
More than 5 months

Farming and stock raising

Mixed farming is carried on in Oregon and Washington. You can see it along the fertile lowland that runs from southern Oregon through Washington (p. 327). This strip includes the Willamette Valley and the lowlands around Puget Sound.

Huge amounts of string beans and other vegetables are grown. Some farmers raise daffodil, gladiola, and iris bulbs for sale.

Washington and Oregon raise many kinds of fruit. Berry farms grow strawberries, loganberries, blackberries, and raspberries. Some are rushed to market. Many are frozen or made into jam and jelly. Southern Oregon has big crops of cherries and pears.

Irrigation has turned some dry valleys of eastern Washington into fruit-growing areas. Apples are the main crop. Washington grows about a fourth of the apples eaten in our country. The fruit trees in bloom are a beautiful sight.

At harvest, the orchards are as busy as beehives. Pickers gather the fruit at just the right time and handle it with care to prevent damage. Many apples are rushed to market in refrigerator cars. But much of the crop goes to packing houses. There the fruit is stored for later sale. Apples then are sold the year round. The growers get better prices this way. If all the apples had to be sold in a few weeks, their price would drop.

Dairying is one of the main industries near the coast. Cattle can graze in green pastures all the year round. Plenty of grass grows because of the rainy climate and mild winters.

Some farmers ship dairy products to nearby cities. But many sell milk and cream to cheese factories and creameries.

Wheat and other grains are raised on the Columbia Plateau. Wheat is Washington's largest crop. The plateau gets only a little rain. So wheat and other grains are grown by dry farming.

Some other crops such as sugar beets grow where lands are irrigated.

Eastern Oregon and Washington have big cattle and sheep ranches. They spread over thousands of acres. But they lack water and grass during the hot summers. Late in the spring the animals are driven to grazing areas in the mountains.

Alaska has some farms, chiefly in the Matanuska Valley. About fifty years ago the Matanuska (mat′ə nü′skə) Valley was covered with forests. But pioneers moved in, cut down trees, and laid out farms.

Some dairy cattle are raised. They supply milk and cream for the city of Anchorage not far away. Farmers grow oats, peas, cabbages, potatoes, and strawberries.

The growing season this far north is very short. But summer days are warm and provide about twenty hours of daylight. Plants shoot up fast, and the crops ripen quickly. Some of the largest vegetables in the world are grown here.

Logs are dragged into position to be moved to the sawmill. At the mill they will be cut into lumber. Once cut, lumber is seasoned, or dried, in stacks.

Lumbering in the Northwest

Lumbering is a main industry in the Northwest. Some lumber is cut in southeastern Alaska. Oregon and Washington are among the leading lumber-producing states. In fact, Oregon produces more lumber than any other state.

Most of the trees are evergreens. They keep their thin, needle-shaped "leaves" the year round. These softwood trees include pine, hemlock, cedar, spruce, and fir. The Douglas fir is the largest and most valuable tree in this region. It grows to a height of 200 feet (60 m) or more. Its huge trunk can produce a large amount of lumber. Many small Douglas firs are used as Christmas trees. Growing them has become a big business.

Trained, expert foresters work in the forests. They decide which trees to cut. Douglas firs are harvested in patches. This is *clear-cutting*. Often the patch is soon replanted. In *selective cutting* the forester marks, for cutting, trees that are crowding young timber. Some "old" trees are marked, too.

The *fallers,* or cutting crew, move in with their power saws run by gasoline motors. They cut a notch in the direction the tree should fall. Then they move to the other side and saw toward the notch. When the tree begins to lean, a logger shouts "Tim-ber-r-r!" This warns that the tree is about to drop. Trained fallers know how to send a tree just where they want it.

Next the branches are sawed off. Then the tree is cut into several logs. They are taken to a loading place. Some are dragged by tractors. Others are carried by cables that are worked by a pulley and engine.

At the loading place some logs are lifted by machinery onto huge trucks. Some are loaded on flatcars of a train. Near a river, some may be towed to the mill by boat.

Huge mill saws rip the big logs into long slabs. Other power saws slice the slabs into boards, perhaps as many as twenty at a time.

Wood chips are unloaded at an Oregon paper mill.

Special machines turn some short logs into shingles or fence posts or material for making boxes. Small trees and wood scraps may be cut into chips to turn into pulpwood. Much pulpwood is made into paper. The paper which you use at school comes from pulpwood. So does wrapping paper and newsprint.

Some forests are on public land, and others are privately owned. Millions of acres belong to the state and national governments. Such forests are found in many parts of our country.

Lumber companies pay to cut timber in these forests. They agree to obey certain rules and the orders of the rangers. The rangers are trained people in charge of state and national forests.

Some forests are owned by lumber companies. In many cases these forests are farms! Trees are being grown as a crop in the Northwest and in other places. You read about this kind of crop in the South.

Many tree farms are in hilly or mountainous areas not suited for crops. Forests are already growing on such lands. The tree farmer takes over to guard the woodlands. New trees are planted in the bare spots. Tree farmers keep watch for fires and spray to control insects. Diseases destroy many trees in the Northwest each year.

FIRE is the forest's worst enemy in every part of our country. Many fires start because campers or sightseers are careless. Many are caused by lightning.

A hot, dry season is the danger time. One spark may be fanned into flames within minutes. The flames can spread very fast.

Fire causes costly damage. It ruins whole forests. It burns away the forest's carpet of needles, twigs, and dead leaves. This is *humus*. It acts like a sponge. It soaks up rain water and melting snows.

When the humus is destroyed, the water rushes down slopes. Water washes away the top soil. This causes floods. The runaway soil may choke reservoirs or do other damage.

People are helping to keep the forests green. Special laws have been passed. Signs are put in forest areas. One says, "No Smoking." Another forbids campfires except in the outdoor stoves.

Forest rangers are on duty all summer in lookout towers. If they see smoke, they check quickly. They have two-way radio phones to call fire fighters. Planes are used more and more to spot forest fires.

Fish, minerals, and oil

Fishing is one of the main industries along the coast. Shrimps, clams, and crabs are gathered along the shores of Washington and Alaska. Oysters are harvested from shallow waters in Puget Sound. Halibut, herring, and salmon are caught.

Many people in the Northwest earn their living in some part of the salmon business. Some catch the fish. Others work in the canneries. Most salmon are canned, though some are frozen, smoked, or sold fresh.

The summer months are very busy. Salmon spend most of their lives in the ocean. From May to November, millions of them move toward the mouths of rivers. They are on their way "back home" to the place where they were born. Many are caught at the start of this long trip up the river.

The salmon's life story is one of constant danger. Salmon eggs are laid on the sandy floor of streams or in quiet lakes. Baby salmon hatch from these eggs. While the fish are still small, they start drifting downstream toward the sea.

Young salmon may travel hundreds of miles. Dangers lurk all the way. The salmon may be gobbled up by bears or raccoons that wade into the streams. They may be snatched by birds or swallowed by larger fish. They may be poisoned by polluted water. Perhaps they will stray into irrigation ditches. Or they may be killed by powerhouse machinery below a dam.

Many salmon reach the ocean. There they feed on small fish and grow larger and larger. At full growth they may weigh twenty pounds (9 kg) or more. At last they leave the sea and begin the long swim upstream.

The salmon's trip back to its birthplace is full of danger. Many are caught in fishing nets. Others are taken by people fishing with hook and line. People come long distances to fish for the Northwest salmon. The salmon that escape must swim upstream against swift currents. They leap over rocks and small waterfalls. They may be killed trying to climb over dams.

Fish ladders have been built beside some dams, such as at Bonneville. Fish ladders are a series of pools built in steps. Salmon can easily jump from one pool to the next. They can make their way safely to the river above the dam.

At last, some salmon reach "home." There they lay their eggs and then die.

Salmon are one of our scarce natural resources. Some years, too many have been caught. So not enough were left to lay eggs upstream. Many salmon have died because of dirty rivers or because dams have blocked their way.

Some mining is carried on in the three Northwest states. All three states have deposits of coal, and gold has been found in each one.

Alaska had an exciting gold rush. In 1896, bits of gold were found on Alaska's west coast. When this news got out, fortune hunters rushed to the region. They pitched tents or put up shacks. Thus the "gold rush" town of Nome began. Later, gold was found farther inland on the Yukon Plateau. The gold miners helped to start the city of Fairbanks. Some gold mining is still carried on near Fairbanks and at Nome.

As the Alaska pipeline carries crude oil from the North Slope to the ice-free port of Valdez, it crosses several rivers like the Tanana. The pipeline can carry 2 million barrels of oil a day.

In 1968 rich oil deposits were found in Alaska's far north. They are buried deep in the earth near Prudhoe Bay. This part of Alaska is tundra. Its low plain is frozen most of the year. During the summer the surface of the tundra thaws. It becomes a spongy swamp with patches of moss. But the deep soil remains frozen.

A number of oil companies made plans for drilling in this far north. Drilling equipment was moved to Prudhoe Bay. At first, planes were used because there was no road. Later, materials were loaded on huge barges at Seattle. Giant tugboats pulled the barges to the far north.

Drilling through the frozen earth was very hard. But the experts proved it could be done. A chief problem was how to get the pumped oil to the refineries. The nearest ones were far to the south near Seattle.

Prudhoe Bay and the Arctic Ocean are frozen most of the year. So tankers could not load at Prudhoe Bay. The oil would have to go overland by pipeline to Alaska's port, Valdez. It is free of ice most of the year.

The huge job of building the pipeline began in 1974. Eight oil companies joined to build the 800-mile (1300 km) pipeline. First, roads and camps for the workers were built. Then the work on the pipeline began.

Thousands of skilled men and women got jobs. Some were Native Americans. There were road planners and road builders. There were truck drivers, welders, computer experts, and secretaries. Many workers in other jobs were needed, too.

Trained foresters would replant trees and plants that were damaged along the pipeline. At Valdez, workers built the tanker terminal where the pipeline was to end.

The pipeline project cost billions of dollars. It took loads of expensive materials. Shipping them to the far north was another big cost. Wages were also very high.

The pipeline was built over miles of frozen tundra. It went through rugged mountains and over rivers. Work went on even when weather was −40°F (also −40°C) or colder.

Before work got under way, there was a long delay. Some people feared that the tundra would be damaged. Caribou herds could also be hurt. But the builders at last won the right to start the pipeline.

The Alaskan pipeline was completed in 1977. In the summer the first oil from the Prudhoe Bay fields began to flow through the new pipeline. At Valdez it was loaded onto a tanker. Then it began its journey to a refinery north of Seattle.

Towns and cities

Most of the Northwest is very thinly settled. Notice how the map on page 187 shows this. Which of the three states has the most people? Use the Reference table on page 435. Where in Washington and Oregon do more people live, east or west of the Cascades?

Towns are scattered along the coast and islands of southern Alaska. The largest towns include Ketchikan (Kəch′ə kan′) and Juneau (jü′nō). Ketchikan is on an island. Juneau faces the sheltered sea waters of the Inside Passage. East of it rises the steep slopes of forested mountains. One of the chief industries in summer is caring for tourists. Fishing and lumbering are also important.

For many years Juneau has been the capital of Alaska. But in the early 1970s the people voted to move the capital. They wanted a more central location. A new capital is planned north of Anchorage in the Matanuska Valley.

Fairbanks is the main city in central Alaska. Find it on the map of the Northwest states. It is at the northern end of the Alaska Railroad and of the Alaska Highway. Many tourists drive north on this highway.

Fairbanks is a trading center for villages in the area. It has offices and warehouses that carry on oil business. Caring for tourists is a leading industry in summer.

Anchorage, Alaska's largest city, is on a narrow arm of the Pacific. Grand mountains rise behind it. This growing city has many businesses and two universities. Near it is a large United States air base.

Alaska depends largely on air transportation to link its scattered cities and towns. So Anchorage is the center of a "spider web" of air lines. Then, too, Anchorage is on a main route to Asia. It links Japan and other parts of the Far East with the United States. The air route between Anchorage and Seattle is a major one.

Seattle is the largest city in the Northwest. Seattle's location on Puget Sound has helped it become a shipping center. It is the chief port for trade with Alaska. Railroads and planes link Seattle with all parts of our country.

Seattle has airplane and missile industries. It manufactures many kinds of wood,

337

The Seattle business district overlooks the dock area. In the lower right you can see the Alaska Ferry coming into port.

metal, and food products. It has furniture factories and fish and vegetable canneries.

This city started on a sheltered bay. It spreads out along Puget Sound and over nearby hills. To the west, across Puget Sound, are the Olympic Mountains. To the east are the Cascades.

Near Seattle is Tacoma. It is a thriving shipping center. It also is a copper-smelting city. The small city of Olympia is Washington's capital. Here in 1977 Dixy Lee Ray took the oath of office as governor. She had once been head of the Atomic Energy Commission.

Spokane is the Northwest's largest city east of the Cascades. It was started near falls on the Spokane (spō kan′) River. Nearby is a pass through the Rocky Mountains. Railroads and highways use this pass.

Spokane is in a thriving lumbering, farming, and mining region. It is the trading and business center for this area. It uses products of the region in many factories. Spokane has woodworking plants for making doors and window frames. It has a huge flour mill. It has fruit, vegetable, and meat canning and packing plants. It also turns out many aluminum products.

Power from the falls on the river pro-

duces electricity for running some factories. Electric power from Grand Coulee Dam on the Columbia is also used.

Near Spokane are vacation lands with lakes, forests, and high mountains. Camping areas and miles of trails attract summer tourists. Caring for them provides jobs for bus drivers and for park and forest rangers. Some people work in restaurants, service stations, and motels.

Portland, Oregon's leading city, is a busy trading center. It has grown up on the Willamette River near where the Columbia and Willamette rivers join. Portland is more than a hundred miles (160 km) inland. But ships can go up the broad, deep Columbia River to Portland's docks. Portland is near one of the few gateways through both the Cascade and Coast ranges. Why is this a good place for a trading center?

Portland's mills and factories turn out lumber, furniture, woolen goods, and chemical products. Also there are flour mills and food canneries.

Portland has so many rose gardens that it is called the "City of Roses." Three fifths of Oregon's people live in the metropolitan areas of Portland, Eugene, and Salem, the capital.

Test each other

Help your class play a Review Game. Look through chapter 24 and decide what facts should be remembered. Write five questions about these main facts. Be sure to write the answers so that you will have them in mind.

When the class is ready, divide into two teams. Then decide on rules for your game. Which team will ask the first question? How will you keep score? See which team can answer the most questions correctly. After a question has been asked, try not to ask it again.

Some other things to do

1. Read in another book about one of the following groups.

    Eskimos   Aleuts
    Tlingits   Nez Percé
    Athabascans   Haidas

2. Make a poster about protecting our forests. Display the best posters in your school hall.

3. Arrange a picture exhibit on your bulletin board to tell the story of lumbering.

Learning more about latitude

East-west lines on maps and globes are called lines of latitude, as you know. Notice these lines on the global map. They show distance north and south of the equator. Notice that the equator is numbered 0°. The other latitude lines are numbered north *and* south from the equator. There is a line of latitude numbered 20°, *north* of the equator, and one with the same number *south* of the equator, for example.

The latitude lines with the lowest numbers mark the east-west lines near the equator.

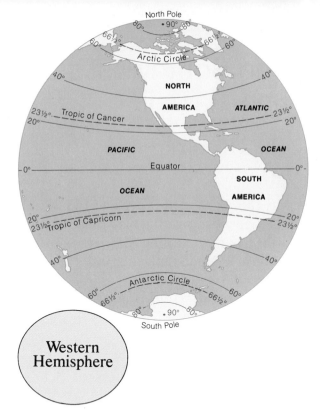

Western Hemisphere

So the region close to the equator is sometimes called the *low latitudes*. The low latitudes are between the two lines of latitude marked $23\frac{1}{2}°$. These two lines have special names, the Tropic of Cancer and the Tropic of Capricorn. Find them on the global map. The low latitude regions are known as the *tropics*.

Find the latitude lines with the highest numbers. They are near the North Pole and the South Pole. The regions near the poles are called the *high latitudes*. The high latitudes are between the lines of latitude marked $66\frac{1}{2}°$ and the poles, which are marked 90°. The lines marked $66\frac{1}{2}°$ are known as the Arctic Circle and the Antarctic Circle. Find them on the global map above. Locate Alaska on the global map on page 354. What part of Alaska is in the high latitudes?

The regions between the low latitudes and the high latitudes are known as the middle latitudes. They are between the latitudes numbered $23\frac{1}{2}°$ and those numbered $66\frac{1}{2}°$. Point to the middle-latitude regions on the global map.

25

The Southwest states and Hawaii

The Hohokams knew what to do

Mr. Garcia handed shovels to Linda and Bruce. He was irrigating his orange grove, and they had offered to help. He showed them how to guide the water into the right furrows.

"This is great!" said Bruce. "We don't do this back home."

"Of course not," replied Linda. "We don't have orange groves. And besides, we don't irrigate."

"You don't have to," answered Mr. Garcia. "Your state gets plenty of rain. But we don't here. The Southwest is pretty dry all summer. Maybe from April to November! These trees will die if they aren't watered deeply every three weeks. So would a lot of crops. We have to irrigate!"

"Where does this water come from?" asked Linda.

"A good question, Linda," replied Mr. Garcia. "From melting snows in the Rockies. The Colorado River brings it on a long journey to a dam. It's stored in a lake behind the dam until it's needed. Canals, ditches, and pipes bring it here to us."

"Wow!" exclaimed Linda, looking at the water filling the furrows.

"Have people always irrigated around here?" asked Bruce.

"I think so, if they've raised crops in the summer," replied Mr. Garcia. "My ancestors did two hundred years ago."

Bruce whistled in surprise. "You mean your ancestors lived here then?"

"Yes, and they kept diaries," said Mr. Garcia. "My great-great-grandparents came from Mexico about two hundred years ago. They were given a huge grant of land for a ranch. It included this land we're irrigating and thousands of acres more. But they didn't grow oranges. They raised mostly cattle. They grew some corn, squash, and beans down by the river and irrigated there. When the river dried up in the middle of the summer, they used water from their well.

"But my ancestors weren't the first people to irrigate in the Southwest. The Hohokams knew what to do a thousand years ago!"

Mr. Garcia was right.

The Hohokams irrigated crops a thousand years ago. These Native Americans lived near a river in what is now Arizona. They built canals and dug ditches to lead river water to their fields.

The Hohokams may have been the earliest farmers in the Southwest. Their descendants are the Papagos and the Pimas. Many Pimas are farming in Arizona today.

Looking at Arizona, Nevada, California, and Hawaii

California is the largest state in the Southwest area. Its long coastline runs along the Pacific for about 840 miles (1350 km). Arizona and Nevada are inland states as the map shows.

Hawaii (hə wī′ē) is far out in the Pacific. It is made up of a string of islands. There are eight main islands. The largest one is named Hawaii. But another island, Oahu (ō ä′hü), is the most thickly settled. The capital of the state, Honolulu, is located on Oahu.

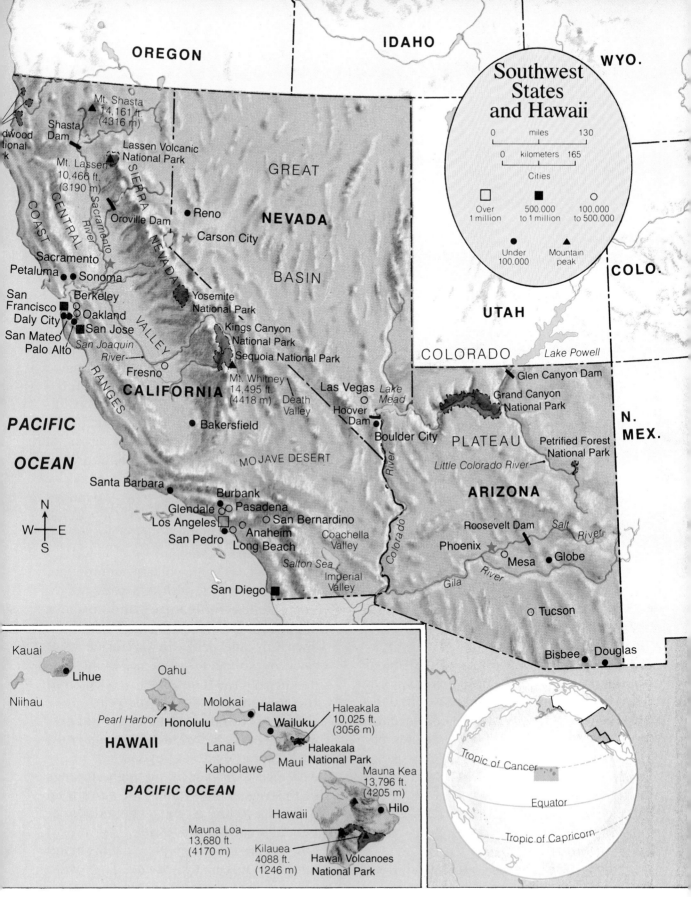

Southwest States and Hawaii

OREGON

IDAHO

WYO.

Southwest
States
and Hawaii

| 0 | miles | 130 |
| 0 | kilometers | 165 |

Cities

| □ | ■ | ○ |
| Over 1 million | 500,000 to 1 million | 100,000 to 500,000 |

| ● | ▲ |
| Under 100,000 | Mountain peak |

COLO.

Mt. Shasta
14,161 ft.
(4316 m)

Shasta Dam

dwood
tional
k

Lassen Volcanic
National Park

Mt. Lassen
10,466 ft.
(3190 m)

GREAT

● Reno

NEVADA

Oroville Dam

★ Carson City

BASIN

UTAH

Sacramento
River

SIERRA NEVADA

COAST

CENTRAL

Sacramento

Petaluma

● Sonoma

Berkeley

San
Francisco

Daly City ○ Oakland

San Jose

San Mateo

Palo Alto

San Joaquin
River

VALLEY

Fresno

RANGES

CALIFORNIA

Yosemite
National Park

Kings Canyon
National Park

Sequoia National Park

Mt. Whitney
14,495 ft.
(4418 m)

Death
Valley

Las Vegas
○

Lake
Mead

COLORADO

Lake Powell

Glen Canyon Dam

Grand Canyon
National Park

N.
MEX.

PACIFIC

OCEAN

● Bakersfield

Hoover
Dam

Boulder City

MOJAVE DESERT

PLATEAU

Little Colorado River

Petrified Forest
National Park

Santa Barbara

N
W   E
S

Burbank

Glendale ○ Pasadena

Los Angeles □

San Pedro

Anaheim

Long Beach

○ San Bernardino

Coachella
Valley

Salton Sea

Imperial
Valley

Colorado

River

Gila

ARIZONA

Roosevelt Dam

Salt

River

Phoenix ★

Mesa ○

● Globe

River

San Diego ■

Bisbee
●

Douglas ●

Kauai

● Lihue

Oahu

Niihau

Pearl Harbor

Honolulu ★

HAWAII

Molokai

Lanai

Kahoolawe

PACIFIC OCEAN

Halawa ●

● Wailuku

Maui

Haleakala
10,025 ft.
(3056 m)

Haleakala
National Park

Mauna Kea
13,796 ft.
(4205 m)

Hawaii

● Hilo

Mauna Loa
13,680 ft.
(4170 m)

Kilauea
4088 ft.
(1246 m)

Hawaii Volcanoes
National Park

Tropic of Cancer

Equator

Tropic of Capricorn

Many of the same things are true for each of these four states. In general they have a pleasant climate and interesting scenery. They are thought of as vacation country by many people.

California, Arizona, and Nevada were a part of the Spanish Southwest. The Spaniards were the first people to explore these lands. Later on, Spanish and Mexican settlers came. Many of their descendants live in the Southwest today.

Some early Spanish ideas and customs still influence ways of living in the Southwest. Rodeos and fiestas are still held. Some ideas from Spanish-Mexican architecture can be seen in many buildings.

Many Native Americans still live in the Southwest. Their people came thousands of years ago. The Hohokams were one of the early groups.

Arizona has the largest Native American population of any state. The Navajo, Hopi, Papago, and Pima are some of its people.

The name *Arizona* is a Native American word said to mean "little spring." A *spring* is a place where water flows out of the ground. Water is very important in the dry Southwest.

Hawaii became a territory of the United States in 1898. The English explorer James Cook and his sailors first visited the islands in 1778. People in many parts of the world did not know about the islands before that time.

The Hawaiians welcomed the visitors with gifts and treated them well. But later when Cook's party returned, fighting broke out. Captain Cook and several sailors were killed.

After people learned about Hawaii, trading ships began stopping at the islands.

One American ship sailed away leaving two sailors behind. The Americans married members of the king's family and became his advisers.

Missionaries from New England started schools in Hawaii. They showed the people new ways of living. Other Americans and people from other countries came and settled on the islands.

In 1898 the United States went to war with Spain. Some battles were fought in the Philippine Islands far to the west of Hawaii. Hawaii was a good stopping place for the ships. Soon Hawaii became a territory of the United States. In 1959, Congress voted to make it the fiftieth state.

These four states have large areas of mountains. The Hawaiian Islands are the tops of mountains. They were formed by volcanoes. Long, long ago volcanoes erupted through the floor of the Pacific Ocean. Slowly they built up the mountainous Hawaiian Islands.

California has some volcanic mountains, too. They are a part of the Cascade range, which extends from Oregon into northern California.

Two Cascade peaks in California were formed by volcanoes. One is Mount Lassen. The other, Mount Shasta, is covered with snow and ice most of the year.

California has part of the Coast Ranges. They are chains of low mountains and hills as in Washington and Oregon.

The Sierra Nevada is the highest range in this region. It extends for more than 400 miles (640 km) along the boundary between California and Nevada.

One part of the Sierra Nevada has many giant trees known as *sequoias*. They were named for the Cherokee leader who devel-

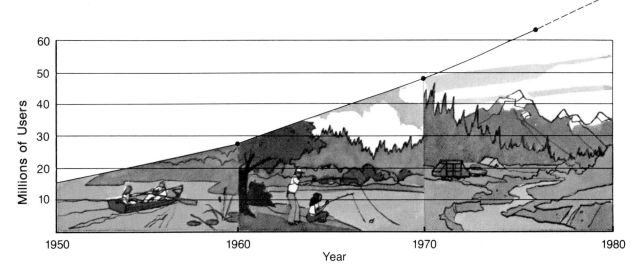

Millions of Users — Year (1950, 1960, 1970, 1980)

What problems are caused by the increased use of our national parks?

oped an alphabet for his people. Sequoias may grow to a height of 300 feet (90 m) and are the tallest living trees. Some are more than 3000 years old. In 1890, Congress set aside part of this area as Sequoia National Park.

Yosemite (yō sem′ə tē) is another wonderland in the Sierra Nevada. An immigrant from Scotland spread the word about its beautiful scenery. He was John Muir, who was born in 1838.

At age 11, John Muir came to America with his family. They settled on a farm in Wisconsin, and John grew to love the out-of-doors. He was interested in plants and flowers. He studied to become a plant expert, a botanist. At about age 30, Muir went to California.

John Muir lived in Yosemite for several years. He studied the plants and trees and wrote magazine articles about the wonders of Yosemite. He urged that it be saved as a park. His articles helped to get Congress to make Yosemite a national park.

John Muir also worked to save forests. He persuaded President Theodore Roosevelt to set aside certain areas of forest. They are known as national forests. Today there are more than 150 national forests in our country. They cover about 190 million acres.

National parks and national forests have many pleasant areas where people may camp or hike. In some places people may go boating, fishing, or swimming. There are many roads on which tourists may drive.

Lumbering and grazing are allowed in some national forests but under strict rules. Rangers are in charge.

Mount Whitney is the highest peak in the Sierras. It has an elevation of 14,495 feet (4418 m).

The Colorado Plateau occupies a large part of Arizona. Its wide tablelands have some volcanic peaks. One of its most colorful areas is Grand Canyon National Park.

Grand Canyon extends through Arizona for about 200 miles (320 km). It was carved out by the Colorado River many thousands of years ago. In 1919, Congress set aside the most colorful half of this area as a national park.

The Pueblos lived in the Grand Canyon area long ago, perhaps in the 1200s. Spaniards in Coronado's party found Grand Canyon when they were exploring the Southwest. Today the Havasupai people live as farmers in one part of the canyon.

The Grand Canyon was formed millions of years ago by the Colorado River.

The Great Basin spreads across most of Nevada. Notice this on the map on page 341. Some basin lands extend into California and Arizona. One area in California is the vast Mojave (mō hä′vē) Desert.

Death Valley is another part of the basin lands. It is along the southeastern border of California. Death Valley is a sun-baked desert with scorching summers. It has the lowest lands in the United States. Part of it is 280 feet (85 m) below sea level.

Forty-Niners gave Death Valley its sad name. They were on their way to the gold fields. They turned off the main trail to take a shortcut and got lost. They could not find water. Many of them died.

California has fertile valleys between the mountain ranges. Central Valley is more than 400 miles long (640 km). It lies between the Sierra Nevada and Coast Ranges. It has rich soil but needs irrigation.

Two desert valleys in California are the Coachella and Imperial valleys. They get only a few inches of rain a year. But irrigation makes farming the main industry.

Snow and rain in the mountains provide the water. Much of it flows into streams and rivers. Water is stored in reservoirs back of dams built on some of the rivers.

The Colorado is the largest river flowing through these states. It starts as a small stream high in the Rockies. On its journey it rushes along the floor of the Grand Canyon. The floor is nearly 2000 feet (600 m) below the canyon rim, or top.

In earlier years the Colorado River caused damaging floods every spring because of melting snows. Today large dams hold back huge lakes. Two are Hoover Dam and Glen Canyon Dam. The saved water is used for irrigation and for many homes and industries. Powerhouses below the dams produce electric power for Nevada, Arizona, and California.

The building of dams and reservoirs brings benefits to users of the water and electric power. People enjoy the huge lakes that are created. But often the lakes cover more than wasteland. Many scenic areas are flooded and lost forever.

Two large rivers flowing through the Central Valley are the Sacramento and the San Joaquin (san wä kēn′). Both begin in the snowfields of the Sierra Nevada. But they start hundreds of miles apart.

Shasta Dam sits across the Sacramento River and forms a large lake. Oroville Dam is on a branch of the Sacramento. Its thick wall reaches more than a mile across a canyon.

Water from Lake Oroville flows south to a place east of San Francisco. There it is pumped into the California Aqueduct, a cement-lined canal. The water flows south to the end of the San Joaquin Valley. It is supplying irrigation water for nearly a million acres of once-dry croplands.

California, Nevada, and Arizona have a variety of climates. Along California's coast, ocean breezes cool the land in summer. They keep the weather mild in winter. They also bring rain clouds. Turn to the drawing on page 317 and review the information about rain clouds. Then study the rainfall map on the same page. Which areas in Arizona, Nevada, and California get the most moisture?

Northern California's coastal lands have very rainy winters. They have a climate much like the coastal lands in the Northwest region.

But much of the land in these states is dry. Water is so needed that scientists are searching for more ways to provide it.

The desert areas have a sunny climate winter and summer. Thousands of tourists visit the desert in winter. Summer days are blistering hot. Temperatures may soar to 115°F (45°C) or higher.

Parts of California and Arizona have a long growing season. In some places crops can grow all year long. Where in these three states is the growing season the shortest? What kinds of lands are found there?

Hawaii has a warm climate all year long. Hawaii is in the low latitudes and so it is in the tropics. Notice this on the map on page 354. These islands have a tropical climate. But the weather is seldom hot. Sea breezes usually cool the islands.

The winds blow across thousands of miles of ocean and gather a great deal of moisture. As they reach Hawaii's mountains, they rise and become even cooler. Most of their moisture falls as rain on the northeastern sides of the islands.

The northeast slopes have a dense tangle of trees, vines, flowers, and ferns. But the southwest areas are much drier. Farms there are irrigated.

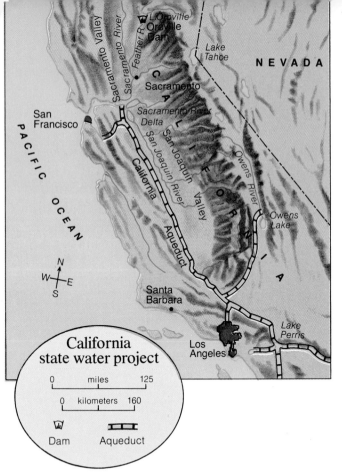

California
state water project

0 miles 125

0 kilometers 160

Dam   Aqueduct

Farming and stock raising

Irrigation makes the Southwest a rich farming region. Yet less than one twentieth of the land is suitable for growing crops. The main kinds of farming are shown on the map on page 319.

Many farms extend over thousands of acres. Most large farms are owned by a company or a group of people. Farms in this area are called ranches, no matter what their size or crops.

Most crops must be irrigated. Canals carry the water from reservoirs to croplands. The map above shows the California Aqueduct. It brings water from Lake Oroville by the Feather and Sacramento rivers to the San Joaquin Valley.

Ditches and underground pipes guide the water from the main canals into fields and orchards. The ditches have small water gates. When it is time to irrigate, the farmer opens the gates and the water runs

into the furrows. Sprinklers are used to water in some areas.

Ranchers use many kinds of machines, even airplanes. Among them are tractors, tree shakers, and cotton pickers. Some farmers use low-flying planes to plant seed, such as rice. The farmers may hire experts to fly low and dust or spray crops to control insects. In the winter small planes may drop food to livestock trapped after a snowstorm.

Cotton is one of the leading crops in Arizona and California. Thousands of acres of cotton are grown. Many cotton ranches are very large. One reason is that costly machinery is needed to raise this crop. Farmers cannot afford to buy such machines for a small farm.

Arizona produces a variety of crops besides cotton. These include citrus fruits, cantaloupes, vegetables, and alfalfa. In what part of the state are the main farming areas? Turn to the map on page 319 and see. The main croplands are irrigated.

California raises more than 200 kinds of crops. Citrus fruits are grown in southern California and in parts of the Central Valley where the climate is mild.

Central Valley farms produce tons of peaches, plums, cherries, apricots, figs, and grapes in its "Fruit Salad Lands." Some fruits are sold fresh. But millions of pounds are canned, frozen, or dried. The hot summer air is just right for drying fruits. Tons of grapes and prunes are dried. Dried grapes are sold as raisins.

Much rice is raised in the northern part of the Central Valley. Some ranches produce sugar beets, and others raise alfalfa. Many truck gardens raise all kinds of vegetables. One of the largest crops is to-

Fields of sugar cane and pineapple cover the Hawaiian landscape. Today machines do much of the planting and harvesting.

matoes. Also tons of strawberries are grown near Anaheim, south of Los Angeles.

Crops can be grown for about 300 days of each year in the desert valleys. So Imperial Valley sends tons of winter vegetables to market. Coachella Valley is famous for its dates and grapefruit.

Hawaii's tropical climate makes sugar cane the state's largest crop. Sugar cane is a kind of giant grass. It looks something like a tall, thick cornstalk. When the stalks are ripe, they are full of sweet juice. Sugar is made from this juice.

The cane is planted by a large machine. It digs furrows and drops pieces of stalk into them. Soon little plants sprout and grow from the stalks. Many fields are irrigated. At harvest, the thick stalks may be twelve to fifteen feet high.

The fields are set afire as harvest begins. This destroys the leaves but does not damage the stalks or the sweet juices inside. After the stalks are cut, they are picked up and hauled to a mill. There they are made into sugar.

In earlier years many workers came from Japan, China, and the Philippines. Most of them stayed on in the islands.

Many of Hawaii's people can trace their ancestors back to those who came to work in the sugar industry.

Pineapples are another famous crop in Hawaii. They are grown on pineapple plantations owned mainly by large companies. Like sugar cane, pineapples are raised from shoots called slips.

Some pineapples are sent to market to be sold fresh. But most are canned, or are crushed for their juice.

Nevada and Arizona have huge cattle and sheep ranches. Some also spread over the hilly back country of California. Most grazing lands are found in the rolling areas not suited to farming.

Hawaii has several large cattle ranches. One has more than 300,000 acres and is one of the largest in the world. It was started by a New Englander. Its first cowhands came from Mexico.

California has a big dairy business and many poultry ranches. The Petaluma area north of San Francisco calls itself the "Egg Capital of the World."

347

Tuna caught off the shores of California is a valuable resource.

Redwoods are giant trees that like very damp air. They grow in the wet coastal lands of northern California. They are one kind of sequoia and are among our tallest and oldest trees. Some redwood forests have been set aside as national parks.

The Southwest has rich mineral and petroleum treasures. Arizona produces more copper than any other state in our country. Its cities of Globe, Bisbee, and Douglas have grown up chiefly because of the valuable copper mines nearby. Nevada also mines copper. Both Nevada and Arizona mine some gold and silver.

California has a number of rich oil fields. Pumps send oil through underground pipes to refineries. One large refining center is in the Los Angeles—Long Beach area district. Another is near San Francisco.

Fishing, lumbering, and mining

Fishing is a major industry in California and Hawaii. Tuna, sardines, halibut, and barracuda are caught off the California coast. Tuna is the largest catch.

Canneries prepare tuna for market. After the fish are cleaned, they are cooked in huge ovens. Skilled workers remove the bones and pack the tuna in cans. The cans are sealed tightly and cooked for more than an hour. Then they are labeled and prepared for shipping.

The waters around Hawaii have many kinds of fish. The catching and canning of tuna provide jobs for many people there.

Lumbering is an important industry in northern California. Redwoods, pines, and Douglas firs are among the main kinds of trees cut.

Many cities, but also much open space

Some parts are a megalopolis, and others are thinly settled. Notice this on the map on page 187. See how far apart the cities are in Arizona and Nevada. What areas in California have the fewest people?

Metropolitan Los Angeles is crowded with cities. This area is a part of a megalopolis which extends as far as San Diego. Look for it on the population map.

Metropolitan San Francisco is another thickly populated area. Find it on the population map. Many cities have grown up around San Francisco Bay.

Mexican pioneers started the first "bay" settlement. Captain Portola and a party of Spaniards and Mexicans discovered San Francisco Bay in 1769. They had marched overland with Father Serra to help start

348

missions in California. Father Serra and his helpers camped at the place they named San Diego. Portola's party went on north to explore. One day some hunters climbed to a hilltop. How surprised they were to see a huge bay spread out below them.

Later the Spaniards built a fort overlooking the bay. It was called the Presidio of San Francisco. Three miles away, a mission was started. Pioneers from Mexico settled near it. Their settlement became known as the pueblo of San Francisco.

San Francisco is a leading seaport on the Pacific. It is at the north end of a peninsula and faces water on three sides. To the west is the Pacific Ocean. San Francisco Bay is to the north and east.

San Francisco's Golden Gate Bridge

San Francisco Bay area

0   miles   4

0   kilometers   5

City areas   Park

Main highways   Bridge

The bay has one of the world's best deep harbors. Coastal hills protect it from ocean storms. The place where the hills break provides the harbor's entrance, called Golden Gate. A high bridge spans Golden Gate. Thousands of people travel across Golden Gate Bridge every day.

Many ships sail through Golden Gate into the bay. When they leave, they may carry such exports as cotton, grain, canned foods, and manufactured goods. Much trade is carried on with Hawaii, the Far East, and Australia.

Many of San Francisco's people earn their living in the trading and shipping businesses. Some have jobs in canneries and quick-freezing food plants. Some people have jobs in the printing, publishing, and tourist industries.

San Francisco is an exciting city to visit. It is built on many steep hills. Special streetcars called cable cars travel up one hill and down another clanging their bells.

The San Francisco airport also serves nearby cities like Daly City, San Mateo, and Palo Alto.

Across San Francisco Bay are other busy cities. They are linked with San Francisco by bridges. Oakland is a trading and shipping center. Berkeley is the home of the huge University of California.

Some bay cities have oil refineries. Tankers unload oil from Alaska at refineries in this area.

San Jose is south of the bay. It was California's first pueblo. The Spanish governor of California founded it for Mexican pioneers. Nine soldiers, five settlers and their families, and one cowhand settled there.

Today San Jose is a large city. Among its

many industries are food processing and electronics.

Los Angeles is the largest city on the west coast. In fact, it is the third largest city in the United States. Many cities are clustered around it.

In the middle 1500s a branch of the Shoshoni people lived in this area. Later, Spanish explorers and missionaries passed through it. Mission San Gabriel and Mission San Fernando were set up not far away.

In 1781 the Spanish governor of California founded Los Angeles. This pueblo was to be a stopping place halfway between the two missions. It was settled by Mexicans. It was given a very long name which meant "The Town of Our Lady, Queen of the Angels." After Mexico won its independence from Spain, the pueblo shortened its name to Los Angeles.

Gradually Los Angeles grew. Railroads brought more people. In the late 1880s two railroads quarreled about fares. One charged only a dollar to travel from Kansas City to Los Angeles. At such a bargain, thousands of people bought tickets. A large number stayed in Los Angeles. Along with nearby cities, Los Angeles has been growing ever since.

This region needed water for its growing population and industries. Los Angeles built a huge aqueduct from a mountain basin in the Sierra Nevada. Los Angeles and nearby cities also banded together to bring water from the Colorado River.

The Los Angeles area is one of the leading industrial centers. It has aircraft and missile plants. The spaceship *Enterprise* was built here. There are electronics firms, auto-assembly plants, oil refineries, food-

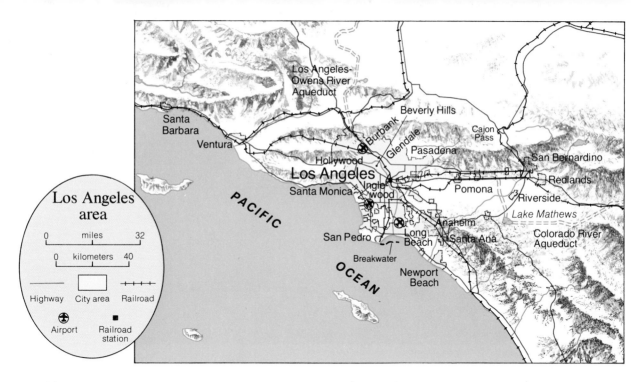

Los Angeles
area

0   miles   32

0   kilometers   40

Highway   City area   Railroad

Airport   Railroad station

packing plants, and many other kinds of factories.

Air pollution is often a problem. Smog is caused by its factories, heavy auto traffic, and weather conditions.

Los Angeles spreads out over more land than any other city in our country. One long, narrow strip extends nearly twenty miles to the ocean harbor. This harbor has been deepened and widened. Ships from all over the world tie up at its wharves.

The large International Airport serves the Los Angeles area. More than a million planes take off and land there every year.

Around half a million Mexican Americans live in Los Angeles. Some take an active part in the city and state governments. The city also has many black residents. One of them, Tom Bradley, was elected mayor in the 1970s. Another, Yvonne B. Burke, represented a Los Angeles district in Congress.

Thousands of people visit Los Angeles and other parts of California every year. Many tourists enjoy the Pueblo de los Angeles. This old section of Los Angeles has been restored. It looks like the pueblo it was long ago. Many people spend the winters in southern California because of its mild climate. Caring for tourists is one of the main businesses.

San Diego and Sacramento are two other California cities. Sacramento is the capital of California. It is the leading manufacturing and trading city for the northern part of Central Valley.

San Diego has a deep harbor. It is a center for aircraft and space industries.

Phoenix is Arizona's fastest growing city and its capital. Phoenix (fē′niks) is in the heart of a rich farming area. Many of its people work in canneries and food-packing plants. Phoenix is also a shipping center for these goods and for the beef cattle raised nearby. But it, too, has much manufacturing. Some plants turn out aircraft. Others produce air conditioning and electronic equipment.

Phoenix grew up in a desert. Water for it and for irrigation is stored at Roosevelt Dam on the Salt River and in other nearby reservoirs.

Both Phoenix and Tucson (tü′son), Arizona, attract many tourists during the winter. People from all over the country enjoy the dry, sunny climate.

351

Diamond Head marks the busy city of Honolulu.

Honolulu is Hawaii's capital and its main seaport. Over half of the people of this state live in Honolulu. Ships from all over the world tie up at the docks of its fine harbor. Freighters unload manufactured goods, gasoline, and foods. Some ships carry away cargoes of fresh and canned pineapples, and sugar.

Tall palm trees line many avenues in Honolulu, and its parks are bright with tropical flowers.

A big airport near Honolulu handles planes that fly the Pacific airways. Hawaii is sometimes called "the crossroads of the Pacific."

A short distance from Honolulu is Pearl Harbor, a naval base. Many people in Hawaii work for the United States armed forces.

Thousands of people visit beautiful Hawaii every year. They are often greeted with the lovely song "Aloha Oe." Sometimes fragrant chains of flowers, or leis (lāz), are hung about their necks.

There are many interesting things to do on the islands. Some people like to visit the sandy beaches. Some tourists fly to other islands and take drives through the countryside. Highways lead past sugar and pineapple plantations, mountain scenery, and beaches. One can travel to see Mauna Loa, the exciting volcano in the island of Hawaii. This volcano is in Hawaii Volcanoes National Park. There is another national park with a volcano on the island of Maui (mou'ē).

Hawaii's people have come from many lands. Visiting Hawaii reminds us again that the people of our country come from many backgrounds. Hawaii has a mixture of people whose ancestors have come from every continent. There are many Japanese Americans in Hawaii. George R. Ariyoshi became governor in 1975. Patsy Takemoto Mink and other Japanese Americans have represented Hawaii in Congress. People from China and the Philippine Islands also helped to build Hawaii.

Some citizens are Hawaiian. Their ancestors were Polynesians, the first people to settle Hawaii. Mrs. Bernice Pauahi Bishop started a school for young people of native Hawaiian background. She was a great-granddaughter of a famous Hawaiian king. Mrs. Bishop also helped to start the Bishop Museum. Here, visitors can see the ways of living of the early Hawaiians.

Questions to test your reading

1. What are the chief mountain ranges in California? What are the main rivers in the Southwest?

2. How does the climate along the coast of northern California differ from the climate in Arizona, Nevada, and the rest of California?

3. How would you describe the climate of Hawaii? Is it the same throughout the islands? Give reasons for your answer.

4. Why did Americans become interested in getting Hawaii?

5. What are the leading farm products of the four states in this chapter?

6. What other industries are also important in this region?

7. What are some of the most famous vacationlands in this region?

What would you say?

1. Why is water so important in the Southwest?

2. How has modern transportation helped to develop the states studied in this chapter?

3. What are some ways in which Hawaii is different from Nevada?

4. What can you do to better understand those whose background or race is different from your own?

A choosing game

Decide on the correct ending for each of the following incomplete sentences.

1. The largest state in this region is (Nevada.) (California.) (Arizona.)

2. The state farthest south in this region is (Arizona.) (Nevada.) (Hawaii.)

3. Hawaii was discovered by (Cook.) (Cabrillo.) (Columbus.)

4. Mount Shasta and Mount Lassen are in the (Cascades.) (Sierra Nevada.) (Coast Range.)

5. Central Valley and Imperial Valley are famous for their (winter sports.) (mineral resources.) (farm products.)

6. California raises huge quantities of (corn.) (wheat.) (cotton.)

7. Hawaii is famous for its pineapples and (alfalfa.) (sugar.) (oranges.)

Some other things to do

1. Read a book about early life in one of these four states. Share what you learn.

2. Find and share a current event about one of these states.

3. Make a products map of one of the four states.

4. Study the "Latitude and Climate" exercise that follows. Be ready to discuss it with your class.

5. Learn all you can about some interesting places to visit in one of the cities listed below. Be ready to take your class on a tour of "your" city.

Los Angeles	Tucson	Honolulu
San Diego	San Francisco	Phoenix

6. Be ready to tell at about what latitude each of these cities is located.

Los Angeles	Seattle	San Francisco
Honolulu	Portland	Anchorage

   You may want to refer to a large wall map of the world.

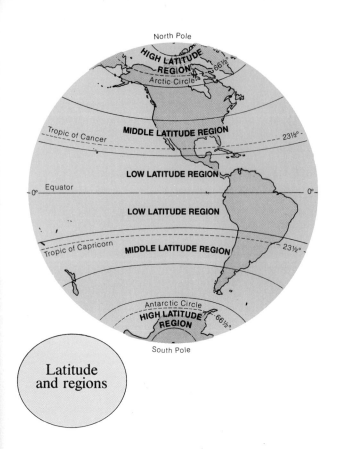

North Pole

HIGH LATITUDE REGION
Arctic Circle
66½°

MIDDLE LATITUDE REGION
Tropic of Cancer   23½°

LOW LATITUDE REGION

Equator   0°   0°

LOW LATITUDE REGION

Tropic of Capricorn   23½°
MIDDLE LATITUDE REGION

Antarctic Circle
HIGH LATITUDE REGION   66½°

South Pole

Latitude and regions

Find the high latitude, or polar, regions. As you can see, one is near the North Pole. The other is near the South Pole.

The region near the equator is hot. The regions around the two poles are cold. So as you travel from the equator toward either of the poles, the climate becomes colder. If you know the latitude of a place or the region in which it lies, you will know something about its climate.

In the low latitude, or tropical, regions the weather may be warm the year round. There is no spring, summer, fall, or winter as we think of them. Which one of our states is in the low latitudes, or tropics?

In which of the regions would you expect to find the coldest and longest winters? The high latitude, or polar, regions have very short summers and cold weather for most of the year. Which state is partly in the high latitudes?

Most parts of our country are in the middle latitudes. They have warm summers and cold or cool winters. What kind of climate does your part of the country have?

5. Learn more about a water project in one of the Southwest states.

6. Sing the song "Aloha Oe" with your class.

7. Make a lei.

8. Find out from what lands your ancestors came. Help members of your class to show this information on an outline map of the world. Pin strings leading from your ancestors' countries to your community.

Latitude and climate

You have learned that we often use latitude lines to divide the earth into regions. There are the low latitude, or tropical, regions; the middle latitude regions; and the high latitude regions.

Look for these regions on the map on this page. Find the middle, or mid-latitude, regions. Notice that one of these regions is north of the tropics and one lies to the south. In which one do you live?

Our American neighbors

26
Canada

England claims Canada

It was late August 1497. A sea captain had come back from a voyage. Everyone was excited.

"Bravo Caboto!" shouted a merchant. "Caboto is a great hero!"

"Yes," agreed his friend. "Caboto sailed near Asia, they say. But he's John Cabot now. He's taken an English name."

"I know," replied the merchant. "But never forget this! He is still a Venetian, Giovanni Caboto!"

The merchant and his friend lived in London. They had come from Venice, Italy. So had Giovanni Caboto. They were all Venetians, the name given to the people of Venice.

Venice was a famous trading center. Ships unloaded imports, such as pepper and spices, from Asia. Young Caboto often had watched.

When the boy grew up, he became a sea captain. He planned to sail to Asia to bring back spices and other treasures.

Caboto took his family to live in the busy port of Bristol, England. He met many merchants and sailors. He became known as John Cabot.

Cabot and his new friends often talked about Asia. They thought that Columbus had landed in Asia, south of China. They did not know that he had reached islands in the Caribbean Sea.

English merchants wanted more goods from the Spice Islands. They thought Cabot could find a shorter route to Asia. So they gave him a ship, a crew, and supplies.

King Henry VII of England gave permission for the trip. Cabot agreed to claim lands for England. He also promised to give the king a share of any riches found.

In May 1497 Cabot set out in his small ship. He sailed west across the northern part of the Atlantic. The map on page 23 shows his route.

Cabot reached a rocky shore of North America. The place was probably Newfoundland. Cabot claimed the land for England.

Cabot sailed along the coast. He saw that the waters were full of fish. Fish were a main food for many people in Europe. Fishing was a leading industry. Cabot returned to England with the good news that he had found rich new fishing grounds.

The next year Cabot sailed west again to search for a route to Asia. But he did not find it. He did not know that two continents were between Europe and Asia.

Cabot did far more than he knew. He claimed Canada for England. He found the rich fishing grounds, the Grand Banks. His news about these fishing grounds sent many people across the Atlantic.

Native Americans had come to Canada much earlier. They had crossed the Bering Strait from Asia into North America. Find the Bering Strait on the map of North America on page 89.

Eskimos are groups of Native Americans who stayed in the far north. They lived mainly along the coast. They became expert at hunting and fishing. The Eskimos call themselves the Inuit (i'nyüət').

Other Native American groups moved farther south. They also lived by hunting and fishing. The largest groups were Algonkin peoples. They included the Cree, Micmac, Naskapi, and Ojibwa groups. Other large groups lived along the Pacific coast. Find them on the map on page 29.

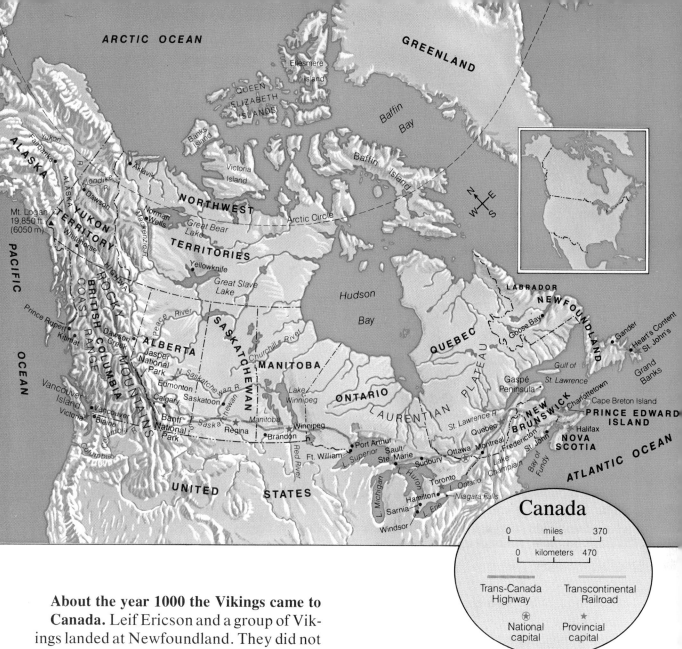

Map labels:

ARCTIC OCEAN

GREENLAND

Ellesmere Island

QUEEN ELIZABETH ISLANDS

Baffin Bay

Banks Island

Victoria Island

Baffin Island

ALASKA

Fairbanks

Yukon R.

Aklavik

NORTHWEST

Arctic Circle

Mt. Logan 19,850 ft. (6050 m)

YUKON TERRITORY

Klondike R.

Dawson

Whitehorse

Norman Wells

Mackenzie R.

Great Bear Lake

TERRITORIES

Yellowknife

Great Slave Lake

Hudson Bay

LABRADOR

NEWFOUNDLAND

Goose Bay

Gander

Heart's Content

St. John's

PACIFIC OCEAN

ROCKY COAST RANGE

BRITISH COLUMBIA

Prince Rupert

Kitimat

Peace River

Churchill River

ALBERTA

SASKATCHEWAN

MANITOBA

QUEBEC

LAURENTIAN PLATEAU

Gulf of St. Lawrence

Gaspé Peninsula

Grand Banks

Jasper National Park

Dawson Creek

N. Saskatchewan R.

Edmonton

Calgary

Lake Winnipeg

Vancouver Island

Victoria

Vancouver

Blaine

Columbia R.

Banff National Park

Saskatoon

Saskatchewan R.

Regina

Brandon

Winnipeg

Red River

Ft. William

Port Arthur

L. Superior

Sault Ste. Marie

ONTARIO

Sudbury

St. Lawrence R.

Quebec

Montreal

Ottawa

NEW BRUNSWICK

Fredericton

Lake Champlain

St. John

Bay of Fundy

NOVA SCOTIA

Halifax

Charlottetown

Cape Breton Island

PRINCE EDWARD ISLAND

ATLANTIC OCEAN

L. Michigan

L. Huron

Toronto

Hamilton

L. Ontario

Niagara Falls

Sarnia

L. Erie

Windsor

UNITED STATES

Canada

| 0 | miles | 370 |
| 0 | kilometers | 470 |

Trans-Canada Highway

Transcontinental Railroad

National capital

Provincial capital

About the year 1000 the Vikings came to Canada. Leif Ericson and a group of Vikings landed at Newfoundland. They did not explore very far inland, though. Not until the voyages of John Cabot, 500 years later, did Europeans begin to explore what is now Canada.

The French come

Verrazano and Cartier were two early explorers. An Italian sailing for France explored the east coast of Canada in 1524. He was Verrazano (ver′ə zän′ō).

Ten years later King Francis I of France sent Jacques Cartier to Canada. Cartier discovered the Gulf of St. Lawrence. He sailed far up the St. Lawrence River in search of a waterway to the Pacific.

Cartier and his party stopped near some rapids. They climbed a steep hill above an Iroquois village. They named the hill *Mont Real,* the French words for Mount Royal. Today Montreal (mont′riôl′), Canada's largest city, is located there.

Cartier claimed the vast region around the St. Lawrence River for France. He called it New France. He tried to start set-

357

tlements but failed. Then the king lost interest in this land.

French fishermen, though, sailed to New France. They caught cod at the Grand Banks. They dried and salted the fish on shore. Then the fish would not spoil.

Some of the French began to trade with Native Americans. They traded knives, kettles, and other things for furs and skins. This was the start of the fur trade in Canada. By the late 1500s the fur trade was thriving.

At this time, English explorers were still searching for a waterway through North America. Two of them were Martin Frobisher and Sir Humphrey Gilbert. British fur traders, too, began to come to Canada. The king of France became worried about what England was doing.

The king sent Samuel de Champlain to New France to start a colony. A few years earlier, Spain had hired Champlain to explore. He sailed to the West Indies and visited Mexico. The king of France heard about Champlain. So he asked him to start a settlement in New France.

Champlain sailed to New France in 1603. He explored along the St. Lawrence River. He visited parts of present-day New England and New York. He found the large lake in New York that is now named Lake Champlain.

In 1608 Champlain started a settlement and named it Quebec. It was at the foot of a high cliff near the St. Lawrence River. Quebec became a leading fur-trading center. Today it is one of the large cities of Canada. Find it on the map of Canada.

More and more French people moved to New France. Trading companies brought fur traders and farmers across the Atlantic.

Seven women arrived in Quebec in 1639 to serve the colony. Six of them were nuns sent by the Catholic Church in France. Three of the nuns came to start a hospital. The other three set up a convent. A *convent* is a school and home for nuns, or sisters, and for girls training to be nuns.

Everyone rushed down to meet the ship that brought the women. Guns at the fort fired a salute.

Marie of the Incarnation was one of the women. She became head of the convent. She taught Native American and French children in a school she had the colonists build. She studied the native languages and wrote school books in these languages. Her letters and other writings were full of facts about life in early Quebec.

Some of the French colonists laid out strip farms. They were on narrow pieces of land facing the St. Lawrence River. The farms went back into the forest for a mile (1.6 km) or more. On such farms neighbors could live close together. They could help each other in time of danger.

Each strip farm had its own piece of river front. The river was the only "highway" in those days. There were no roads through the forests. Earlier, Native Americans had taught the colonists how to build canoes. They had shown them waterways to use in going from one place to another.

Other settlements were started in the St. Lawrence River Valley. They were trading centers for New France. Some Native Americans called this area "Canada." The word Canada probably comes from the language of the Iroquois people. It means "a group of huts."

France ruled New France for about 150 years. The fur trade grew. The trappers

Since the days of the colonists, the St. Lawrence River has grown in importance. Now called the St. Lawrence Seaway, it has many locks to help large ships travel its entire length.

and traders pushed farther north and west.

At first French and Native American trappers brought furs to the coast. There the furs were put on ships bound for Europe. In time the French built trading posts farther inland. Algonkin and Huron hunters trapped animals in the forests. At the trading posts they traded the furs for supplies.

The Algonkins and Hurons had been nomadic hunters. They had moved from place to place. Now some of the groups stayed near the trading posts and built homes. This changed their way of life.

Russia and Spain tried to start a fur trade in Canada. In the early 1700s Russia sent a Danish explorer, Vitus Bering, to the west coast. On the map on page 327, find the places named after this explorer.

The Spanish also explored the west coast. They traveled north from their lands in the Old Southwest.

The British gain Canada

About 1670, British fur traders set up a company in eastern Canada. It was the Hudson's Bay Company. The English king gave it all of the land around the rivers that flowed into Hudson Bay. The company's land included about a third of Canada. It took in lands already claimed by France.

The Hudson's Bay Company built many trading posts. British traders followed the French way of trading with Native Americans. The company's business grew and grew. French fur traders lost much business to the English.

There were bitter quarrels over land and over the fur trade. War between France and England broke out in 1689. Battles were fought now and then until 1763. In Canada the last part of this war is called the Seven Years' War. In the United States it is known as the French and Indian War.

Visitors can get a feeling for Montreal's past by taking a carriage ride through the narrow cobblestone streets of Old Montreal.

Some battles took place in Canada. Some were fought west of the Appalachians. George Washington and other colonists helped the British in a part of this war.

The British won the war. Then France had to give up New France.

More settlers come

The British gained French Canada in 1763. They dropped the name New France. They called the large French region the Province of Quebec.

During and after the American War for Independence, thousands of Loyalists fled to the Province of Quebec. They were the people who stayed loyal to England during the war. They settled mainly along the Great Lakes and the upper St. Lawrence River. A river's upper part is nearest where the river starts. The area where the colonial Loyalists settled had been mainly French.

In 1791 the British began to use the name "Canada" for their lands north of the

United States. They divided the Province of Quebec into two parts, Upper Canada and Lower Canada.

Upper Canada was the area along the upper St. Lawrence River and Lake Ontario and Lake Erie. Upper Canada had many English settlers by this time.

Lower Canada was northeast of Upper Canada. It included the cities of Quebec and Montreal. It had most of the French-speaking people. They kept on using the French language. They followed French customs.

The Strickland sisters wrote about life on the frontier in Upper Canada. The two women settled there in the early 1800s. They are known by their married names—Catherine Parr Trail and Susanna Moodie.

Each of them wrote a book about pioneer life. The books were used as a guide for immigrants to Canada.

Catherine wrote that frontier women like herself were independent. She said that they were not worried about "what Mr. and Mrs. So and So thinks or says."

Explorers and fur traders learned much about western Canada. Its vast lands stretched west and north of Upper Canada. Little was known about them.

One explorer of Northwest Canada was Alexander Mackenzie. He came to Canada from Scotland at age 14 and began working for a fur-trading company.

In 1789 Mackenzie and a cousin set out to explore the northwest. He went with a small party led by guides from the Chippewa people. The explorers pushed through the wilderness for many miles. They reached a stream that is now named the Mackenzie River. They followed it to its mouth at the Arctic Ocean.

On another trip, Mackenzie explored along the Peace River. He made his way through the Rocky Mountains to the Pacific Ocean. He was looking for a water route to the Pacific. On the map of Canada on page 357, find the places explored by Mackenzie.

Mackenzie wrote a book about western Canada. It was published in 1801.

George Vancouver left home in England at age 13. He was a sailor with Captain Cook on two voyages. In 1792 Vancouver explored and mapped the Pacific coast. He visited a large island near the western mainland of Canada. It is Vancouver Island, named for him. Find it on the map. About how far is it from the eastern coast of Canada?

Many fur traders paddled canoes up rivers, exploring as they went. They learned about the prairies west of Upper Canada.

Thomas Douglas was a member of a Scottish noble family. He heard about the good prairie farmland. He bought a large piece of this land from the Hudson's Bay Company. Douglas helped many farm families move from Scotland to Canada's prairies. In 1812 these families started homes near Fort Garry, a fur-trading post in the Red River Valley. Their log huts were the first homes in what is now the city of Winnipeg. Find Winnipeg on the map of Canada.

Pioneer men and women faced many problems. They nearly froze during the cold winters. They did not have furniture or warm houses. One pioneer woman built beds of boxes for her family. They slept on these "beds" for a year.

During winter months, food ran low. The pioneers almost starved. But Native Americans helped them. They showed the settlers how to hunt buffalo for meat. They taught them how to make warm robes from buffalo hides.

Nancy McClung was age 7 when her family moved to Manitoba. Find Manitoba on the map. The family left their Ontario farm and headed west in ox-drawn wagons. She became Canada's first author of a best-selling book. She was also a leader in the struggle to get the vote for Canadian women.

The pioneers in the west were often ready to give up. There were no towns or cities nearby. So it was hard to get supplies and sell their farm products. The rivers were the only roads to the faraway cities. After many years of struggling with this problem, the pioneers heard good news. They learned that a railroad would be built across Canada.

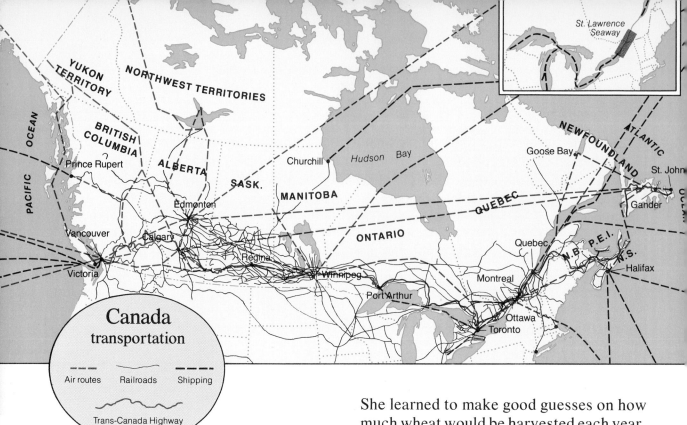

St. Lawrence Seaway

YUKON TERRITORY
NORTHWEST TERRITORIES
BRITISH COLUMBIA
ALBERTA
SASK.
MANITOBA
ONTARIO
QUEBEC
NEWFOUNDLAND
N.B.
P.E.I.
N.S.
PACIFIC OCEAN
ATLANTIC OCEAN
Hudson Bay
Prince Rupert
Churchill
Goose Bay
St. John
Edmonton
Gander
Vancouver
Calgary
Regina
Quebec
Victoria
Winnipeg
Montreal
Halifax
Port Arthur
Ottawa
Toronto

Canada
transportation

--- Air routes   ~~~ Railroads   - - - Shipping

〰〰 Trans-Canada Highway

A railroad across Canada opened up the west. It was completed in 1885. This railway went across Canada from the Atlantic to the Pacific. It joined the prairie towns with eastern cities. It linked far western British Columbia with the rest of Canada.

This was the start of Canada's vast means of travel and shipping. Today Canadians can ship and travel by road, water, rail, and air. The map shows this.

The prairies had been thinly settled. Huge areas were almost without people. These were good farmlands, though. After the railroad was built, more people moved west from eastern Canada.

Cora Hind rode on the new railway to get to Winnipeg in 1882. This was before the Canadian Pacific Railroad was completed to the Pacific coast. Cora Hind was the first woman typist west of the Great Lakes. She became a famous writer for a Winnipeg newspaper. She wrote about agriculture.

She learned to make good guesses on how much wheat would be harvested each year. Then the railroad could arrange to have cars to haul the wheat at harvest time.

People from many parts of the world also came to the prairies. In 1896 gold was found along the Klondike River in the Yukon. Nearly 30,000 people rushed to the gold fields. Most did not find gold, but many stayed in western Canada. They became farmers, miners, lumberjacks, and shipbuilders.

Life in Canada changed for the Native Americans. First their ways of hunting and fishing changed. They began to use European weapons. Then farmers settled on the prairies. The Native Americans moved farther west and north. The Canadian government set aside certain lands for their hunting and fishing. In time, most of them moved to reservations.

The Native Americans on the reservations were poor. Disease killed hundreds every year. In the mid 1900s Native Americans began to demand help. They won the rights other Canadian citizens had. With money from the government

Canadian lawmakers meet in the houses of Parliament located in Ottawa, Canada's capital.

they built clinics and schools. They opened their own businesses.

In the mid 1800s fur traders and whale hunters had moved into Inuit lands. The Inuit, or Eskimos, went to work for the Europeans. They began to hunt with guns. But their old way of life did not change much for a while. Then oil and mining companies began to look for petroleum and minerals in the far north. Some of the Inuit continued to hunt and fish. But many of them found other work. Today most of Canada's 17,500 Inuit live and work in the towns and cities. In Canada today, native groups are claiming their old lands. They want to share in the wealth found there.

Immigrants from many lands came to Canada. The first groups were from France, England, Scotland, Ireland, Germany, and the United States. Between 1894 and 1914 about three million more people moved to Canada. A large number were from Germany, Austria, Hungary, Russia, and Italy. About a million people came from Britain. Another million were from the United States.

Another large group of immigrants reached Canada after World War II. More than 1,387,000 arrived from more than forty countries. The largest number came from Britain, Germany, Italy, and the Netherlands.

More than 125,000 Asians have settled in Canada. Many are from China and Japan. Most of them live in British Columbia.

Canada's government

Canada received its constitution in 1867. The British Parliament passed the British North American Act that year. It became Canada's constitution. It set up a federal form of government. Canada's own Parliament was to make the laws for the country. A governor-general represented the British king or queen.

In 1931 Canada was given full independence. The British monarch is still honored as king or queen of Canada but has no power to rule.

Ottawa is the capital of Canada. It is in the southeast, not far from Montreal. Find Ottawa on the map of Canada on page 357.

The government of Canada is similar to that of Great Britain. Laws are made by the Canadian Parliament. It has a House of Commons, elected by the people, and a Senate. Senators are appointed to serve to age 75. The House of Commons has more power than the Senate.

The Canadian Rockies are a part of a mountain chain that runs through North and South America.

Laws are carried out by the prime minister and cabinet. The prime minister is leader of the party that wins the most seats in the House of Commons. The prime minister and cabinet also tell Parliament what laws are needed.

Canada has a Supreme Court and courts for the provinces. A province is like a state in the United States.

Each of the ten provinces has its own government, too. It has a one-house legislature. The head of the government is called the premier.

From the very start, some French Canadians disliked the national government. They wanted the province of Quebec to be independent. This call for independence is still heard in Quebec today.

A look at Canada

Canada is a huge country, larger than the United States. It is the largest country in the world after the Soviet Union.

Study the map of Canada. Notice that the country extends from Newfoundland in the Atlantic to Vancouver Island in the Pacific. It extends north to the Arctic Ocean and south to the border of the United States. This huge country has many kinds of lands.

Eastern Canada has hilly lands and low mountains. Some of them are a part of the Appalachians. They are thickly forested. Along the St. Lawrence River and the Great Lakes are lowlands. There

are also lowlands just south of Hudson Bay. As you read about Canada, use the North America Landforms map on page 89 and the map of Canada on page 357.

The Canadian Shield is a hilly, rocky region. It curves around Hudson Bay. It extends all the way up into the Northwest Territories. The eastern part of the Canadian Shield is the Laurentian Plateau. A *shield* is a huge area of solid rock. On top of this rock, there are layers of other kinds of rocks.

Long ago glaciers moved across the Canadian Shield. They scraped away most of the top soil. So this land is not good for farming.

Wide plains sweep across the central part of Canada. They are the Canadian part of the North American central plains. Grasslands cover the southern part of these plains.

North of the grasslands is an area of evergreen forests with thousands of lakes. It has many kinds of wildlife.

Still farther north are flat plains known as the tundra. They extend to the Arctic Ocean. The tundra is frozen most of the year. In the summer the soil thaws a little. Then the tundra is a wet marshland.

Along the northern coast are the Arctic islands. They are lonely lands, where few things grow.

The Canadian Rockies rise west of the central plains. They are a part of a great chain of mountains. The chain extends through North and South America. Two

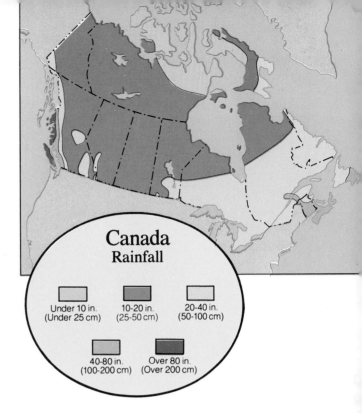

Canada
Rainfall

Under 10 in. (Under 25 cm)
10-20 in. (25-50 cm)
20-40 in. (50-100 cm)
40-80 in. (100-200 cm)
Over 80 in. (Over 200 cm)

beautiful national parks are in the Canadian Rockies. They are Banff National Park and Jasper National Park.

Along the Pacific coast there are other mountains. They are like the coastal ranges in Oregon and Washington.

The long St. Lawrence is Canada's most valuable river. On the map on page 357 notice how this river widens near the Gulf of the St. Lawrence. Ships can go up the river almost 1000 miles (1600 km) to Montreal.

Ships can now travel over 1200 miles (1930 km) farther inland. They can move across the Great Lakes from the St. Lawrence Seaway. It is a series of canals and locks between Montreal and Lake Ontario. The Seaway opens the upper St. Lawrence River to ships. See the inset map on page 362. Use the map of Canada to find how the Seaway joins the Atlantic Ocean and the lower St. Lawrence with the Great Lakes.

The Great Lakes are the largest and most important lakes in Canada. Which four are shared by Canada and the United States? Use a map to name these lakes.

Niagara Falls is between Lake Erie and Lake Ontario. Niagara's waters crash to the river below with great power. Some of this power is used to make electricity.

Canada's climate differs from region to region. A big country usually has many kinds of climate.

The climate of southern Canada is about like that in the northern parts of the United States. Winters are cold, and summers may be quite hot. Crops, such as wheat, hay, vegetables, and fruits, grow well in southern Canada.

Farther north, winters are long and cold. Summers are cool. Still farther north the weather is very cold most of the year. In the wide belt of forests, snow covers the ground month after month. The long winters on the tundra are bitterly cold. Along the Pacific coast, the weather is mild most of the year.

Study the rainfall map on this page. Eastern Canada gets from 20 to 40 inches (50 to 100 cm) of rainfall a year. Its lands have enough rain for growing many crops.

The central plains are drier lands. About how much rain do they get? The southern plains grow a lot of wheat. Wheat does not need as much rain as some other crops.

Heavy rains fall along the Pacific coast. The climate there is much like that in western Oregon and Washington.

Light snow falls along the Pacific and Atlantic coasts, on the central plains, and on the areas north of the plains. The Rocky Mountains and the shores of the Gulf of St. Lawrence are heavy snow areas. Some places near the Great Lakes also get much snow.

365

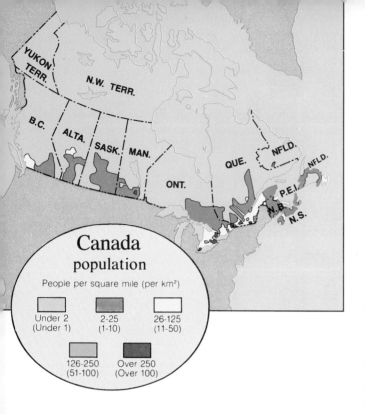

Canada
population

People per square mile (per km²)

Under 2 (Under 1)	2-25 (1-10)	26-125 (11-50)
126-250 (51-100)	Over 250 (Over 100)	

Canada has a small population for a large land. The United States has almost ten times as many people as Canada. Look at the above map of Canada's population. What color shows the areas of largest population? Why do such large numbers of people live in these places?

Canada is an urbanized country. More than half of its people live in the metropolitan areas of the large cities. Most of the cities are in southern Canada. This is the most densely populated region. It has the largest of Canada's 600 airports and most of the factories.

The Atlantic provinces

The four Atlantic provinces are in eastern Canada. They are Nova Scotia, New Brunswick, Prince Edward Island, and Newfoundland. Find each one on the map of Canada (page 357). Notice that eastern Labrador is part of Newfoundland. Which of the Atlantic provinces share borders with the state of Maine?

The Atlantic provinces have rocky coasts. Prince Edward Island is mostly a plain. The other three provinces have rocky hills nearly covered by thick forests. What does the rainfall map on page 365 tell about the climate of the Atlantic?

Nova Scotia is both a peninsula and an island. The island is Cape Breton Island. Nova Scotia is nearly surrounded by water. The Atlantic Ocean, the Gulf of St. Lawrence, and the Bay of Fundy border it.

Find the Bay of Fundy on the map. Notice that it is a long, narrow arm of the sea. It is about 180 miles (290 km) long. Ocean tides come all the way into the Bay of Fundy. High tides may be 50 feet (15 m) high by the time they reach the narrowest part of the bay.

The name Nova Scotia means New Scotland. Nova Scotia's first European settlers came from Scotland in 1629. Later, French people settled in Nova Scotia. They were called Acadians. When England was at war with France in the 1700s, the Acadians were forced to leave their homes. Some of them moved to what is now our state of Louisiana.

Halifax is the capital of Nova Scotia. It is the largest city in the Atlantic provinces. Find it on the map on page 357. The harbor of this fine seaport is open all the year round. This is not true of the ports on the St. Lawrence River. They are blocked with ice and are closed in winter.

New Brunswick lies across the Bay of Fundy from Nova Scotia. Cartier stopped at New Brunswick in 1534. He found a land full of beautiful meadows. In the 1780s many Loyalists from the United States settled in New Brunswick. You read earlier that others settled in Upper Canada. Many

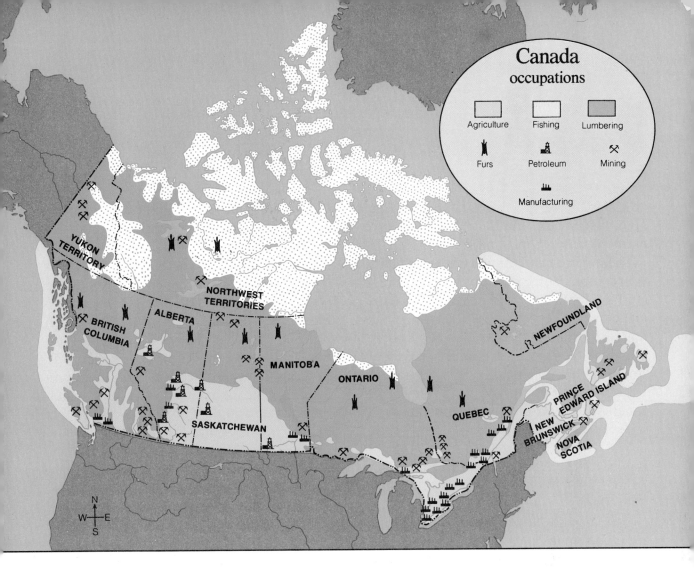

people in New Brunswick today are descendants of the Loyalists.

Fredericton is the capital of this province. Saint John, its largest city, is located on the Bay of Fundy. The harbor at Saint John, like the one at Halifax, is open all year round.

Prince Edward Island is small but thickly populated. In 1763 the British named the island for the son of King George III. Earlier the Micmacs had called it Abegweit, which means "cradled on the waves."

Charlottetown is the capital of Prince Edward Island. Fine oysters caught in the waters around the island are shipped from Charlottetown. There are many farms on the island. There are also fine beaches and camping areas.

Newfoundland is closer to Europe than any other part of America. It was the first place in America visited by the Vikings. Cabot reached it almost 500 years later.

The first cable across the Atlantic was laid between Ireland and Newfoundland. It was completed at the town of Heart's Content, Newfoundland, in 1866. The first wireless messages across the Atlantic were sent from England to Newfoundland in 1910.

St. John's is the capital of this province. It has a fine harbor and is a busy seaport.

Manufacturing is important in the four Atlantic provinces. Wood products are the chief manufactured goods. Trees are cut and sent to sawmills and to pulp and paper mills. Most of the logs are ground up.

367

They are treated and then made into paper. Newsprint is one of the leading paper products. It is the kind of paper on which newspapers are printed. Nova Scotia. New Brunswick, and Newfoundland have many pulp and paper mills.

Fishing is a main industry in the Atlantic provinces. Some people work on the fishing boats. Others build or repair boats or make fishing nets. Many work in the plants that dry, can, or freeze fish for export. Some of these people live in villages on small sheltered bays.

Cod, mackerel, herring, and salmon are caught in the Gulf waters. Lobsters are taken from the sea.

Much fishing is done at the Grand Banks. The Grand Banks are a feeding ground for millions of cod and other fish. The Banks' shelf of underwater land curves around Newfoundland's coast for about 200 miles (320 km). The water that covers the shelf is fairly shallow. Then the shelf slopes downward, and the water deepens.

Farming and mining are important in the Atlantic provinces. Farmers grow oats, barley, hay, vegetables, and fruit. Apples are a main crop in Nova Scotia. Potatoes are a big crop in New Brunswick and on Prince Edward Island.

Gypsum is mined in Nova Scotia. It is used for making plaster. Sand and gravel, coal, gold, silver, copper, lead, and zinc are also found in these provinces.

Much iron ore is now being mined in Labrador. The ore is hauled out on a railroad built through rugged mountains. At the Gulf of St. Lawrence, the ore is loaded on ore boats. Much of it goes to steel mills in the United States.

The Province of Quebec

The largest province of Canada is the Province of Quebec. Find it on the map on page 357. It extends more than 2000 miles (3200 km) from north to south. One part of it is the Gaspé peninsula, which borders New Brunswick. About four-fifths of the people of Quebec have French ancestors. Many are descended from early French settlers. Most of them have kept their French language and culture. Students go to schools where lessons are taught in French. The people listen to and watch French radio and TV programs. They have French holidays and French customs.

Some people in southern Quebec are farmers. They live on the plains along the St. Lawrence River. The soil is fertile, and plenty of rain falls. Farmers can raise good crops here. They grow potatoes and apples. Some farmers have many maple sugar trees. In the early spring, they tap the trees for sap. The maple sap is made into syrup and sugar.

Dairy farmers sell much milk and cream. They grow corn, hay, and oats for cattle feed during the long winters. Beef cattle are also raised. So are hogs and poultry.

North of the farm belt is the Laurentian Plateau. It has such minerals as copper, iron, gold, and zinc. It also is the richest source of asbestos rock in Canada. This rock contains tough asbestos fibers that will not burn. They are used in boots, suits, and gloves for fire fighters. They are used in making roof shingles and linings for furnace pipes, too.

Forests cover about half of Quebec. Many people work as loggers. Others have jobs in the pulp and paper mills.

Quebec *(above)* was built on a cliff overlooking the St. Lawrence River. Montreal *(right),* Canada's largest city, is also on the St. Lawrence.

Montreal is the largest city in Quebec and in Canada. Find it on the map of Canada. It is on an island where the Ottawa River joins the St. Lawrence.

Land and air routes extend from Montreal in all directions. Its busy harbor is about 1000 miles (1600 km) inland from the Atlantic Ocean. The St. Lawrence River connects Montreal with the seaports of the world. Every year millions of tons of wheat are shipped from Montreal. This city is the largest grain port in the world.

More than half of Montreal's people work in factories, mills, and refineries. Among the products they make are electrical equipment, clothing, paper goods, aircraft, and railroad cars.

Montreal has a number of universities. In some, French is the language spoken. In others, English is used.

The old city of Quebec is the capital of Quebec province. It's the oldest city in Canada. Quebec is on the St. Lawrence River about 400 miles (640 km) from the Gulf of St. Lawrence. Its name comes from the Algonkin word *kebec.* It means "the river narrows here." Long after this city began, the name Quebec was given to the entire province.

Quebec's Upper Town is high above the St. Lawrence. A stone wall was built around it in the early 1800s. A part of the wall and the old fort still stand. Lower Town is along the river front. It has large stores and factories and also some old, narrow streets.

Several million tourists visit Quebec and Montreal every year. In fact, tourists come to many parts of Canada. Caring for tourists is a growing industry.

Toronto is often called the commercial center of Canada.

The Province of Ontario

The large province of Ontario is west of Quebec. Find it on the map on page 357. Notice that it extends north to Hudson Bay. Four of the Great Lakes border it on the south. Ontario extends farther south than any other province. Its most southern part is across a river from Detroit.

The Laurentian Plateau covers a large part of Ontario. Notice this on the map of Canada. It is a region of vast forests. Some of the trees are made into lumber. Most, though, go to the pulp and paper mills.

The southern part of Ontario's Laurentian Plateau has such minerals as gold, silver, copper, and nickel. More nickel is mined in this region than anywhere in the world. Nickel is a tough metal that does not rust.

Uranium ore and platinum are also mined in Ontario. Uranium is needed to produce atomic energy. Platinum is a valuable silverish white metal. It is used in making chemicals, glass, and jewelry.

Some farming is carried on in southern Ontario. Farmers raise herds of beef and dairy cattle. They raise corn, hay, and other feed crops. Tobacco, fruit, and grapes grow near the Great Lakes.

Manufacturing is centered in the southern part of Ontario where there are many cities. Southern Ontario is one of the most densely populated areas in all of Canada.

Toronto, the capital of Ontario, is on Lake Ontario. It is the second largest city in Canada. Toronto began in the late 1700s as a small settlement named York.

Toronto has a good harbor. The waterfront is ten miles (16 km) long. Toronto's factories and mills turn out all kinds of products. Among them are paper goods, processed foods, iron, steel, and chemicals.

Toronto is a publishing center. Many books and several national magazines are published in this city. It is also a center of education. It has several universities, including the University of Toronto.

The prairie provinces

The three prairie provinces are in central Canada. They are Manitoba, Saskatchewan (sas kach′i won), and Alberta. Find them on the map of Canada. Which one is nearest to Ontario? Which of the three is farthest west?

Plains extend across these provinces. They reach from the Laurentian Plateau on the east to the Canadian Rockies on the west.

The prairie provinces have more than three-fourths of all Canadian farmland. Wheat is the main crop. And most of Canada's oats and rye are grown here. Farmers use combines and other large machines in the grain fields.

From the air the wheat fields look like a huge checkerboard. The planted fields are green in the spring and gold in the late summer. Unplanted strips or squares look gray. They are left fallow to store up moisture for the next planting.

On the drier lands farther west are some irrigated farms. Water is brought from lakes and rivers. These drier lands have

Alberta is famous for its wheat. What mountains form a natural boundary along the western edge of the province?

many cattle ranches. The prairie provinces raise about two-thirds of the beef cattle in Canada.

Thick forests cover the area north of the plains. Each year many trees are cut down by loggers. Some lumber is used for making furniture. Much of it, though, goes to pulp and paper mills.

Mining is a fast-growing industry in the prairie provinces. Workers mine nickel, zinc, copper, and gold. Most of the mining is done in the rocky region north of the central plains. Saskatchewan is the center of potash mining. Potash is used in making fertilizer.

Petroleum and natural gas are found in the prairie provinces. Alberta is Canada's leading supplier of these products. This province has some oil refineries. It also has plants where oil is used in making such products as fertilizer and plastics.

Pipelines carry much of the oil and gas to refineries in distant cities. One line extends

371

from Alberta to Montreal. It is more than 2000 miles (3200 km) long.

Cities are far apart in the big prairie provinces. About half of the people in these three provinces live in cities or their suburbs.

Winnipeg, the capital of Manitoba, is on the Red River of the North. Its name comes from a Cree word that means "muddy waters." Winnipeg is sometimes called "The Gateway City." It is a main railroad center between eastern and western Canada.

Winnipeg is a leading center for buying and selling grain. It also has large stockyards where beef cattle are bought and sold. Many people work to prepare for market the foods that are raised nearby. They work in flour mills, meat-packing plants, and creameries where butter and cheese are made.

Regina is the capital of Saskatchewan. Its name means "Queen." It was given in honor of Queen Victoria, who ruled Britain for 63 years in the 1800s.

Regina (ri jī′nə) has many factories. There are oil refineries and meat-packing plants. Other plants make sheet metal and wood products.

Edmonton, the capital of Alberta, is known as the "Gateway to the North." The highway that leads to Alaska goes through Edmonton. Many tourists stop there on their way to and from Alaska.

Edmonton is one of Canada's main oil centers. It has refineries, chemical plants, food-processing plants, and flour mills.

Nearly 125,000 Native Americans live in the prairie provinces. This is almost half of the Native Americans in Canada. Many own or work on farms and cattle ranches.

The Province of British Columbia

British Columbia is on the Pacific coast of Canada. Find it on the map on page 357. It includes Vancouver Island and other islands off the coast. British Columbia is nearly covered by the Canadian Rockies and the Coast Range.

British Columbia has a rugged coastline. There are hundreds of sheltered bays and inlets. They have been carved out by glaciers and streams.

British Columbia produces about one half of Canada's lumber. The western slopes of the Coast Range are rainy lands. Thick forests grow in the mild climate.

Many people in British Columbia work in wood-products plants. Others have jobs in food-processing plants, oil refineries, and chemical plants.

Other people work at fishing, farming, or mining. The largest catch is salmon. Other catches include cod, herring, and halibut. Fish canneries and freezing plants are busiest during the months of May through September. More fish are caught during this time than during the cold months.

British Columbia has only a little land for raising crops. The inland Okanagan (ō′ka-nä′gən) Valley has good soil and plenty of irrigation water. It is noted for its apple, apricot, pear, peach, and cherry orchards. There are also some farms on Vancouver Island.

Gold, silver, copper, lead, and zinc are mined in British Columbia. In 1858 gold was found along the Fraser River. Over

Victoria uses flowers to spell out a greeting to visitors.

20,000 miners rushed into the area. Most went back home. Others went to work in mines and on farms.

Caring for tourists provides jobs in Victoria and Vancouver. About three-fourths of the people in British Columbia live in or around these two cities. Find them on the map of Canada.

Victoria, the capital, is on Vancouver Island. It was started as a trading post by the Hudson's Bay Company. Flowers thrive in its mild moist climate. Victoria is famous for its flower gardens.

Vancouver is a busy shipping center. It is the western "end of the line" for the cross-country railroads and the Trans-Canada Highway. It is also Canada's chief western seaport.

Canada carries on much trade with countries in Asia. Lumber, salmon, and many kinds of manufactured goods are exported. Japan is one of Canada's leading customers.

Vancouver is the leading manufacturing city west of Ontario.

Canada's territories

Yukon Territory and the Northwest Territories are cold lands. Find them on the map. They have long, bitterly cold winters and short, cool summers.

The few towns are hundreds of miles apart. In winter, mail and supplies must come in by plane. Snowmobiles may be used for short trips.

Yukon Territory is mountainous. The highest peaks are in the southwest not far from Alaska. Mount Logan is almost as high as Mount McKinley, the highest peak in North America.

The Alaska Highway winds through the southwest part of the Yukon. Notice this on the map on page 357. The highway brings many tourists to the towns along its route. One of these towns is Whitehorse, the capital. It is a tourist center. It is also a trading center for the mining camps.

Eskimo students enjoy a sack race during recess. Would it be hard to get to the finish line in the snow?

The Northwest Territories cover nearly a third of Canada. They stretch north to the Arctic Ocean. They include many frozen islands that are within the Arctic Circle. Find some of these islands on the map.

The southern part of the Northwest Territories is forested. The far north, though, is too cold for trees to grow. Yellowknife is the capital of the Northwest Territories.

Nearly half of the 30,000 people that live in the Northwest Territories are Native Americans. Among them are the Eskimos. Many Native Americans live in inland villages in the central region.

Most of the Eskimos live in villages near Hudson Bay or on the Arctic islands. They work in mining, fishing, and other industries. Some Eskimos have set up businesses of their own.

A few Eskimos live in small groups in remote areas. They hunt and trap in the old ways. Some still use kayaks (kī'aks), or skin-covered boats, for fishing and dog sleds for traveling.

The Canadian territories have many rich natural resources. Gold, silver, lead, zinc, and copper are found there, especially in the Great Slave Lake area. Pioneers are developing mines. Some supplies and machinery are flown in. Others are shipped during the summer on barges on the Mackenzie River.

Oil and natural gas are pumped near Norman Wells. But huge deposits of oil and gas are said to lie under the Arctic Ocean. Engineers are studying ways to develop the oil fields in the far north. But there are no roads or pipelines to carry the oil and gas to the south.

Canada, a good neighbor

Canada and the United States are friendly neighbors. The two countries border each other for more than 3000 miles (4800 km). Yet on this long border there is not a single fort. Canada and the United States live together in peace and friendship.

Several monuments honor the friendship between Canada and the United States. One is the beautiful Peace Arch at Blaine, Washington.

Sentences to complete

In List A are the beginnings of sentences. The endings are in List B. On paper copy the complete sentences.

List A

1. The oldest city in Canada is
2. The capital of Canada is
3. Canada's largest western seaport is
4. Rocky land around Hudson Bay is the
5. A city once named York is
6. The largest grain port in the world is
7. The Prairie provinces are
8. The Atlantic provinces are
9. The largest province is

List B

Ontario	Saskatchewan
Canadian Shield	Montreal
Prince Edward Island	Nova Scotia
Vancouver	Alberta
Newfoundland	Ottawa
Toronto	New Brunswick
Quebec	Manitoba

In what order?

Below is a list of important events. Make a time line for these events. What date will you write at the left end of the line? What date will be at the right end?

Canada got its own government

Cabot claimed Canada for England

England won New France

Mackenzie explored the Northwest

Cartier explored along the St. Lawrence

Champlain started Quebec

Using maps

1. Turn to the map of the Chief Regions of the Earth on page 354. In which two regions is Canada? In which region is southern Canada?
2. Find Canada on the map of North America on page 89. What east-west line on the map crosses Hudson Bay? Would you expect the climate near this line to be colder or warmer than at latitude 50°N? Why?
3. What part of Canada has about the same rainfall as North Dakota? Look on the maps on pages 259 and 365 to find out.
4. Find the Saskatchewan, Churchill, Peace, and Mackenzie rivers. Which is the longest? About how long is it?

What do you think?

1. Why were rivers very important in Canada's early days?
2. Why do we say that fish and fur helped Canada's exploration?
3. Why does Canada have a small population? What facts about land and climate give you some clues? Why is southern Canada the most thickly populated area?
4. Why can the Gulf of St. Lawrence be called "Canada's front door"?
5. Why can we think of the areas in the far north as "the lands of tomorrow"?

Things to do

Read in an encyclopedia about one of these topics. Write a summary report.

nickel	asbestos	Inuits
uranium	potash	Canadian city

27

Mexico

Long ago in Mexico

The Aztecs lived in northern Mexico long ago. They were also known as the Mexica people. They lived in a dry land, and food was scarce. Slowly the Aztecs wandered to the south. They were looking for a better place to settle.

After many years they reached a wide green valley. But stronger people held the best places. The Aztecs were pushed out, time after time.

Years passed. Then one day Aztec leaders were resting at the edge of a shallow lake. A legend tells that they saw an eagle. It had a snake in its beak. The eagle swooped down on a small island in the lake. It perched on a thorny cactus and began to eat the snake.

One leader said, "This is a sign from the gods to settle here. We must be brave. If we are as brave as the eagle, we will conquer our enemies."

About 1325 the Aztecs started a village on the island. They named it Tenochtitlán (tā noch′tē′tlän).

Aztec farmers thought of a way to make more land. They wove rafts of reeds and twigs. They scooped up mud from the lake and piled it on the rafts. Then they planted vegetables and trees on the rafts. They planted corn, beans, squash, peppers, avocados, and tobacco.

In time, the trees pushed their roots deep into the shallow lake. The roots kept the islands from floating. Workers filled some spaces between the islands with twigs and mud to make more land. They left other spaces as waterways to be used as streets. Drawbridges joined the island city with the shore of the lake. The drawbridges could be moved away from the shore in time of danger.

The warrior Aztecs built a very great empire. All Aztec men had to serve in the army. In the 1400s they began to defeat other groups to the north and the south. The Aztecs built an empire that spread over central Mexico.

The defeated peoples had to pay the Aztecs with cloth, deer hides, and food. Gold, silver, jade, and jewels came to Tenochtitlán, too. There they were made into fine ornaments. Some soldiers from the defeated armies had to work as slaves.

Tenochtitlán was the capital of the big Aztec empire. It had large stone buildings with fine gardens. One palace had more than one hundred rooms. It was the home of the ruler, Montezuma (mon′ti zü′mə).

In the center of the city was a walled plaza. It had huge stone pyramids. On top of them were temples where the Aztecs honored their gods. There were hundreds of priests to lead the temple ceremonies. Some young women were trained for such duty, too.

Most of the people lived in adobe houses. The houses were painted white and trimmed in bright colors. The city also had great marketplaces. Some women ran booths in the market.

The Spaniards in Mexico

Stories spread that the Aztecs had great wealth. It was said that Montezuma ate from gold plates and drank from gold cups. It was said that Aztec palaces were built of gold on streets paved with silver. Some stories were true. Others were not.

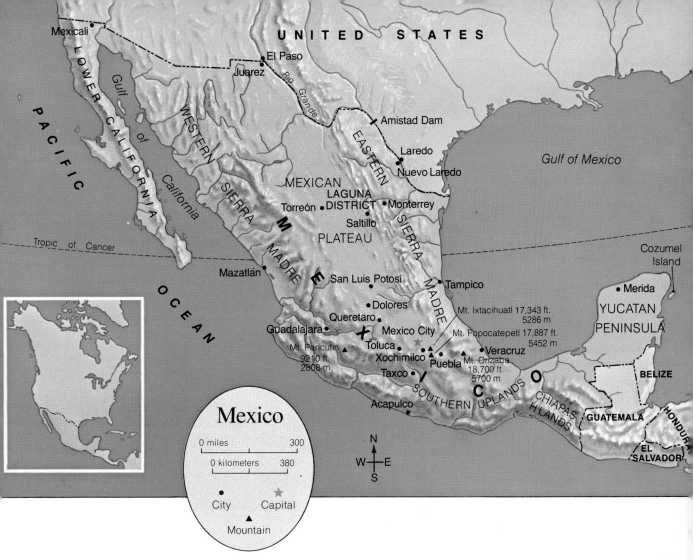

Mexicali

El Paso
Juarez

UNITED STATES

LOWER CALIFORNIA

Gulf of California

PACIFIC

OCEAN

Tropic of Cancer

Mazatlán

WESTERN SIERRA MADRE

MEXICAN
LAGUNA
DISTRICT
Torreón
Saltillo
PLATEAU

San Luis Potosí

Dolores

Guadalajara

Mt. Paricutin
9210 ft.
2808 m

Queretaro

Toluca
Mexico City
Xochimilco
Taxco
Puebla

Acapulco

SOUTHERN UPLANDS

EASTERN SIERRA MADRE

Amistad Dam

Laredo
Nuevo Laredo

Monterrey

Rio Grande

Tampico

Mt. Ixtacihuatl 17,343 ft.
5286 m
Mt. Popocatepetl 17,887 ft.
5452 m
Veracruz
Mt. Orizaba
18,700 ft.
5700 m

Gulf of Mexico

Cozumel
Island

Merida

YUCATAN
PENINSULA

CHIAPAS HLANDS

BELIZE

GUATEMALA

HONDURAS

EL
SALVADOR

Mexico

0 miles 300
0 kilometers 380

N
W—E
S

• City   ★ Capital

▲ Mountain

a good harbor. Cortés named it Veracruz. He built a fort there. His soldiers defeated some native groups that lived nearby.

Montezuma II was the ruler of the Aztecs. He heard reports about Cortés and was puzzled. Was this the ancient Aztec white god who was to come back one day?

Montezuma sent some very fine gifts to Cortés. Messengers brought him gold and jeweled masks and necklaces. There were bright robes and hats with fine feathers.

Cortés shot off a cannon to impress the messengers. They rushed back to Montezuma full of fright. He sent more presents. One was a gold plate the size of a wagon wheel. Another was a large silver plate. There were beautiful gold and silver figures and a bow with gold arrows.

Many Spaniards believed these tales. One was Hernán Cortés. He was a daring Spanish soldier living in Cuba.

The governor of Cuba asked Cortés to sail to Mexico. He was told to explore and to hunt for gold. He was also told to claim land for Spain and to trade with the native people.

Cortés took eleven ships with 650 people to Mexico. Many horses, guns, and cannon were on the ships, too. The Spaniards explored the southern coast of Mexico. They sailed as far south as the Yucatan Peninsula. Find it on the map above.

Then Cortés turned northward. In 1519 he and his people landed at a place that had

Teotihuacán, the "city of the gods," was destroyed long before the Spaniards came. Today visitors still marvel at the ruins of the largest of the pre-Columbian cities in Mexico.

Cortés was pleased. Now he wanted more than ever to reach the rich Aztec city. It was far inland.

Along the way, thousands of native people joined Cortés. They were enemies of the Aztecs. Only with their help could Cortés succeed.

After long weeks of marching, Cortés reached Tenochtitlán. Montezuma did not fight. He still thought that Cortés might be a god. He gave his guests a palace in which to live. He made sure that they were served plenty of fine food.

In time Montezuma began to plot against Cortés. But Cortés plotted, too. He took Montezuma prisoner but treated him like a king.

After several months, fighting broke out. Many Spaniards lost their lives in the rush to leave the city. The angry Aztecs even threw stones at Montezuma. He had urged them to let the Spaniards go. Montezuma died a few days later.

Far from the city, Cortés made new plans. He found more allies among the Aztecs' enemies. About a year later he returned. This time Cortés destroyed Tenochtitlán. Its people gave up. So did other Aztec cities. By the end of 1521, the

Spanish had conquered the whole Aztec empire.

An important woman in the Spanish conquest of Mexico was Malinche. She was called Doña Marina by the Spaniards. Malinche learned the Aztec language in her home town. She was taken prisoner by the peoples of Tabasco. She learned the language of the Mayas from them. When Cortés landed, she became his interpreter. An *interpreter* tells a person who cannot speak a language what another person says in that language. Malinche told the Spaniards what the native people were saying. She also told the native people what the Spaniards said.

Malinche was important to Cortés in many ways. She helped the Spaniards and some native people make plans for the conquest. Both the Spaniards and some native people depended on her.

Spain rules Mexico

Spain began to govern the land, which they called New Spain. The king of Spain made Cortés the governor of the colony. Cortés decided to build the capital of New Spain at Tenochtitlán. He forced Aztecs to do the hard work. They cleared away the ruins and filled in the canals. They built a new capital. It was called Mexico City. Find it on the map on page 377.

The king of Spain gave Cortés and the other conquerors huge areas of land. Cortés took Mexico's best land for himself. He spent much time exploring and hunting for more gold.

After a few years, the king replaced Cortés. He sent a viceroy (vīs′roi), or chief governor, to rule Mexico. A viceroy had great power as long as he pleased the king.

Many colonists sailed to New Spain. Among them were Spanish officials and soldiers. Missionaries came to teach the native people about the Christian religion.

Some Spanish settlers were given large grants of land for ranches. The native people had to do most of the ranch work. They raised the crops and cared for the cattle. Whole villages worked for landholders. Some villages had to send young people to a labor center. Some people were forced to work in mines. Other villages had to give part of their crops or other goods to the nearest Spanish official.

Men and women from Spain came to live in Mexico. Many families settled on farms. Men and women worked together in preparing the land and caring for crops. Women spun wool and made silk for clothing.

When husbands were away, wives ran the plantations. They were leaders in their community and in government. Some women became workers in the church.

One famous woman was a nun named Sor Juana Inés de la Cruz. "Sor" means sister. Sor Juana was born in a small town near Mexico City in 1651. She learned to read at age three. At age 13 she went to live with an aunt in Mexico City. She became known as one of the most brilliant persons in the city.

When Sor Juana was 17, she became a nun and lived in a convent. There she got together a huge library and collection of musical instruments. She did experiments in science and studied mathematics. She was most famous for the poetry she wrote. She is known today in Mexico as one of the country's greatest poets.

Spain governed Mexico for about three hundred years. The viceroy had more and more power. The laws were strict. They were unfair to most of the people.

Towns had a council and a mayor. But these offices were controlled by the richer people. On large estates the landholders ruled as kings.

Miguel Hidalgo's statue stands atop Independence Church in his hometown of Dolores Hidalgo.

Spain tried to run its colonies for its own benefit. Other European nations had the same plan for their colonies. New Spain would send minerals, hides, wool, and other raw materials to Spain. The colony was to buy manufactured goods from Spain. Only Spanish ships were to be used.

Spain had a hard time enforcing these trade laws. Goods were smuggled into and out of New Spain. Smuggling also took place in the English colonies. Many Spanish treasure ships were lost at sea. They were taken by Spain's enemies or by pirates.

Most of the people in New Spain were poor. They could not own land or get an education. They had no chance to improve their lives.

In time, Mexican leaders began to work for independence. Word had spread that the Thirteen Colonies had won freedom from England. This encouraged Mexicans to try to win independence from Spain.

Also, by 1800, Spain was no longer such a powerful nation. It was having problems in Europe. Mexican leaders thought this would be a good time to act.

A few patriots set up secret groups. They read books about winning freedom. The books had been smuggled into Mexico. One of the patriots was a priest, Father Hidalgo (hi dal′gō).

Father Hidalgo lived in the village of Dolores. Most people there were poor farm workers. He tried to help them earn a better living. But Spanish officials stopped his work.

The patriot priest worried about the many poor people in Mexico. He knew there had to be a change. Otherwise the people could never have a fair chance.

Father Hidalgo called all of his people to arms. It was about midnight on September 15, 1810. Father Hidalgo had just come back from a secret meeting. He went to the church and rang the church bell.

Father Hidalgo talked to the villagers about freedom. He told them it was time to overthrow the Spanish rulers. He urged them to join others in fighting for freedom. The priest then ended with stirring words. He led the villagers in what became known as "El Grito de Dolores." These Spanish words mean "the cry of Dolores." This was a war cry for freedom. It ended with Spanish words that mean "Long live independence."

These daring words were passed from village to village. Before long, thousands of people joined Hidalgo's army. But they had only clubs and farm tools. They were no match for the well-armed Spanish troops. So they lost most of the battles.

Father Hidalgo was captured and put to death. This sad event stirred more people to fight for freedom. Other brave leaders took his place. In time almost everyone in Mexico, rich and poor, joined the revolt. In 1821 the Mexicans won independence. Father Hidalgo's dream had come true.

Mexico City's most important public square, the Zócalo, is on the site of the old Aztec capital. Facing the Zócalo is the National Palace. The president and other lawmakers have offices in the Palace.

Mexico celebrates September 16 as Independence Day. The church bell that was rung at Dolores is called Mexico's Liberty Bell. Today it hangs in the National Palace in Mexico City.

Every September 15 about midnight, crowds gather in the plaza in front of the National Palace. They are there for Independence Day.

The president of Mexico rings the bell. Then he leads the people in the famous "El Grito de Dolores."

An independent Mexico

Free Mexico had to try to find ways to solve many problems. People could not agree on a new leader. A Spanish army officer got control. He became a dictator. Soon he was driven from power.

In 1823, Mexican leaders wrote a constitution. This constitution provided for a central government and for state governments. A president was to be the head of the central government. A congress was to make the laws.

A president and a congress were elected. But only a few people had the right to vote. Most of the native people and mestizos (mes tē′zōs) did not. The *mestizos* were people who had both Native American and Spanish ancestors.

Leaders often quarreled. At times strong army leaders took over the government. Other times wealthy landowners had control. Often these leaders did not follow the constitution.

That was a sad time for Mexico. During those years the country lost nearly half of its land to the United States. It lost Texas and our Southwest.

In the mid 1800s, Benito Juárez became president of Mexico. The ancestors of Juárez (hwä′res) were of the Zapotec group.

The Zapotecs had lived in southern Mexico for a long time. They were expert builders. They had developed a calendar and a form of writing.

Juárez was born in a poor Mexican village. His parents died when he was young. Friends helped him to get an education. He studied hard. At last he became a lawyer. Later he served as governor of his state.

Juárez was one of Mexico's greatest presidents. He urged many reforms. Perhaps the chief one was land reform.

Most of Mexico's land was owned by wealthy people and the Catholic Church. Juárez thought that some large farms should be divided. Poor people could then own the smaller farms.

The powerful landowners did not like this plan. They blocked the land reforms.

Still, the work of Juárez was not forgotten. After his death in 1872, his plans for land reform were made a part of the nation's constitution.

Porfirio Díaz became dictator of Mexico in 1876. Except for four years, Díaz (dē′äs) ruled until 1911.

The Revolution of 1910 caused more problems. At last, in 1917, a new constitution was adopted. The country was divided into 31 states. Mexico became the United Mexican States.

Mexico has a three-branch government like that of the United States. The president is the head of the central government. The Mexican Congress has two houses. There is a Supreme Court and a system of lower courts.

Mexico City is the capital. It is in a district of its own, a Federal District.

Spanish is the official language in Mexico. It comes from the old Latin language. Mexico is sometimes called a Latin American country.

A closer look

Mexico is directly south of the United States. A part of the border between Mexico and the United States is formed by the Rio Grande. Find this river on the map (page 377).

Mexico stretches a long way from north to south. It borders two Latin American countries. Find them on the map.

Mexico also extends many miles from east to west. Find the Yucatan Peninsula on the east. Cortés explored along its coast before he founded Veracruz. Find Veracruz on the map.

Find Lower California on the map. A

382

town on this peninsula is about as far west as San Diego, California. A map of North America will show that this is true.

Mexico has plateaus, mountains, and lowlands. A wide plateau extends through central Mexico. Ranges of high mountains surround it on three sides. Plateau lands and mountains cover about two thirds of Mexico.

Low plains extend along the eastern coast. They stretch from the Rio Grande to the Yucatan Peninsula. Grasslands cover the northern plains. Thick forests and jungles cover much of the southern plains.

The Mexican Plateau covers about a third of the country. It extends from the Rio Grande to the area around Mexico City. Find the plateau on the map.

The plateau is a high land. Its elevation is about 3000 feet (900 m) above sea level in the north. It rises to about 8000 feet (2400 m) in the far south. The plateau has mountains and hills. Between them are many valleys.

Valuable minerals are found in some lower mountains on the plateau. Among them are copper, gold, silver, and lead. Mexico has been one of the leading silver-mining countries since the 1500s.

Two ranges of mountains run north and south through the country. They are the Eastern Sierra Madre and the Western Sierra Madre. They meet south of Mexico City. They are a part of the long chain of mountains that extends through North and South America.

There are many old volcanoes in this area. Some have not erupted for a long time. One quiet volcano is snow-capped Mount Orizaba (ō′ri sä′bä). Its name is a Native American word meaning "Moun-

The village of Paricutín had to be abandoned when Mexico's newest volcano, also called Paricutín, erupted. Lava flows buried the town. The volcano grew more than 1500 feet (460 m) in eight months.

tain of the Star." Find Mount Orizaba on the map. It is the highest peak in Mexico. What is its elevation?

Find the second and third highest peaks. What are their names? How high are they?

Paricutín is Mexico's youngest volcano. Find it on the map. This volcano began in a corn field one winter afternoon in 1943. That day, a farmer was plowing. He felt the soil grow hot. In a short time, the earth began to spit out hot rocks and smoke.

Paricutín's lava shot hundreds of feet into the air. Soon it formed a new cone-shaped mountain. The lava buried two villages and the fields for twenty miles (32 km) around.

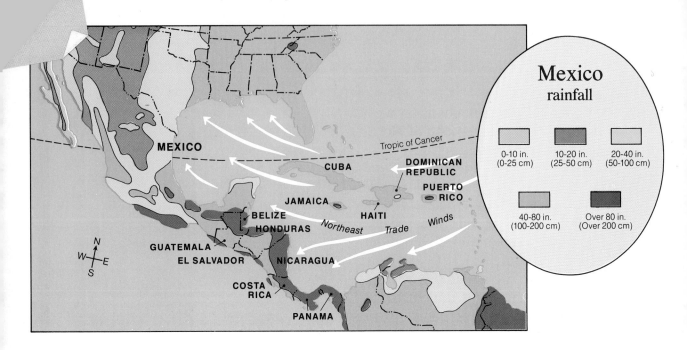

Mexico
rainfall

0-10 in.
(0-25 cm)

10-20 in.
(25-50 cm)

20-40 in.
(50-100 cm)

40-80 in.
(100-200 cm)

Over 80 in.
(Over 200 cm)

Mexico has both a hot climate and a cool climate. About one-half of Mexico is south of the Tropic of Cancer. Notice this on the map on page 377. You might expect, then, that this area would have a hot climate. But climate depends in part on elevation. Highlands have a cooler climate than lowlands. For example, Mexico City is on a high plateau. It has an elevation of 7575 feet (2300 m). Its climate is comfortable all year. Veracruz is on a lowland on the Gulf of Mexico. Its climate is hot.

Study the rainfall map above. Notice which parts of Mexico get the most rain. Locate Mexico City on the map on page 385. About how much rain does Mexico City get? How much rain does Guadalajara receive? How much rain does Monterrey receive?

Mexicans live in villages, towns, and cities. Study the population map. What areas of Mexico are the most thinly settled? Their climates and lands are among the reasons why the population is small.

What areas are thickly settled? They have some large cities, many towns, and hundreds of villages.

Three-fifths of the Mexican people live in towns and cities of more than 2500 people. Most of the other people live in villages. A village is called a *pueblito* (pweb lē′tō), a Spanish word for "little town."

A visit to a pueblito

Raul Munoz (mü nyôz′) had invited his cousin Carmen to visit his pueblito. The Munoz family greeted her at the door with the words, "Buenos dias." The words mean "Good day," or "Good morning."

It was Sunday, so the whole family was at home. There were Raul's mother and father, his grandmother, and his two younger sisters.

The Munoz house was built of adobe. It had a roof made of curved tiles. The floor was made of lovely light blue tiles. Bright pictures covered the walls. There were many flowers in the house, too.

The kitchen was at one end of the house. Orange-red peppers were hung there to dry. They would be used to season some foods.

384

The Munoz family enjoyed a meal together. They had *enchiladas* (en′chi-lä′dəs). These are made with *tortillas* (tôr-tē′yəs), which are thin cornmeal pancakes. The tortillas are filled with meat, chicken, or cheese and covered with a sauce. The family also ate rice and *frijoles refritos* (frē′hōlz rē frē′tos). These are beans that are boiled, mashed, and then

Some farming communities still use the old ways of working the land.

fried. Squash was served, too. For dessert there were avocados, mangoes, and bananas.

While they were eating, Carmen talked about her family. She said that her older sister was studying in Mexico City. She

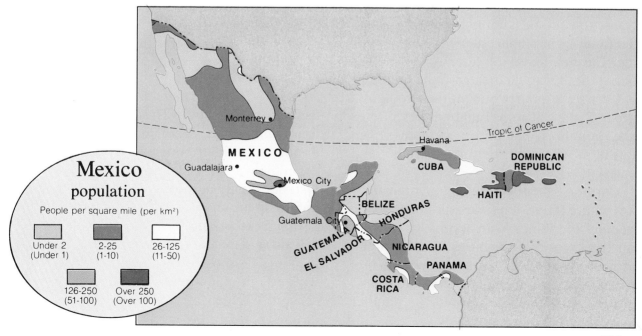

385

Open-air markets are popular places to shop. They also serve as meeting places for friends. What kinds of things are being sold at this market?

wants to become a dentist. She told about her family's new apartment in a large building. Carmen had a job after school taking tickets at the movie theater in the building.

Carmen's mother bought their food in a grocery store near the building. Sometimes she bought fruits and vegetables from farmers, who sold them from trucks and carts.

Carmen described the big open-air market where they sometimes shopped. Many people sold things from booths. Others sat on the ground with things to sell spread around them. At the market they could buy many kinds of fresh and cooked foods. There were baskets, pottery, leather goods, and toys for sale, too.

Raul said that their village had a market. On Saturdays the farm families brought their goods to market to sell or trade. They also visited friends at the market.

After dinner, the family walked to the plaza. It is the center of the pueblito. The church and some stores face it. Nearby is the school.

The family visited with neighbors and friends. Carmen met some of Raul's friends from school. They spent a lot of time looking over a new truck. The father of one of Raul's friends had just bought it.

On the way home Carmen asked Raul to visit her family in the city. She would take him to an art show in one of the parks and perhaps get tickets for a soccer match.

Raul said that he would come after planting time. Almost everyone in the village worked in the fields during planting season. Carmen offered to help the next day.

Twine is made from the fibers of the sisal plant, an important Mexican crop. The leaves of the plant are crushed by a machine. Then the pulp is washed out of the fibers before the fibers are allowed to dry.

Some main industries

Only a small part of Mexico's land is good for growing crops. But the farmers are able to raise most of Mexico's food. This is partly because many farmers now use machines and improved ways of farming.

Also, farmers can plant crops on land that they could not use before. Jungles have been cleared in parts of the hot lowlands. These areas are just right for growing bananas, sugar cane, and rice.

Irrigation has changed the dry northwest. Farmers in this region can now grow cotton, wheat, and winter vegetables. The Laguna District is one of these areas in northern Mexico. Its farmers grow about half of Mexico's large cotton crop. Find the Laguna District on the map on page 377.

Dams have been built on some of the rivers. Reservoirs behind the dams store water for irrigation.

The Amistad Dam is on the Rio Grande on the border between Mexico and the United States. The two countries worked together to build it.

Some of the best farmlands are in the southern plateau region. Farmers there raise corn, beans, other vegetables, fruit, and coffee. Corn and beans are the largest crops. They are two of the main foods in Mexico. Crops such as cotton, sugar cane, coffee, fruit, and winter vegetables are exported.

Cattle ranching is a very old industry in Mexico. The Spaniards brought the first cattle to Mexico in the 1500s.

Thousands of beef cattle are raised in the northwest. Grass grows thinly in these dry lands. It takes hundreds of acres to feed a large herd. So cattle ranches are huge.

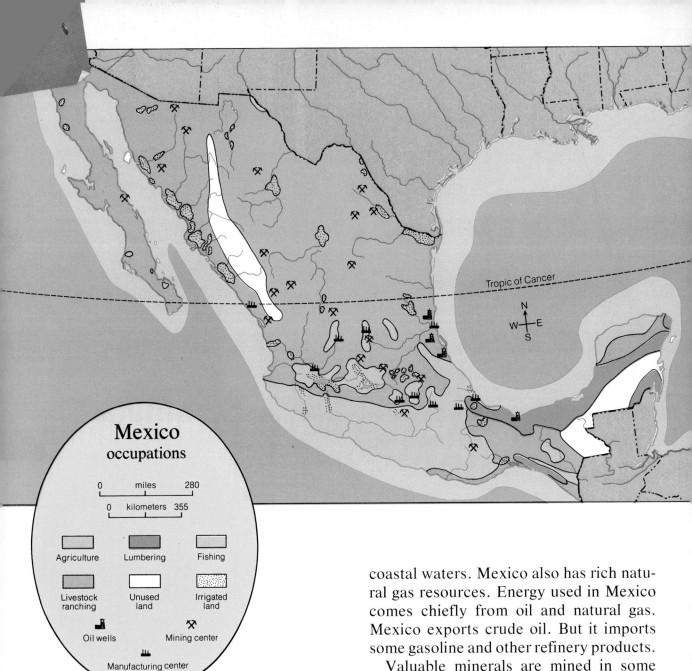

Mexico
occupations

0   miles   280

0   kilometers   355

Agriculture	Lumbering	Fishing
Livestock ranching	Unused land	Irrigated land
Oil wells		Mining center
	Manufacturing center	

Tropic of Cancer

Dairy cattle, sheep, goats, horses, hogs, turkeys, and chickens are also raised.

Use the map of Mexico's occupations to find the lands used for farming. What other occupations are carried on? Where?

Oil wells and mines add to Mexico's wealth. Oil is found along the eastern coastal plain. Engineers have found new pools of oil. They lie under the shallow

coastal waters. Mexico also has rich natural gas resources. Energy used in Mexico comes chiefly from oil and natural gas. Mexico exports crude oil. But it imports some gasoline and other refinery products.

Valuable minerals are mined in some lower mountains on the plateau. Among them are copper, gold, silver, and lead. Mexico is a leading producer of silver.

Mexico's natural resources are used in its growing industries. These include the making of chemicals, clothing, iron, steel, and auto parts. Foods are processed, too.

Another leading industry is the making of handcrafted items. Expert workers make silver jewelry, glassware, pottery, baskets, and leather goods. Many of these goods are exported or sold to tourists.

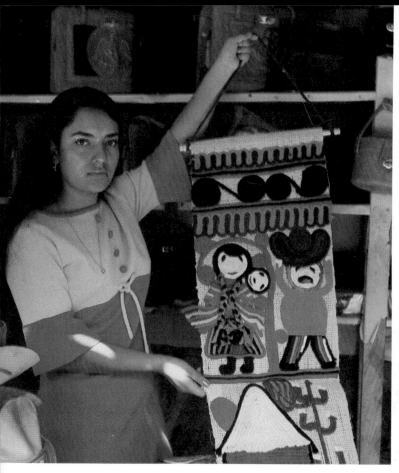

Mexico has a variety of industries. Handicrafts and manufacturing are both important. Does our country also have a variety of industries? Name some of them.

Some manufacturing centers

Monterrey is the third largest city in Mexico. It has hundreds of factories and mills. Find this city on the map.

Coal and iron ore are mined near Monterrey. They are brought to its busy steel mills. Many people in Monterrey work in factories that make iron and steel products. Others work in places that make textiles, plastics, and cement.

Veracruz on the east coast is the chief seaport. Tons and tons of exports are shipped out of its harbor. Highways and a railroad connect Veracruz with Mexico City and other manufacturing centers.

Factories in Veracruz produce cement, flour, shoes, and textiles. Workers here also prepare seafood for market.

Other cities are busy manufacturing and trade centers. One that is famous for the making of pottery and glass items is Guadalajara (gwä′dä lä hä′rä). Guadalajara is Mexico's second largest city. Its workers also make textiles, clothing, flour, and iron and steel goods.

It is also a trading center for farms and cattle ranches nearby.

Tampico is a leading oil-refining center. It is also the chief port for exporting oil.

Puebla has many factories. This city is known for its brightly decorated tiles. Its people turn out fine pottery, glass products, and cotton goods.

Taxco (täs′kō) is the center of the silver industry. People from all over the world come there to buy hand-made articles of silver.

389

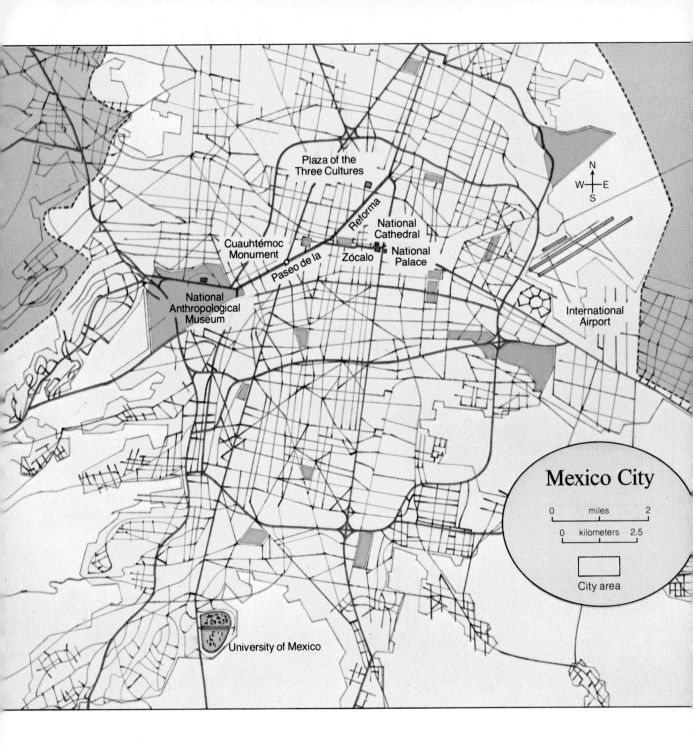

Map labels:
Plaza of the Three Cultures
Reforma
National Cathedral
Cuauhtémoc Monument
Paseo de la
Zócalo
National Palace
National Anthropological Museum
International Airport
University of Mexico

N
W — E
S

Mexico City

0   miles   2
0   kilometers   2.5

City area

Mexico City

Mexico City is the largest city in the country. It is also one of the largest and oldest cities in North America. The Mexico City area has a population of more than 12 million people.

Mexico City was founded by the Spanish in 1521. That was almost a hundred years before the Pilgrims came to America.

Find this city on the map of Mexico. Notice that it lies far south on the Mexican Plateau. It is in a bowl-like region with high mountains at the rim.

This is Mexico City's Plaza of the Three Cultures. What items of Aztec, Spanish, and modern culture can you find?

Mexico City is the leading manufacturing center of the country. The city area has more than 25,000 factories.

All kinds of products are manufactured. They include autos, chemicals, textiles, machinery, and iron and steel products.

This exciting city is partly old and partly new. Constitution Plaza is in the heart of the old city. It is also called the Zocalo. It is in the same place as the main square of the old Aztec capital.

The National Palace faces the Zocalo. The Spaniards built the palace in the 1600s as the viceroy's home. Today this block-long building is the center of Mexico's government. The president and other officials have offices there.

The National Cathedral is another famous old building on the Zocalo. This huge church was built during Spanish times, too.

Mexico City has many modern stores and office buildings. Some of them look out on tree-lined avenues.

One famous avenue is the Paseo de la Reforma. It has small park-like circles where some streets cross it. These tiny parks have statues of Mexican heroes. A statue of Cuauhtemoc stands in one circle. He was the last Aztec emperor. He fought bravely until his capital was captured by the Spanish.

One museum in the city is called "The House of the Ancients." It shows much about the early peoples of Mexico. In it are tools, dishes, and other things dug up from ruins.

The University of Mexico is in Mexico City. It was founded in the 1500s. Its library building is decorated with bright murals.

Ancient pyramids rise a few miles from Mexico City. They were built more than 2000 years ago by native people.

One is the Pyramid of the Sun. It covers about 11 acres. Huge blocks of stone form steps that climb 200 feet (60 m) to the top.

The ancient city of Teotihuacan (tā′ō-tē′wä kän′) was located in this area. The Pyramid of the Sun was one of its largest buildings.

Acapulco's beautiful beaches, mild climate, and fine hotels make it a favorite of tourists.

Many tourists visit different parts of Mexico every year. They shop at colorful open-air markets in the cities and villages. They enjoy folk dances, art, and music. They walk through flower-filled parks and streets. Some may see a bullfight. Many people take vacations at the beaches. Acapulco is one famous resort area. Visitors to Mexico see a country that combines riches from Native American and Spanish cultures.

Mexico has close ties with the United States. The largest number of tourists come from the United States. And most of Mexico's trade is with the United States.

Many people from Mexico now live in the United States. Many United States citizens are of Mexican descent. Mexican Americans often call themselves Chicanos (chi kä′nōs).

Mexico and the United States are working together on special projects. They are working together in trade, use of energy, and better ways of farming. They are good neighbors.

Who? What? Where? How? Why?

1. Who were the Aztecs?
2. Where did the Aztecs build their capital? What did they call it?
3. How did the Aztecs make more land?
4. How did the Aztecs become rich?
5. What name was given to Mexico by the Spanish conquerors?
6. Where did the Spanish build their capital? What did they call it?
7. Why did New Spain revolt against Spain?
8. What was Father Hidalgo's part in the revolt?
9. Who was Juárez?
10. How did Juárez help change Mexico?
11. Why is Mexico called a Latin American country?

When?

On paper copy the events listed below. In the chapter find when each event happened. Then write the correct date before each event.

1. _____ Mexico won independence from Spain.
2. _____ Cortés conquered the Aztecs.
3. _____ The Aztecs built Tenochtitlán.
4. _____ Cortés landed at Veracruz.
5. _____ Hidalgo held the meeting that started the revolt against Spain.

Using maps

1. Find Mexico on the map on page 354. In what two regions does it lie? Which part of Mexico is in the low latitudes?

2. The map on page 377 can help you answer these questions.
   What cities are on the border between the United States and Mexico?
   In which direction is Mexico City from Veracruz? from Monterrey? from Acapulco?
   How many miles (kilometers) long is Lower California?
   What body of water separates Lower California from the rest of Mexico?
   What part of Mexico is farthest east?

Some questions to think about

1. What does the word culture mean? What does the following sentence mean: "Mexico is a mixture of the cultures of its native peoples and the Spanish people."

2. Does the United States also have a mixture of cultures? If so, how is the mixture different from that of Mexico?

3. Tourists who visit Mexico meet many kinds of workers. Listed below are only a few of these workers. How many more can you add to this list? Write them on your paper.

   airplane pilots   tour guides
   hotel clerks   bus drivers

Which ending will you choose?

There are ten beginnings of sentences in List A. The endings are in List B. Write each complete sentence on your paper.

List A

1. Mexico is divided into
2. A huge plateau covers
3. Low plains extend
4. Monterrey has
5. Spain governed Mexico
6. Juárez was one of
7. Some Mexican foods are
8. Mexico City is the
9. Guadalajara is famous
10. The Spaniards brought the first cattle to Mexico

List B

a. for three hundred years.
b. a third of Mexico.
c. along the eastern coast.
d. for pottery and glass items.
e. the capital of Mexico.
f. thirty-one states.
g. Mexico's most famous presidents.
h. busy steel mills.
i. tortillas, frijoles, and enchiladas.
j. in the 1500s.

Things to do

1. Make a timeline of the events listed in the exercise "When?".

2. Have a class exhibit showing pictures of things tourists can bring from Mexico.

3. Look in an encyclopedia to find out about piñatas (pē nyä′täs). Then make a class piñata.

28

Central America and the West Indies

Yesterday and today in Central America

A guide led a group of tourists along a jungle trail. Ahead they saw thick stone walls rising above the trees.

"The great Maya city of Tikal once stood there," explained the guide.

"That must have been long ago," said one tourist.

"About two thousand years ago," answered the guide. "Perhaps as early as the year 250 B.C."

"And the walls still stand after all that time?" asked another tourist. "That's amazing!"

"It really is," added a third tourist. "And they had no machines to help. How did they do it?"

"We all wonder about that," replied the guide. "The Maya were a remarkable people."

The Maya built cities in Central America and southern Mexico. These were not places for people to live all of the time. They were mainly places to worship the Mayan gods. The cities were places for market days and for celebrations. Find Central America on the map.

The cities had tall stone pyramids with temples on top. They had long, low palaces with many rooms. Some palaces had stone carvings and tall stone pillars. The palaces were for the rulers and the priests.

Some of the Mayan priests were scientists. They worked in round buildings, or observatories. They studied the stars.

Nearly every city had a ball court. The court had one high stone ring. It looked somewhat like a basketball hoop. The players on two teams tried to send a rubber ball through the ring. They could use only their knees and their hips. They had to try hard to score even one point. The game ended when one team scored.

Most of the Maya were farmers who lived in villages. The farm people came to the cities only once in a while. They built their village houses of mud with roofs of grass or leaves. The houses were on top of mounds. This kept them dry during the rainy season.

Some Maya were builders or stone carvers. Some were painters or weavers. Others were potters. Maya traders carried on business with other groups of Native Americans.

The Maya developed a number system and invented a calendar. They figured out when there would be an eclipse of the sun. They studied the stars and the planets. The Maya had a writing system, too. They carved their history and their religious ideas on tall stone pillars. Modern-day scientists have learned much about the Maya from these stone pillars.

The Mayan civilization thrived until the 800s. Then the people began to give up their cities. No one knows why. Some experts think that the farmers rose up against the rulers and priests. Others think that the farmland became too poor to raise crops.

Today more than 1,500,000 Maya still live in Central America and southern Mexico. They still speak the Mayan language. Many wear Mayan clothing and follow old customs.

Explorers from Spain first came to Central America in 1501. The next year Columbus visited it. He was making his fourth and last voyage. He sailed along the coast

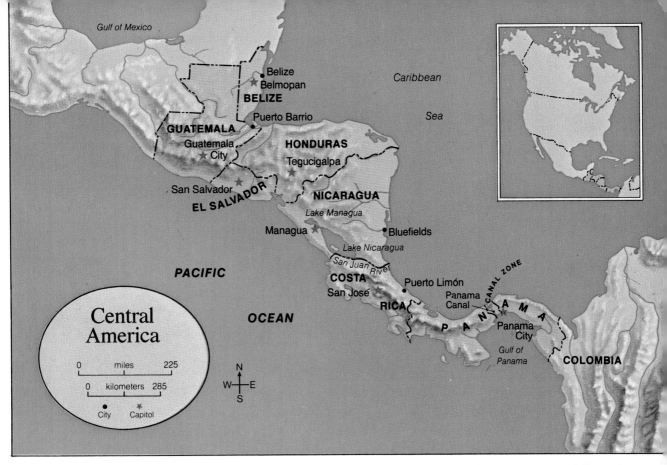

Map labels:
Gulf of Mexico
Caribbean Sea
Belize
Belmopan
BELIZE
GUATEMALA
Puerto Barrio
Guatemala City
HONDURAS
Tegucigalpa
San Salvador
EL SALVADOR
NICARAGUA
Lake Managua
Managua
Bluefields
Lake Nicaragua
San Juan River
PACIFIC
OCEAN
COSTA
San José
RICA
Puerto Limón
Panama Canal
CANAL ZONE
PANAMA
Panama City
Gulf of Panama
COLOMBIA

Central America

| 0 | miles | 225 |

| 0 | kilometers | 285 |

● City   ★ Capitol

N W—E S

of Central America. He was looking for a waterway through the land.

Later, Balboa and other Spaniards came. They, too, were hunting for a waterway to Asia. They claimed land for Spain and looked for gold. They also conquered many Native American groups.

By 1522 Cortés had become interested in Central America. He had conquered Mexico. He dreamed of winning more land, gold, and glory.

Cortés sent soldiers to Central America. The bows and arrows of the Native Americans were no match for the Spaniards' guns and cannon.

By 1525 Cortés had conquered the people who lived in Central America. He called this whole area Guatemala (gwä′ti-mä′lə). It took in most of present-day Central America.

Spain ruled the colony of Guatemala for 300 years, then Spain's control ended.

This map shows the republics of Central America. Which is the smallest? What country borders Mexico on the north?

In 1821 Central America declared its independence. Guatemala, El Salvador, Costa Rica (kos′tə rē′kə), Honduras, and Nicaragua (nik′ə rä′gwə) were formed. At first they became parts of Mexico. The next year, though, they founded the United Provinces of Central America.

Beginning in 1838 the provinces broke away to form independent countries. Later, Panama became independent, too. Find each of these countries on the map of Central America.

English is the official language in Belize (be lēz′). This country was once known as British Honduras. The other six countries use Spanish as their official language. Many of the Native Americans in Central America still speak their old languages.

Guatemala, like most Central American countries, is a blend of old and new. Tropical forests exist a few miles from large cities.

A look at Central America

Central America is south of Mexico and is part of North America. On the map on page 354, notice that Central America is in the low latitudes. It is south of the Tropic of Cancer. So it is in the tropics.

Tropical lands have about the same temperature the year around. They do not have four seasons as we know them.

The climate in Central America depends partly on elevation. Lowlands have the hottest weather. Highlands, as a rule, are more comfortable.

Hot, low plains along the Caribbean Sea are mostly jungle. They have a thick growth of trees and underbrush. Wild parrots and other brightly colored birds nest in the trees. Monkeys chatter and howl as they swing from tree to tree. Lizards and snakes crawl in the damp undergrowth. Alligators and turtles live along the swamps and rivers.

Farther inland there are fewer swamps. Wild pigs roam about. Cat-like pumas slink through the forests.

Along the Pacific coast, there are drier plains. They cover a narrow strip of land between the sea and the mountains.

Mountains cover much of the region of Central America. The highest ranges are near the Pacific coast. Many of them have volcanoes, and a few are still active.

Some of the lands near the volcanoes have earthquakes. Some earthquakes have caused great loss of life and property.

Most of the people in Central America live in the mountain valleys. There the climate is mild and cool. The valleys and some sloping areas have good farmland. The soil is rich. Long ago these lands were covered by lava and volcanic ash. As time passed, wind and rain broke up the lava and ash. They became part of the soil and helped to make it fertile.

Central America's tropical highlands have an ideal climate for growing coffee. The bright red color of these coffee berries shows that they are ripe.

Many kinds of crops are grown. Among them are corn, beans, bananas, coconuts, and cacao. Cacao beans are used to make cocoa and chocolate.

Coffee is an important crop in Central America. Most of it is grown on the lower mountain slopes. Coffee needs a mild climate. The tropical highlands have such a climate. Coffee needs plenty of water, too. But it must have well-drained soil. Rain drains off quickly from the slopes.

Coffee trees are small and look somewhat like bushes. They have shiny dark-green leaves. When coffee berries are ripe, they are bright red. They look like polished cranberries. Two small beans are inside each berry. They are dried and roasted before they are ground for coffee.

The countries of Central America

The countries of Central America have many of the same problems. They are growing very fast. The populations of most of the countries probably will double in less than 25 years.

Small farms cannot support larger and larger families. So people are moving in great numbers to the cities. This has meant a shortage of houses, jobs, and schools.

The countries are trying to solve these problems. More use of their natural resources could help. Central America has rich farmland, great hardwood forests, and mineral deposits. Many of these resources have been hardly touched. They could provide jobs for people in rural areas and in cities.

One big problem is the lack of roads. Jungles and mountains make road building very costly. But there must be roads to develop the natural resources.

Guatemala, on the border of Mexico, has thick forests. Its name means "full of trees." It is third largest in area. But it has more people than any other country in Central America.

About half of its people are Native Americans. A large number of them are descended from the Maya. They still follow ancient Mayan customs. The other Guatemalans follow Spanish-American customs.

Most of the Native Americans live in small villages. Most of their houses are one-story and made of adobe. The ground is sometimes the floor. The roof may be thatched with palm branches or grass.

These people raise most of their own food. Nearly every family has a patch of corn. Some keep goats and chickens.

Each village has a market. Many people grow or make things to sell on market day. Some weave beautiful cloth, rugs, and blankets. Others make leather goods and pottery.

Families carry their goods to market. They strap their loads on their backs or place them in large baskets. The baskets are balanced on their heads.

The whole family enjoys market day. They sell some things and buy others. They have a good time visiting, too.

Many of the village people work on farms and plantations. Workers on Guatemala's small farms grow corn, beans, rice, wheat, and cotton. Those on large plantations grow coffee, sugar cane, rubber, and bananas. Coffee makes up about half of Guatemala's exports.

Guatemala City is the capital of Guatemala. It is the largest city in Central America. It is a big industrial center. Find this city on the map.

Guatemala City has many Spanish-style buildings. Some are houses. These are usually one-story buildings with thick adobe walls. They are often painted light colors. Their rooms are built around a patio, or open-air court.

Many tourists visit Guatemala City. They come from all over the world. Thousands come from the United States. Some tourists come to see the ruins of ancient Mayan cities.

Many Guatemalans make their living caring for tourists. Some sell hand-made items at the markets and shops.

Belize was at one time known as British Honduras. It belongs to Great Britain. Most of the land in Belize is covered with thick forests and swamps. But some farm-ing is done. Farmers grow sugar cane, grapefruit, and oranges. Logging is also a leading business.

Nearly half of the people of Belize are descendants of African slaves. Many live in Belize City, the largest city, and in Belmopan (bel′mō pän′), the capital.

Honduras was named by Columbus, who landed on its shores. He found deep water off the coast. So he named the land Honduras. "Hond" means "deep" in Spanish.

Tegucigalpa (te gü′si gäl′pä) is the capital of Honduras. It means "silver hills." This city is located in a high valley near silver mines.

Most of the people in Honduras are *mestizos*. They are a mixture of Spanish and Native American. Some of the people are also descendants of African slaves.

About three-fourths of all Hondurans live in rural villages. Most are poor. Many cannot read or write.

Honduras is mostly a mountainous country. But it does have some low coastal plains. Bananas are grown on the northern coastal plain. Bananas make up about half of the country's exports.

Bananas grow in hot lowland areas where jungles have been cleared. Bananas grow on green plants that are from 10 to 25 feet (3 to 8 m) tall. Small pieces of banana root are planted about 20 feet (6 m) apart. Green spongy stalks shoot up. Large bright green leaves unfold near the top of each curved stalk.

The plants grow rapidly for 12 to 15 months. Then buds appear at the end of the stalks. The leaves of the buds open up, showing rows of small flowers. Some of the flowers turn into bananas.

398

Some of these flowers will grow into bananas. Green bananas are cut, packed, and shipped to faraway places. They will ripen on the way to market.

Each plant produces just one bunch of fruit. A single bunch may have a hundred or more bananas.

A banana plantation is a busy place at harvest time. Workers move through the rows of tall plants. Each worker has a partner. They cut the stalks so that they bend down. Then the bunches of bananas are lowered and cut. The fruit is picked while it is green. Green bananas keep well on their way to market.

Oxcarts and trucks take the bananas to railroad cars. They are hauled to ports. Then they are packed in refrigerator ships. Bananas are shipped to many countries. Huge quantities are exported to the United States.

San Salvador is a very modern city. It has many department stores much like those in our country.

El Salvador is the smallest country in Central America. The capital is San Salvador. El Salvador is a mountainous land. But it has fertile valleys.

Over half the people live in rural areas. They are farmers and ranchers. Coffee is their leading crop. El Salvador exports a large amount of coffee. Other farm products include beans, corn, rice, and sugar cane. Cotton and textiles are also produced and exported.

Nicaragua extends across the middle of Central America. Spanish explorers named Nicaragua after the Nicarao people. Today the Native American culture has blended with the Spanish. Only a few groups follow their old way of life.

Most of the people in Nicaragua live in the central highlands or near the west coast. The city of Managua (mä nä′gwä), the capital, is near the west coast. It takes its name from the large lake that it faces. The city is on a low plain. It has a hot climate.

Cotton is Nicaragua's leading export crop. Coffee is raised on hilly lands and low mountain slopes. Bananas and sugar cane are grown on some lowlands.

Dense forests cover most of the low plains along the Caribbean Sea. This region is one of the wettest places on earth. It gets as much as 300 inches (750 cm) of rain a year.

The country of Costa Rica is south of Nicaragua. Its name means "rich coast" in Spanish. Explorers gave it this name because Native Americans told stories about gold and other riches nearby.

Almost three-fourths of the people in Costa Rica live on a high plateau in the central part of the country. The soil is rich. The climate is good for growing crops. San José (san hō zā′), the capital, is on this plateau.

Agriculture is a leading industry. All kinds of crops are raised. They include corn, beans, and tobacco. Bananas, sugar cane, and coffee are main crops. Coffee is a leading money crop. So is cacao.

Cacao beans grow on evergreen trees. After the trees are about five years old, they begin to blossom. As the blossoms drop off, purplish-yellow pods form. They are round in shape. By harvest time they may be about 12 inches (30 cm) across. They look somewhat like melons.

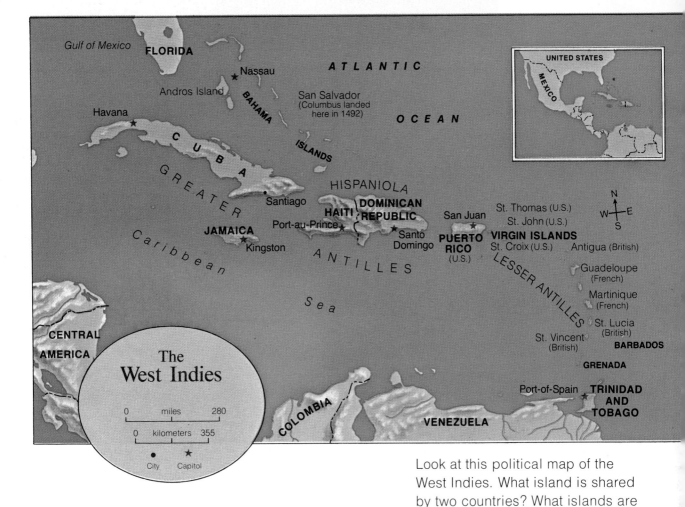

The West Indies

miles 0 — 280
kilometers 0 — 355

● City   ★ Capitol

Look at this political map of the West Indies. What island is shared by two countries? What islands are a part of the United States?

Many cacao beans are inside the pods. The beans are dried and shipped to factories. They are crushed and made into cocoa products.

Panama occupies the bridge of land known as the Isthmus of Panama. Find it on the map on page 395. Spanish colonists named the country Panama, which means "plenty of fish."

In the early 1900s the United States leased, or rented, some land in Panama. It was a strip of land ten miles (16 km) wide through the center of the country. It was called the Panama Canal Zone.

The Panama Canal was built through this zone. It was completed in 1914.

Ships from all over the world use the canal. It saves them the long trip around South America. Find the Panama Canal on a map.

Farming and fishing are important in Panama. Rice is the main crop. Shrimp, oysters, and sponges are caught in the waters around Panama.

The capital and largest city of the country is Panama City. It is near the site of the old Spanish village of Panama.

The West Indies

The Caribbean Sea has a long chain of islands called the West Indies. This island chain is more than 2000 miles (3200 km) long. The chain is a curve that begins near Florida. It ends off the coast of Venezuela (ven′i zwā′lə), South America. Locate the West Indies on the map above.

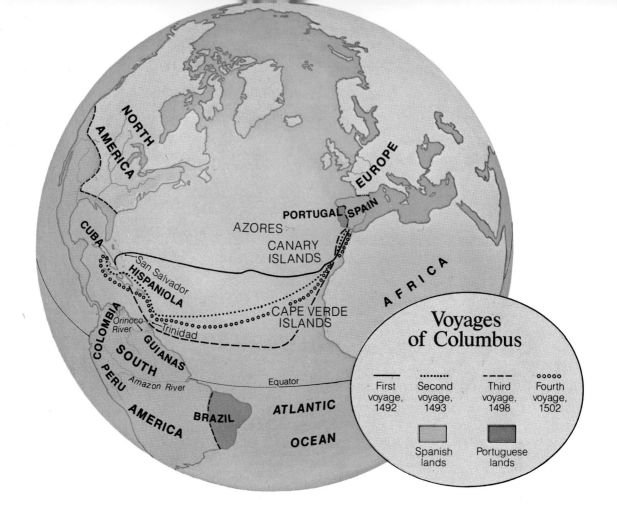

Voyages of Columbus

First voyage, 1492	Second voyage, 1493	Third voyage, 1498	Fourth voyage, 1502

Spanish lands

Portuguese lands

Most of the islands are the tops of a sunken range of mountains. The four largest islands are Cuba, Hispaniola (his′pən yō′lə), Jamaica (jə mā′kə), and Puerto Rico (pwer′tō rē′kō). Which one is nearest to Florida? Which one is closest to Central America?

Columbus discovered and named the West Indies in 1492. He thought that he had reached the Indies, which are in Asia. He claimed the islands for Spain. Look at the map of his voyages above. How many did he make? In what way was his third voyage different from the others?

During the early 1500s Spanish colonists settled the islands. They conquered the native peoples, the Arawaks and Caribs. The Spaniards started the sugar industry. At first they tried to force the Arawaks and Caribs to raise this crop. But their plan did not work. Later the Spaniards brought slaves from Africa to do work in the sugar fields.

England, France, and the Netherlands also wanted lands in the West Indies. Pirates from those countries attacked and robbed Spanish treasure ships. Spaniards were shipping much gold and silver from Panama to Spain.

In time, England seized the Bahama Islands (bə hā′mə), Jamaica, and Trinidad. Find these islands on the map on page 401. France and the Netherlands claimed some small islands off the coast of South America. Later, the western third of Hispaniola, now the country of Haiti, became a French colony. Today most of the islands in the West Indies are independent.

Most of the West Indies are in the low latitudes. The Bahamas are just north of the Tropic of Cancer. The other islands are in the tropics. The islands have a warm climate winter and summer. During the winter many tourists come. Caring for tourists is the main industry on many of the islands.

The West Indies are in the trade-wind belt. The northeast trade winds bring heavy rain. The winds cool as they rise to cross the mountains. So the winds drop rain on the northeast sides of the islands.

As the air goes down the other side of the mountains, it is warmed. It drops only a little moisture. So the southwest sides of the islands are drier.

From August to October, there are often storms called hurricanes. A hurricane may be hundreds of miles wide. Some are so powerful that they smash buildings and tear down trees. Such a storm can leave whole towns in ruins.

A closer look at some islands

The Bahamas are coral islands formed by small sea creatures. When corals die, their limestone skeletons are left. The skeletons have been piling up, layer upon layer, for thousands of years. Huge masses of coral skeletons have collected. In one

Many people vacation in the West Indies each year. The friendly people and interesting places appeal to tourists. A number of visitors enjoy skin diving and snorkeling among the coral reefs.

The canal in the background leads from the Gulf of Mexico to Havana's protected harbor.

area they have formed the Bahamas. Find these islands on the map.

The Bahamas are low and flat. They do not have much fertile soil. So only a little farming is done. Some people make a living by fishing. Many workers care for the thousands of tourists who come to the islands each year. Nassau (nas′ô) is the capital and largest city.

Cuba is the largest country in the West Indies. The main island is more than 700 miles (1125 km) long. There are also more than 1600 smaller islands. Find Cuba on the map. Notice that this long curved island is at the entrance to the Gulf of Mexico.

Mountains cover about one-fourth of the main island. Some of the mountains are along the coast. This part of the island is

rugged and beautiful. The rest of the land is a rolling plain.

Havana is the capital of Cuba. It has a fine harbor and is the chief seaport. Some narrow streets and old thick-walled buildings remain from Spanish days.

Spain ruled Cuba for nearly 400 years. The country became independent in 1898. Then it developed close ties with the United States.

Doctors and scientists began a fight on yellow fever in Cuba. After many tests, they found that mosquitoes spread the disease. The big job, then, was to get rid of these insects.

Scientists from Cuba and the United States worked together. They drained swamps, the mosquitoes' breeding places. The scientists helped to improve conditions in cities and on farms.

The close ties between Cuba and the United States were broken in 1959. Fidel Castro led a revolt against the government of Cuba. Soon he turned Cuba into a Communist country. Trade with the United States stopped.

Agriculture is the main industry found in Cuba. The country has fertile soil, plenty of rain, and a long growing season. Many kinds of crops can be raised. Sugar cane is the leading crop.

Harvest time is a busy season for the sugar-cane workers. They cut the cane stalks close to the ground. They remove the tops and strip off the leaves. Then they rush the stalks to mills where sugar is made.

Tobacco is grown on many hillsides. Workers cover the plants in some fields with thin white cloth. This protects them from the burning sun. The tobacco leaves are dried and used in making cigars.

Coffee is grown on some hilly lands. So are oranges, grapefruit, pineapples, and cassava (kə sä′və). Cassava roots are used in making tapioca.

South of Cuba is the beautiful island of Jamaica. Find it on the map. Jamaica is famous for its scenery. In fact, long ago Columbus was charmed by its beauty. It has many lovely mountains. Some of its peaks rise more than a mile (1.6 km) above sea level.

Farming is Jamaica's chief industry. Once sugar was the only important crop. But now coffee plantations and cattle ranches cover the higher lands. Banana and sugar plantations are on the plains along the coast. So are farms that grow vegetables and fruits.

Haiti and the Dominican Republic are on Hispaniola. Find Hispaniola on the map. It is a mountainous land. Some of its peaks are 10,000 feet (3000 m) above the sea.

Haiti (hā′ti) was once a French colony. Its capital, Port-au-Prince, has a French name. French is still its official language.

Haiti is densely populated. Most of its people are descendants of slaves. The slaves were brought to work on the sugar plantations.

Farming is the main industry. Such crops as sugar cane, tobacco, cotton, and coffee are raised.

The Dominican Republic is an agricultural land, too. On its plains are sugar, cotton, and tobacco plantations as well as smaller farms. Farther inland are cattle ranches.

The country's capital and chief city is Santo Domingo. It is the oldest city in the Western Hemisphere. One of its churches was built in 1512. It is said that Columbus is buried beneath this church.

The Virgin Islands are east of Puerto Rico. They are made up of two groups. One group belongs to Britain. The other is a part of the United States.

There are about fifty Virgin Islands in the American group. Only a few are settled. The three largest ones are St. Thomas, St. Croix (sānt kroi′) and St. John. Many tourists visit these islands every year.

Puerto Rico has been a territory of the United States since 1898. Before that time it was governed by Spain. Puerto Rico manages its own affairs. It elects a governor and representatives who make the laws.

The people of Puerto Rico are citizens of the United States. Their rights are protected by the Constitution. They are free to move to any state whenever they wish. Many Puerto Ricans have moved to

The University of Puerto Rico's oldest campus is in San Juan.

our large cities, such as New York and Chicago.

Hills and mountains cover three-fourths of the island. A narrow coastal plain and inland valleys are the only low areas.

Puerto Rico is one of the most densely populated areas in the world. More than a million people live in San Juan (san hwän′), the capital and largest city.

Manufacturing is important in Puerto Rico. There are more than 2500 factories. They turn out chemicals, food products, clothing, and electrical machinery. Many of the factories are owned by companies on the United States mainland.

Farming is also important. Sugar cane is the main crop. Coffee and bananas are grown and exported, too.

Caring for tourists, especially from the United States, is the work of many people.

What's missing?

On paper write the numbers 1 through 8 in a column. After each number write the word or words that complete the sentence correctly. Choose from the list below the sentences.

1. Most of the West Indies are in the tropics, or _____ latitudes.
2. Storms known as _____ whip across the West Indies.
3. The four largest islands of the West Indies are _____, _____, _____, _____.
4. Both _____ and _____ have territory in the Virgin Islands.
5. French is the language of _____.
6. Puerto Rico is a territory of the _____.
7. The Bahamas were formed by millions of sea creatures known as _____.
8. Tapioca is made from the roots of the _____ plant.

Cuba	cassava
United States	Haiti
low	hurricanes
fish	Puerto Rico
Jamaica	coral
high	Hispaniola
Great Britain	Bahamas
cacao	

Let's review the West Indies

1. Where are the West Indies? Why were they given that name?
2. What kind of climate do the West Indies have?
3. What explorer first claimed the West Indies? for what country? when? Was he the first person to set foot on these islands?

Reviewing Central America

1. Who were the Maya?
2. Name at least three things that show that the Maya had a great civilization.
3. What Spaniard led the conquest of Central America?
4. In what part of Central America are the hot, wet lowlands?
5. On what kind of land is coffee grown? are bananas grown?
6. What is one of Central America's big problems?

Name the country

On paper, number from 1 to 6 in a column. After each number write the name of the Central American country that completes the sentence correctly.

1. _____ has the most people.
2. A canal cuts through _____.
3. _____ was once called British Honduras
4. _____ is the smallest country in area.
5. The name of _____ means "rich coast."
6. The capital of _____ is Tegucigalpa, and bananas are this country's chief export.
7. The capital of _____ is Managua, and cotton is the leading export crop.

What do you think?

1. How has climate influenced ways of living in Central America?
2. Why are coffee, bananas, and cacao called "money crops"? Why do people grow money crops as well as food for themselves?
3. How would more and better roads help Central America solve its problems?

Using maps

1. Is Central America north or south of the equator?
2. What Central American country is an isthmus?
3. What bodies of water do most Central American countries face?
4. Which West Indies islands are part of the United States?
5. Which is closer to South America, Jamaica or Trinidad?
6. Use the scale of miles (or kilometers) to measure the distance from the tip of Florida to (a) Havana, (b) Hispaniola, (c) Trinidad, and (d) Nassau.

Things to do

1. Find out about the quetzal (ket säl´) bird. What was its place in Mayan culture? How is it used as a symbol?
2. Read in another book about the Maya. Help your class plan and draw or paint a mural about them.
3. Make a diorama of Central America. Show jungles, mountains, plateaus, and lowlands. Be sure to show the plants and animals that live there.
4. Share with your class a report on one of these topics.
   coral   sponges   the cassava plant
   Be sure to include pictures with your report.
5. Read how doctors and scientists conquered yellow fever. Some members of the class may want to dramatize this story.

29
South America

Planning for freedom

One afternoon in the early 1800s Simón Bolívar was talking with a friend.

"I have made up my mind," Simón Bolívar (bō lē′vär) said. "I know what I must do!"

"What do you mean?" asked his friend.

"Spain has ruled most of South America for nearly 300 years," answered Simón. "It's time to be free, and we will be! I'll spend my whole fortune for the cause if it is needed."

"Those are bold words, Simón," replied his friend. "And dangerous ones, too."

"Of course!" agreed Simón. "Spain has strict laws and armies to enforce them. But nothing is going to stop me. I will join the patriots. We will plan for weapons and soldiers and . . ."

"Soldiers! Where will you get soldiers? People will be afraid to side against Spain," said the friend.

"We will meet secretly. Many people will join us in secret."

"This may cost your life, Simón," warned the friend.

"Whatever the cost, I am ready," declared Simón. "I have made up my mind. I shall lead the revolt against Spain."

Simón Bolívar had been in Europe for a time. During those months he thought much about freedom. He knew that the English colonists had shown great courage in fighting for their freedom.

Bolívar returned to a South America that was ready for revolt. It was a land with a long and colorful history.

Explorers find South America

Both Spain and Portugal claimed land in South America. Columbus reached the coast of Venezuela in 1498 on his third voyage. He and his crew went ashore and claimed the land for Spain. See the map on page 402.

Two years later Pedro Cabral (ka vräl′) landed on the coast of Brazil. He was leading a fleet of ships from Portugal to Asia. He planned to sail around Africa. But winds blew the ships off course to the west. He claimed Brazil for the king of Portugal.

In 1519 Spain hired Magellan to hunt for a waterway to Asia. He reached what is now Argentina. Then he sailed south to the tip of the continent. There he found a strait. A *strait* is a narrow body of water that connects two larger bodies of water.

Magellan sailed through the rough waters of this strait. Later it was named after him. Find the Strait of Magellan on the map of South America.

In 1526 Spain sent Sebastian Cabot on a voyage west. He was a son of John Cabot, who had claimed Newfoundland for England.

Cabot sailed down the coast of South America. He reached a body of water that seemed to go far inland. But then he found that it was a river. Some Native Americans along the river wore silver necklaces. So Cabot named the body of water "Rio de la Plata." Rio de la Plata (rē′ō dā lä plä′tä) is Spanish for "River of Silver."

In 1535 Pedro de Mendoza, a Spanish soldier and explorer, led settlers to Argentina. They started a settlement on the

20° | Tropic of Cancer | 70° | 60° | 50° | 40° | 30° | 20°

CUBA
HISPANIOLA
WEST
**PUERTO
RICO**

10°
INDIES
Caribbean   Sea

CENTRAL
Barranquilla
AMERICA   Maracaibo   ○ La Guaira
Lake
Maracaibo   ★ Caracas   *ATLANTIC*
Medellín
Orinoco   River   Georgetown   Paramaribo
VENEZUELA   **GUYANA**   **SURINAM**   ★ Cayenne
Bogotá   ★   **FR.
GUIANA**
Buenaventura
COLOMBIA

0°   **ECUADOR**   Rio   Negro   Equator   *OCEAN*
Quito
Guayaquil   Amazon   River   Belém
○ Manaus

PERU   **B   R   A   Z   I   L**   Recife □

10°   Lima   ○   São   Francisco   River   Salvador ■
Callao ●   Cerro de Pasco
● Cuzco
El Misti ▲   Lake
Titicaca
19,167 ft.   ★ La Paz   **MINAS
GERAIS**
(5842 m)   Brazília ★
BOLIVIA
★ Sucre

PACIFIC   ○ Potosí   Volta Redonda
20°   Chuquicamata   **PARAGUAY**   São Paulo □ □
Paraguay River   Rio de Janeiro
Tropic of Capricorn   Antofagasta   Asunción ★   Iguassú   Santos ●
Falls

● Tucumán   Paraná   River

Mt. Aconcagua   River
22,835 ft.   Rosario ■   **URUGUAY**
30°   *OCEAN*   ▲ (6960 m)   Mendoza
Valparaiso   Buenos Aires ★ ● Montevideo
Santiago   La Plata   Rio de la Plata

Concepción   Colorado River

**South
America**

0   miles   600

0   kilometers   760

Cities

□   ■   ●
Over   500,000   100,000
1 million   to 1 million   to 500,000

○   ★
Under   National
100,000   capital

40°   **FALKLAND
ISLANDS**
(British)
Strait of
Magellan
Punta Arenas ●
TIERRA DEL FUEGO
Cape Horn

50°   90°   80°   60°   50°   40°   30°   20°   10°

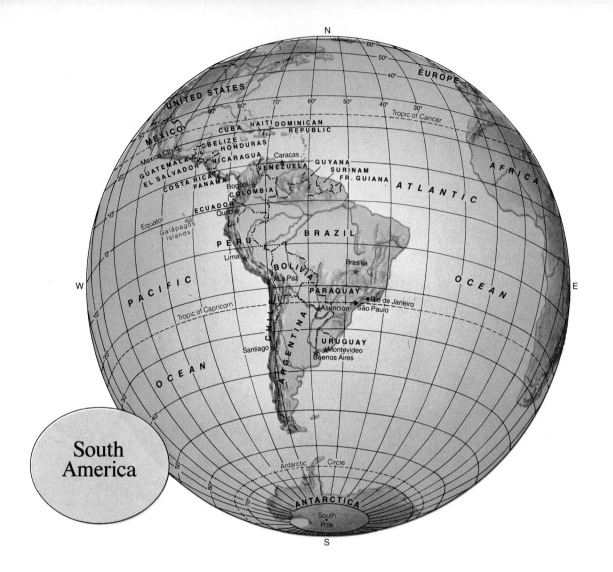

South America

muddy banks of a shallow bay. They called it Buenos Aires (bwā′nəs er′ēz). These are Spanish words for "good air." Soon the Spaniards moved farther inland. Later a settlement at Buenos Aires grew to be a large city.

The Spaniards heard tales of gold and silver. One hunter for treasure was Francisco Pizarro. He was a Spanish explorer who had settled in Panama. He learned that Inca people, who lived in the Andes Mountains, had great wealth. He had heard about their vast stores of gold and silver.

Pizarro tried over and over to find the Inca lands. At last, his exploring party reached the Inca capital.

410

The Inca

The Inca peoples had built up a great civilization. They were building towns about the year 400. This was long before Europeans had heard of South America. The towns were in what is now the country of Peru.

Hundreds of years later the Inca founded a kingdom. They conquered one Native American group after another. By 1500 the Inca empire stretched north to Ecuador, south to Chile, and into Bolivia and Argentina. It had a population of a few million people. Find the area of the Inca empire on the map of South America on page 409.

Cuzco (küs′kō) was the capital of the empire. It was built in a high mountain valley. It had many temples, palaces, and other large buildings.

The Inca knew how to construct fine buildings. Some were built of huge stones. Thousands of workers had to haul the stones to the building sites.

The Inca also made roads throughout their empire. They paved them with flat stones. They stretched bridges that were made of ropes and poles across deep canyons.

Inca farmers grew such crops as potatoes, squash, corn, peanuts, beans, tomatoes, and cotton. They farmed in the valleys. They also laid out terraced fields on mountain slopes.

Many people were experts with crafts. They knew how to weave and how to make clay and metal products. They made jewelry, tools, and weapons of silver, gold, copper, and bronze.

Officials kept in touch with all parts of the empire. The people had to give part of their crops to the government. They also had to spend some time working for the ruler.

Pizarro arrived in the Inca empire in 1531. By this time the Inca had great power. The Spaniards captured Atahualpa (ä′tä wäl′pä), the Inca ruler. He offered to pay much gold and silver to be set free. He sent for enough gold to fill a room and silver to fill two rooms.

Pizarro was pleased, but greedy. He wanted all of the Inca wealth. He had Atahualpa put to death. Then he began to govern the people. By 1569 the Spaniards ruled the whole Inca empire. They sent shiploads of gold and silver to Spain.

Cuzco, Peru, was once the capital of the Inca Empire. Nearly half of Peru's people are Native Americans.

More and more settlers

By the mid-1600s Spain had control of much of South America. Colonists chose land where Native Americans already lived. The Spaniards started cities and farms on this land. The Native Americans had to move. In the Spanish colonies the Native Americans were forced to do much of the work. They put up the buildings, raised the crops, and tended the cattle and sheep.

Some Native Americans fought back. Many fled into the mountains. They settled in places that were hard to reach.

Other countries also had an interest in South America. For many years Portuguese ships had stopped in Brazil. They took on loads of brazilwood. This wood was used in making red dye.

In the mid-1500s the Portuguese built a settlement in Brazil. They chose a place on the coast and called it Salvador. Some settlers started farms and plantations. Others looked for gold. Late in the 1600s some gold was found near the coast. Soon there was a gold rush to southeastern Brazil. A few gold seekers wandered west all the way to the Andes. But they did not find gold.

In the early 1700s diamonds were found in Brazil. This news brought some people to the colony.

English, French, and Dutch colonists also came to South America. They settled along the hot, wet northeast coast. Guyana (gi ä′nə), Surinam (sür′i näm′), and French Guiana are now in this area. The colonists began to grow sugar cane and tobacco.

Farming became a big industry in South America. Food was raised for the settlers and the workers. Sugar cane, coffee, cotton, tobacco, and cacao were raised as money crops. They were sold to European countries.

Some colonists had slaves from Africa. The slaves worked on the large farms.

Through the years other groups of Europeans moved to South America. Some Asians came, too. But most South Americans today are descendants of people who lived in the colonies. Their ancestors were Native Americans, Africans, Spanish, and Portuguese. Many of the people are descendants of two or more of these groups.

Patriot Simón Bolívar is a hero to the people of South America. In the city of his birth, Caracas, Venezuela, his statue stands in Plaza Bolívar.

Independence

In time, many people in the colonies wanted independence. They were tired of paying high taxes. They had no chance to change unfair laws. They were just as unhappy with Spain as the people were in Mexico and Central America.

More and more people wanted freedom. About this time, Bolívar and other patriots planned the revolt against Spain.

Simón Bolívar was born in Caracas, Venezuela, in 1783. His wealthy parents died when Simón was young. They left him their fortune.

A tutor, or private teacher, was hired for Simón's lessons. His name was Simón Rodríguez. He was strict with the five-year-old boy. He insisted on good manners and plenty of study. After lessons, though, there was time for play. Rodríguez often took his young pupil swimming, riding, and hiking.

As the boy grew older, he began to study history. Rodríguez talked much about freedom. He said that all people should be free. He told how the new United States had gained its freedom. Simón never forgot these stirring ideas.

When young Bolívar was 16, he was sent to Spain to attend college. There he was married. Bolívar brought his wife back to Venezuela. Before the year was over, she died of yellow fever.

Bolívar was broken-hearted. He could not forget his grief. He went back to Europe. He began to take an interest in politics. He met people who thought that South America was ready for independence. It was at this time that Bolívar decided to lead the revolt against Spain.

In 1807 the young patriot returned to South America by way of the United States. He talked with President Jefferson. He visited several American cities.

Bolívar joined a group of patriots in Venezuela. They drove the Spanish officials from Caracas (kə rä′kəs). They declared Venezuela free. Find Venezuela and Caracas on the map on page 409.

The Spanish won back this land, and Bolívar had to flee. But he did not give up. He went from place to place to get support. He raised and equipped armies. He led troops in more than 200 battles. The revolt spread throughout Spain's South American colonies.

Manuela Saenz (sä′enz) was one of the many people who helped Bolívar. She raised money for the patriots. She also traveled with the armies. She served as a spy when the patriots needed to learn about Spanish plans.

The struggle for freedom dragged on and on. At last, by 1824, Bolívar's armies had won. They had freed Venezuela, Colombia, Peru, Bolivia, and Ecuador.

Bolívar dreamed of a united South America. He hoped everyone would work together to solve problems. But his dreams did not come true. He had a hard time just to keep order and often needed to govern harshly. At last, he had to give up his work.

The South American people honor Bolívar as a great hero. He is called the Liberator because he led South America to freedom.

José de San Martín was another brave patriot. San Martín (sän′ märtēn′) was born in what is now Argentina. He was educated in Spain in a military school. San Martín returned to South America when

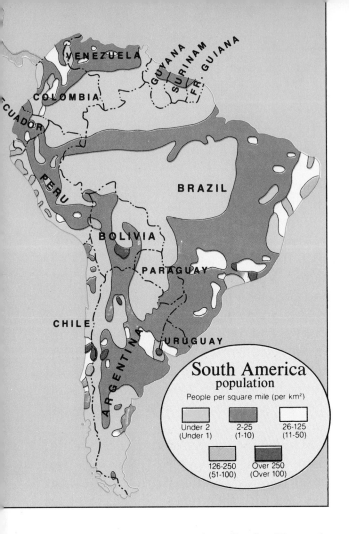

South America
population
People per square mile (per km²)

Under 2 (Under 1)	2-25 (1-10)	26-125 (11-50)
126-250 (51-100)	Over 250 (Over 100)	

the revolt broke out against Spain. He took charge of patriot armies in the south. By 1816 these armies had freed Argentina. Then he marched across the Andes into Chile. His armies joined the Chilean armies led by Bernardo O'Higgins. By 1818 the armies had freed Chile. Then San Martín helped free Peru.

Brazil won its independence without a war. Brazil was a Portuguese colony. It became independent in 1822. Its first ruler was a member of the royal family of Portugal. It became a republic in 1889.

Paraguay (par′ə gwā) declared its independence from Spain in 1813. Uruguay became free in 1828 with the help of Argentina. Guyana was a British colony until 1966. Surinam remained a Dutch colony until 1975. French Guiana still belongs to France.

The land regions of South America

Most of South America is east as well as south of North America. You can see this if you look at the map on page 418. Notice the north-south line that passes between New Orleans and New York City. Almost all of South America is east of this line.

South America is smaller than North America. The continents are somewhat alike in shape. Both continents have ranges of high mountains that stretch in a north-south direction. In North America the mountains are the Rockies. In South America they are the Andes (an′dēz).

Ranges of old, worn-down mountains also extend through the eastern part of both continents. The two continents have wide areas of plains.

Most of South America is south of the equator. Find the equator on the map of South America. Through what South American countries does it pass?

The equator is a line that map-makers draw on maps. It is halfway between the North Pole and the South Pole. This east-west line is marked 0°. It divides the earth into the Northern Hemisphere and the Southern Hemisphere. South America lies mostly south of the equator. So it is said to be in the Southern Hemisphere.

Countries south of the equator have seasons that are just the opposite of those north of the equator. For example, Argentina is having summer when we are having winter. July is a winter month there. January is a summer month.

Tropic of Cancer

Caribbean   Sea

ATLANTIC

OCEAN

Lake
Maracaibo

ORINOCO BASIN

Orinoco River

Magdalena River

GUIANA
HIGHLANDS

Rio   Negro

Amazon   River

Equator

A   M   A   Z   O   N   B   A   S   I   N

A N D E S

BRAZILIAN

HIGHLANDS

São   Francisco   River

El Misti
19,167 ft.
(5842 m)

Lake
Titicaca

PLATEAU OF BOLIVIA

MINAS
GERAIS

PACIFIC

ATACAMA   DESERT

GRAN   CHACO

Paraguay River

OCEAN

Tropic of Capricorn

River

Iguassu
Falls

Paraná

Uruguay   River

▲ Mt. Aconcagua
22,835 ft., (6960 m)

DRY
PLAINS

PAMPA

Rio de la
Plata

Colorado   River

PATAGONIA

Strait of
Magellan

FALKLAND
ISLANDS
(British)

TIERRA DEL FUEGO
Cape Horn

South America
landforms

0	miles	600

0	kilometers	760

Plains   Plateaus   Hills

Mountains

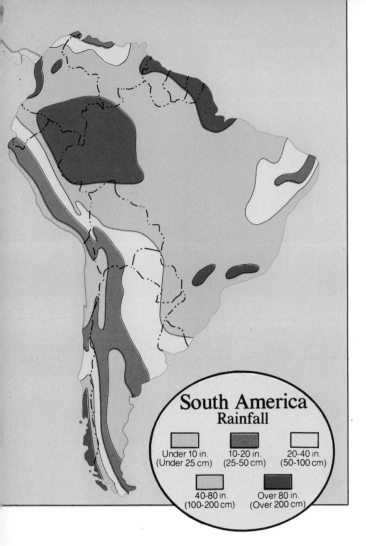

South America
Rainfall

Under 10 in.
(Under 25 cm)

10-20 in.
(25-50 cm)

20-40 in.
(50-100 cm)

40-80 in.
(100-200 cm)

Over 80 in.
(Over 200 cm)

About three-fourths of South America is in the tropics. The tropics extend from the Tropic of Cancer to the Tropic of Capricorn.

Climate in the tropics depends partly on the elevation of the land. Tropical lowlands are hot and wet. Tropical highlands and plateaus are cooler and drier.

Nearly a fourth of South America is in the mid-latitudes. The southern mid-latitudes are between the Tropic of Capricorn and the Antarctic Circle. Notice this on the map. In the mid-latitudes the weather usually changes from season to season. Winters may be cold, and summers hot.

The Andes Mountains run the entire length of South America. Look at the landforms map. The Andes begin on the Caribbean coast. They end on the windswept island of Tierra del Fuego (tyer′ə del fwā′gō). Many Andes peaks are vol-

Southern Chile is a country of many mountains. Some of these Andean peaks, like Llaima, are active volcanoes.

canoes. The lands near them often have earthquakes.

Many fertile valleys and rolling plateaus are between the mountains. They are much lower than the mountains. But they are still highlands. Narrow valleys are tucked in between the mountains. Their rich soil and mild climate are good for farming.

Vast plains cover a large area east of the Andes Mountains. In the tropics most of these plains have dense jungles. Some thickly forested plains extend along the northeast coast. They are known as the Orinoco Basin.

Other forested plains extend far inland through Brazil. This vast region is known as the Amazon Basin. Find the Orinoco Basin and the Amazon Basin on the land-forms map.

Broad plains sweep over much of Argentina. They are in the mid-latitudes and have a cooler climate than the tropical plains.

Study the rainfall map. Notice that Argentina's plains get much less rain than do the tropical plains. This drier, cooler region has tall grasses and many farms and ranches.

Much of the eastern part of the continent consists of highlands. Find the Guiana Highlands and the Brazilian Highlands on the map. The eastern mountains are much lower than the Andes. A part of the eastern highlands is covered by tropical forests. Another part is rolling hills. Still another is a fairly flat plateau.

The Amazon is the largest river in South America. Its source is high in the Andes. It is fed by melting snows. Many streams join the Amazon as it rushes swiftly down the steep slopes. Trace the Amazon River on the landforms map.

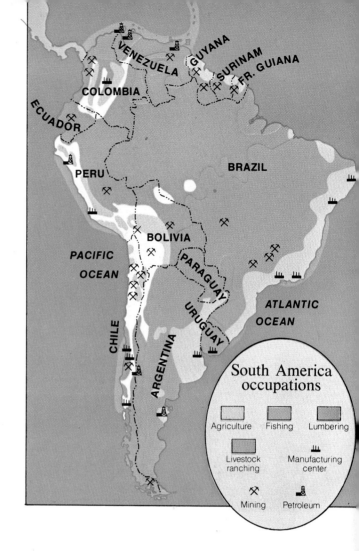

South America occupations

Agriculture   Fishing   Lumbering

Livestock ranching   Manufacturing center

Mining   Petroleum

The Amazon becomes very wide and deep. Ocean-going ships can sail up the river for more than 2000 miles (3200 km). But the Amazon is not a busy waterway. It flows across hot, rain-soaked tropical plains. Few people live in this region.

The Orinoco is the second largest river in South America. Find it on the map. It flows east and north across 1600 miles (2575 km) of highlands, plains, and swamps. Its waters flow into the Atlantic.

Far to the south are three other important rivers. They are the Paraná (pä′rä nä′), the Paraguay, and the Uruguay. Find each on the map. Notice that all three empty into the Rio de la Plata. What large city is located at the mouth of the river?

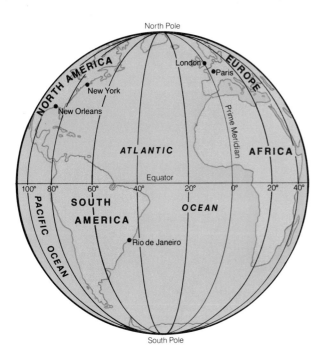

Longitude

You have learned that lines of latitude are east-west lines that circle the globe. The global map on this page shows only one line of latitude. Point to it. What is it called?

The equator is the starting point for measuring latitude. It is the 0° line of latitude.

Notice that this map shows a number of north-south lines. They are *meridians of longitude.* Notice how they extend from the North Pole to the South Pole.

The *prime meridian* is the starting point for measuring longitude. It is the 0° line of longitude. What large city in England does it pass through?

Notice how the other meridians are numbered both east and west of the prime meridian. Is the United States east or west of 0° Longitude? Which of these cities is east of 0° Longitude: Paris, New York, Rio de Janeiro?

Using a map

Use the global map above to help you answer these questions.

1. Which extends farther east, North America or South America?

2. Is South America in the west longitudes or the east longitudes?

3. Find the meridian that marks 40° West Longitude. Which continent does it pass through, North or South America?

4. Look for the meridian that marks 80° West Longitude. Does it cross the equator near the east coast or the west coast of South America?

Who, why, what, and where?

1. Who were the Inca? What city was their capital?

2. Why is it said that the Inca had a great civilization?

3. Why did the Spanish want to conquer the Inca?

4. Why did the Spanish colonists rebel?

5. What South American countries won freedom from Spain?

6. Who were two chief leaders in the fight for independence?

7. Where are South America's highest mountains? Where are there ranges of low mountains?

8. Why are parts of South America sparsely populated?

9. Where are two regions of dense tropical forests? What are they called?

Making a chart from a map

Use the map of South America occupations to make a chart. On paper write in a column the names of the countries of South America. Beside the name of each country, write the chief occupations of its people.

Add other occupations to your chart as you read about these countries.

418

Brazil

Brazil is the largest country on the continent. It covers almost half of South America. It has 21 states and four territories. Find Brazil on the map of South America. Name the countries that border it.

Most of Brazil is in the tropics. You can see this by looking on the map. The lowlands are hot the year round. The plateaus are cooler and drier.

Some areas have a rainy climate. Find these lands on the rainfall map. How much rain falls in the area around the Amazon River?

The Amazon and its tributaries flow through Brazil. A few Native American villages are scattered along the rivers. One city, Manaus, is located far up the river.

The Amazon Basin surrounds the river. It spreads over a huge area of low plains. Notice that it is in the heart of the tropics. Because of its hot, rainy climate, trees, shrubs, and ferns grow rapidly. It is covered by dense jungles.

Much wildlife lives in the jungle. There are hundreds of kinds of bright-feathered birds. Parrots and macaws screech from perches high in the trees. Monkeys chatter and scream as they swing from branch to branch. Large cat-like jaguars and the slow-moving sloths live in this region, too. So do giant butterflies and many mosquitoes. Snakes crawl through dark undergrowth. Some kinds of snakes often swim in the rivers.

Brazil's highlands rise sharply near the east coast. There are hills and mountains in this region. Find the highlands on the landforms map.

Some highlands are rich in minerals. Gold has been mined for about 300 years. The chief minerals today include bauxite, manganese, chrome, and iron ore. Bauxite is used in making aluminum. The steel industry uses manganese and iron. Brazil has one of the largest steel mills in Latin America.

The highlands are also famous for diamonds and other precious stones. Some diamonds are sold as jewels. Many are used in manufacturing.

Farming is Brazil's most important industry. Brazilian farmers are among the world's leading food producers. More and more farmland is being cleared. But much rich land has not yet been touched.

There are long stretches of cleared lowlands along the northeast coast. Farmers grow bananas, cacao, sugar cane, and cotton. Beans, citrus fruits, corn, rice, and tobacco are raised on farms throughout Brazil. After the United States, Brazil produces more oranges than any other country in the world.

Coffee is grown on the hills east of the coastal mountains. The coffee plantations are called fazendas. Coffee is one of Brazil's leading exports.

Ranchers raise cattle, sheep, and horses. Ranches are mainly in the plains region.

Manufacturing has expanded greatly since the 1940s. This is partly because of the growth of hydroelectric power. Textile-making is the leading industry. Brazilian factories also make chemicals, cement, railroad cars, autos, and appliances. Other main products are shoes, paper, glass, machinery, and processed foods.

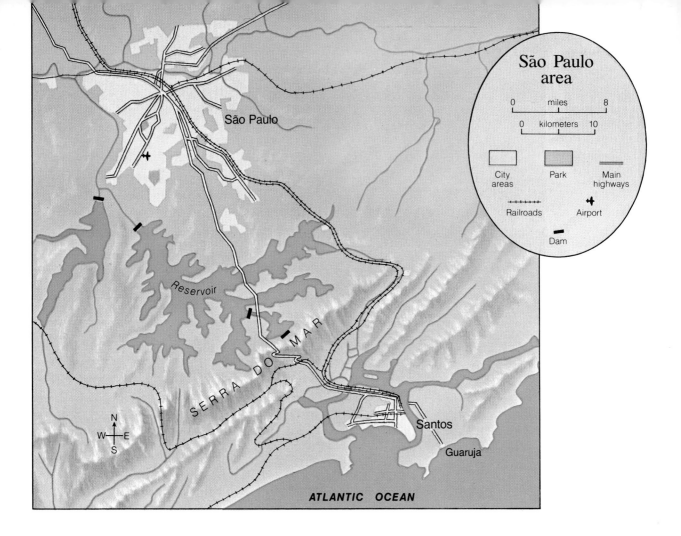

São Paulo area

0 miles 8

0 kilometers 10

City areas   Park   Main highways

Railroads   Airport

Dam

São Paulo

Reservoir

SERRA DO MAR

N
W E
S

Santos

Guaruja

ATLANTIC OCEAN

São Paulo is the name of a city and of a state. São Paulo (souɴ pou′lō) is the leading industrial region in Brazil. Half of the country's textile mills are in this state. Find the city of São Paulo on the map. It is Brazil's largest city and the center of the coffee business. São Paulo is in the highlands near the coffee plantations.

Santos is a busy seaport near the city of São Paulo. It ships millions of sacks of coffee. Much of the coffee goes to the United States. Santos also exports many products manufactured in São Paulo. How far is São Paulo from Santos? Use the map of the São Paulo region to find out.

The city of Rio de Janeiro looks out on a bay. One Portuguese explorer sailed into this bay in January 1502. He thought the bay was the mouth of a river. So he named it Rio de Janeiro (rē′ō dā zhə nār′ō), meaning "River of January."

Rio de Janeiro is surrounded by hills and mountains. On one hill stands a large statue of Christ. It is as tall as an eight-story building.

Rio de Janeiro, sometimes called Rio, has many fine modern buildings. Some are tall skyscrapers like those in our largest cities. Many are apartment houses or hotels, or perhaps fine stores and office buildings. Most of the business buildings are crowded together on the level land near the bay. But thousands of homes are perched on hillsides. Some are in the valleys that run back between the mountains.

Rio has grand old homes, churches, and palaces that were built in colonial days. Some sidewalks are very wide and are

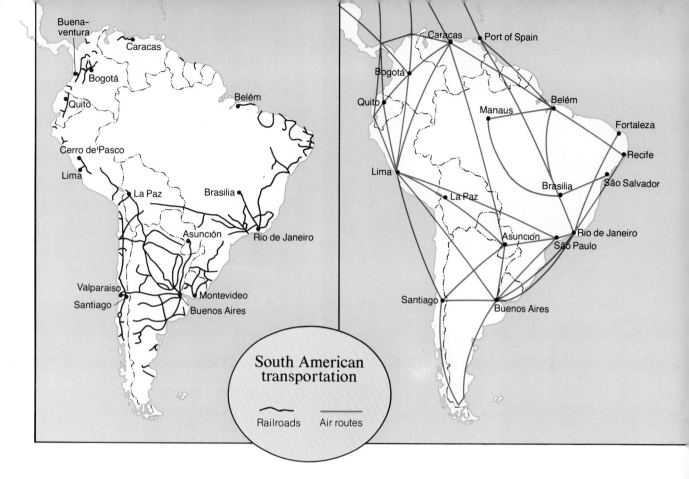

South American
transportation

Railroads   Air routes

paved in the early Portuguese way. They have many tiny colored stones fitted together in designs. Tourists like to stroll along these colorful sidewalks.

They also enjoy visiting the tall island called Sugar Loaf. This mass of rock has smooth, steep sides and soars high above the sea. From its top, visitors have a good view of Rio and of the islands in the bay. Getting to Sugar Loaf's summit is quite an adventure. One must travel through the air in a box-like car, that moves on strong cables, or steel ropes.

Rio de Janeiro is the third largest city in South America. It has grown large because of its fine location and large, deep harbor. It is located in one of the richest sections of Brazil. Nearby are many mineral resources as well as miles and miles of coffee plantations and farms.

Because it is near raw materials, Rio has become a busy industrial center. It has

flour mills, textile mills, oil refineries, and many factories, large and small. Among the goods made are clothing, shoes, textiles, furniture, foods, and iron and steel products.

Rio depends largely on railroads to bring raw materials to its factories. They also haul farm products to its harbor to be shipped overseas. Rio is at the hub of most of Brazil's railroad lines. From it, railroads reach out in many directions. Notice this on the railroad map. But only a small part of Brazil has railroads. No railroad line reaches across the vast interior.

The other map shows the main airways that link the South American countries. Why is air travel so important?

From 1808 to 1960 Rio de Janeiro was Brazil's capital. It was even the capital of Portugal for a time. In the early 1800s Napoleon tried to conquer Europe. When his armies marched toward Portugal, the

421

Brasília, the new capital of Brazil, is in the interior of the country. Oscar Niemeyer, the famous Brazilian architect, designed many of the buildings.

king and many wealthy Portuguese fled to Brazil.

At that time Rio de Janeiro was just a small town. The king had workers build fine palaces and public buildings. Wide avenues and parks were laid out. It became a beautiful city.

The king went back to Portugal in 1821 after Napoleon's defeat. He left his son Pedro to rule Brazil. The next year Pedro said that Brazil was independent from Portugal. He was crowned the emperor. Later many people turned against Pedro. So he fled to Portugal. He left his young son Pedro in Brazil. When the boy grew up, he became emperor as Dom Pedro II.

Dom Pedro governed Brazil for nearly fifty years. The country prospered. Railroads were built. Coffee trees were planted. A big rubber industry grew, but then died out in the early 1900s. The rubber came from trees growing wild in the Amazon rain forests. Many German and Italian immigrants helped develop the land.

Dom Pedro welcomed rich and poor to the palace. He traveled to other countries. He was eager to learn things that would help Brazil.

By 1850 Brazil had about eight million people. About three million of them were African slaves. Through the years many slaves were freed. In 1888 the last of the slaves—about 700,000—were set free. The law was signed by Princess Isabel. She was ruling while her father, Pedro II, was in Europe for medical treatment. The next year Brazil became a republic.

Brasília, a planned city, was made the capital in 1960. It is on the central plateau about 600 miles (965 km) northwest of Rio. Find Brasília on the map.

Leaders chose a spot on an almost empty plain. They hoped that a new inland capital would bring many settlers to this region. A huge lake was dug to surround the city on three sides. Houses, offices, and schools were built. A modern highway links the city with the coast.

Argentina and Chile

Argentina is South America's second largest country. Its capital and chief city is Buenos Aires. Find Argentina (är′jən tē′nə) and Buenos Aires on the map.

Northern Argentina has a fertile plain called the Gran Chaco (grän′ chä′ kō). It has hot, rainy summers that change the plains into steamy swamps. Its hot, rainless winters burn the grasses and dry up the streams. Cotton and sugar cane are grown on parts of the Gran Chaco.

To the south and west are wide plains called the Pampa. They stretch for about 300 miles (480 km) west of Buenos Aires. They have a mild climate and fertile soil. Most of Argentina's crops are grown on the Pampa. Among them are wheat, corn, and alfalfa. Flax fields spread over some areas. Flax seeds are crushed to make linseed oil. The oil is used in making paint and other products.

Millions of cattle are raised on the Pampa. Argentina exports more beef than any other country in the world. Cattle rais-ing is Argentina's oldest industry. It dates back to the days of the early Spanish colonists. The cowhands in Argentina are known as gauchos.

Patagonia in the south is a high, dry, windy plateau. It extends all the way south to the Strait of Magellan. Some very large sheep ranches are in this region. So Argentina is a world leader in producing sheep and wool.

West of the Pampa and north of Patagonia are dry plains. They extend far west to the Andes. They have fertile soil but are drier than the Pampa. Many irrigated crops are grown on these rich plains. Water is brought from mountain streams.

Four out of five people in Argentina live in urban areas. Many work in factories. Most of the workers process the products of farms and ranches. For example, they tan hides or pack meat. Textiles, automobiles, and trucks are made. So are electrical goods, chemicals, furniture, and petroleum products.

The ancestors of most of Argentina's people came from Europe. Many, of course, were from Spain. A large number of immigrants came from Germany and Italy.

Argentina is one of the continent's richest countries. Yet it has faced serious problems over the years. One problem has been a big jump in prices from month to month. Goods that cost $100 in January might cost $400 by December. A general rise in prices is known as *inflation.*

Inflation has hit many countries in recent years. It has been a problem in our country, too.

Americans worry about inflation when prices go up about one-tenth in a year. At

Buenos Aires *(top)*, the capital of Argentina, is a coastal city. Santiago *(bottom)*, the capital of Chile, lies in the mountains in the central part of the country.

that rate, goods costing $100 in January would cost $110 in December. Think, then, how hard it would be for people when prices double every few months.

Wages for some workers increase in a time of inflation, too. But many people with low incomes are hurt by rising prices.

From time to time, military rulers have taken over Argentina's government. One takeover took place in 1955. President Juan Perón had to leave the country. He came back in 1973 and was elected president again. His wife, Isabel, was elected vice-president. She became president when Juan Perón died the next year. Isabel Perón was the first woman to be the head of a national government in the Western Hemisphere. But military rulers soon took over again.

Chile is a long narrow country on the Pacific coast. The name Chile (chil/i) comes from the Native American word *chilli*. It means ''place where the land ends.'' Find Chile on the map on page 409.

Mountains and hills cover about three-fourths of Chile. The Andes Mountains stand like high walls along the entire eastern border. Low mountains and hills extend along the Pacific coast.

Chile's northern region is a hot, dry desert. Day after day, scorching winds blow across it. Years go by without even a sprinkle of rain.

This dry land has valuable mineral deposits. The chief ones are copper, iron ore, and nitrate. Mining these minerals is Chile's leading industry. Chile produces about four-tenths of the world's copper. Nitrate is used in making medicines, fireworks, and fertilizers. Borax is also mined. It is used in certain medicines and soaps and also in glass products.

Southern Chile is a cold, rainy region with much fog. Much of it is covered by mountains. Forests thrive on the lower slopes. Some sheep are raised on the lands at the foot of the mountains.

Most of the people of Chile live in the middle region. Middle Chile extends for about 700 miles (1125 km) from north to south. The northern part has warm, dry summers and mild, rainy winters. The southern part is cooler, and rain falls the year round. This area has thick forests.

Santiago (sän′ti ä′gō) is the capital of Chile. It is in middle Chile. So is Valparaíso, the chief seaport and a manufacturing center. Concepción (kōn sep syōn′), another industrial center, is there, too.

More and more people are working in the factories and mills. They make such products as textiles, clothing, wood products, paper, and appliances. Chile also has a steel industry.

Some people are farmers. Among the main crops are wheat, fruits, vegetables, and grapes. Some crops are irrigated. Why? Study the rainfall map on page 416. What does it tell about Chile's rainfall?

Three middle countries

Paraguay is between Argentina and Brazil. Find Paraguay on the map. It is divided into two parts by the Paraguay River. To the west are the grassy plains of the Gran Chaco. They extend across Paraguay and into northern Argentina. Few people live in this region.

East of the river is a rolling fertile land of farms and cattle ranches. Corn, rice, sugar

Paraguay is noted for the fine embroidery its artisans make.

cane, oranges, and cotton are grown.

Along the Paraguay River are forests where quebracho (kā brä′chō) trees grow. Wood from these trees is cut into chips and soaked in water. The water is then used in making animal hides into leather.

Yerba maté (yer′bə mä′tā) trees also grow in the forests. The leaves are gathered and used to make a kind of tea called maté.

Asunción (ä sün syōn′) is the capital of Paraguay. It is a small, quiet city on the banks of the Paraguay River.

More than nine-tenths of the people of Paraguay are mestizos. You learned that a mestizo has both Native American and white ancestors.

Uruguay is a small land in the middle latitudes. Find it on the map. It has warm summers and cool winters. Cattle and sheep raising are Uruguay's leading industries. Seven-tenths of the land is used for livestock. Huge quantities of meat, hides, and wool are exported.

425

Native American herdsmen tend their llamas in the Bolivian highlands.

Some crops are raised, too. These include wheat, corn, oats, and flax.

Montevideo (mon′ti vi dā′ō) is the capital, chief seaport, and industrial center of Uruguay. Over a third of the people live in this city. Many work in meat-packing plants, flour mills, textile mills, and tanneries. A *tannery* is a place where hides are treated and made into leather. Montevideo is also a vacation resort.

Bolivia is sometimes called the "land of the sky." Find Bolivia on the map. This country is named after Simón Bolívar. Three-fourths of the people live on a high plateau in the Andes Mountains. More than half of all Bolivians are Native Americans. Many others are mestizos.

Over half of Bolivia is covered by low plains. These plains are good for growing some crops. But most of the farmers live on the plateau where the climate is cold and dry. They can grow only a few crops. Their chief one is potatoes. More than 200 kinds of potatoes are raised. Cattle, sheep, pigs, and llamas are raised, too.

426

Llamas are cousins of camels. They are about four feet (120 cm) tall and have no humps. Like camels, llamas can go without water day after day.

Llamas are used in the mountains of South America. They are sturdy pack animals. They can climb steep mountain trails. Long trains of llamas take goods to markets. Each animal can carry a load up to 100 pounds (45 kg).

Llamas are useful in other ways, too. Their thick coats can be sheared and spun into yarn. The yarn is woven into cloth. Their hides may be made into sandals. Their meat can be eaten.

Sucre (sü′krā) is the capital of Bolivia. But most government offices are in La Paz. This city is in a valley on the high plateau.

South of Sucre is the old city of Potosí. During Spanish times, it was famous for a nearby silver mine. Today tin-ore mines are being worked there. Bolivia produces about one-eighth of the world's tin. This metal has many uses. One is for coating steel cans known as "tin" cans. Because of the tin coating, food keeps well in tin cans.

Northern countries

Peru is the third largest country in South America. It is the land of the Inca. Find Peru on the map.

There are three main regions in Peru. Near the coast are strips of desert plain and low hills and mountains. Many rivers and streams flow from the Andes to the Pacific across this region. Water from these rivers is used to irrigate fields of cotton, rice, and sugar cane. This is the country's main farming area.

High in the Peruvian Andes are the ruins of the "lost city of the Inca," Machu Picchu. Lima, Peru's present capital, lies on the coast.

East of the Andes is an area of hot, wet plains. It is almost covered with tropical forests. Few people live there.

The Andes highlands separate these two regions. Between the towering peaks are narrow valleys, deep canyons, and high basins. About half of Peru's people live in the highlands. Most of them make their living by farming. The main crops are corn, potatoes, and coffee.

Lima (lē′mə) is the capital of Peru. It was founded by Pizarro in 1535. Lima was the capital of Spain's vast South American colonies. Much gold was shipped to Spain from Lima.

There are rich deposits of minerals in Peru's mountains. They include copper, lead, zinc, iron, gold, and silver.

The copper deposits are very rich. The most famous copper mine is nearly 15,000 feet (4600 m) above sea level. It is hard for miners to work in such a high altitude because the air is very thin. Many native people have always lived in the high mountains. They are used to the thin air and are expert miners.

The waters off the coast of Peru are filled with fish. So Peru has a very large fishing industry.

Nearly half of the people in Peru are Native Americans. Almost as many are mestizos. More Native Americans live in Peru than in any other country. An old Inca language is used in Peru along with Spanish.

Ecuador has a Spanish name that means "equator." Find Ecuador on the map. Notice that the equator runs through it. Ecuador is a small country, but it has three

Quito, the oldest of the South American capitals, is high in the Andes. Steep narrow streets are part of old Quito. Other sections of the city are very modern.

very different regions. A hot, rainy plain is along the Pacific coast. Some of its thick jungles have been cleared. Crops of cacao, cotton, rice, bananas, and sugar cane are raised.

The Pacific plain has a fast-growing population. Almost half of the people now live there. Guayaquil (gwī′ə kēl′) is located on the plain. It is the country's largest city and chief seaport. It is fifty miles (80 km) inland on a river.

The Andes Mountains rise east of the coastal plains. In the mountains are high valleys and plateaus with a pleasant climate. Almost half of the people live in them.

Quito (kē′tō), the capital of Ecuador, is on one of the plateaus. Its elevation is more than 9000 feet (2700 m) above sea level.

Ecuador's other plains lie east of the Andes and are covered by jungles. Few people live there.

The Galapagos (gə lä′pə gəs) Islands are part of Ecuador. These islands are in the Pacific Ocean 600 miles (1000 km) west

of Ecuador. Some very unusual creatures live on the islands. There are rare birds and huge lizards. Giant tortoises are found there. Some weigh about 500 pounds (225 kg). Some are more than 200 years old.

Colombia faces both the Pacific Ocean and the Caribbean Sea. Find it on the map. Colombia has hot lowlands along its coast. In the northeast are plains that cover more than half of the country. Inland are the high Andes Mountains. Another range of mountains is in the northwest.

Colombia is rich in resources. It is one of the leading oil producers in South America. It also mines most of the world's emeralds. Emeralds are precious green stones. More gold is mined in Colombia than in any other South American country. It has the largest deposit of platinum in the world.

Coffee is Colombia's main export crop. Cotton, sugar cane, corn, bananas, rice, potatoes, and cacao are also grown.

Bogotá is the capital. It is partly old and partly new. Its older buildings go back to Spanish days. Some of the older streets are very narrow. The new sections of the city have wide avenues.

Medellín is a fast-growing manufacturing center. It is one of the chief textile-making cities in South America.

Venezuela is in the northern part of South America. Find it on the map. Long ago, Spanish explorers sailed along the coast of this land. They saw Native American houses built on stilts above the waters of Lake Maracaibo (mar′ə kī′bō). This sight reminded them of the houses along the canals in Venice. So they named the land Venezuela, which means ''little Venice'' in Spanish.

Venezuela is in the tropics. In the west are the Maracaibo lowlands. They have dense jungles and a hot, damp climate.

Also in the west are the Andes Mountains. Most of the people in Venezuela live in the mountain valleys and plateaus.

To the east between the Andes and the Orinoco River there are low, nearly level plains. They are mainly cattle-grazing lands.

The Guiana Highlands rise in the southeast. They have some of the richest deposits of iron ore that have been found.

Great stores of petroleum lie beneath Lake Maracaibo. This body of water is not a real lake, though. It is a protected area of shallow water off the coast. Many oil derricks rise above the water. They are built on high platforms set on poles driven into the lake.

Crude oil and oil products provide about nine-tenths of Venezuela's exports. Some of the income from oil pays for fine highways and schools.

The city of Maracaibo is on the shores of Lake Maracaibo. It is the center of the oil industry.

Caracas, the capital, is in a high inland valley. Because of its elevation, Caracas

Venezuela is one of the world's leading producers of petroleum. Most of its oil comes from reserves underneath Lake Maracaibo.

The large city of Caracas is located in a high mountain valley.

has a comfortable climate. A winding highway through the mountains connects Caracas and the city of La Guaira, the chief seaport.

Simón Bolívar was born in Caracas. The people of Venezuela are proud of his deeds. They have a museum in the old stone house where the famous patriot was born.

Guyana, Surinam, and French Guiana are southeast of Venezuela. Two of them are republics. But French Guiana is governed as a part of France.

Guyana was the British colony of British Guiana from 1815 to 1966. Before that time it was a Dutch colony.

Surinam was once called Dutch Guiana. It became independent from the Netherlands in 1975. You remember that the English took New Netherland from the

Dutch in 1667 and renamed it New York. At that time the English gave Surinam to the Dutch for their loss of New Netherland.

These three lands have dense tropical forests inland from the coast. Most of the people live on the coastal plain. The chief crops are rice, sugar cane, cacao, and fruits.

Over half of the people in Guyana are East Indians. More than a third of Surinam's people are from the East Indies, too. These three lands also have many people whose ancestors came from Africa as slaves.

Neighbors working together

Countries of the Western Hemisphere hold meetings to solve problems. In the late 1800s, delegates from countries in North and South America met in Washington, D.C. They talked about problems that the two Americas shared.

In 1910 the Pan American Union was formed. In 1948 the name was changed to Organization of American States (OAS). One chief purpose of the OAS is to work for peace. The main OAS office is in Washington, D.C. Most of the countries in the Western Hemisphere are members of the OAS. Delegates from the countries meet each year.

The people of the Americas work with each other in many ways. Countries trade with one another. Students study in each other's countries. Tourists visit many places in the Americas. The people of the Americas have learned much from one another.

Review questions

1. What is Brazil's Amazon Basin like?
2. What minerals are found in Brazil's highlands?
3. Where is Argentina? How is the Pampa different from Patagonia?
4. What are the three main regions in Chile? Where do most of the people live? Why?
5. Why is Peru called the land of the Inca?
6. Why are llamas so useful in the mountainous regions?
7. Which countries have large Native American populations?
8. What are some of Colombia's natural resources?
9. Where is Venezuela? What is its most important product?
10. What lake in Venezuela is connected to the Atlantic Ocean by a narrow channel?

Which are partners?

On paper write the numbers 1 to 10 in a column. Read each of the ten items. After its number, write the word or words from the list that belong to it.

1. The largest city in Brazil
2. The capital of Argentina
3. A cowhand in Argentina
4. The capital of Spain's South American colonies
5. A planned city in Brazil
6. A tea-like drink made from leaves
7. Metal that is found mainly in Colombia
8. The birthplace of Simón Bolívar
9. A beautiful city called a river
10. The capital of Chile

List

Caracas	Rio de Janeiro
São Paulo	maté
gaucho	Quito
Bolivia	Montevideo
platinum	Buenos Aires
Brasília	nitrate
Santiago	Lima

Things to do

1. Read in another book about one of these topics

The Andes	Guyana
Bolívar	Pizarro
San Martín	Mendoza
Surinam	Magellan

2. Learn more about the animals and birds that live on the Galapagos Islands. Then make a poster showing at least three of the creatures that live there. Tell about the animals in captions. Display some posters on the bulletin board.

3. Find out more about the life of a gaucho on the Pampa or of a sheepherder in Patagonia. Write and illustrate a story about an adventure of a gaucho or sheepherder. Be ready to share your story.

4. Help your class make a large outline map of South America. You can do this by projecting a political map slide on a large paper. Trace the outline of the continent, the boundaries of the countries, and the largest rivers. Label the countries and main rivers. Draw pictures of the main products of each country. Place the pictures on the map in the correct locations.

Using latitude and longitude

A global map will help you learn more about latitude and longitude.

1. Locate the equator and the prime meridian on the map on page 418.

2. Lines of latitude are called *parallels*. Parallels of latitude that are south of the equator are called the south latitudes. Use the maps on pages 409 and 410. Find the parallel of 20° South Latitude. What countries in South America does it cross?

3. Look for the parallel of 40° South Latitude. Now find the meridian of 60° West Longitude. Notice where they cross. Is this closer to Brazil or to Argentina?

4. Find the parallel of 10° South Latitude and the meridian of 80° West Longitude. Notice where these lines cross. Is this nearer Lima or São Paulo?

5. Which countries are entirely within the south latitudes?

6. Which countries in South America are entirely in the north latitudes?

7. On a sheet of paper write the approximate latitude and longitude of each city.

	latitude	longitude
Montevideo	___	___
Asunción	___	___
São Paulo	___	___
Brasília	___	___
Lima	___	___

8. Find the distance between Montevideo and the following places. Write them on a sheet of paper. Use the map on page 409.

	miles	kilometers
Caracas	___	___
La Paz	___	___
Quito	___	___
Manaus	___	___
Bogotá	___	___

Use the map on pages 254–255 to answer items 9 and 10.

9. Is the United States in the north latitudes or the south latitudes?

10. On a sheet of paper write the approximate latitude and longitude of each city as you did for cities in exercise 7.

Seattle	Boston
Philadelphia	New Orleans
Los Angeles	

432

Geography dictionary

altitude The height above sea level.

bay Part of a large body of water that reaches into the land.

branch A river that flows into a larger river. Also known as a tributary.

canyon A deep, narrow valley with high, steep sides.

cliff A high, steep wall of rock.

climate The kind of weather a place has year after year.

continents The seven largest bodies of land on the earth.

current The flow of a stream of water.

delta Land built up of soil deposited at the mouth of a river.

divide A high ridge of land that separates river systems.

downstream The direction in which a river flows.

elevation The height above sea level.

equator An imaginary line around the earth halfway between the North Pole and South Pole. The equator is shown by a line on maps.

falls A fall of water from a high level to a lower level. Also a waterfall.

fiord A long, narrow arm of the sea that reaches inland and usually has steep sides.

glacier A large body of ice that moves slowly over land.

globe A small model of the earth that usually has a map of the world on it.

growing season The number of days when the weather is warm enough for crops to grow without damage from frost.

gulf Part of a large body of water that reaches into the land; larger than a bay.

harbor A sheltered body of water where ships may anchor safely.

hemisphere Any half of the earth's surface.

hill A raised and somewhat rounded part of the earth's surface; smaller than a mountain.

iceberg A floating mass of ice that has broken from a glacier.

island Land entirely surrounded by water; smaller than a continent.

isthmus A narrow strip of land that connects two larger bodies of land.

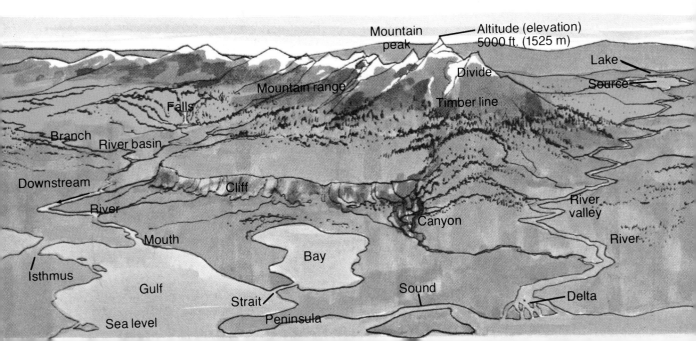

jungle Land thickly covered with bushes, vines, and trees.

lake An inland body of water.

latitude Distance north or south of the equator, measured in degrees.

longitude Imaginary east-west lines that circle the globe.

mountain High rocky land with rather steep sides and with a sharp, pointed peak or a rounded top; higher than a hill.

mountain range A long row of mountains.

mouth (of a river) The place where a river empties into a larger body of water.

North Pole The point on the earth that is farthest north.

oceans The earth's five largest bodies of water.

peninsula The part of a larger body of land that is almost surrounded by water.

plateau A region of high land that is not as level as a plain.

prairie A large area of level or rolling grass-land.

river A stream of water that flows through the land.

river basin The land drained by a river and its branches.

river valley Low land through which a river flows.

sea A large body of salt water, smaller than an ocean, partially or entirely enclosed by land.

sea level Level with the surface of the sea.

season A part of the year when the weather from day to day is somewhat alike. Winter is a season.

sound A long, narrow body of water that separates one or more islands from a mainland.

source (of a river) The place where a river begins.

South Pole The point on the earth that is located farthest south.

strait A narrow body of water that connects two larger bodies of water.

tide The regular rise and fall of ocean water that occurs about every twelve hours.

timber line The place on a mountain above which trees cannot grow because of the cold.

tundra The vast, level, treeless plains in the cold arctic regions.

volcano A mountain with an opening through which steam, ashes, and lava are forced.

Pronunciation key

The way to pronounce many difficult words is shown where they first occur in this book. This is done by showing in parentheses after the word how to pronounce it. For example, Cartier (kär′tyā). When you use the Key to help you pronounce the word, say the syllable marked with ′ with more force. If a syllable is marked with ′, say it with a little less force. Say the unmarked syllables with even less force.

a	hat, cap	ėr	term, learn, burn	oi	oil, voice	u	cup, butter
ā	age, face	i	it, pin	ou	house, out	u̇	full, put, foot
ã	care, air	ī	ice, five	th	thin, both	ü	rule, move, food
ä	father, far	o	hot, rock	ᵺH	then, smooth	ū	use, music
e	let, best	ō	open, go				
ē	equal, be	ô	order, all				

ə represents:
a in about
e in taken
i in pencil
o in lemon
u in circus

Reference tables

Table 1 • The United States

No.	State	*Date	Abbre-viation	Nickname	Area square miles (square kilometers)		Population (projected, 1980)	Capital
1	Delaware		Del.	Blue Hen	2,057	(5,328)	655,000	Dover
2	Pennsylvania	**	Pa.	Keystone	45,333	(117,412)	12,157,000	Harrisburg
3	New Jersey		N.J.	Garden	7,836	(20,295)	8,300,000	Trenton
4	Georgia		Ga.	Empire State of the South	58,876	(152,489)	5,191,000	Atlanta
5	Connecticut		Conn.	Nutmeg	5,009	(12,973)	3,551,000	Hartford
6	Massachusetts	Original Thirteen States	Mass.	Bay	8,257	(21,386)	6,277,000	Boston
7	Maryland		Md.	Old Line	10,577	(27,394)	4,782,000	Annapolis
8	South Carolina		S.C.	Palmetto	31,055	(80,432)	2,731,000	Columbia
9	New Hampshire		N.H.	Granite	9,304	(24,097)	878,000	Concord
10	Virginia		Va.	Old Dominion	40,815	(105,711)	5,229,000	Richmond
11	New York		N.Y.	Empire	49,576	(128,402)	19,789,000	Albany
12	North Carolina		N.C.	Tar Heel	52,712	(136,524)	5,482,000	Raleigh
13	Rhode Island		R.I.	Little Rhody	1,214	(3,144)	1,027,000	Providence
14	Vermont	1791	Vt.	Green Mountain	9,609	(24,887)	504,000	Montpelier
15	Kentucky	1792	Ky.	Bluegrass	40,395	(104,623)	3,372,000	Frankfort
16	Tennessee	1796	Tenn.	Volunteer	42,244	(109,412)	4,259,000	Nashville
17	Ohio	1803	Ohio	Buckeye	41,222	(106,765)	11,675,000	Columbus
18	Louisiana	1812	La.	Pelican	48,523	(125,673)	3,975,000	Baton Rouge
19	Indiana	1816	Ind.	Hoosier	36,291	(93,994)	5,872,000	Indianapolis
20	Mississippi	1817	Miss.	Magnolia	47,716	(123,584)	2,245,000	Jackson
21	Illinois	1818	Ill.	Prairie	56,400	(146,076)	12,256,000	Springfield
22	Alabama	1819	Ala.	Cotton	51,609	(133,677)	3,565,000	Montgomery
23	Maine	1820	Me.	Pine Tree	33,215	(86,027)	1,016,000	Augusta
24	Missouri	1821	Mo.	Show Me	69,686	(180,487)	5,070,000	Jefferson City
25	Arkansas	1836	Ark.	Wonder	53,104	(137,539)	2,052,000	Little Rock
26	Michigan	1837	Mich.	Wolverine	58,216	(150,779)	10,031,000	Lansing
27	Florida	1845	Fla.	Sunshine	58,560	(151,670)	8,280,000	Tallahassee
28	Texas	1845	Tex.	Lone-Star	267,339	(692,408)	12,812,000	Austin
29	Iowa	1846	Iowa	Hawkeye	56,290	(145,791)	2,908,000	Des Moines
30	Wisconsin	1848	Wis.	Badger	56,154	(145,439)	4,930,000	Madison
31	California	1850	Calif.	Golden	158,693	(411,015)	24,226,000	Sacramento
32	Minnesota	1858	Minn.	Gopher	84,068	(217,736)	4,245,000	St. Paul
33	Oregon	1859	Oreg.	Beaver	96,981	(251,181)	2,421,000	Salem
34	Kansas	1861	Kans.	Sunflower	82,264	(213,064)	2,334,000	Topeka
35	West Virginia	1863	W.Va.	Mountain	24,181	(62,629)	1,634,000	Charleston
36	Nevada	1864	Nev.	Silver	110,540	(286,299)	673,000	Carson City
37	Nebraska	1867	Nebr.	Corn Husker	77,227	(200,018)	1,570,000	Lincoln
38	Colorado	1876	Colo.	Centennial	104,247	(270,000)	2,636,000	Denver
39	North Dakota	1889	N.D.	Flickertail	70,665	(183,022)	600,000	Bismarck
40	South Dakota	1889	S.D.	Coyote	77,047	(199,552)	658,000	Pierre
41	Montana	1889	Mont.	Treasure	147,138	(381,087)	721,000	Helena
42	Washington	1889	Wash.	Evergreen	68,192	(176,617)	3,958,000	Olympia
43	Idaho	1890	Ida.	Gem	83,557	(216,413)	761,000	Boise
44	Wyoming	1890	Wyo.	Equality	97,914	(253,597)	342,000	Cheyenne
45	Utah	1896	Utah	Beehive	84,916	(219,932)	1,234,000	Salt Lake City
46	Oklahoma	1907	Okla.	Sooner	69,919	(181,090)	2,787,000	Oklahoma City
47	New Mexico	1912	N.M.	Land of Enchantment	121,666	(315,115)	1,088,000	Santa Fe
48	Arizona	1912	Ariz.	Grand Canyon	113,909	(295,024)	2,164,000	Phoenix
49	Alaska	1959	none	none	586,400	(1,518,776)	352,000	Juneau
50	Hawaii	1959	none	Aloha State	6,424	(16,638)	874,000	Honolulu

* Date and order in which they became states

** In the order in which they signed the Constitution, 1787-1790

Table 2 • Our lands beyond our boundaries

Place	Date of annexation	Area square miles (square kilometers)		Population 1975	Capital
American Samoa	1900	76	(197)	30,000	Pago Pago
Guam	1899	212	(549)	111,000	Agana
Pacific Islands under					
U.S. trusteeship	1947	8,511	(22,043)	116,000	
Puerto Rico	1899	3,435	(8,897)	3,128,000	San Juan
Virgin Islands	1917	133	(344)	100,000	Charlotte Amalie

Table 3 • Our North American neighbors

Country	Year of independence	Area square miles (square kilometers)		Population 1975	Capital
Belize	1969	8,867	(22,966)	119,000	Belmopan
Canada		3,851,809	(9,976,185)	22,998,000	Ottawa
Costa Rica	1821	19,575	(50,699)	2,000,000	San José
Cuba	1898	44,218	(114,525)	9,200,000	Havana
Dominican Republic	1844	18,703	(48,441)	4,697,000	Santo Domingo
El Salvador	1821	8,260	(21,393)	4,100,000	San Salvador
Guatemala	1821	42,042	(108,889)	5,400,000	Guatemala City
Haiti	1804	10,714	(27,749)	4,750,000	Port-au-Prince
Honduras	1821	43,277	(112,087)	2,800,000	Tegucigalpa
Jamaica		4,244	(11,424)	2,100,000	Kingston
Mexico	1821	761,602	(1,972,549)	60,145,000	Mexico City
Nicaragua	1821	49,759	(139,699)	2,155,000	Managua
Panama	1903	29,762	(77,083)	1,708,000	Panamá
Trinidad and Tobago	1962	1,980	(5,128)	1,100,000	Port-of-Spain

Table 4 • Our South American neighbors

Country	Year of independence	Area square miles (square kilometers)		Population 1975	Capital
Argentina	1816	1,072,070	(2,776,661)	25,050,000	Buenos Aires
Bolivia	1825	424,163	(1,098,582)	5,634,000	La Paz, Sucre
Brazil	1822	3,286,478	(8,511,978)	107,500,000	Brasília
Chile	1818	292,257	(756,946)	10,700,000	Santiago
Colombia	1819	439,513	(1,138,339)	24,717,000	Bogotá
Ecuador	1822	109,483	(283,561)	7,200,000	Quito
French Guiana		35,135	(91,000)	50,000	Cayenne
Guyana	1966	83,000	(214,970)	800,000	Georgetown
Paraguay	1811	157,047	(406,752)	2,625,000	Asunción
Peru	1824	496,223	(1,285,218)	15,839,000	Lima
Surinam		55,144	(142,823)	425,000	Paramaribo
Uruguay	1828	72,172	(186,925)	2,764,000	Montevideo
Venezuela	1811	352,143	(912,050)	11,993,000	Caracas

Table 5 • Metropolitan* areas of 300,000 or more population (1975)

Akron, Ohio	667,000	Harrisburg, Pa.	427,000	Phoenix, Ariz.	1,221,000
Albany-Schenectady-		Hartford, Conn.	732,000	Pittsburgh, Pa.	2,322,000
Troy, N.Y.	798,000	Honolulu, Hawaii	705,000	Portland, Oreg.-Wash.	1,083,000
Alburquerque, N.M.	385,000	Houston, Tex.	2,286,000	Providence, R.I.-Mass.	904,000
Allentown, Pa.-N.J.	624,000	Indianapolis, Ind.	1,139,000	Raleigh-Durham, N.C.	469,000
Anaheim, Calif.	1,700,000	Jacksonville, Fla.	693,000	Reading, Pa.	305,000
Atlanta, Ga.	1,790,000	Jersey City, N.J.	578,000	Richmond, Va.	585,000
Austin, Tex.	397,000	Johnson City, Tenn.-Va.	401,000	Riverside-San	
Bakersfield, Calif.	350,000	Kansas City, Mo.-Kan.	1,299,000	Bernardino, Calif.	1,226,000
Baltimore, Md.	2,148,000	Knoxville, Tenn.	435,000	Rochester, N.Y.	971,000
Baton, Rouge, La.	412,000	Lancaster, Pa.	343,000	Sacramento, Calif.	880,000
Beaumont, Tex.	351,000	Lansing, Mich.	445,000	St. Louis, Mo.-Ill.	2,367,000
Binghamton, N.Y.-Pa.	304,000	Las Vegas, Nev.	331,000	Salt Lake City, Utah	783,000
Birmingham, Ala.	791,000	Little Rock, Ark.	348,000	San Antonio, Tex.	982,000
Boston, Mass.	2,890,000	Long Branch, N.J.	492,000	San Diego, Calif.	1,585,000
Bridgeport, Conn.	395,000	Los Angeles, Calif.	6,987,000	San Francisco-	
Buffalo, N.Y.	1,327,000	Louisville, Ky.-Ind.	888,000	Oakland, Calif.	3,140,000
Canton, Ohio	400,000	Madison, Wis.	302,000	San Jose, Calif.	1,174,000
Charleston, S.C.	371,000	Memphis, Tenn.-Ark.-		Seattle, Wash.	1,407,000
Charlotte, N.C.	593,000	Miss.	867,000	Shreveport, La.	349,000
Chattanooga, Tenn.-Ga.	392,000	Miami, Fla.	1,439,000	Spokane, Wash.	306,000
Chicago, Ill.	7,015,000	Milwaukee, Wis.	1,409,000	Springfield, Mass.-	
Cincinnati, Ohio-		Minneapolis-St. Paul,		Conn.	549,000
Ky.-Ind.	1,381,000	Minn.-Wis.	2,011,000	Stockton, Calif.	300,000
Cleveland, Ohio	1,967,000	Mobile, Ala.	403,000	Syracuse, N.Y.	648,000
Columbia, S.C.	365,000	Nashville, Tenn.	748,000	Tacoma, Wash.	416,000
Columbus, Ohio	1,069,000	Nassau-Suffolk, N.Y.	2,657,000	Tampa-St. Petersburg,	
Dallas-Forth Worth, Tex.	2,577,000	New Brunswick, N.J.	464,000	Fla.	1,348,000
Davenport, Iowa-Ill.	370,000	New Haven, Conn.	593,000	Toledo, Ohio-Mich.	779,000
Dayton, Ohio	836,000	New London, Conn.-R.I.	760,000	Trenton, N.J.	318,000
Denver, Colo.	1,413,000	New Orleans, La.	1,094,000	Tucson, Ariz.	444,000
Des Moines, Iowa	328,000	New York, N.Y.-N.J.	9,561,000	Tulsa, Okla.	586,000
Detroit, Mich.	4,424,000	Newark, N.J.	1,999,000	Utica-Rome, N.Y.	334,000
El Paso, Tex.	424,000	Newport News-		Washington, D.C.-Md.-	
Flint, Mich.	519,000	Hampton, Va.	347,000	Va.	3,022,000
Fort Lauderdale, Fla.	848,000	Norfolk, Va.	773,000	West Palm Beach, Fla.	455,000
Fort Wayne, Ind.	373,000	Oklahoma, City, Okla.	746,000	Wichita, Kans.	385,000
Fort Worth. See Dallas		Omaha, Nebr.-Iowa	573,000	Wilmington, Del.-N.J.-	
Fresno, Calif.	446,000	Orlando, Fla.	583,000	Md.	518,000
Gary, Ind.	643,000	Oxnard, Calif.	438,000	Worcester, Mass.	378,000
Grand Rapids, Mich.	564,000	Paterson, N.J.	452,000	York, Pa.	348,000
Greensboro, N.C.	764,000	Peoria, Ill.	354,000	Youngstown, Ohio	549,000
Greenville, S.C.	525,000	Philadelphia, Pa.-N.J.	4,807,000		

*A metropolitan area includes the central city plus surrounding urban areas.

Index

444

Credits

Graphic Design and Production
Edit, Inc.

Cover Design
Hayward Blake & Company

Maps
Leon Bishop: 212, 247, 390
Cartographic Services Associates:
187, 259, 269, 270, 273, 288,
291, 303, 304, 306, 365, 366,
385, 414, 416
Robert C. Forget: 14, 29, 35, 55, 89,
90-91, 149, 254-255, 264, 286,
313, 327, 341, 409, 415
Lowell Stumpf: 101, 167, 258, 263,
289, 317, 319, 332, 349, 357,
362, 384, 388, 418, 421
Jack Wallen: 330, 346, 351

Illustrations
Edit, Inc.: 25, 27, 59, 186
Dan Siculan: 8, 9, 12-13, 31, 37,
49, 100, 103, 104, 109, 110, 111,
122, 140, 144, 161, 176, 190,
191, 226-227, 245, 343, 433
George Suyeoka: 183, 194, 235
239, 299, 318, 329
Jack Wallen: 44, 50-51, 66-67,
114, 164, 173, 175

Photographs
Wally Aaron: 265 left
American Iron and Steel Institute:
96 left
American Printing House for the
Blind: 232 left
Peter Arnold: 201 bottom
Björn Bölstad, 38
Vic Cox, 347 left
W. H. Hodge, 315 top
James H. Karales, 188
Richard Weiss, 284
AT&T Photo Service: 236
James Ballard: 180 bottom left and
bottom right, 265 right, 266, 298
J. N. Bartfield Art Galleries, Inc.,
New York: 105
Bausch & Lomb: 80
The Bettmann Archive, Inc.: 20,
132, 222, 229, 262
Black Star:
Steve Allen, 3 right, 159 right
Dennis Brack, 1, 233, 248
Craighead, 389 left
Tom Ebenhoh, 221
Victor Engelbert, 383, 391, 392,
424 top, 425, 428
Bob Fitch, 207
John Hyre, 397
John Launois, 359, 370
Dan McCoy, 4 right, 253 right
Ernest Manewal, 416, 424
bottom
Claus Meyer, 411, 422
Bert Miller, 274 bottom right
Charles Moore, 184 bottom, 213,
333, 336 left
Kosti Ruohomaa, 260 right
Flip Schulke, 403 right
Erik Simonsen, 224 bottom
Ted Spiegel, 95 bottom left, 279,
399
Bill Strode, 374
John de Visser, 360, 369 bottom,
371
Fred Ward, 4 left, 209 right, 251,
378 bottom, 403 left, 404, 406
D. Wilson, 205
Doug Wilson, 217, 223

Collection of the Boatmen's
National Bank of St. Louis:
130-131
Brokaw: 2 left, 7 left
Courtesy of Brown County Library:
43 bottom
Camera Hawaii:
Werner Stoy, 189 bottom
Chessie System, The B & O
Museum: 219
City of Chicago, Howard Simmons:
204
Chicago Historical Society: 115
Chicago Sun-Times: 232 right
The Church of Jesus Christ of
Latter-Day Saints, Salt Lake
City: 151
Jed A. Clark, 3 left, 99 bottom
Cincinnati Art Museum: 164
Bernie Cleff: 278 left
The Cleveland Museum of Art, Gift
of Mr. and Mrs. Lawrence S.
Robbins: 56
Colonial Williamsburg Foundation:
34, 45 middle and bottom, 52, 57
Confederation Life Insurance
Company: 22
Continental Corporation: 76 bottom
Historical Paintings Collection of
the Continental Insurance
Company: 73
Culver Pictures, Inc.: 201 top
Dallas Museum of Fine Arts: 16
Denver Public Library, Western
History Department: 143
DRT Library at the Alamo: 147
Ford Motor Company: 183
Grant Heilman: 3 left, 99 top, 180
top, 302
Courtesy, The Henry Francis du
Pont Winterthur Museum: 39
Historical Pictures Service,
Chicago: 84, 244
Historical Society of Pennsylvania:
51, 61
Idaho Historical Society: 138
Illinois Bell Telephone Company:
237
Image, Inc.:
Harold Twitty, 292
The Image Bank: 324
Morton Beebe, 373
Gerald Brimacombe, 274 top
Josephus Daniels, 378 top
Cliff Feulner, 363
Gerard Gscheidle, 429
Larry Lee, 290, 364
Richard Magruder, 385
Richard and Mary Magruder,
380
William Rivelli, 334
Leonard Lee Rue III, 336 right
Eric Schwerkardt, 430
John Lewis Stage, 5 left, 323
top, 355 right
Luis Villota, 400, 412
Independence National Historical
Park Collection, Philadelphia:
77 top, 81, 123
International Harvester: 179 top
and right
Jeroboam, Inc.:
Andy Mercado, 179 bottom
Karen R. Preuss, 86
David Kelley: 54, 63 right
Robert Knopes: 338
The Kosciuszko Foundation: 72
Lexington Historical Society: 62

Library of Congress: 18, 46, 69 top,
70, 74, 75, 83, 108, 112, 119 top
left, 163 bottom, 166 left, 184
top, 224 top
Louisiana State Museum: 116
Steve McCutchon: 189 top
Milt and Joan Mann: 95 bottom
right, 241, 260 left, 278 right, 307
left, 314, 347 right
Marconi Wireless Telegraph
Company, Ltd.: 238 left
The Mariners Museum of Newport
News, Va.: 13
The Metropolitan Museum of Art,
Rogers Fund, 1942: 211
Milwaukee Public Exhibit: 45 top
Milwaukee Public Museum: 26
Missouri Historical Society: 87, 129
Montana Historical Society,
Helena: 127
Dan Morrill: 3 right, 159 left
David Muench: 4 right, 124, 253 left
Museum of Art, Rhode Island
School of Design (Museum Works
of Art Fund): 43 top
Museum of the City of New York:
24, 185
Museum of Fine Arts, Boston: 55
Nancy Palmer Photo Agency:
Kenneth Murray, 323 bottom
National Aeronautics and Space
Administration: 4 left, 209 left,
240
National Gallery of Art, Washington,
Gift of Edgar William and Bernice
Chrysler Garbisch: 82
National Historical Park: 172
National Maritime Museum: 120
National Portrait Gallery, London:
78 bottom left
Navy Combat Art Gallery: 192-193
New Hampshire Historical Society:
170-171
New Mexico Department of
Development: 141, 145
The New York Historical Society:
47, 231
Nick Nicholson: 352
Oak Ridge National Laboratory:
293
Oregon State Highway Travel
Division: 136-137
Painting by A. Lassell Ripley.
Copyright—The Paul Revere Life
Insurance Company: 63 left
Pennsylvania Academy of Fine
Arts: 78 top left
Pennsylvania Historical and
Museum Commission:
Newbold H. Trotter, 109
Photo Researchers: 282
Jim Amos, 348
William Carter, 95 top
Dick Davis, 381
Carl Frank, 389 right
Allen Green, 268
Esther Henderson, 295 right
Russ Kinne, 287 left, 321 left, 349
Tom McHugh, 427 bottom
Michael Philip Manheim, 41, 238
right
Irvin L. Oakes, 94
Carl Purcell, 387
Rapho-Guillumette/Esther
Henderson, 295 left
Joe Rychetnik, 328
Abram G. Schoenfeld, 97 right

James R. Simon, 93
Ted Streshinsky, 321 right
John Henry Sullivan, Jr., 2 right,
33 right
Gianni Tortoli, 128
Plimoth Plantation: 40
State Capitol, Richmond, Virginia:
78 right
Permanent Collection, Roswell
Museum and Art Center: 19
Leonard Lee Rue III: 336 right
San Jacinto Museum of History
Association: 148
Scott's Bluff National Monument:
133
Shostal Associates: 119 bottom
Eric Carle, 2 right, 33 left, 92, 296
Ed Cooper, 119 top right
Art D'Arazien, 256
Robert Ellis, 69 bottom
Tony Linck, 27
Sophia Smith Collection, Smith
College 163 top left and top right
Stock, Boston:
Hammond, 2 left, 7 right
J.P. Rabot, 396 right
Franklin Wing, 30
Supreme Court Historical Society,
Washington, D.C.: 249 bottom
Texaco: 96 right
The Thomas Gilcrease Institute of
American History and Art, Tulsa,
Oklahoma: 28, 134-135
Tuskegee Institute: 181
United Nations: 199
U.S. Capitol Historical Society:
National Geographic
Photographer, George F. Mobley,
234, 249 top left, top right, and
center
Painting by Carl Rakeman.
Courtesy of the Federal Highway
Administration/U.S. Department
of Transportation: 106
U.S. Naval Academy Museum: 77
bottom
U.S. Postal Service: 230
Van Cleve, Inc.:
Glen Donahue, 309
John Lund, 305
John McClurken, 287 right
David Muench, 153, 344
Virginia State Library: 65, 76 top,
75 left
Wappelo County Historical Society,
Ottumwa, Iowa: 154, 156
Courtesy Wells Fargo Bank: 155
Wide World: 203 left
Woodfin Camp & Associates:
Craig Aurness, 274 bottom left
Marc and Evelyn Bernheim, 386
Dan Budnik, 203 right
Daily Telegraph, David
Adamson, 5 left, 355 left
George Hall, 369 top
Sylvia Johnson, 307 right
Loren McIntyre, 426, 427 top
Albert Moldway, 396 left
William S. Weems, 242
World Health Organization: 195
Wright Bros. National Memorial.
Photo courtesy Library of
Congress: 224 top
Leo de Wys, Inc.: 97 bottom left
Everett C. Johnson, 97 top left
Yale University Art Gallery: 71

EFGH083210
Printed in the United States of America